SOCIO-ECONOMIC PROFILE OF RURAL INDIA

[Series III]

Volume One

Socio-Economic Profile of Rural India (Series I)

VOLUME 1 : **South India**
Edited by V.K. Agnihotri

VOLUME 2 : **North East India**
Edited by C. Ashokvardhan

VOLUME 3 : **Western and North Central India**
Edited by Rajendra Vora

VOLUME 4 : **Eastern India—Bihar, West Bengal, Orissa and Uttar Pradesh**
Edited by C. Ashokvardhan

Socio Economic Profile of Rural India (Series II)

VOLUME 2 : **North East India (Assam, Manipur, Tripura and Nagaland)**
Edited by S.C. Patra, Ashish Vachhani

VOLUME 4 : **Eastern India (Orissa, Jharkhand, West Bengal, Bihar and Uttar Pradesh)**
Edited by C. Ashokvardan

VOLUME 5 : **North and Central India (Punjab, Haryana, Himachal Pradesh and Madhya Pradesh)**
Edited by Raj Mohini Sethi

ABOUT THE EDITORS

Dr. C. Ashokvardhan belongs to the 1980 batch of the Indian Administrative Service and was allocated to the Bihar Cadre. He retired in November 2013 and is currently Member, Fifth State Finance Commission, Bihar.

Dr. Ashokvardhan has been mainly interested is revenue laws and land reforms and he holds a nationwide reputation in this domain. His works have been published by LBSNAA, Mussoorie and NIRD, Hyderabad. His reputation is also that of a trainer of revenue laws at various centres of learning, including the LBSNAA. During his prolonged stint as Principal Secretary. Revenue and Land Reforms in Bihar, he drafted a number of pro-poor revenue laws which have received wide acclaim.

Dr. Varunendra Vikram Singh, Faculty, Centre for Rural Studies: Ph.D., Sociology Department, Lucknow University, Lucknow. Awarded Junior Research Fellowship and also Senior Research Fellowship by Anthropological Survey of India, Government of India, Kolkata. Did Certificate Course in 'Computer Basics & Internet'. Passed National Stock Exchange's Certification in 'Financial Markets with expertise in Derivative & Capital Market.' Did an International Course on Management of 'Common Property Resources' from IIM, Ahmedabad. Organized and contributed to several seminars and workshops of national importance. Worked as Researcher in National Institute of Administrative Research, LBS National Academy of Administration, Mussoorie. Has several Reports and Research papers published in scientific journals and also edited published and Co-authored books to his credit. Areas of Interest are in the field of Land Reforms, Land Markets, Elementary Education, Tribal Development, Common Property Resources, Financial Management and Land Resources Management in India.

SOCIO-ECONOMIC PROFILE OF RURAL INDIA

[Series III]

VOLUME ONE

(Haryana, Punjab, J&K, Rajasthan and Himachal Pradesh)

Edited by

C. Ashokvardhan

Dr. Varunendra Vikram Singh

Published for

Lal Bahadur Shastri National Academy of Administration

Centre for Rural Studies

Lal Bahadur Shastri National Academy of Administration

Mussoorie

by

CONCEPT PUBLISHING COMPANY PVT. LTD.

NEW DELHI-110059

ISBN-13: 978-93-5125-249-8 (Series-III)
ISBN-13: 978-93-5125-250-4 (Vol. I)

First Published 2017

Published and Printed by

Concept Since 1974

Concept Publishing Company Pvt. Ltd.
Regd. Office:
A/15-16, Commercial Block, Mohan Garden,
New Delhi-110059 (INDIA)
Phones : 25351460, 25351794, *Fax* : 091-11-25357109
Email : publishing@conceptpub.com
Website: www.conceptpub.com

Editorial Office: H-13, Bali Nagar, New Delhi-110 015, India.

Cataloging in Publication Data--*Courtesy:* D.K. Agencies (P) Ltd. <docinfo@dkagencies.com>

Socio-economic profile of rural India. Series III / edited by C. Ashokvardhan, Dr. Varunendra Vikram Singh.
volumes cm
Includes bibliographical references and index.
Contents: volume 1. Haryana, Punjab, J&K, Rajasthan and Himachal Pradesh
ISBN 9789351252498 (series)
ISBN 9789351252504 (vol. 1)

1. India—Rural conditions. 2. India—Economic conditions. I. Singh, Varunendra V. (Varunendra Vikram), author. II. Centre for Rural Studies (Lal Bahadur Shastry National Academy of Administration) III. Title.

HN683.5.S63 2016 DDC 307.720954 23

Dr. Prem Singh, IAS
Centre Director,
Centre for Rural Studies,
LBS National Academy of
Administration, Mussoorie

Foreword

This volume tends to develop on the state profiles of the socio-economic development of five States, viz., Haryana, Punjab, J&K, Rajasthan and Himachal Pradesh. IAS Officer Trainees, as part of their field exposure, carry out village assignments where they have a direct interface with stakeholders and where they try to capture the current status of development in select rural pockets of a given State. The discussion is further elevated to the State level, where we take inputs from State experts.

Like its predecessor volumes, this volume deals with the key issues of socio-economic development for different sectors. The focus is on sectors such as education, poverty, food security, unemployment, housing, sanitation, nutrition and health, which play an important role in the betterment of the conditions of the deprived and the disadvantaged. There is a special focus on social inclusion. Exclusions and deprivations are closely tied in with traditional structures of domination at the micro-level.

Aggregate economic growth does not often sufficiently capture the living conditions of the people. Hence, an understanding of the processes which impact different aspects of the lives of the people is imperative.

I compliment the IAS Officer Trainees, authors of the State Papers and the editor for the painstaking work carried out by them. I also thank Dr. Varunendra Vikram Singh who made it possible to bring out this volume in its present shape.

Dr. Prem Singh, *IAS*

Lal Bahadur Shastri National Academy of Administration (Govt. of India) Mussoorie - 248179
EPABX : (0135) 2222000, 2632374, 2632489, 2632405, 2632236, 2632367 Fax : (0135) 2632350, 2332720
Website: http://www.lbsnaa.gov.in

Preface

The present volume is a compilation of State Papers on Jammu & Kashmir, Punjab, Haryana, Rajasthan and Himachal Pradesh. The Papers have been designed in a backdrop of the socio-economic surveys conducted by IAS officer trainees in select villages. Such surveys, over the years, have become an integral part of their training with a focus on empirical, down to earth, real life scenario. It provides a unique opportunity of career development, in as much as theoretical and academic training is dovetailed with an exposure to the rural challenge—the fight with deprivation and the attempt to lift the rural populace from its present morass. The OTs are exposed also to the silver linings, where governmental and societal efforts have, over a period of time, registered successes on various fronts of poverty alleviation. Development is no longer the prerogative of the Government. It is a combined end-product of official and non-official contributions in planning, execution and monitoring. There has also been an appreciable spurt in the development activities of self-help groups. It is a fact that State's presence in key sensitive areas combined with local initiative tends to brighten our hope for the future.

Yet another conclusion that broadly emerges from the papers is that we have to move in terms of sustainable development. What comes as sporadic, in between or transient may conglomerate in some perceptible improvement for the time being. Nevertheless, in the absence of sustainable foundations, the effort may go waste and the beneficiary individual or group may slide back to deprivation. Development is an on-going process, with concurrent evaluation and monitoring as its integral part. It is an outcome of concerted activities designed in a planned manner. Here too, planning has to come from below. The planning goals may have to be prioritized in the light of availability of funds, but invariably, the decentralized planning processes are the best.

Unfortunately, on account of various factors, the cooperative movement failed to make much dent. One could say, in a similar vein, that Panchayati Raj Institutions and Urban Local Bodies which were envisaged as bodies of local governance (with an elected component) could not be strengthened. Devolution of funds, functions and functionaries remains a far cry as general bureaucracy is, by and large, reluctant to budge. There is a manifest lack of political will in bringing local bodies to an enviable position. There are training and manpower development gaps, which hardly get adequate attention.

While the record of representative democracy has been manifestly strong, India's track in ensuring better living standards for its people has been strikingly unsatisfactory. A large number of people are poor even by the most modest standards of living; universal literacy is yet to be realized; there is a high drop-out rate from schools and a very small proportion of the population move on to higher education. What is needed is much greater public engagement with the demands for justice and development which has been quite limited in India. The benefits of growth have gone to a small proportion of the population while the bulk of the people experience little or no trickle-down benefits from growth. Growth is important for achieving development, but this requires public policies that can ensure the fruits of economic growth reach everyone. Fast economic growth is essential for the generation of public revenues for investment in social services especially public health care and public education. Economic development cannot be disengaged from social development since such growth would neither be possible nor sustainable in the long run unless it translates into a general improvement in living standards and enhancement of people's well-being.

"Jobless growth" has adversely affected the bulk of the working classes who have not benefited from the modest growth in employment opportunities. Services sector has expanded at the cost of the manufacturing sector, which has been plagued by political and technological limitations. Although, unemployment of males and females has declined in the rural areas, the informalization of workers has continued unabated. Certain sectors such as construction and trade have recorded a higher share in employment, but these sectors have served the purposes of a few surplus-earning individuals and have not impacted the working population as a whole. The semi-skilled and educated labour force has not received any desirable employment. Unless significant attention is paid to the primary and secondary sectors, the rate of unemployment will take a longer period to fall and the casualization of workers will increase.

There has occurred a feminization of poverty as a result of the agrarian crisis. Liberalisation has seen a general neglect of the agricultural sector through the dismantling of subsidies, weakening of credit provision, rise in input prices, and price fluctuations owing to integration with the world market. The crisis has triggered migration, mostly of males, from villages to towns and cities. Women increasingly constitute the mainstay of the workforce in agriculture. A general decline of agriculture, therefore, means greater depression for women.

Food security remains a challenge in both developed and developing countries. In the period 1990-92, there were about 816 million undernourished people in the world—a figure that fell to 777 million by 1997-99. However, progress was unequal. The average rate of decline in the number of chronically undernourished has slowed in the last year—from 8 million a year in 1999 to 6 million a year in 2001. Consequently, the annual reduction required to reach the World Food Summit target of having the number of undernourished people by 2015 is now 22 million per year. Counting the current rate, it will take more than 60 years to reach the target (FAO, 2001a).

A considerable literature documents the social and economic importance of land access, and especially secure and long-term access for individuals and families as well as the broad access to land at the macro-level for the country's development prospects. Yet, large number of rural families in many developing countries are completely landless, in the sense that they lack secure and meaningful possession of land. Women's economic development and their rights to land are intrinsically linked. More than half of all women in the developing world still work in agriculture. Africa's women produce 78 per cent of the continent's food, mainly through subsistence agriculture and small landholding. In India, 86 per cent of rural women workers work in agriculture as compared with 74 per cent of rural male workers. In addition, females head a large percentage of households: 20 per cent in Bangladesh and India and 30 per cent in Sub-Saharan Africa. Among the poor, women and women-headed households are the most vulnerable and account for a growing majority of the extreme poor. Land ownership can ensure safety, status and adequate housing and food security for women and children.

Land rights clearly confer direct economic benefits to women. Land is a key input into agricultural production. It can be a source of income from rental or sale, and can be used as a collateral for credit that can be used either for consumption or investment purposes. Women's land rights almost always require strengthening, under both formal and customary law. On this topic—in which "land law" may overlap and interact with "family law", the limitations of formal law are particularly evident. While legislative reform has an important role to play in creating "space" for progressive change it is clearly not sufficient. Cultural action, advocacy and education including literacy will play crucial roles.

Land reforms were poorly implemented and failed to realize their objectives. There was a perceptible lack of political commitment to land reforms. There were loopholes in land reforms laws. The bureaucratic machinery evinced antipathy for the tenant and the agricultural labourer. Cases protracted in courts of law. Due to these formidable factors, land reforms failed on all three counts: to deliver justice, achieve economic efficiency and effect radical change in the rural power structure. Where limited gains were delivered to the tenants and landless poor, the failure to tie up provision of financial/technical and input assistance to improve cultivation of land led to the frittering away of the benefits of reforms.

C. Ashokvardhan

Acknowledgements

This volume is an upshot of the socio-economic assignments submitted by the IAS Officer Trainees during the year 2003 to 2010. The book came out in its present shape is basically by the encouragement of Sri Padamvir Singh, the Director-*cum*-Chairman of the Centre for Rural Studies, LBS National Academy of Administration, Mussoorie. I am also grateful to Dr. Prem Singh, Centre Director, Centre for Rural Studies, who took keen interest and supported at all stages beginning from compilation of socio-economic reports, selection of authors for writing the state papers and selection of the editor of the volume to its final stage of publication. Now, it is my pleasing obligation to thank all the IAS Officer Trainees whose socio-economic assignments had been utilized for preparing the data base for writing the state papers.

In the last but not least, I would like to appreciate the cooperation made by the faculty members of the Centre for Rural Studies and contributions made by the staff of the Centre for Rural Studies who accepted various tasks of secretarial assistance during time to time. I also am obliged to express thanks to Sri Nitin Mittal, Publisher, Concept Publishing Company Pvt. Ltd., New Delhi. I hope that this volume will prove to be of vast meaning for the planners, policy makers and academicians.

Varunendra Vikram Singh
Centre for Rural Studies,
LBS National Academy of Administration,
Mussoorie, Uttarakhand

Contents

List of Boxes

List of Tables

List of Contributors

Professor (Dr.) Bashir Ahmad Dabla, Department of Sociology, University of Kashmir, Srinagar, J&K.

Dr. C. Ashokvardhan, IAS (Retd.), Officers Flat No. 35/60, Bailey Road, Patna, Bihar.

Professor (Dr.) Shyam Nand Singh, Head, Political Science, MDS University, Ajmer, Rajasthan.

Professor (Dr.) Sucha Singh Gill, Centre for Research in Rural and Industrial Development, Chandigarh.

Professor (Dr.) Surinder Kumar, Director, GIRI Institute of Development Studies, Lucknow.

Satish Kumar, Research Faculty, Centre for Research in Rural and Industrial Development, Chandigarh.

Introduction

C. ASHOKVARDHAN

State papers included in this volume tend to capture the current socio-economic scenario in the States concerned along with perspectives, paradigm shift over a period of time and vision ahead. Starting from the premises laid down by IAS OTs and taking a cue from empirical findings in select villages, there has been an endeavour to generalize on the same. Facts and figures, taken mostly from official sources, tend to build up a rather wholesome edifice of fast, inclusive and sustainable growth. While the challenge ahead and constraints have been taken into account strategies too have been delineated to meet goals and objectives on a time-frame.

The proportion of the population depending mainly on agriculture has been falling, but it is still too large. There is a need for those currently engaged in agriculture to shift to higher productivity non-agricultural occupations. This can only happen if the non-agricultural sector can provide gainful employment not only to the growing number of people who will be entering the labour force, but to those moving out of agriculture. To be truly inclusive, the growth process must lead to job creation. All this calls for a certain degree of policy restructuring as well. Policies aimed at supporting the diversification of agriculture and greater involvement of the private sector in marketing agricultural produce are called for.

Distributional concerns have traditionally been viewed as ensuring an adequate flow of benefits to the poor and the most marginalized. Inclusiveness is not just about bringing those below an officially fixed poverty line to a level above it. It is also about a growth process which is seen to be fair by various socio-economic groups. Inclusiveness must address the concern of groups such as the Scheduled Castes, Scheduled Tribes, Other Backward Classes, Minorities, the differently abled and other marginalized groups. Women can also be viewed as a disadvantaged group for this purpose.

Another aspect of inclusiveness relates to correcting regional imbalances. Many of the erstwhile backward States have begun to show significant improvement in growth performance. However, both the better performing and other States are increasingly concerned about their backward regions and districts, which may not share the general improvement in living standards experienced elsewhere.

The current debate is also around empowerment and participation. People are no longer prepared to be passive recipients of benefits doled out by the Government. They are slowly beginning to demand those benefits and opportunities as rights and they also want a say in how they are administered. This brings to the fore issues of governance, accountability and people's participation. This also covers areas like access to information about government schemes, knowledge of the relevant laws and how to access justice. The growing concern with governance has also focused attention on corruption.

A fairly wide gamut of the rural socio-economic scenario has been covered in the State papers. The following sectors come out striking as we tend to comprehend the growth profile of a given State:

1. Agriculture and Horticulture,
2. Livestock,
3. Rural Development,
4. Employment and Skill Development,
5. Education, and
6. Health.

It will be my endeavour to reflect on the above sectors in the light of the findings arrived at in the State papers as also in the light of studies carried out elsewhere.

1. AGRICULTURE AND HORTICULTURE

There are formidable challenges, for example, a shrinking land base, dwindling water resources, the adverse impact of climate change, shortage of farm labour, and increasing costs and uncertainties associated with the volatility of international markets. The key drivers of agricultural growth remain:

1. Viability of farm enterprise and returns to investment that depend on scale, market access, prices and risk;
2. Availability and dissemination of appropriate technologies that depend on quality of research and extent of skill development;
3. Plan expenditure in agriculture and infrastructure which together with policy must aim to improve functioning of markets and more efficient use of natural resources; and
4. Governance in terms of institutions that make possible better delivery of services like credit, animal health and of quality inputs like seeds, fertilizers, pesticides and farm machinery.

In addition, certain regional imbalances must be clearly addressed. A national priority from view of both food security and sustainability is to fully extend Green Revolution to areas of low productivity in the eastern region, where there is ample ground water. Rain-fed areas continue to be at a disadvantage.

Agriculture contributes to about 22 per cent of the State Domestic Product in Rajasthan. 70 per cent of the population of the State depends on agriculture as a source of livelihood. The south-east and eastern parts of the Aravalli Hills are productive for agriculture purposes, having clay loam type soil. Rajasthan's position in the country's agriculture is as follows:

- Stands at fourth position after Uttar Pradesh, Punjab and Andhra Pradesh in foodgrain production;
- Second in production of gram and the largest producer of moth-bean;
- Second largest producer of total oilseed and the largest producer of mustard, third position in soyabean production and fourth position in groundnut;
- Fifth largest producer of wheat and largest producer of all coarse cereals; and
- Largest producer of guar, seed spices.

The agriculture sector in Rajasthan faces the following challenges—

- Increasing gap between demand and availability of water;
- Scanty and uncertain rainfall affecting agriculture in particular and economy in general;
- Deteriorating quality of land and underground water;
- Low value agriculture;
- Large gap between potential and realized yield of crops and high inter-year variation in productivity;
- Mono-cropping in western dry region and southern tribal belt of the State, limiting the scope for diversification;
- Low share of vegetable and fruit crops, seed spices and medicinal plants, depriving the benefits of value addition and extra employment for the rural masses; and
- Out of 90 lakh female workers engaged in on-farm work, nearly 50 per cent are with sub-optimal workdays. Generation of full employment opportunities through labour intensive agriculture activities in areas like horticulture and agro-processing, is a great challenge.

Agriculture dominates the economy of Himachal Pradesh, though only a little over 10 per cent of the total land area is cultivated. The population pressure on cultivated land is high and holdings of most of the cultivators are small and scattered. Most of the holdings are self-cultivated. About 18.5 per cent of the cultivated area is under irrigation and remaining 81.5 per cent is rainfed. Agro-climatically, the region is more suitable for growing off-season vegetables and temperate fruits.

In 2012-13, 15 per cent of State Domestic Product was generated by agriculture and allied sectors. In the same year, the foodgrains production achieved a record level of 15.68 lakh MT, while the production of potato and vegetables was 1.83 lakh MT and 13.80 lakh MT.

The emphasis in Himachal Pradesh is on increasing productivity levels besides diversification towards high value crops. Due to increasing shift to commercial crops, the area under foodgrains is gradually declining which reduced to 798.31 thousand hectares in 2012-13.

Emphasis has been laid on the distribution of seeds of high yielding varieties to the farmers. In this connection, adoption of plant protection measures is of paramount importance.

In order to maintain fertility of the soil during each season, soil samples are collected from the farmers and analysed in the soil testing laboratories. During 2012-13, 1.23 lakh numbers of soil health cards were issued.

Organic farming is becoming popular, being suitable, environmental friendly and health conducive to all concerned. For organic farming, incentive @ Rs. 10,000 per hectare (50%) and for certification 10,000 per hectare is being provided for three years. Fertilizer is a single input which helps in increasing the production to a great extent. The level of consumption of fertilizers has increased in the State to 48,129 tonnes in 2012-13. In view of the propensity of farmers to borrow money, credit flow for purchase of inputs is being made available by the banks. 5,84,568 Kisan Credit Cards were issued by the banks in 2013. Moreover, from 2013-14, the existing NAIS has been withdrawn by the Government of India and in place a new C.S.S. of NCIP will be implemented. The regulated markets established in the State provide useful services to farmers. A modernized market complex at Solan is functional at present.

Total area under tea is 2,300 hectares with a production level of 8-10 lakh kgs. Under agriculture mechanization, new farm implements/machines and testing of these machines are popularized among the farmers. Seed village programme has been initiated in the State in order to meet local seed requirement besides facilitating supply of seeds at lower cost and in shorter time. The Government has a project on production of cash crops by Adoption of Precision in Farming Practices through Poly House Cultivation. The NABARD has sanctioned a project of 154.92 crores for 4 years from 2008-09. 13,500 poly houses were constructed by March 2014.

Himachal Pradesh has gained reputation for the cultivation of off-season vegetables and production of quality vegetables seeds. There is a high demand for off-season vegetables in the plains.

The following key reforms are being promoted in Himachal Pradesh:

1. Providing innovative restructured autonomous bodies at the district level (Agriculture Technology Management Agency) and at Block level (Farmer's Advisory Committee, Block Technology Team), which are flexible, promote bottom up and participatory approaches, and are farmer driven. They also facilitate public-private partnership;
2. Convergence of line departments, programmes and operating on gap filling mode by formulating Strategic Research and Extension Plan (SREP) and Annual Work Plans;
3. Encouraging Multi-agency Extension Strategies involving *inter alia* public/private extension service providers;
4. Moving towards integrated, broad-based extension delivery in line with farming systems approach;
5. Adopting Group approach to extension operating through Farmer Interest Groups (FIGs) and Self-Help Groups (SHGs);
6. Addressing gender concerns (mobilizing farm women into groups for capacity building, etc.); and
7. Moving towards sustainability of extension services (e.g. through beneficiary contribution).

Himachal Pradesh is extremely rich in horticulture, apiculture and floriculture. The concept of progeny-cum-demonstration orchards and nurseries as growth centres were developed right from the First Five Year Plan. Presently, 94 such units are in operation in all parts of the State which have played commendable role in the proliferation of fruit plantation. These units occupy about 1,394 acres of land on which 1 lakh progeny trees of different species have been planted as a source of bud wood for propagation of planting material for supply to the fruit growers. Together these will produce 40 lakh elite fruit plants of different kinds in nurseries during plan period.

Training and extension is an important programme for the transfer of technology to the farmers for increasing horticultural production. This programme is also very important for human resource development to meet the skilled manpower need of the horticulture industry. This scheme aims at organizing training camps/workshops/seminars/courses/study tours, etc., for the farmers as well as for the technical officers and field functionaries of the department of horticulture, to provide skill development and to extend services to farmers.

Fruit and vegetable preservation is a basic necessity for the horticulture industry. About 20-25 per cent of the fruit production goes waste unless it is utilized for fruit processing. Moreover, the processing grade and substandard fruits not only receive very low prices in the market but also affect the rates of good quality fruits adversely, thereby causing economic losses to the fruit growers. The only solution to overcome this problem is to utilize such fruits in the manufacture of value added processed products like juices/juice concentrates, jam, jelly, squashes, alcoholic beverages, etc. The Government of Himachal Pradesh is, therefore, implementing a scheme for the utilization of unmarketable surplus fruits in 8 small fruit processing units with an installed capacity of 500 MT.

For getting remunerative price of their produce, the orchardists need market advisory services, proper marketing and quality control facilities and smooth transport system, besides, adequate knowledge of maturity standards, training in the post-harvest operations like picking, grading, packing and market intelligence. This scheme has the objective to provide such facilities to the farmers. To achieve better results, the Government of Himachal Pradesh will establish/facilitate post-harvest management infrastructure like farm access, road network, ropeways, local markets, modern grading and packing houses, CA storage, pre-cooling and cool chain systems up to consuming markets.

Himachal Pradesh offers very rich potential for the development of bee-keeping because of large areas under horticulture, agriculture and forest. There is a big demand for honey produced, in the country as well as abroad. As a cottage industry, it is possible to adopt bee-keeping on commercial lines by the farming community for getting additional income to improve their economic status. Besides honey production, the honey bees are also recognized as an important source of pollination for increasing crop productivity. During the plan period, bee-keeping scheme of the Government will be strengthened to intensify establishment of nucleus apiaries of Italian bee, new beehives and modern tools, honey processing, Agmark laboratories and attractive package and marketing infrastructure.

Commercial floriculture is one of the main thrusts of the Twelfth Plan in Himachal Pradesh. The potential existing in the form of diverse climatic conditions in various regions of the State can be exploited for the cultivation of wide range of flowers, ornamental plants and production of flower seeds/bulbs, etc., for year round supplies to the domestic as well as export market. About 2,500 growers are involved in the floriculture activities producing flowers worth Rs. 77 crore in an area ot 860 hectares. Protected cultivation of quality flowers like carnation, gerbera and rose have opened new avenues of self-employment among farmers of lower and mid-hill areas of the State. The objectives of the scheme would be area expansion under diversified floriculture and strengthening marketing infrastructure by introducing new flowers of economic viability and ensure availability of improved material. The agro-climate conditions prevailing in many parts of Himachal Pradesh provide ample scope for the cultivation of mushroom, both for domestic consumption as well as for export purposes. Presently, about 900 growers are engaged in small scale cultivation of mushroom. Besides this, 40 compost production and growing units and 10 spawn production units have been established in the private sector. About 6,000 MT mushrooms are being produced in the State annually. Mainly two types of mushroom, viz., white button mushroom (*Agaricus bisporous*) and oyster mushroom (*Pleurotus* spp) are being cultivated. During recent years, cultivation of milky mushroom (*Calocybe indica*) is also being taken up by growers in the warm areas of the State. Mushroom cultivation activity is being promoted by four projects at Solan, Palampur, Bajaura and Dharbaggi through transfer of technology and supply of quality pasteurized compost. Another project is being installed at Duttnagar in Shimla district to popularize this activity in the upper areas of Shimla district, adjoining areas of Kullu district and Kinnaur district.

Being indoor activity, the main objective of the scheme is to prepare and distribute 2,500 MT pasteurized compost during the Twelfth Plan from departmental units with a target to achieve annual production level of 6,200 MT. It will be achieved by establishing modern composting infrastructure for cultivating high yielding strains of mushroom.

Potential for Agriculture in Jammu & Kashmir

- Organic Basmati Rice, Rajmah, off-season vegetables, potatoes, aromatic and medicinal plants.
- Virus free potato seeds for all seasons.

- Development of commercial floriculture, production of virus free quality seeds for flowers and vegetables, aromatic and medicinal plants.
- Mushrooms round the year, honey by-products, fodder intensification, etc.
- Wide range of flora available to boost bee-keeping.
- Boost to quality saffron production.
- Jetropha (Biofuel) cultivation on waste lands and rainfed areas of Jammu region under NWDPRA.

Limitations/Constraints in Agriculture in Jammu & Kashmir

- Hilly Terrain.
- Small and fragmented land holdings.
- Fragile soil in hilly areas susceptible to soil erosion.
- Limits to mechanized farming and transportation of products.
- Extreme limits to irrigation of cultivated land.
- Single cropping season in temperate/high altitude areas.
- Inadequate and unorganized marketing infrastructure.
- Distant market for export outside the State.

Paddy is the main crop of the Kashmir region followed by maize and wheat. Maize is the major crop of the Jammu region followed by wheat. Barley is the major crop of the Ladakh region followed by wheat. The economic contribution of agriculture to the State's GDP is steadily declining. Even then agriculture plays a significant role in the overall socio-economic fabric of the State. Boosting agricultural growth is very essential for inclusive growth because this sector sustains livelihood of 70 per cent of the population. However, agriculture contributes only 16.67 per cent to the State's Gross Domestic Product (constant prices). Low contribution of agriculture to GSDP is mainly because productivity of major agricultural crops is very low in comparison to other States and rest of the country. Technology deficit in agriculture seems the main cause. Yield per hectare of foodgrains, fruits and vegetables is far below the country level averages. Yield rates of principal crops like rice, maize and wheat for the year 2012-13 are 2,095 kg/ha 1,648 kg/ha and

1,596 kg/ha respectively. The corresponding figures are 2,462 kg/ha for rice, 2,552 kg/ha for maize and 3,118 kg/ha for wheat as per fourth advance estimates for the year 2012-13 for India.

J&K is endowed with varied agro-climatic conditions for growing a variety of horticulture crops like fruits and vegetables, plantation crops and floriculture. Kashmir's agriculture has an international identity. The world's high quality saffron is grown in the valley and its major intensity is in Pulwama and Budgam districts. Nearly 98 per cent of the total area in the State under the crop is cultivated in the Kashmir area. Its cultivation in the Jammu division is confined to a few pockets of the district Kishtwar. The State holds first position in the country in the production of saffron. Saffron is the world's most expensive spice and the most popular ingredient for colouring and flavouring butter, cheese, confectionery, baked food and medicines. However, both the area and production of saffron and also its productivity has substantially decreased over the years. Black zeera, another famous crop in the world, is also produced in some pockets of J&K.

The favourable climatic conditions and fertile soil of the State provide immense scope for the promotion of the horticulture sector. Moreover, this sector is labour intensive in nature and provides employment opportunities to a sizeable number in the processing of its produce and contributes considerably towards the State economy. Apple, pear, walnut, almond, cherry, apricot and a large variety of other fruits are grown in the State. The State holds first position in the production of temperate fruits like apple. As per information available for the year 2012-13 production of fruits was 17.42 lakh metric tonnes which accounts for more than 2 per cent of total fruits of 812.85 lakh metric tonnes for 2012-13 produced in the country. Export of fruits outside the State during 2012-13 was 7.21 lakh metric tonnes constituting 41.39 per cent of total fruit production. In fact, export of fruits forms the base for the State's trade. For 2012-13, the Horticulture department has reported 355.29 (2013-14) thousand hectares of land under fruit cultivation compared to 6,982 thousand hectares in the country for 2012-13.

Availability of water is most critical in increasing productivity in agriculture. The water use efficiency in agriculture is very low due to substantial conveyance and distribution losses. As a result around 60 per cent of the cultivated area in the State is without irrigation. The percentage of gross irrigated area to gross cropped area in the State is 41.91 per cent for 2012-13 as against 44.91 per cent at the national level for 2010-11. Similarly 43.62 per cent net area sown is irrigated for 2012-13 compared to 44.92 per cent for India for 2010-11. The State provides tremendous scope for the promotion of all agriculture related sectors like mushroom, apiculture, floriculture, fisheries, sericulture development, etc.

The net area sown in J&K during 2013-14 was 741 thousand hectares whereas the gross area sown (total area sown under different crops) was 1,160 thousand hectares. The mode of irrigating the crops mainly is the canals. About 89 per cent of the net area irrigated is through canals while tanks, tube wells and other means are also used.

Comparison of crop yield of J&K with the largest producing Indian States and some other countries for the year 2012 shows the agricultural backwardness of the State as given in Table 1.

Table 1: Comparison of Crop Yield to Other States

Sl. No.	*Crop*	*Yield of J&K (Qtls/ha)*	*Higest Yield States in India*	*Yield (Qtls/ha)*	*World's Highest Yield Countries*	*Yield (Qtls/ha)*
1.	Paddy/Rice	20.85	Punjab	39.52	China	66.61
2.	Wheat	14.04	Punjab	50.17	UK	73.60
3.	Maize	16.48	Tamil Nadu	53.72	USA	88.50
4.	Oilseeds	8.24	Gujarat	17.23	UK	35.88

Source: Economic Survey, 2014-15, Directorate of Economics and Statistics, J&K.

J&K is well known for its horticultural produce both in India and abroad. The State offers good scope for the cultivation of horticultural crops, covering a variety of temperate fruits like apple, pear, peach, plum, apricot, almond, cherry and sub-tropical fruits like mango, guava, citrus, litchi, phalsa and berete. Besides, medicinal and aromatic plants, floriculture, mushroom, plantation crops and vegetables are also cultivated in the State. Apart from this, well known spices like saffron and black zeera are also cultivated in some pockets of the State. As a result, there is a perceptible change in the concept of horticulture development in the State. There are around 7 lakh families comprising of about 33 lakh people which are directly or indirectly associated with horticulture. Horticulture development is one of the thrust areas in agriculture and a number of programmes have been implemented in the past, resulting in the generation of higher incomes in the rural areas, thereby improving the quality of life in villages. Looking at the specie-wise details of area under fruit for the year 2013-14, it is observed that the largest area of 45.34 per cent (1,61,364 hectares) is occupied by apple out of the total area of 3,55,921 hectares under fruit. Walnut is the next major fruit occupying 26.86 per cent in the overall area under fruit.

Food processing industry offers tremendous opportunity for commercial exploitation of horticulture in J&K but commercial processing is around 1 per cent only due to lack of post-harvesting and processing facilities as well as unscientific packaging. Therefore, opportunities are open for exploiting the potential under processing, with individual, joint venture and Government efforts.

The area under fruits in J&K has increased from 2.95 lakh hectares in 2007-08 to 3.60 lakh hectares in 2014-15 (estimated). The production was expected to increase from 17.13 lakh MT in 2009-10 to 22.76 lakh MT in 2014-15 which could not happen due to unexpected rains and floods of September 2014.

One hectare of land planted with fruit trees provides an additional employment for one thousand man-days, thereby generating employment for over 6 crore man-days by planting fruit trees on 65,000 hectares. Some hands assist the farmers in marketing their produce; others help in providing the seeds, the plant materials and insecticides and chemicals to the farmers so as to ensure that the plants are protected from diseases and pests; others assist in the picking/harvesting of fruits. The cultivation of fruits is labour intensive and requires a significantly higher labour force, starting from the stage of planting the trees to the point of marketing. The manpower requirement in the cultivation and marketing of apples as well as field crops is met by employing paid workers and the support of family members.

Floriculture has a vast scope and potential in the Kashmir valley, which is evident from the fact that during the year 1996, an area of 80 hectares was under flower cultivation in J&K, which has currently expanded to the level of 350 ha, with an annual turnover of about Rs. 1,350 lakhs. Further more than 1500 youths are directly engaged under the commercial floriculture sector in Kashmir Division. Moreover, an area of about 9.297 hectares has been covered under protected cultivation, in private sector by raising Tubular Structure

Poly Houses; High Tech Poly Houses, Shade Net Houses, etc. Development of commercial floriculture has been assigned a top priority by the Government, under Technology Mission and RKVY, as it holds a tremendous potential for employment generation.

In Haryana, as more and more culturable area was brought under cultivation, irrigation facilities were increased by expanding canal infrastructure and increase in the number of tubewells. This led to increased intensity of agriculture and more area under high productivity crops. The Green Revolution package was used to increase the productivity of land.

The gross area sown in 1966-67 was 45.99 lakh hectares which increased to 63.57 lakh hectares in 2010-11. The share of area under wheat and paddy crops against the gross area sown in the State was 59.15 per cent during 2010-11. This was about 80 per cent of the total area sown under foodgrain crops. This highlights a major change in the cropping pattern since the inception of Haryana in 1966-67. The area under wheat and paddy was 16.16 per cent and 4.17 per cent respectively of the gross area sown in 1966-67, which increased to 39.17 and 18.99 per cent respectively in 2009-10. Another important change in the cropping pattern of the State is that the area under sugarcane has come down whereas cotton and oilseeds have registered an increase in the area over the period. However, dry crops like gram, bajra and oilseeds still dominate the agricultural scene, especially in less irrigated districts of Mahendergarh, Rewari and Bhiwani. The highest percentage of area under wheat was registered in district Jhajjar (52.11%) in 2009-10, followed by Faridabad (50%). The lowest percentage of area under wheat was registered at 15.30 in district Mahendergarh. Districts Karnal, Kurukshetra, Kaithal, Panipat, Ambala and Yamunanagar, the core region of Green Revolution, have emerged as the major rice producing districts in the State. Other important rice producing districts are Sonepat, Jind, Fatehabad and Panchkula. The only district where rice failed to make its entry was Mahendergarh. Districts Rewari, Bhiwani, Gurgaon and Mewat have little area under this crop.

Sugarcane has lost its importance as a commercial crop in Haryana over time, except in districts Yamunanagar (11.57%), Kurukshetra (4.95%) and Ambala (4.83%). Cotton has emerged as a major commercial crop in districts Sirsa, Hisar, Fatehabad, Jind and Bhiwani whereas oilseeds play an important role in agriculture in Mahendergarh, Rewari, Bhiwani, Mewat, Rohtak and Gurgaon.

The cropping intensity in the State has reached 184 in 2010-11. The agricultural cropping pattern in the State is thus dominated by paddy-wheat rotation, causing degradation in soil fertility and fall in the underground water level.

Most of the area under major crops has been brought under high yielding varieties, recording 97.4, 64.6, 80.0 and 96.2 per cent respectively for wheat, paddy, maize and bajra in 2010-11. The foodgrain production, thus reached an impressive level of 166.29 lakh tonnes during 2010-11, as compared to a meagre production of 25.95 lakh tonnes in 1966-67, registering an increase of about 6 times.

To have a holistic approach in horticulture development from seed to post-harvest management, a State Plan scheme was started in the year 2009-10 for non-NHM Districts with the following objectives:

1. To provide holistic growth of horticulture sector in diverse agro-climate conditions;
2. To cover more area under horticulture by promoting horticulture to new untapped areas;
3. To establish synergy among multiple ongoing and plan programmes; and
4. To promote development and dissemination of ongoing and latest technologies.

The benefits which were seen in NHM Districts specially with regard to the development of clusters and creation of infrastructure in horticulture shall be replicated in the non-NHM Districts to give benefit to the farmers of these districts. During 2014-15, this scheme was implemented as per the provisions and guidelines of the National Horticultural Mission scheme. The activities which have been undertaken including the development of nurseries, vegetable seed production programme especially potato, cluster-based area expansion programme for fruits, vegetables, spices and aromatic plants, tours, trainings, shows, seminars, field days, water conservation techniques like farm ponds, bee-keeping, protected cultivation, marketing infrastructure, farm mechanization and pre- and post-harvest management practices. The assistance shall be available both for the farmers/entrepreneurs and public sector. The percentage of assistance is exactly as per the norms of National Horticulture Mission prescribed by the Government of India and ranges from 25-100 per cent. The main focus is on vegetable cultivation under poly houses.

Horticulture Bio-Technology Centre was started in Haryana in 2008-2009 with the primary objective of multiplication of plants through tissue culture technology and application of biotechnology in the field of horticulture. In 2013-14, a provision of Rs. 80.00 lakh was made and a full-fledged tissue culture laboratory in the name of Horticulture Biotechnology Centre is established adjoining Horticulture Training Institute, Uchani, Karnal. For 2014-15, the budget proposed is Rs. 80.00 lakh and the finances shall be borne by the State Government.

The scheme was formulated with the following objectives:

1. To popularize the tissue culture plants of horticultural crops.
2. To make available the quality seed of potato equivalent to breeder seed through micro tuber technology.
3. To make available the plants and seeds at remunerative prices to the farmers of the State.
4. To keep monitoring the ill effects of earlier adopted packages and practices by adopting DNA finger printing and virus indexing.

With the introduction of this scheme there are efforts for a systematic and planned production of tissue culture plants and potato tubers. Under this programme, micro tubers production of potato and tissue culture plants of banana have already been produced and distributed to farmers in 2008-09, 2009-10, 2011-12, 2012-13 and 2013-14.

Lately, agricultural activities have begun to show signs of fatigue in Punjab. Today, Punjab is at the crossroads, as the existing production pattern and marketing systems are out of tune with the immediate and long-term supply and demand situation in both national and international markets. A package of dynamic, pro-active and responsive policies and action programmes is required to revive Punjab's agriculture, so as to meet the increasing pressures of free trade, liberalization and globalization. The State envisages to have a vibrant, dynamic agricultural sector which is well integrated with the rural economy on the one side and domestic and international markets for the supply of food and fibre on the other. The major approach of the State is to ensure growth and sustainability of agriculture in the State with a thrust on conservation of natural resources, especially land and water, crop diversification and post-harvest handling of produce to improve the quality of produce, minimize the cost of production and improvement in income of farmers.

Against an expenditure of Rs. 739.10 crore during the Eleventh Five Year Plan, an outlay of Rs. 1412.76 crore has been provided in Twelfth Five Year Plan. An expenditure of Rs. 224.41 crore, Rs. 268.11 crore and Rs. 368.26 crore was incurred during 2012-13, 2013-14 and 2014-15 respectively. An outlay of Rs. 412.72 crore is provided in the Annual Plan 2015-16.

Punjab is predominantly an agricultural State where irrigation plays an important role in sustaining its growth and economy. The strategy in the irrigation sector is to rehabilitate the existing canal system and undertake measures such as lining of canals and water courses for minimizing the seepage losses and for the conservation of water. The canal surface water distribution system consists of 14,500 km of canals/distributaries comprising six major systems in the State namely, Sirhind Canal system, Bhakhra Main Line, Bist Doab Canal, Upper Bari Doab Canal, Sirhind feeder and Eastern canal. The canal system which is one of the oldest in the country has outlived its life and its carrying capacity has been sub-optimized.

Horticulture which includes fruits, vegetables, root and tuber crops, mushroom, floriculture, medicinal and aromatic plants, etc., is very significant in improving land-use, promoting crop diversification, generating employment and above all providing nutritional security to the people. Punjab will become a leading State in horticulture research with the setting up of Post Graduate Institute of Horticulture Research and Education in Amritsar. With the establishment of this Institute, crop diversification process in the State will scale new heights.

The main schemes/programmes included in the Punjab Annual Plan (2015-16) are as under:

1. National Horticulture Mission; and
2. Catalytic Development Programme Under Sericulture.

In Punjab, sericulture is under the administrative control of the

Directorate of Horticulture, Punjab. The agro-climatic condition of some pockets of Punjab is quite conducive for the cultivation of Mulberry silk.

2. LIVESTOCK

At the national level, livestock sector has received much less resources and institutional support. Livestock extension remains grossly neglected. The country still lacks adequate facilities and the infrastructure for disease diagnosis, reporting, epidemiology, surveillance and forecasting. Livestock markets are underdeveloped, which is a formidable barrier to the commercialization of livestock production.

Integrated Sample Survey (2011-12) revealed that total livestock population of Jammu region had demonstrated an increase of 8.40 per cent over the year 2009-10 and reached to 78.908 lakh from 72.79 lakh. Kashmir region also witnessed an increase of 4.63 per cent as livestock population had reached to 74.994 lakh from 71.67 lakh. However, in Ladakh region livestock population slipped by 1.44 per cent from 6.60 lakh to 6.5 lakh during the same period.

Average milk yield per day animal during 2011-12 was 5.643 kg for cross-cow, 2.594 kg for local-cows, and 4.895 kg for buffaloes and 0.605 kg for goats.

During 2010-11, the total estimated milk production for Jammu & Kashmir was 1609.247 thousand MT. During the year 2011-12, the total estimated milk production for the State was 1614.57 thousand MTs constituting 982.05 thousand MT (60.83%) of cross-cow milk, 237.19 thousand MT (14.69%) of local-cow milk, 293.70 thousand MT (18.19%) of buffalo milk and 101.62 thousand MTs (62.94%) of goat milk.

Average per capita availability of milk in J&K was 370.10 gms per day which is higher than the national average of 356 gm per person per day in 2010-11.

Average wool yield per annum is 26.218 kg for cross-breed sheep and 17.495 kg for local-breed sheep.

During 2011-12 the total wool production estimated for the State was 75.295 kg which consisted of 61.586 lakh kg (81.79%) from cross-breed sheep and 13.709 lakh kg (18.20%) of local-breed sheep.

During the year 2010-11, the total wool production estimated for the State was 73.819 lakh kg.

Total availability of wool per person per annum is 629.978 gm for the State as a whole which included 515.278 gm from cross-breed sheep and 114.700 gm from local-breed sheep.

Total number of laying birds (hens+ducks) in J&K was 36.866 lakh out of which 84.30 per cent (31.079 lakh) are of Desi category while 15.70 per cent (5.787 lakh) are of improved stock as per ISS estimates for 2011-12.

Estimated total egg production in the State for 2011-12 was 6519.758 lakh out of which 6122.661 lakh (93.91%) were laid by hens and 397.097 lakh (6.09%) by ducks and estimated total egg production of the State for 2010-11 was 6209.333 lakh.

Total egg availability per person was worked out to be 55 (number) per year for the State as a whole as per the ISS report 2011-12 against 53 (No.) for 2010-11.

As per the Integrated Sample Survey Report (ISS), 2011-12, total estimated meat production of J&K was worked out to be 322.781 lakh kg consisting of 80.79 per cent of (260.762 lakh kg) red meat and 19.21 per cent (62.019 lakh kg) of white meat. As per the latest Integrated Sample Survey Report (ISS), 2010-11, total estimated meat production of J&K was worked out to be 308.986 lakh kg.

As per estimated results of ISS survey 2011-12, the meat availability was worked out to be 2.701 kg per person per year against 2.650 kg for 2010-11.

Meat production registered a growth from 308.986 lakh kg to 322.781 lakh kg in 2011-12 over the previous year resulting into 4.47 per cent growth.

Fisheries sector occupies a very important place in the socio-economic development of J&K. It has been recognized as an employment source of cheap and nutritious food, besides being a source of livelihood for a large section of economically backward population of the country. The total fisherman population in the State as per livestock census 2003 was around 31,000. It is presently estimated at 93,000. The 27,781 km length of rivers/streams facilitate farming of more than 40 million tonnes of fish. As against this, the State has only 0.07 lakh hectares under reservoir area. There is a big gap between the demand and supply of fish. Fish is a valuable element of diet of the local people throughout the year. There is also a demand for fish from the defence personnel and tourists. There are 1,248 lakes including waterbodies and water is spread into 0.40 lakh hectares of area which gives an indication of the potential for fisheries in the State.

Poultry production has assumed importance as a major agro-based industry which provides:

- Part-time/whole-time source of earning to the unemployed youth; and
- Highly nutritious animal protein in the form of quality poultry meat and eggs.

The main objective in this sub-sector is to increase poultry meat and egg production by:

- encouraging private enterprises with the requisite technical guidance; and
- providing fast and specific diagnosis of poultry diseases in order to reduce risk of loss to farmers.

The last decade has witnessed tremendous growth in the poultry sector. The poultry farming has come in a big way in Jammu, Kathua, Udhampur, Pulwama and Budgam districts, with large number of educated unemployed youth taking up poultry farming as sustainable means of earning their livelihood.

As per the official estimates, the achievements made in poultry development during last three years are as in Table 2.

Table 2: Achievements in Poultry Development

Sl. No.	*Particulars*	*Unit*	*2008-09*	*2009-10*	*2010-11*	*2011-12*	*2012-13*	*2013-14*	*2014-15 (ending Dec., 2013)*
1.	Production of day old chicks	Lakh Nos	3.29	4.9	6.18	6.35	6.21	6.21	5.545
2.	Breeding birds sold	Lakh Nos	1.24	1.5	1.61	1.92	1.66	1.67	1.117

Source: *Ibid.*

The agro-climatic conditions in the State are conducive for wool and mutton production. This is a primary occupation of migratory tribes. The contribution of livestock to the State economy is quite significant and the sheep and goat population constitutes about 56 per cent of the total livestock. The local Kashmir wool which was primarily used for manufacturing of Namdas and coarse blankets obtained from cross breed sheep; finds its way into the market for making of fine quality tweeds, pullovers and blankets, etc.

The Government of India sanctioned 229 buildings (70 hospitals and 159 veterinary dispensaries) at a cost of Rs. 28.87 crore under the scheme "Establishment and Strengthening of Veterinary Hospitals and Dispensaries" (ESVHD) with central share of Rs. 21.65 crore (75%) in the last financial year against the released amount of Rs. 12.49 crore out of which 74 buildings have been completed so far and the remaining buildings are expected to be completed during the current financial year.

71 Mobile Veterinary centres (Animal Husbandry Jammu 26, Animal Husbandry Kashmir 26, Sheep Husbandry Jammu 09 and Sheep Husbandry Kashmir 10) have been sanctioned alongwith creation of 214 posts of various Non-gazetted and Class IV categories. The mobile ambulatory vehicles shall be fitted with GPS, so as to rationalize and monitor the services to be delivered by the mobile centres.

With a view to timely reporting of disease outbreak and for its effective monitoring, surveillance and ultimate eradication, a Centrally Sponsored Scheme "National Animal Disease Reporting System" (NADRS) has been taken up for implementation. So far 158 nods have been established out of which broad band connectivity has been provided to 60 nods. The scheme was launched in the month of January 2013 and the State will be important constituent of the National Informatics System reporting disease profile and development activities as well. The investment in this activity is being supplemented with assistance under the Centrally Sponsored Scheme "ASCAD" State/District Plan and Non Plan.

Haryana holds a very prominent place in the country for its livestock wealth. The State is proud of being the home tract of the famous breeds of Haryana cows and Murrah buffaloes. According to the 2007 census, the total livestock population in the State is 90.50 lakh consisting of 15.52 lakh cattle, 59.53 lakh buffaloes, 5.38 lakh goats, 0.39 lakh camels, 1.34 lakh pigs, 2,033 lakh horses, ponies donkeys, mules and others. Besides this, there is 287.86 lakh poultry population. Animal power still remains the main source of the draught power in the State to perform various agricultural operations particularly on the small and medium size farms owned by the small and marginal farmers. With this livestock and poultry wealth, Haryana has contributed significantly towards India attaining top position in milk production in the world and fifth top position in poultry production. An outlay of Rs. 14800.00 lakh had been proposed for the Annual Plan 2014-15, which included Central Share of Rs. 1800.00 lakh under Centrally Sponsored Schemes.

Milk production during 2010-11 was 62.67 lakh tonnes. The per capita per day milk availability in the same year was 680 grams in the State, which was the second highest in the country. Production of eggs was 39,644 lakh and that of wool 12.87 tonnes during the same year (*Economic Survey of Haryana*, 2012, p. 28).

In Himachal Pradesh, indigenous cows (non-descript local) are being upgraded by cross breeding programme by breeding with Jersey and Holstein bulls so that the exotic blood level is maintained. The artificial insemination by frozen semen technology is being adopted in cows and buffaloes. Three cattle farms located at Kothipura (Bilaspur), Kamand (Mandi) and Palampur (Kangra) are being run to produce genetically superior breeding bulls.

Artificial insemination facility is being provided through 2,084 veterinary institutions in the State. In the remote areas, where it is not possible to introduce artificial insemination technique, natural service with improved breed of bulls is being carried out. To give boost to cross breeding programme, "HP Livestock Development Board" has been formed by getting 100 per cent grant from the Government of India.

The following measures will be taken for genetic upgradation of livestock during the plan period:

1. Artificial insemination facility in the State will be further strengthened to cover most of the breedable cows and buffaloes for cross breeding purpose. The refresher courses will be arranged for in-service veterinary officers and para-vets to improve the artificial insemination services;

2. Progeny tested semen straws and embryos will be imported to enhance genetic potential of the indigenous animals; and
3. The first Embryo Transfer Laboratory for livestock is being established at Palampur and the technique will be strengthened by imparting training to more veterinary officers in the field of ETT.

Poultry farming plays an important role in improving the socio-economic status of rural population. The scale of eggs on day-to-day basis helps in providing supplementary income as well as nutrition of high protein without incurring extra expenditure. Six poultry farms, six extension centres and two hatcheries are working in the State for the benefit of the farmers. A project for poultry development is also functioning in the State covering 3 districts namely Shimla. Una and Bilaspur. For the development of poultry, the following programmes are being undertaken in Himachal Pradesh:

1. Existing hatcheries will be strengthened by way of renovation of infrastructure along with replacement of old machinery.
2. Carrying capacity of existing hatcheries for rearing of parent stock will be increased so that more number of chicks are available for distribution for self-employment generation and boosting of nutritional status of the beneficiaries.
3. The Government of India will be requested to extend 200 broiler unit schemes presently being implemented for SC families, and also to BPL families of other categories.
4. Efforts will be made to encourage establishment of poultry farm in the private sector to increase population of poultry birds and egg/broiler meat production.

Sheep rearing is one of the main occupations of the people of Himachal Pradesh. Rampur Bushari and Gaddi breeds of Himachal Pradesh are famous for indigenous carpet wool production in the country. In rural areas, 37 per cent of agricultural families rear sheep. The local sheep is crossed with good quality rams of Rambouillet, Russian Merino so that the quality as well as quantity of wool production is increased.

To bring desired increase in quality and quantity of wool produced by the indigenous sheep, the Government has maintained four sheep breeding farms and one ram centre located at Karchham (Kinnaur), Jeori (Shimla), Tal (Hamirpur) and Sarol (Chamba). The high yielding rams of exotic Russian Merino and Rambouillet breeds are sold at nominal rates from these farms to interested sheep breeders to carry out cross breeding of indigenous sheep with these exotic breeds. The ram centre, Nagwain (District Mandi) provides rams during breeding season to sheep breeders and at the end of breeding season, these rams are brought back to the ram centre, so that farmers are saved from the cost of maintaining these rams.

There are ten sheep and wool extension centres in various parts of Himachal Pradesh. These extension centres are also making available pure exotic rams from the State farm or cross-breed ram from improved flock of sheep breeders to interested farmers. These extension centres are also managing health care of sheep flock of their respective regions. Two wool analysis laboratories located at Tal (Hamirpur) and Sarol (Chamba) are also working. These laboratories help in grading of wool and thereby ensuring good price to the sheep owners.

The following measures would be undertaken for the development of sheep and wool in Himachal Pradesh:

1. Existing sheep breeding farms will be strengthened by renovating the infrastructure; and
2. To nullify the adverse effect of in-breeding in the sheep being reared in the farms, efforts will be made to import pure breed Rambuillet/Merino Rams. Cross breeding programme with pure breed of exotic rams will continue to cover maximum number of sheep population.

Himachal Pradesh is blessed with some of the finest rivers, viz., Sutlej, Beas and Chenab originating from the permanent glaciers and spring-beds. The rivers and their branches are bestowed with exotic trout, mahaseer, snow trout, loaches, indigenous lesser barilas and mirror carps. Besides, there are many natural lakes located in the higher reaches, man-made impoundments harbouring more than 78 species of fish belonging to sisordac, belonidae, ophiocephalidae and masteermbelidae in a series of pounds dotted especially in sub-mountainous region.

Fisheries in Himachal Pradesh are artisanal in character involving roughly 12,500 families of fishermen engaging from localized subsistence fishing to highly mobile and intensive fishing. The activities are mainly 'capture' in character where the fishermen operate varied types of fishing devices in open waters.

Objectives of Twelfth Five Year Plan

1. To increase fish production by judicious management of all the culturable water resources;
2. To develop reservoir fisheries with an aim to increase per hectare production from the open impoundments;
3. To undertake breeding programme of Indian and exotic carps, Mahseer, Trouts and other sub-temperate species for augmenting the seed stocking programme in reservoir, rivers and streams alongwith their tributaries and also to produce/purchase fish seed from outside the State so as to accomplish seed stocking as per norms;
4. To protect and conserve reservoir and lacustrine fishery;
5. To promote game fishery with particular emphasis on the promotion of angling tourism;
6. To promote commercial farming of rainbow trout in the high altitude areas;
7. To promote aquaculture by providing technical and financial assistance to the farmers;
8. To generate employment opportunities in the fishery sector and ameliorate the conditions of fishermen; and
9. Improvement in health status of local population especially women and children by ensuring easy availability of animal protein food.

While most of the schemes implemented during the Eleventh Five Year Plan are proposed to be continued, greater emphasis will be on the quality of the execution of the schemes in the Twelfth Plan with an equally strong focus on management and conservation of the resources.

The fish production from reservoirs shall be sustained at a level of 1,000 MT every year to ensure viable livelihood to 4,000 reservoir fishermen families through quality fish seed stocking and enforcement of fisheries legislation. New self employment opportunities shall be created for 3,750 fishermen and 1,050 fish farmers so as to associate these fishermen/fish farmers to increase fish production. The concept of fish culture in cages in reservoirs shall be popularized and used as a tool to increase fish production from the reservoir sector during Twelfth Five Year Plan.

The animal husbandry sector in Rajasthan is harbouring a fabulous livestock wealth, providing subsidiary source of income to a large number of small farmers, marginal farmers, BPL families and agricultural labourers. Distribution of livestock wealth is more egalitarian compared to land. Marginal farmers constitute core livestock production centre. Over 50 per cent of all species are owned by marginal farmers. Livestock sector is extremely livelihood intensive and a major source of sustenance.

Dairy provides milk production as supplementary nutrition and generates income on regular basis. In Rajasthan there is shortage of water in most of the areas and the State faces famine/drought almost every second or third year. This brings agriculture under threat and farmers become insecure. In such situations, animal husbandry provides income and nutrition for their sustenance. Milch animals including goats are mainly looked after by women. Animal Husbandry provides not only recognition to them but also leads to their increased participation in the economy and the availability of cash income which helps them for their socio-economic development. Livestock production in general and cattle and buffaloes in particular is highly woman oriented.

In Rajasthan animal husbandry is not merely a subsidiary to agriculture but is a major economic activity specially in arid and semi-arid areas, thus providing the much needed insurance against prominently occurring scarcity conditions. Next to crop production animal husbandry is the most important activity in Rajasthan. Livestock sector has also the highest potential for rural self-employment with the lowest possible investment and risk. Development of livestock sector, therefore, is critical to rural prosperity.

As against twenty-five well defined breeds of cattle and seven buffalo breeds in the country, Rajasthan is endowed with the finest drought hardy milch breeds (Rathi, Gir and Tharparkar), dual purpose breeds (Kankrej and Haryana) and the famous breeds of Nagori and Malvi.

During the last few years Rajasthan has focused on expansion of health and breeding services by creation/upgradation of institutions and development infrastructure. Veterinary Polyclinics have been started in all districts in the State. The Government has also focused on awareness for breed improvement and disease control. Special efforts have also been made to combat the problem of infertility in cattle and buffaloes.

Rajasthan is second highest milk producer in the country but average production is comparatively lower than other neighbouring States. It is due to large number of scrub bulls and low productive animals. Hence, efforts have been made for breed improvement through expansion of artificial insemination adopting different modes and distribution of improved quality bulls, bucks and rams of indigenous breeds as per breeding policies and castration of scrub bulls.

Rajasthan has also focused on conservation and development of indigenous cattle breeds like Tharparkar, Gir, Kankaraj, Rathi and Shaiwal. For this purpose the newly established University of Veterinary and Animal Sciences, Bikaner has developed four cattle farms and is developing fifth. For expansion of extension and training facilities, the Government has established new Pashupalak Training Institute in Jodhpur and strengthened State Livestock Management and Training Institute, Jaipur. Veterinary University, Bikaner is also establishing Research-cum-Training centres in ten districts with target to have centres in each District.

The State faces frequent drought/famine, which results in shortage of fodder and decline in animal production. The gap between the production and actual requirement of dry as well as green fodder in the State is about 50 per cent. Hence, there is a need for integrated efforts for fodder and quality seed production.

Rajasthan has established mobile veterinary units in every district and Tehsil to provide services in outreach villages every month and in emergency. The State has strengthened infrastructure facilities of veterinary health institutions and training institutions under centrally sponsored Establishment and Strengthening of Veterinary Hospitals and Dispensaries Scheme, Rural Infrastructure Development Fund

(RIDF) of National Bank of Agriculture & Rural Development (NABARD) and Rashtriya Krishi Vikas Yojana (RKVY). The State has developed cold chain maintenance system for vaccine transport and storage to sustain quality of vaccine to develop proper immunity for prevention of contagious diseases.

To combat infertility in cattle and buffaloes, infertility camps are organized under RKVY, SCSP and TSP by selecting 50 animals for a camp. Under RKVY and the State Plan, Veterinary University is also developing education, training, research and technology infrastructures.

Efforts will be made to double the milk yield through breed improvement activities and better health practices in Rajasthan. Integrated Livestock Development (ILD) centres under Public Private Partnership (PPP) mode will be established to expand the outreach services in those areas where no institutional facility of the Government is available. For the conservation and propagation of indigenous cattle like Sahiwal and Haryana in the State, departmental farms will be strengthened with the help of PPP. District/Tehsil Mobile Veterinary Units, insurance of livestock as well as livestock breeders, fodder development activities will be strengthened. For increase in meat and wool production in the State a small Ruminant Development Cell (sheep and goat) will be established.

Objectives

- Increase animal protein availability.
- Improvement of outreach services in remote areas having no veterinary health and breeding facilities.
- Enabling the small producer to have better forward and backward linkages specially marketing of livestock and products, participate in the process of globalization, growth and modernization of the livestock sector.
- Development of fodder resources and to reduce cost of production and ensure sustainable production throughout the year.
- Improvement of quality assurance facilities.
- To utilize livestock sector as a tool for economic and social development and gender equity.

As the sub-sector of agriculture, livestock has left a mark in the rural economy in Jammu & Kashmir and provides gainful employment to marginal and small and landless farmers. It is considered as the booming eco-friendly sector and so, besides covering domestic biodiversity, it is a means of producing food in dry lands without depleting ground water resources. This sub-sector contributes about 11 per cent to the State economy.

There were 98.993 lakh livestock in the stock in 2003 which makes their density 98 animals per sq. km of area. There were 926 animals per 1,000 population in J&K and average livestock was 6 animals for 44 in the year 2001.

Animal husbandry plays an important role in Punjab's rural economy by contributing approximately 13 per cent to the State GDP. The State has extensive veterinary infrastructure for animal health care through which it is providing quality health services to the livestock owners and also giving impetus on improving animal breeds which includes production of better quality of semen and also providing artificial insemination services at the doorstep of the farmers. Surveillance and monitoring of livestock diseases has been one of the major activities of animal health care delivery system in Punjab. There has been an overall increase of 10.9 per cent in the total bovine population in the nineteenth livestock census 2012 as compared to the previous census of 2007. Milk production in Punjab has doubled during the last two decades from around 5.3 million tonnes in 1992-93 to 9.7 million tonnes in 2012-13. The per capita availability of milk in the State is the highest in the country.

Diversification of State agriculture through allied activities comprising animal husbandry, commercial dairying and fisheries has acquired added significance in the reduction of income disparities between the rural and urban population. Livestock keeping along with marketing services, manufacturing of livestock products, inputs and other subsidiary and supporting industries offer a great scope for gainful employment to the expanding labour force, small and marginal farmers and agricultural labour and thereby helping in raising the standard of living of rural population especially of weaker sections of the society.

In the recent past, agriculture in Punjab has reached saturation point and the need for its diversification became important. In this context, dairying has come to the centre stage as a potential alternative.

Dairying is no longer a complementary vocation and has assumed the status of a full fledged vocation.

At present, Punjab produces 9.72 million MT of milk annually, which is about 9 per cent of the total milk production of the nation. The per capita availability of milk in the State is highest in the country, which is recorded as 961 gm per day. Daily milk production is about 266.00 lakh litres. There are 79 Milk Plants (11 in the cooperative sector and 68 in the private sector) with aggregated daily milk handling capacity of 82.39 lakh litres.

The following thrust areas have been identified:

1. Capacity building and landholding of those people who eke out their livelihood with a small dairy unit to make their activity gainful and sustainable.
2. Introducing new dairy training programmes specially designed for educated unemployed youth who are not in a position to start their own dairy farm.
3. Education and training of farmers for diverting them towards commercial dairy farming with special focus on improving quality of milk and value addition at farm level by providing dairy entrepreneurship training.
4. Assisting farmers in establishing commercially viable units of dairy farming for milk production with special stress on economical and scientific animal housing, herd management system, mechanization and remunerative market of milk.
5. Strengthening infrastructure for quality and clean milk production and establishment of farm milk cooler at farm level.
6. Educating consumers about the quality of milk and milk products.
7. Quality Control in animal feeds and supplements.

Management of fisheries in natural waterbodies is done under the Punjab Fisheries Act 1914 and the Punjab Fisheries Rules 1985 framed thereunder. Various conservation measures have been adopted under this Act to have the sustainable fish yield. Besides, the fish production in the natural waters is also increased by stocking fish seeds in these waters.

By adopting the measures indicated above, the fish production has jumped to 6,560 kg/per/ha/per year and fish farming has emerged as suitable alternative to agriculture as returns from fish farming are far more remunerative than agriculture and any other allied activity.

To develop pisciculture in the State, the Government provides various types of inputs to enhance fish production in village ponds and tanks which are given as under:

1. Fish seed from Government Fish Seed Farms in the State;
2. Training of aspirants in fish farming;
3. Extension activities for transfer of technology in respect of fish production to the grass root level; and
4. Subsidy on various items such as excavation of fish ponds renovation of old ponds and first year inputs, etc., and also arrange liberal loans from the financial institutions.

3. RURAL DEVELOPMENT

The true potential of MGNREGA as an instrument of social transformation is yet to be fully realised. There have been many problems in infusing the system with the new culture of demand-driven, rights-based, decentralised decision-making. There are problems that arise from the sheer scale of the programme. At the same time, new opportunities have arisen because of advances in Information Technology that allow us to get rid of inefficiencies and corruption in a manner quite inconceivable in the past. More than 8 crores muster rolls and over 12 crores job cards have been placed online. But there is still a large scope for further systemic improvements.

A large proportion of MGNREGA workers are small and marginal farmers, the productivity of whose lands has been so decimated over the years that they have been compelled to work under the MGNREGA. The real success of MGNREGA will be in raising the agricultural productivity of millions of those farmers who will then be able to return once again to farming and will no longer depend on MGNREGA for their survival.

The advent of MGNREGA has resulted in a significant structural break in rural wage increases. The tightening of the labour market post-MGNREGA is a positive indicator of poverty alleviation and also signals a pressure for technological advances that raise farm productivity in areas of relative labour shortage. This is the process of agrarian transformation the world over.

Nearly 80 per cent of the works under MGNREGA are focused on soil and water conservation on the lands of small and marginal farmers. It is clear that MGNREGA is making a potential contribution to raising their incomes through improved agricultural productivity and also reducing the need for small and marginal farmers to work on MGNREGA sites.

The major weakness so far has been that States have not set up effective systems of recording demand. As demand gets better recorded, there needs to be a corresponding increase in the supply of work. This requires strengthening of capacity at the cutting edge level of implementation. Unfortunately, the main implementation agency under MGNREGA, the Gram Panchayat, is badly lacking in capacities to plan and implement high quality works under MGNREGA.

In Himachal Pradesh, after analyzing the wage employment provided and the nature of assets created under the scheme, the following objectives have been set for the Twelfth Five Year Plan:

1. To ensure guaranteed wage employment to every household whose adult members volunteer to do unskilled manual work under the scheme;
2. Creation of durable directly productive economic assets like water conservation works, irrigation schemes, horticulture, plantation and land development, etc., on community as well as private land of the target group families;
3. To strengthen the rural livelihood resource base for enhancing farm productivity through convergence initiatives;
4. Effective involvement of PRIs in the selection, planning and execution of schemes; and
5. To ensure internet connectivity in all Gram Panchayats and cent per cent operationalization of MGNREGA-MIS.

Strategy

1. Intensive IEC activities will be undertaken to make all rural

masses aware of their entitlements under MGNREGA so that they could avail all benefits under the scheme;

2. There would be a shift from the creation of community welfare assets like rural roads/paths to the creation of durable directly productive economic assets like water conservation works, irrigation schemes, horticulture, plantation and land development, etc., on community as well as private land of the largest groups.
3. MGNREGA funds will be dovetailed with the schemes of other departments like agriculture and horticulture for enhancing the farm productivity and creation of durable and good quality assets.
4. Orientation and training programmes for PRI members will be organized so that these institutions could play an important role in the selection, planning and execution of MGNREGA works.
5. Adequate ICT infrastructure will be provided upto Gram Panchayat level to ensure connectivity and operationalization of MIS.

Expected Outcomes

1. It is expected to generate about 8 crore person days during the Twelfth FY Plan.
2. 100 per cent operationalisation of MIS.
3. Creation of rain water harvesting structure in each household in rural areas.

The success of MGNREGA has been impressive in Rajasthan. Presence of effective grass root NGOs and their ability to mobilize the poor, transparent administration and persistence of drought situation has made Rajasthan a leading State in the implementation of the scheme. Recently, the State has created an infrastructure building fund under the scheme and increased the guaranteed days of jobs to 150 days. This will not only improve the infrastructure in the State but also contribute to the well-being of the people.

Initiatives taken for effective implementation in Rajasthan:

- Work allocation in groups of 5 (self-formed groups by labourers) and daily measurement of work by mate and intimation to the labourer.
- Rationalization of task based on quick Time and Motion Studies.
- Uniform task issued based on type of soil.
- Inspection norms being strictly enforced.
- Inspection of Muster Rolls by NGOs and any public representative is allowed.
- Staggering of Muster Roll.
- Issuance of e-Muster Roll.
- Generation of wage list through MIS.
- Wage card to labourers.
- GR Rules issued.
- Ombudsman appointed for 18 districts.
- Technical Manual, Accounts Manual and Social Audit Manual issued.

About 69 per cent women workers are involved in MGNREGA employment. Several facilities are also provided like crèche facility, water facility, etc. There are equal wages for males and females in MGNREGA.

The number of registered BPL families is too less in Punjab. In fact, the entire list has been exhausted for the construction of houses under Indira Awaas Yojana and the State has not been able to utilize the funds earmarked for this scheme. 11.30 per cent of the total population in Punjab is below poverty line. In rural areas, the percentage of people below poverty line is 7.40 per cent and in urban areas, it is 17.60 per cent. These poverty ratios are based on per day per capita consumption expenditure of Rs. 37.12 in rural areas and Rs. 48.71 in the urban areas of Punjab.

A special NREGA Cell has been established at the State headquarters to coordinate the implementation of this programme all over Punjab. The Government of India has now decided to fix the wage rate under NREGA on the basis of consumer price index which will be implemented on 1st April every year and will be applicable for the whole financial year. An outlay of Rs. 660.00 crore as State share and Rs. 5940.00 crore as central share has been provided in the Twelfth Five Year Plan 2012-17. Against an outlay of Rs. 247.50 crore an expenditure of Rs. 210.54 crore was incurred during 2014-15 in Punjab. An outlay of Rs. 233.00 crore including central share of Rs. 212.00 crore is provided for the annual plan 2015-16.

The National Rural Livelihood Mission works on five critical dimensions of rural livelihood and human development:

- Strengthening the package of credit-*cum*-technology support to strengthen rural livelihood.
- Empowering institutions of the poor that will fundamentally alter the balance of power in rural India.
- Facilitating the poor to complete on more equal terms in the market so that they can derive real benefits from the new opportunities opening up in rural India (rather than being at the receiving end).
- Improving the quality of human development programmes such as drinking water, sanitation and housing by making higher private investments possible through a credit component being added to the subsidies being currently provided.
- Imparting the much needed skills to the rural population to meet the demands of both the growing rural and urban economies and ensuring placement of skilled workers in appropriate jobs.

NRLM will aim at supporting 1 crore youth in the Twelfth FY Plan in this manner. The focus will be on youth from IAP districts, J&K, North Eastern States, districts/Blocks with high SC population and minority concentrated districts. The initiative will also aim at enrolling as many girls as possible.

The self-employment and microenterprises sub-component would pursue multiple streams:

- Micro-entrepreneurs and enterprises directly nurtured by Rural Development and Self-Employment Training Institutes (RUDSETIs).
- Micro-entrepreneurs through apprenticeship and nurturing

by practicing micro-entrepreneurs (as under Kudumbasree in Kerala).

- Working with other training partners, including CBOs, CSOs and so on.

These models envisage transforming unemployed youth into confident self-employed entrepreneurs through a short duration experiential learning programme followed by systematic long duration hand-holding support/apprenticeship. In the Twelfth FY Plan it is proposed to nurture 30 lakh entrepreneurs from among the poor to set-up micro-enterprises.

In Himachal Pradesh, keeping in view the weaknesses or constraints in the past, the following goals/objectives have been set to be achieved during the Twelfth FY Plan:

- Inclusion of every BPL HH in SHG/federation under SGSY/NRLM.
- Scientific analysis based income generation activity selection at all levels, i.e., Panchayat/Block/District level.
- Intervention with restpect to infrastructure creation/marketing linkages and adequate findings based on proper scientific analysis.
- Development of strong monitoring and evaluation system.
- A strong convergence with banks so as to make the financial services people-friendly.
- It is expected that about 55,000 BPL families will be provided financial assistance in the form of loan and subsidy during Twelfth FY Plan. These families will take up self employment ventures to enhance their income.
- Besides this, skill development training to about 71,225 rural BPL youths will be provided and they will be able to get employment in various trades.

In Rajasthan, the SHG movement is about 15 years old and about 3.5 lakh SHGs are reported to have been formed across the State by various departments/agencies. However, many (about 30-35%) SHGs are apparently defunct. SHGs have been formed mainly by the

Department of Women and Child Development (about 65%) and Voluntary Agencies (about 35%). The SHG movement in Rajasthan involves about 40 lakh women, out of whom almost 70 per cent are from disadvantaged sections like BPL, SC, OBC, etc.

The SHG movement in Rajasthan has vast potential of addressing two very critical areas, viz., 'Woman Empowerment' and 'Poverty Alleviation'. But, this potential is yet to be fully realized because the Government has not yet looked at the SHGs as 'strategic intervention' within the State. Banks have also not been very forthcoming in providing credit to the SHGs, which has had a demoralizing effect at times.

There are two critical issues that are working as 'impediments' in realizing the full potential of SHG movement within Rajasthan.

In Rajasthan, under NRLM, the endeavour would be to reach out, mobilize and support 5 million BPL households across the State by facilitating and pro-actively supporting self-managed SHGs and their federal institutions and livelihood collectives. NRLM's long-term dedicated and responsive support would be provided to them along with facilitation support to enable them to come out of poverty. In addition, the poor would be provided increased access to their rights, entitlements and public services. Efforts would be made to empower them socially and economically and reduce their vulnerability by mitigating their risks.

In Rajasthan, the interested rural BPL youth would be offered skill development after counselling and matching aptitude with job requirements, and placed in jobs that are remunerative, self-employed and entrepreneurial oriented. The poor would be provided skills and financial linkages and nurtured to establish and grow with micro-enterprises for products and services in demand. The SHGs will also be able to act as a bridge between banks and the poor who otherwise are not able to link with banks individually. NRLM has provision for payment of interest subsidy as incentive to all SHGs that repay their bank's loans on time. Strengthening of livelihoods of about 6 million families would need significant amount of credit from banks. The banks can continue lending to the poor/SHGs only if they repay bank loan on time. The State government will reimburse 50 per cent of the interest paid by the SHGs to Banks.

The Rajasthan Gramin Ajeevika Vikas Parishad (RGAVP) is implementing livelihood projects (RPLP, MPoWeR, NRLP and

NRLM) in the State to alleviate extreme poverty in the rural areas through creation of institutional platform for poor women. At the time of village entry, a dedicated Block level team of RGAVP (Project Facilitation Team) analyses major gender issues/women related issues in the village and prepare strategy to address the same. All projects have standard processes for the identification of the poorest women/widows/women suffering from violence/women with disability/migrants and women from other vulnerable category. These identified women are organized into SHGs and it is ensured that all women have access to financial institutions and banks. RGAVP provides continuous handholding support till the women get sustainable livelihood and get economically and socially empowered.

Gender sensitization and gender equality have been integral part of capacity building and training for staff recruited under different projects. A comprehensive training module for village organization (VO) which is primarily responsible for the inclusion of vulnerable and left out women, had been developed incorporating women's rights, laws and entitlements under various Government programmes.

Special projects proposed for inclusion of victims of human trafficking and women at risk, will also be taken up on pilot basis in two districts, i.e., Dungarpur and Udaipur.

At the national level, as against the target of 7,98,967 habitations for coverage under NRDWP (National Rural Drinking Water Programme) during the Eleventh Plan, the coverage on 31 March 2012 was 6,65,034 (83%).

The difficulty has been that even as coverage becomes universal, there is a growing problem of 'slipback', with habitations suffering a fall in the watertable and water quality, especially given the growing dependence on groundwater. Water quality has emerged as a growing concern, chemically due to geogenic leaching (arsenic and fluoride) and biologically due to bacteriological contamination. The fact that the same aquifer is being tapped for both irrigation and drinking water, without any coordinated management of the resource, has greatly aggravated availability of drinking water. Lack of convergence with sanitation, on the other hand, compromises water quality, even as it makes provision of improved sanitation difficult.

Poor operation and maintenance have resulted in high rates of attrition and dilapidated facilities. This has happened mainly because primary stakeholders do not feel a sense of ownership over the facility created and in the absence of sufficient support structures and professional capacities, upkeep suffers. On the other hand, where people have been centrally involved, they have both paid for the service provided and felt a stake in maintaining the assets, garnering adequate support for the same.

All the 16,997 villages in Himachal Pradesh as per census 1991 were provided with safe drinking water facilities by March 1994. Thereafter, the focus shifted from village to habitation. As per the survey of 2003, which was finalized during March 2005, total 51,848 habitations have been identified of which 20,112 were categorized as fully covered (FC), 9,389 habitations as non-covered and 22,347 as partially covered (PC). These 31,736 habitations have been categorized as slipped back habitations as per revised guidelines of the Central Government.

With the coming in force of the National Rural Drinking Water Supply guidelines w.e.f. 1-04-2009, after realignment/mapping of habitations, there are 53,201 habitations in Himachal Pradesh. Out of these, 19,743 habitations (7,632 habitations with population coverage >0 and <100 +11,841 habitations with 0 population coverage) are having inadequate drinking water. The criteria of the coverage of habitations have been changed to the coverage of population to ensure water security at household level.

A target to cover 10,725 habitations (5,000 habitations under State sector and 5,725 habitations under central sector) besides installation of 10,000 hand pumps during Twelfth Five Year Plan has been kept in Himachal Pradesh.

The coverage status of rural habitations by rural water supply and sanitation in Punjab as on 31 March, 2015 is given in Table 3.

Table 3: Rural Water Supply and Sanitation

Particular	*Habitations*		
	Main	*Other*	*Total*
Fully Covered Habitations	10989	2495	13484
Not Covered Habitations (NC)	32	70	102
Partially Covered Habitations (PC)	1276	471	1747
	12297	3036	15333

Source: Department of Planning, Govt. of Punjab, 2015.

Presently, 99 per cent of rural population has been covered with supplies of potable drinking water. Moreover, 8,200 habitants get 70 lpcd service level. The State government has notified Punjab State Rural Water Supply and Sanitation Policy 2014. The main aim of the policy is to provide (a) 100 per cent coverage of all households in rural areas of Punjab with at least 70 lpcd of potable water, supplied through 24x7 piped and metered individual water supply connections and (b) to ensure that 100 per cent rural households have access to and use safe sanitation facilities that do not contaminate the environment, particularly ground water.

Heavy metal contamination in ground water is an emerging challenge for the State. As per recent report the samples of 3,937 habitations have been found contaminated with various toxic metals like uranium, nickel and aluminium. To provide safe drinking water, 1,824 Reserve Osmosis (ROs) have already been set up. Besides, the State government is installing 561 RO systems under the NABARD project of Rs. 88.74 crore. The State has a proposal to provide safe drinking water in 1971 quality affected habitations by installing 1,829 RO systems.

As per Census 2011, the State has 70.4 per cent coverage of Individual Household Latrines (IHHL) in rural Punjab. A total 33,15,632 households exist in rural Punjab, out of which 23,34,205 households are having individual latrines. Year 2012 survey reveals that 8,38,950 IHHL are yet to be constructed in the rural areas of the State; out of which 2,22,555 and 6,16,395 are BPL and APL respectively. Implementation of Second World Bank project and convergence of the project with Swachh Bharat Mission (Gramin) would ensure individual toilets for every household in the State by 2018.

4. EMPLOYMENT AND SKILL DEVELOPMENT

In agriculture, at the national level, there has been an increase in the absolute number of people employed during 1996-2000 to 2009-10, although in the second half of the decade the proportion has declined marginally. The vast majority of States have also experienced a decline in employment in agriculture between 2004-05 and 2009-10. However, since the total fall in employment in agriculture in the latter half of the decade was only 14.08 million, the distribution of this decline among the States did not lead to a significant shift of workers out of agriculture to industry or services.

This does not indicate that temporary migration from rural to urban areas was not occurring. This may be because workers do migrate from rural to urban but only for temporary periods during the lean season for agriculture and move back during the peak reason. Therefore, this workforce is not available for work in manufacturing or modern services due to lack of appropriate skill set. Their migration reflects rural distress, driven by the fact that 84 per cent of India's farmers are small and marginal, tilling less than 2.5 acres of land.

The cornerstone of the manufacturing policy for the Twelfth FY Plan is to create 10 million additional jobs in the manufacturing sector by focusing on labour-intensive manufacturing and by suitable amendments to the labour regulatory framework, so that manufacturing becomes a genuine engine of employment growth in the country. If focused on more productive and quality (organized and self-employed) employment in the manufacturing and services sector, additional 50 million job opportunities can be created in the non-farm sector. But this will need a huge effort in the form of skill development aligned to the market needs. In particular, manufacturing, construction, trade, transport, hospitality and financial services are the promising sectors where skill development can lead to a faster growth in employment opportunities.

As more skilled people come back to the labour force after completing their education and training to join the workforce, those underemployed in agriculture will be drawn out to fill the job opportunities created by the non-farm sector.

The following strategies for expanding and scaling up the skill development have been chalked out in the Twelfth FY Plan:

- Expanding outreach to bridge all divides.
- Improving quality through better infrastructure, new machines and technology and trainers.
- Defining standards for outcome driven training programmes and regular monitoring.
- Introducing flexibility by adopting global standards and dynamic processes to suit the requirement of both national and international users.

- Developing strong partnerships between all stakeholders, encouraging private partners through incentives.
- Creating enabling environment and monitoring training programmes to achieve outcomes.

Table 4: Unemployment Rate as per Usual Principal Status in J&K in comparison with the neighbouring States All India as per 68th Round of NSS

State	*Rural*			*Urban*			*Rural+Urban*		
	Male	*Female*	*Persons*	*Male*	*Female*	*Persons*	*Male*	*Female*	*Persons*
J&K	2.7	16.6	3.9	4.7	25.6	7.8	3.2	20.2	4.9
H.P	1.8	1.8	1.8	2.1	11	4.2	1.8	2.2	2
Punjab	2.3	6.1	2.6	2.8	5.1	3.1	2.5	5.6	2.8
Haryana	2.6	4.2	2.8	4	5.6	4.2	3.1	4.8	3.2
Delhi	9.4	0	7.8	3.4	4.8	3.6	3.9	4.3	4
All India	**2.1**	**2.9**	**2.3**	**3.2**	**6.6**	**3.8**	**2.4**	**3.7**	**2.7**

Source: National Sample Survey (NSS), 2011-12.

As per the 68th Round of NSS July 2011 to June 2012, based on Usual Principal Status (UPS), J&K has the highest unemployment rate of 4.9 per cent in comparison to its neighbouring States, viz., Punjab (2.8%), H.P. (2.0%), Delhi (4.7%), Haryana (3.2%). All India figures for unemployment rate stood at 2.7 per cent only. Unemployment rate for males in J&K was 3.2 per cent only whereas that of females was 20.2 per cent which is far too high when compared to the unemployment of females in neighbouring States, viz., Punjab (5.6%), Haryana (4.8%), Delhi (4.3%), H.P. (2.2%). The problem of unemployment amongst females is predominant in J&K based on Usual Principal Status has revealed the gap between unemployment rate of females in J&K (20.2%) and that of All India level (3.7%) is huge.

Unemployment rate in the urban areas of J&K based on 68th Round of NSS stood at 7.8 per cent as against 3.9 per cent in rural areas. The unemployment amongst urban male (4.7%) is higher than that of rural males (2.7%) in J&K. Rural female unemployment in J&K stood at 16.6 per cent which is far too high as compared to the neighbouring States, viz., Punjab (6.1%), H.P. (1.8%), Haryana (4.2%) and All India figures of 2.9 per cent only.

J&K has certain inherent strengths that can be utilized to improve the income of its people and to provide gainful employment opportunities on sustainable basis, which are:

- (i) Strong base of traditional skills not found elsewhere;
- (ii) Untapped natural resource; and
- (iii) A natural environment which has been very profitably utilized by other countries for high income-environment friendly tourism industry.

In order to sustain growth and employment in its economy, the State Government should articulate an Employment Policy focusing on:

- (i) Improving the productivity of, and thereby income of, those engaged in industries based on traditional skills,
- (ii) Shifting the agricultural work force to high value-added/high income agriculture/horticulture;
- (iii) Transforming the service industry in the State, driven by tourism, from informal and low income to modern by setting up a world class tourism infrastructure, largely on the basis of private investment and entrepreneurship; and
- (iv) Creating a vibrant self-employed-professional workforce, which does not depend on government jobs, or for off-take of its services by government alone.

The policy would need to incorporate the following objectives:

1. To exploit the full growth potential of the sectors and sub-sectors which are important to the State's economy.
2. To create necessary infrastructure and extension services for diversification of agriculture and setting up new enterprises in manufacturing or services sector.
3. To rehabilitate people who have suffered loss in employment due to the slow down in the economy.
4. To assist the self-employed workers to upgrade themselves through provision of credit, marketing, technological and training facilities.

The following 8 sectors of economy have been identified in J&K for the generation of gainful employment opportunities on sustainable basis:

- Agriculture (including horticulture, floriculture, food processing and animal husbandry),
- Handlooms and handicrafts,
- Industries (including small scale industries and rural industries),
- Tourism and travels,
- Education and health,
- Large infrastructure projects (roads and railways),
- Information technology and telecommunication, and
- Construction Sector.

Extending support to entrepreneurs to set up small and medium enterprises for self employment would appear to be the most effective and durable way of doing this. A large number of workers in J&K have traditionally been self-employed in activities such as handlooms and handicrafts, tourism, horticulture, food processing, etc. The disturbed conditions prevailing in the State have affected them adversely to varying degrees. While some of the workers have suffered loss of employment, majority are working at very low levels of income and productivity. Also, in many of the identical areas, especially horticulture and food processing, a large potential for growth lies untapped waiting to be exploited.

Different sectors and sub-sectors of the State's economy would require different kinds of interventions for revival/growth depending upon the nature of the activity, the impediments to growth and the institutions that are in place to encourage or promote growth. Specific interventions through Government schemes and the special employment programmes like PMRY, REGP, SGSY, NREGS and J&K Self Employment Scheme would be important for giving better employment orientation to growth of the State economy.

The Industrial Training and Vocational Education Department, Haryana provides skill training to the youth of the State making them able to get better job opportunities or they can opt for self-employment. There is a 20 per cent reservation for SC students in all the institutes being run under this department, but there is a need to provide training to more youths of weaker sections of the society to make them economically self-sufficient. Additional wings are being established in this scheme exclusively for the SC students in Government ITIs under the Scheduled Castes Sub Plan (SCSP). Admissions have been made in 14 wings namely Adampur, Panipat, Kalka at Bitna, Meham, Hansi, Kurukshetra, Narnaul, Hassangarh, Gohana, Ganaur, Narwana, Ferozepur Zirka and Sadhora till session 2013-14. The construction work of wings of Government ITIs Sadhora and Nagina has been completed under this scheme during the year 2014-15.

All courses running in the Government Industrial Training Institutes in Haryana are to be affiliated with the National Council of Vocational Training (NCVT). Machinery, equipments and furnitures are provided in these institutes as per norms prescribed by NCVT. To keep pace with the changing technology and liberalization of economy, outdated and worn out machinery has to be replaced with modern updated machinery. Some units of the Government ITIs are still to be affiliated with NCVT. There is deficiency of machinery, equipment and furniture in these units and this will have to be made up urgently. The students will be able to get better employment after getting the intensive computer training in industries including information technology sector. Hence, many Government ITIs have been converted into societies to provide functional, financial and managerial autonomy. Several Government ITIs have been upgraded into Centres of Excellence. Different courses of 1 year to 3 years duration are running in the Government Industrial Training Institutes in different trades.

The Department of Industrial Training, Haryana is imparting skill based training to unemployed youth through a network of 134 Government ITIs (103 Co-Educational and 31 for Women) and 95 Private ITIs with 42,892 sanctioned seats in Government ITIs and 13,076 seats in private ITIs.

The following programmes/schemes are being undertaken aiming at industrial expansion skill development and employment in Himachal Pradesh during the Twelfth FY Plan period:

- Creation of new industrial infrastructure by establishing three new industrial estates which would accommodate 250 new industrial units providing employment to 3,000 persons.

- Adequate support to the rural artisans through various centrally sponsored and State schemes for the promotion or development of handloom and handicrafts. 35,000 rural artisans are proposed to be trained in different trades during the Twelfth FY Plan period.
- Enhancing productivity and competitiveness through capacity building of the small enterprises for the promotion of village industries. This would be achieved through the establishment of 2,500 SSIs with the employment of 25,000 persons in the small scale industrial units.
- Tapping potential belts of the State for intensive sericulture activities and encouraging tussar sericulture to ensure utilization of wild oak leaves for cocoon rearing. Twelfth Plan envisages production of 900 MT of reeling cocoon and generation of 35 lakh man-days.
- Upgradation of existing industrial and social infrastructure in the industrial areas and the areas of industrial concentration.
- Qualitative improvement in the extension services so that the industrial activities in the backward areas of the State also generate maximum employment opportunities.
- Facilitate creation and augmentation of farm gate infrastructure, supply chain and other logistics including storage and processing capacity and development of human resources for the promotion of food processing industry in Haryana.
- Effective promotion of cleaner technology of scientific exploitation of minerals and adoption of best environment management system.
- Improving service delivery system through Baddi-Barotiwala-Nalgarh Development Authority to ensure speedy development of Baddi-Barotiwala-Nalgarh area. Tap resources through various schemes of the Ministry of Commerce and Industries for the upgradation of industrial infrastructure especially in the areas of industrial concentration in the districts of Solan, Sirmaur and Una.
- Completion of the implementation of handloom clusters in Gohar, Kangra, Reckong Peo, Rampur, Janjehli, Jawali and

Tissa as sanctioned by the Government of India under the Integrated Handloom Development Scheme.

- Implementation of new Centrally Sponsored Scheme—Revival, Reform and Restructuring Package of Handloom Sector on 90:10 sharing basis.
- Providing self-employment opportunities to the rural unemployed youth through the implementation of "Swarojgar Yojana" through Khadi and Village Industries Board.
- Convergence with MNREGA to promote sericulture in the State and productivity improvement through Catalytic Development Programme of CSB.
- Effective implementation of PMEGP with an objective to create employment opportunities providing training to young entrepreneurs through Entrepreneurship Development Programme (EDP), Industrial Awareness Programmes (IAPs) and Industrial Awareness Workshops (IAWs).
- Setting up of State Food Processing Mission (SFPM) and District Food Processing Missions at the district level. Preparation of Vision Document outlining SWOT analysis for fostering and promoting FPI in the State. Collaborating with the Polytechnics, ITIs and other Training Institutes and NGOs for providing training in the field of Food Processing Industry.

Growth in employment, especially in the organized sector, has not been commensurate with growth in the economy. To enhance the employability of the youth in the State, the Government of Punjab created a separate Department of Employment Generation and Training in March 2007.

Manpower survey of unemployment has been completed for 22 districts. Mass counselling programmes providing educational and vocational guidance to youth are being organized since 2008 in all the districts. The department is also the nodal office for providing training to the youth. There are 16 training camps where basic training is given to the youth. Each camp is commanded by Lt. Col. (Retd.) as an Adjutant-*cum*-Training Officer. During 2014-15, training has been provided to 8,784 candidates. An expenditure of Rs. 506 crore was incurred during 2014-15 and Rs. 7.45 crore is provided for the Annual Plan 2015-16.

Construction Skill Development Centre has been set up in collaboration with Larsen & Toubro (L&T) and Driving & Automotive Skill Centre set up in collaboration with Tata Motors in Lambi Block, district Muktsar, provide training in different trades, i.e., mason, bar bender, carpenter, plumber, welder and electrician. During 2013-14, training has been provided to 70 candidates.

16 C-PYTE centres have been set up in the State for training of youth for job in army and para-military forces. During the year 2013-14, these centres imparted training to 9,273 candidates and 8,784 candidates in 2014-15.

Maharaja Ranjit Singh Armed Forces Preparatory Institute, Mohali has been established at a cost of Rs. 10.00 crore to facilitate placement of youths in defence services. Every year the Institute imparts training to prepare students of + 1 and + 2 for various jobs at officers level in the armed forces. During 2014, 41 students were trained for NDA. During 2013, 7 cadets successfully made their way to the NDA. 22 cadets joined NDA in 2014, among them one cadet stood first in the entire country. Against an actual expenditure of Rs. 1.80 crore incurred during 2014-15, an outlay of Rs. 3.00 crore has been provided for the Annual Plan 2015-16.

To tackle the problem of unemployment, a Marine Academy at Rup Nagar will be set up to train about 600 students from science background and prepare them for various trades of Navy. An outlay of Rs. 5.00 crore is provided in Annual Plan 2014-15.

The youth of the State are being provided Skill Development Training through the following institutions under the State Skill Development Mission constituted in Employment Generation and Training Department, Punjab.

(i) State Institute of Automotive and Driving Skill Mahuana District Muktsar Sahib.

(ii) Construction Skill Development Centre.

(iii) Foreign Employment and Training Bureau.

(iv) Centre for Employment and Training of Punjab Youth (C-PYTE).

(v) Maharaja Ranjit Singh Armed Forces Preparatory Institute, Mohali.

(vi) Punjab Police Security Corporation.

(vii) Apparel Textile Design Centre Khuni Majra.

(viii) Marine Academy.

The Government of Punjab accords highest priority to the skill development of youths in the State. For the effective implementation of various skill development schemes across various departments, Punjab Skill Development Mission has been constituted on 2nd September, 2014 by the Department of Technical Education and Industrial Training with three bodies—Governing Council, State Steering Committee and State Executive Committee.

Punjab Skill Development Mission will bring the necessary synergy, oversight and effective coordination in the implementation of various skill development schemes. An overarching MoU has been signed with NSDC to improve the employability skills of the beneficiaries participating in skill development schemes. The State has carried out an extensive exercise to weed out the obsolete course in ITIs and introduce a new course. It has planned to take its current capacity of 22,000 student to 40,000 in a phased manner. An amount of Rs. 267.92 crore has been earmarked for skill development of 1,21,000 youth under the following Skill Development Scheme:

Skill Development Scheme is a component of Skill Development Mission. The objective of the scheme is to provide vocational training to school leavers, existing workers, ITI graduates, etc., to improve their employability by optimally utilizing the infrastructure available in the government, private institutions and the industry. For the implementation of the scheme, the GoI provides funds for the reimbursement of training cost and assessment fee as well as for administrative expenses. The training is provided by Vocational Training Providers (VTPs) registered with DGE&T, GoI and its assessment is done as per the pre-defined parameters by the assessing bodies, approved by GoI. There are 87 assessing bodies approved on the panel. An outlay of Rs. 2.50 crore is provided under Skill Development Mission/Initiative Scheme for the Annual Plan 2015-16.

5. EDUCATION

There is a need for a clear shift in strategy from a focus on inputs and increasing access and enrolment to teaching—learning process and its improvement in order to ensure adequate learning outcomes. In this context, States need to set up transparent and reliable systems for tracking attendance in a meaningful way and work on effective strategies for boosting and sustaining high levels of attendance throughout the school year.

While there has been a decline in the percentage of out-of schools children (OOSC) across gender and social categories, Muslim, scheduled caste and scheduled tribe children, need greater and focused attention. The number of OOSC who are physically and mentally challenged remain a cause of concern.

The number of elementary schools that do not comply with the Right to Education (RTE) norms for the required PTR (pupil-teacher ratio) is fairly high. School-wise analysis based on District Information System for Education (DISE) 2009-10 indicated that 46 per cent of primary and 34 per cent of upper primary schools have poor PTRs.

Another serious challenge is the presence of teachers without professional qualifications approved by the National Council of Teacher Education (NCTE) as required under the RTE Act.

Only 4.8 per cent government schools have all the nine facilities stipulated in the RTE Act, approximately one-third of the total schools have up to seven facilities, and about 30 per cent schools do not have even five of these facilities. Keeping in view the RTE stipulations, these facilities have to be provided in all schools in a time-bound manner.

The biggest concern in elementary education is the poor level of student learning—be it scholastic and co-scholastic/non-cognitive.

At the heart of the issue of quality are the weak teaching processes and transaction between teachers and learners that are neither child friendly nor adopt child centred approach to curriculum. The capacity, motivation and accountability of teachers to deliver quality education with significant and measurable improvements in learning outcomes of students need to be critically and urgently addressed.

Improving learning outcomes is crucial for inclusive growth and, therefore, a major focus of the Twelfth Five Year Plan has been on measuring and improving learning outcomes for all children, with a clear recognition that increasing inputs (number of schools, classrooms, teachers, and so on) will by themselves not enough to ensure quality education for all children.

Pre-service and in-service training of teachers has been mounted on a mission mode during Twelfth FY Plan. In particular, modular teacher training programme should be developed so that para teachers can attend training courses during the summer and winter vacations and get formally qualified over a three to five years period. In-service training using technology and innovative delivery methods could address the problem of poor quality of existing teachers.

Thrust areas during the Twelfth Five Year Plan in Himachal Pradesh are as follows:

- Minimization of drop out rate to zero level at elementary stage of education (Class I to VIII) in the State.
- To achieve the targeted level of 100 per cent enrolment of children of age 6-14 as per SSA goal to universalize the elementary education in the State.
- To improve quality of education at elementary level.
- To ensure that all district as well as Block offices are properly equipped with required facilities such as telephone, fax, photostat and computer hardware and introduce web-based monitoring of different programmes implemented by the department for ensuring faster and reliable exchange of information/data.
- To ensure availability of proper infrastructure for all district or Block offices as well as in all primary elementary schools of the State.
- To enhance the capacity of existing teaching man power by imparting better training to improve their teaching skill or technique so that they could handle the children more efficiently.

Haryana is implementing the centrally sponsored scheme of Sarva Shiksha Abhiyan (SSA) in financial partnership with the Central Government. The financial partnership in Twelfth FY Plan period between the State and Central Government has been approved by the State in the ratio of 65:35 during 2008-09 to 2014-15. This scheme is to be implemented through a State level society and the work has been entrusted to Haryana State Project Director (SPD). The objectives are to be achieved by various inputs, i.e., provision of teachers, opening of schools, alternate school facilities, quality improvement programmes, provision and strengthening of infrastructure, etc.

Under this scheme (sharing basis), an outlay of Rs. 25,000 lakh as Central Share and Rs. 35,000 lakh as State Share has been proposed during the year 2014-15.

Though Rajasthan's per capita income is relatively low, it spends around 4.5 per cent of GSDP on education, and this ratio has been increasing over the past decade. Furthermore, Rajasthan allocates more than half of its education budget to elementary education, with a strong pro-poor focus, and this share has gone up in recent years.

Literacy rate of the State as per 2011 Census is 66.11 per cent. The female literacy rate is 52.12 per cent the decadal literacy rate of India and Rajasthan are shown in Table 5 :

Table 5: Comparative Literacy Rate

Year	*Decadal Literacy Status of India and Rajasthan*					
	Total Literacy Rate		*Male Literacy Rate*		*Female Literacy Rate*	
	India	*Rajasthan*	*India*	*Rajasthan*	*India*	*Rajasthan*
1951	16.67	8.95	24.95	14.44	7.93	3.00
1961	28.30	18.12	40.39	28.08	15.33	7.10
1971	34.45	22.57	45.95	33.87	21.97	10.01
1981	43.56	30.09	56.37	44.76	29.75	13.99
1991	52.21	38.55	64.13	54.99	39.29	20.44
2001	65.38	60.40	75.85	75.70	54.46	43.85
2011	72.99	66.11	80.89	79.19	64.64	52.12

Source: Census, 2011.

Progress in education is Rajasthan has been made possible by the interaction of a number of factors. The key factors include:

- Progressive national policies that mandated State actions, starting with the landmark National Educational Policy of 1986 which set up the framework for partnership between the Union and the State Governments. Significant changes in the Indian educational context have occurred over the 1990s including the recognition of universal elementary education (UEE) as a legitimate demand and State commitment towards universalizing elementary education, clearly demonstrated in the 86th Constitutional Amendment (2002), which makes education for children between the ages of 6-14 years a Fundamental Right. Derived from this, the Right to Education Act 2009 seeks to mandate proactive action on the part of the State *vis-à-vis* every child of the country in the 6-14 age group *via* Article 21A.

- Strong civil society and NGO activism to champion the causes of women and socially disadvantaged groups, has led to the development of innovative models to address issues in education (such as Lok Jumbish or community education project and Shiksha Karmi or Para Teacher for remote communities) in partnership with the State. These successful models were scaled up by Centrally Sponsored Schemes (CSS) like the District Primary Education Programme (DPEP) of the 1990s and National programme for Universal Elementary Education (Sarva Shiksha Abhiyan or SSA) of the 2000s.
- Effective partnership with external agencies that provide exchange of ideas, support and additional financing; with three external partners—the World Bank, Department for International Development (DFID), and European Commission (EC)—pooling up.

In Rajasthan, the following quality interventions in elementary education are noteworthy:

Although the State has achieved substantial improvement in school access and infrastructure but quality of education and learning levels of children still remain a challenge. Principles given in National Curriculum Framework (NCF) 2005 and provisions of RTE Act 2009 put focus on key areas of quality of education. These areas are mainly linked to improvement in classroom processes, curriculum revisions, teacher education and minimum standards for a school.

Teacher recruitment in the quality of teacher development as per the provisions of RTE.

Improvement in the quality of teacher training by making them relevant and modular. Resource support from civil societies working for teacher education will be ensured to address large number of teachers. Head Teachers will go through training on school management with a quality focus to be able to run schools effectively.

All the quality interventions require rigorous research based planning and implementation. Research based academic institutes such as SIERT, State Institute of Educational Management and Training (SIEMAT), and Institute of Advanced Studies in Education (IASE) have been designed to guide implementing agencies such as Department of Elementary Education (DOEE) and SSA. SIERT has been declared as 'Academic Authority' for the State under RTE Act. DIETs are the extended hands of SIERT at district level of work as mentor and provide academic support. Paradigm shift in the structure and redefining the functions of the institutes will help the State to face recent challenges in the field of elementary education.

Section 24 and 29 of RTE Act and Rule 20 of "Right of Children to Free and Compulsory Education Rules 2011" talk about the duties of teachers. With an effective monitoring system in place and regular academic support to teachers a campaign would be undertaken for capacity building of teachers to perform as per the duties given in Right to Education Act 2009.

Enhancing the present school academic support will be one of the focus of the Plan period with more human and financial resources for this. Capacities of the supervisory system will be enhanced to become effective mentors of teachers with a quality focus.

The Government of Rajasthan is rigorously piloting all the aspects of the implementation of CCE (Continuous and Comprehensive Evaluation). It is envisaged that by the end of Twelfth Five Year Plan CCE will be part of school processes in the entire State.

The Government is planning to establish library in all the schools which will enhance the teaching learning processes in the schools.

Section 21 of RTE Act lays down the details of provision and constitution of school management committees to establish community ownership in the management of the schools. SMCs of all government schools in Rajasthan have been constituted as per RTE provisions.

Provision of inclusion of 50 per cent females as members in the committee gives the opportunity to mothers to participate in the management of the schools of their children.

In Rajasthan, elementary education has been transferred to Panchayati Raj Institutions.

Public Private Partnership would be encouraged in the teachers training, girls education, adoption of schools, etc. During the Twelfth Plan, there would be deeper engagement with NGOs as well as corporate partners. Bhamashah scheme will be restructured to encourage private as well as community partnerships.

The literacy rate of Punjab at 69.69 per cent (as per 2001Census) increased to 76.70 per cent in 2011 showing decadal growth of 7.01 per cent. The literacy rates over the years in the State are given in Table 6:

Table 6: Literacy Rates by Sex in Punjab (in %)

Sl. No.	*Year*	*Persons*	*Males*	*Females*
1.	1971	34.12	42.23	24.65
2.	1981	43.37	51.23	34.35
3.	1991	58.51	65.66	50.41
4.	2001	69.69	75.23	63.36
5.	2011	76.70	81.50	71.30

Source: Census of India 2001 and 2011.

The State has notified RTE rules under which every habitation has to be served with a primary school within one km radius and upper primary school within 3 km radius. As per school mapping done in 2011-12, there are 65 villages which do not have access to a primary school within one km radius and 57 villages which do not have access to UPS within 3 km radius. Primary to upper primary school ratio in the State is 2.13:1.

There are two levels of school education, i.e., elementary education (primary 1-5 classes and middle 6-8 classes) and secondary education (high 9-10 classes and senior secondary 11-12 classes). There are total 29,182 government, government aided, affiliated and non-affiliated schools, out of which 13,185 are government primary schools, 2,885 government upper primary schools, 1,817 high schools and 1,613 senior secondary schools.

Punjab is successfully implementing the national programme of Mid-Day Meal in the schools for 240 days in an academic year. Currently, the programme covers 11.05 lakh children in Government, Government Aided Schools, Local Bodies, Special Training Centres and National Child Labour Project (NCLP) for 13,642 Institutions (classes I-V) and 6.98 lakh children of 6712 Government/Government Aided Schools (classes VI-VIII). Mid-Day Meal in the districts of Amritsar, Patiala, Moga, Bathinda, Sangrur, SAS Nagar and Shaheed Bhagat Singh Nagar is being provided to students through the NGOs under municipal limits.

The Government of Punjab has by and large fulfilled its obligations under the Right to Education Act. The Rules have been notified. The guidelines for admission of 25 per cent students belonging to weaker sections have been issued. Household survey has been done for the identification of out of school children in the age group of 6-14 and 9,087 children have been identified.

Under Right to Education Act 2009, private schools are required to admit students belonging to weaker sections into class-I to the extent of 25 per cent of the strength and provide free education till elementary level. These schools will be reimbursed the expenditure incurred on these students by the State government. Right to Education Act 2009 has been enacted by the Central Government and, therefore, there should be provision for sharing of burden by the Central Government.

Under Sarva Shiksha Abhiyan, 236 new primary schools, 855 new upper primary schools and 25,253 additional class rooms have been completed. Under Sarva Shiksha Abhiyan, 6,863 posts of Upper Primary Teachers (1,851 Science and Math, 2,273 SST and 2,739 language) and 3,798 posts of Primary Teachers have been sanctioned. All these sanctioned posts have been filled and all are in position.

As a consequence of sustained investment in education sector in Jammu & Kashmir, there has been an exponential growth of the institutional network. The number of educational institutions in public sector reached 24,265 and those in private sector 5,292 in the State. The total enrolment has also increased to 27.41 lakh out of which the enrolment in primary classes is 10.97 lakh, in High/Higher Secondary schools 9.38 lakh.

With the planned interventions and sustained efforts, considerable progress has been made in J&K in the field of literacy. Census 1961 put the literacy rate of the State at 11.03 per cent which increased to 18.58 per cent during 1971 Census. In 1981, the literacy rate was recorded at 26.67 per cent and the projection for 1991 was made at 45 per cent as no census was carried out during the later period. During the decade 2001-2011, literacy rate increased from 55.50 per cent to 68.74 per cent in J&K as against 64.84 per cent to 74.04 per cent at the national level.

Gender differential exists both in the rural and urban areas of Jammu & Kashmir but it is high in rural areas. This can be attributed to a number of factors like social dogmas, engagement of girl child in agricultural and other domestic activities, etc. At the national level, the gender gap in literacy has decreased drastically from 25.06 per cent in 1961 to 21.59 per cent in 2001 and further to 16.68 per cent in 2011. Contrary to this, the gender gap in literacy increased in the State from 12.71 per cent in 1961 to 23.60 per cent in 2001. Accordingly, the Government, both at the national and State levels made all out efforts to reduce the gender gap in literacy. A number of steps for the accomplishment of the goal of bridging gender gap in literacy were taken up and these include National Programme for Education of Girls at Elementary Level (NPEGEL), Establishment of Kasturba Gandhi Balika Vidyalayas (KGBVs), Free Text-Books/ scholarships, community mobilization, establishment of women ITIs and women wings in the existing ITIs, reservation of half of the seats for females in the Medical Colleges, focus on adult female illiterates under the Saakshar Bharat Mission (SBM), etc. As a result of these measures, the State has been able to break this impasse and put a halt to the ever increasing trajectory of gender gap for the first time during the decade 2001-2011 when the gender gap got reduced to 20.25 per cent. This was possible only due to higher rate of increase in the

Table 7: Gender gap in literacy 1961-2011

Sl. No.	Census year	Male		Female		Gender gap in literacy
		Male literacy rate	Increase in literacy %age over the preceding census year	Female literacy rate	Increase in literacy %age over the preceding census year	
1.	1961	16.97	—	4.26	—	12.71
2.	1971	26.75	9.78	9.28	5.02	17.47
3.	1981	36.29	9.54	15.88	6.60	20.41
4.	2001	66.60	30.31	43.00	27.12	23.60
5.	2011 (Provisional)	78.26	11.66	58.01	15.01	20.25

Source: Census, 2011.

female literacy, viz., by 15.01 per cent as against 11.66 per cent recorded for males during 2001-11.

Ever since the launch of Sarva Shiksha Abhiyan (SSA), Mid-Day Meal Scheme (MDMS) and initiation of host of steps like provision of free text-books, scholarships, various educational facilities at an easy reach, etc., Jammu & Kashmir has been able to reduce the drop-out rate. The dropout rate at primary level has declined to 6.24 per cent and at Upper Primary level declined to 5.24 per cent. It is hoped that the dropout rate will certainly come down further and that too quite steeply in near future.

The Sarva Shiksha Abhiyan (SSA) is primarily a flagship programme aimed at achieving universalization of elementary education, enrolment of all Out of School Children (OoSC) in schools by 2012, retention of all OoSC in Upper Primary stage by 2012, thrust on quality education and bridging gender and social category gaps in enrolment, retention and learning besides development of schools infrastructure. To achieve the goals of the above mentioned interventions, a survey named "TALAASH" to identify OoSC was conducted throughout J&K in 2012-13. After collection, compilation and analysis of data the OoSC population was found as 59,061. In 2013-14, 9,242 OoSC have been main-streamed into nearby schools. Rest of the children proposed to be main-streamed were 49,819 in different interventions like NRBC level I, II, III, RBC-KGBV, CWSN and residential facility.

For nomadic population in Seasonal Centres, the progress made during 2013-14 was upto the mark. 30,183 children belonging to nomadic group were covered under 1,228 Seasonal Centres. However, for 2014-15 the proposed children for nomadics in 1,290 Seasonal Centres were 32,271, but MHRD approved only 5,032. The issue has been taken up with the MHRD. As per information received there are 29,350 habitations in the State. 10,894 Primary Schools have been sanctioned by the MHRD till date. Ninety nine residential schools under KGBV for girl students have been opened in economically and educationally backward areas.

A pilot programme called "Learning Enhancement through Active Pedagogy (LEAP)" has been launched in all the upper primary schools of the State. Under this programme, learning corners in science, mathematics, social science and languages were established up to 2014-15 in 9,673 UPS of J&K. In these learning corners, students with the help of their teachers prepare teaching-learning materials (TLM) and displays in learning corners which are used during class room transactions, thus enhancing the creative side of the children which is generally ignored. Two sets of free uniforms were provided to 10,87,678 children at the rate of Rs. 400 per child during 2013-14. 8,245 Upper Primary Schools have been provided Mathematics and Science Kits during the year. For the year 2013-14, free supply of text books to 7,53,330 children (including BPL, SC, ST, Boys, Girls, etc.) in Primary and Upper Primary schools (through BOSE) has been made.

In 2013-14, to enhance quality education, in-service teacher training was provided to 7,124 teachers and to strengthen BRCs and CRCs, training was provided to 2,000 BRCs and CRCs.

For accomplishment of the goal of bridging gender gap in literacy, National Programme for Education of Girls at Elementary Level (NPEGEL) is a focused intervention aimed at enhancing girl education. This intervention provides for the development of "Model School" in every cluster with more emphasis on girl enrolment especially dropouts and never enrolled once. It provides need-based incentive like stationery, books, sports equipments, etc., for girls in the identified schools. So far 593 Model Schools have been established under this intervention.

Kasturba Gandhi Balika Vidyalaya (KGBV) is yet another initiative for enhancing girl education. It is a scheme for setting up residential schools at upper primary level for adolescent girls belonging to SC, ST, and OBC community. Under this intervention, the enrolled girl students are provided with free boarding and lodging facility including their day-to-day expenses. So far 99 KGBVs have been established.

The Government of Jammu & Kashmir rolled out "Beti Anmol" scheme during 2011-12 with a view to arrest post matric dropout rate of girl students belonging to Below Poverty Line (BPL) and enhancing their employment prospects. Under the scheme, an amount of Rs. 5,000 is to be given as incentive to the girl students of Educationally Backward Blocks, who pass their Matriculation examination and get themselves enrolled in the 11th class. The incentive is given in the shape of a bank deposit the amount of which is encashable only after the students pass their 12th class examination. Beti Anmol scheme is presently catering to the girl students hailing from 97 educationally backward Blocks of the State. The ultimate objective of this new initiative is to encourage the education of the girl students in the State. The scheme is operative from academic session 2011-12 both for winter and summer zones. 5,955 girls students were provided incentive during 2012-13 and 5,355 girls students were provided incentive during 2013-14, ending March 2014.

In keeping with the Constitutional provisions to raise the level of nutrition of children and enable them to develop in a healthy manner, the Government of India launched the scheme "National Programme of Nutritional Support to Education (NP-NSPE)", commonly known as Mid-Day Meal Scheme (MDMS) during the year 1995. MDMS was expected to enhance enrolment, retention, attendance of children in schools apart from improving their nutritional levels. This was extended to upper primary (classes VI to VIII) children at the national level in 3,479 EBBs in 2007 and then universalized at the elementary level in the year 2008. MDMS is primarily managed and implemented by School Management/Village Education Committees.

During 2011-12, 2012-13, 2013-14 and 2014-15, 41.92 lakh students have been covered under MDM Scheme. 2,258 kitchen-*cum*-stores were constructed during 2011 to 2013 and funds for the construction of 6,000 more such kitchen-*cum*-stores have been released during the year 2012-13. Besides, 29,437 number of cook-*cum*-helpers engaged till date against 33,268 of PAB approval.

A new initiative for adult literacy has been taken at the national level and 20 districts of J&K, having less than 50 per cent Literacy Rate as per Census 2001, were approved under the Saakshar Bharat Mission Programme. This is another major flagship scheme and focuses on the female adult literacy in the age group of 15 years.

J&K has adopted the norm of 1 km distance for the purpose of the establishment of a primary school to serve the requirements of the community to the desired extent. As a result, the State has been able to provide primary schools within the easy reach of students. Similarly, with regard to the upgradation of schools, the policy framework has been liberalized. The State is now performing better in the field of education as compared to many other States of the country, despite many constraints. Besides, focus on teacher education by incurring the budgetary provisions under SSA/RMSA and State Sector, exposure visits of teachers to other States have been the latest initiatives in getting the teachers acquainted about the strides made by other States in quality education.

6. HEALTH

At present, India's health care system consists of a mix of public and private sector providers of health services.

In such a scenario, rural areas are rather poorly served. Health care services are quantitatively inadequate. At the start of the Eleventh Plan, the number of doctors or nurses per lakh of population was only 45 against the desirable number of 85 per lakh population. Similarly, the number of nurses and Auxiliary Nurse and Midwives (ANMs) available was only 75 per lakh population against the desirable number of 255.

Quality of health care varies considerably in both the public and private sectors. Regulatory standards for public and private hospitals are not adequately defined and, in any case, are ineffectively enforced.

The lack of extensive and adequately funded public health services pushes a large number of people to incur heavy expenses on services taken from the private sector. Out of pocket expenditure arises even in the public sector hospitals since patients are required to buy many medicines.

The total expenditure on health care in India taking both public, private and household out of pocket (OOP) expenditure was about 4.1 per cent of GDP in 2008-09 (National Health Accounts 2009), which is broadly comparable to other developing countries at similar levels of per capita income. However, the public expenditure on health was only about 27 per cent of the total in 2008-09 (NHA 2009), which is very low by any standard.

Public expenditure on core health (both Plan and Non-Plan and taking the Centre and the States together) was about 0.93 per cent of GDP in 2007-08. It has increased to about 1.04 per cent during 2011-12. It needs to increase much more over the next decade.

The Eleventh FY Plan had suggested governance reforms in public health system, such as performance—linked incentives, devolution of powers and functions to local health care institutions and making them responsible for the health of the people living in a defined geographical area. NRHM's strategy of decentralisation, PRI involvement, integration of vertical programmes, inter-sectoral convergence and health systems strengthening have been partially achieved.

Despite efforts, lack of capacity and adequate flexibility in programmes forestall effective local level planning and execution based on local disease priorities. Professional procurement agencies on the lines of Tamil Nadu are still not in place.

While the private sector can continue to operate for those who can afford it, an expansion of good quality affordable public sector care is essential.

Health sector expenditure by the Centre and the States, both Plan and Non-Plan, will have to be substantively increased. The provision of clean drinking water and sanitation should have high priority in health related resource allocation.

The doctor-patient ratio in Jammu & Kashmir is 1:2104 as against the recommendations of the World Health Organization (WHO) of 1:1000, which is grossly insufficient. Against the sanctioned strength of 6,609 doctors in Government health institutions, 5,839 posts have been filled up. In addition to this, 1,432 MBBS and AYUSH doctors have also been hired on contractual basis under the National Health Mission.

Similarly, against the sanctioned strength of 20,664 posts of paramedical staff, 17,504 are in position and 4,374 paramedics engaged on contractual basis under NHM.

With the establishment/upgradation of new health institutions, 458 posts of Medical Officers have been created. These posts are in the process of being referred to the recruiting agency for making selection.

There are 5,532 Government health institutions at primary, secondary and tertiary levels including newly sanctioned 826 sub-centres, 371 NTPHCs and 87 ISM Dispensaries.

It is evident from the year-to-year analysis of figures regarding the patient load that the general masses have once again shown inclination towards the public health services. Table 8 reflects the workload during the last three years.

Table 8: Workload during Last Three Years

Sl. No	Particulars	Unit	2012-13 (March 2013)	2013-14 (March 2014)	2014-15 (ending Jan. 2015)
1.	OPD*	lacs	226.16	259.94	216.26
2.	IPD	lacs	9.93	12.45	7.18
3.	Major Surgeries	lacs	1.18	1.47	0.91
4.	Minor Surgeries	lacs	4.06	4.93	4.42
5.	Institutional Deliveries	%age	86.91%	83.77%	85.20%
6.	Immunization {DP, Measles (1st+2nd), BCGW) 2nd Booster}	lacs	1.69	7.05	5.49 (ending Feb, 2015)

* OPD includes old and new cases, ante-natal check-up, Immunization, etc., during a year.

Source: Economic Survey, 2014-15, Directorate of Economics & Statistics, J&K

The health system in Jammu & Kashmir has dramatically changed from what it was a decade ago. Infant Mortality Rate which indicates the death of children before the age of one year per thousand live births is a sensitive indicator of the health and nutritional status of population. Reducing Infant Mortality Rate (IMR) is the major objective of National Health Mission (NHM). The State has achieved a significant improvement in the IMR over the period. The IMR has fallen from 52 in 2006 to 37 in 2014. The Fertility Rate which measures the number of children born to a woman during her entire reproductive period has also come down to 1.9 from 2.3. Leprosy and Polio are nearing elimination. As a result of various interventions taken up under NRHM, mother and child health indicators in the State except few have improved

Table 9: Trend Analysis of Health Indicators

Year	Infant Mortality Rate (IMR)		Neonatal Mortality Rate (NMR)		Early Neonatal Mortality Rate (ENMR)		Total Fertility Rate (TFR)	
	J&K	National Average	J&K	National Average	J&K	National Average	J&K	National Average
2011	41	44	32	31	26	24	1.9	2.4
2012	39	42	30	29	23	24	1.9	2.4
2013	39	42	32	31	26	24	1.9	2.4
2014	37	40	29	28	24	22	1.9	2.3

Source: Sample Registration System (SRS) Bulletin September, 2014.

and are relatively better than the national average. The trend analysis of these indicators is shown in Tables 9 and 10.

Table 10: Other Health Indicators

Indicators		*National Average*	*J&K*
Maternal Mortality Ratio (MMR)		212	70
Birth Rate		21.4	17.5
Death Rate		7	5.3
Child Sex Ratio (0-6 years) Census 2011		914	856
Life Expectancy (In years) Census 2011	Male	63.95	66.5
	Female	67.08	69.3

Source: SRS 2013.

In order to improve the Infant Mortality Rate, Sick New Born Care Units (SNCUs) have been set up in 15 District Hospitals, New Born Stabilization Units (NBSUs) in 76 First Referral Units (FRUs) and New Born Baby Corners (NBCCs) in 279 PHCs. This is a major intervention in the promotion of child health particularly by providing essential and emergency new born care facilities. Efforts have also been made to strengthen the Neonatal Intensive Care Units (NICUs) in Lal Ded Hospital, GB Pant Hospital in Srinagar and SMGS Hospital in Jammu. These units have been provided support in terms of equipments, drugs, etc. Home based neonatal care (HBNC) has also been initiated to tackle the problems of infant mortality rate. State Trainers, District Resource Persons (DRPs) and ASHAs have been trained in HBNC. The Thirteenth Finance Commission Award has supplemented a budget provision of Rs. 27.22 crore for reducing the Infant Mortality Rate as a major initiative in this direction.

National Health Mission has proved successful in the implementation of various schemes with a focus on improvement of maternal health indicators. The State has achieved 3+ANC at 87 per cent, institutional deliveries have improved from 55 per cent in 2007-08 to 85.11 per cent in 2013-14 which is better than the National Average figure of 72.9 per cent. The birth rate in J&K has also come down by 1.0 from 18.6 (per 1,000) in 2009 to 17.5 in 2014 as against the national average of 21.4. Maternal Health Schemes like Janani Suraksha Yojna (JSY) and Janani Shishu Suraksha Karyakram (JSSK) mainly focus on the promotion of institutional deliveries. Mothers and children together constitute 57.5 per cent of total population.

Major Achievements in 2013-14 and 2014-15

- Establishment of five new Medical Colleges (3 in Jammu and 2 in Kashmir) have been approved to be set up.
- Two State Cancer Institutes (one each to Jammu and Srinagar) have been approved to be set up.
- 3 Tertiary Cancer Care Institutes for Kishtwar, Udhampur and Kupwara have been approved.
- Super Speciality Hospital Jammu at a cost of Rs. 120.00 crore was completed and commissioned. The IPD services in 5 disciplines and OPD in 8 disciplines started.
- Super Speciality Hospital Srinagar at a cost of Rs. 120.00 crore is nearing completion.
- National Urban Health Mission (NUHM) launched in the State. In Phase-I, it will cover 7 towns namely, Srinagar, Anantnag, Baramulla, Sopore, Jammu, Udhampur, and Kathua.
- Rashtriya Swasthya Bima Yojana (RSBY) was successfully launched in two districts on pilot basis and extended to ten more districts of the State. Under this Scheme, the health insurance is given to the BPL families with cashless hospitalization up to Rs. 30,000 per family per annum.

In order to provide better health services to the people of Haryana and to achieve goals of reduction in Maternal Mortality Rate (MMR), Infant Mortality Rate (IMR), Total Fertility Rate (TFR) and increase in Institutional Deliveries, many steps have been taken.

More than 2,000 doctors including specialists have been recruited through the Departmental Selection Committee. Dental surgeons have been positioned in each Primary Health Centre. Free medicines are being supplied to all the patients. Fixed Cost Surgery Package Programme has been launched in all the District Hospitals in Haryana from July 2009. Under this programme, free surgical facilities are being provided for BPL families and residents of urban slums. All surgeries of obstetrics cases, eye, cleft lip/palate, etc., are absolutely free for all. 2,60,169 surgeries took place in District Hospitals up to 30 November, 2012. Due to impact of these initiatives, there is an increased load of 32 per cent in outdoor patients, occupancy and indoor patients and increase in institutional deliveries to 84.2 per cent (CRS-November 2013) as compared to 59.2 per cent in January

2010. Contribution of Government Hospitals in institutional deliveries is 47.10 per cent as compared to 22.34 per cent in 2008. Haryana Swasthya Vahan Sewa No. 102 scheme to provide Referral Transport was launched on 14 November, 2009, to provide free transport services for pregnant women, roadside accident victims, BPL patients, war widows, freedom fighters. Under this scheme 13,41,838 calls have been attended upto 31 October, 2013. From 1 January, 2014, a new scheme with the name of Mukhya Mantri Muft Ilaj Yojana has been started in which free surgeries to all the residents of Haryana, free basic laboratory investigations, free indoor services, free drugs, free transport facility and free dental treatment are provided. Free transport facility to cancer patient in Haryana Roadways Buses is being provided. It is also proposed to open new Primary Health Centres, Community Health Centres and upgradation of existing health institutions. During 2013-14, one PHC, 11 Polyclinics, 4 Dispensaries and 11 Urban Health Centres were opened. For upgrading the skills of the staff in position, it is also proposed to conduct the TOTs of Doctors, Staff Nurses, ANMs & ASHA workers at the State Institute of Health & Family Welfare to ensure for further dissemination of knowledge at District and Block levels.

In Rajasthan, the following steps have been taken to improve maternal and child health services:

(A) Maternal Health

There is reduction of 133 points in MMR from 388 (SRS, 2004-06) to 255 (SRS 2010-12) in Rajasthan and rise in institutional delivery from 28 per cent in 2005 to 80 per cent. Following interventions have been taken by the State Government to improve maternal health services.

Rajasthan Janani Shishu Suraksha Yojana was launched on September 12, 2011 in Rajasthan. It entitles all pregnant women free deliveries including caesarian. Free of cost facility to pregnant women and neonatal for investigations, treatments, medicines and referral transport facility both from home and returning back to home is being provided. In this year 11,86,320 pregnant women availed free medicines, 9,55,860 availed free laboratory tests and 8,06,121 availed free referral services under the scheme.

Institutional Deliveries and Janani Suraksha Yojana (JSY) was launched in the year 2005 with the objective of increasing institutional deliveries. Under this scheme, cash incentive is given to the beneficiary on delivery at a Government health institution and JSY accredited private hospitals. In the year 2013-14, 13,73,419 institutional deliveries conducted and 11,07,115 women have benefited under JSY up to March 2014.

So far, 1,665 health institutions in Rajasthan have been identified to strengthen ensured comprehensive reproductive and child health services on 24×7 basis. These delivery points comprise 7 Medical Colleges, 31 District Hospitals, 359 CHCs, 475 PHCs and 793 Sub Centres. Gap analysis of these points has been done in terms of infrastructure, equipments, human resources, capacity building, electricity and water supply. Training on priority basis is being imparted to the staff of these delivery points.

For strengthening referral transport services, 400 Janani Express ambulances have been deployed at PHC level. 200 new Janani Express vehicles procured and delivered from State fund additionally. Priority is given to remote PHCs so that IMR and MMR can be reduced. The existing '104' facility is being used for making calls for utilizing the services of 'Janani Express'.

The Weekly Iron and Folic Acid Supplementation (WIFS) scheme is a community based intervention that addresses nutritional (iron deficiency) anemia amongst adolescents (boys and girls) in both rural and urban areas. The Programme aims to cover 35 lakh students of class 6 to 12 studying in 34 thousands schools and 9 lakh out of school girls of the age between 10 to 19 years through 61,119 Anganwari Centres (AWC). Under the programme, weekly Iron Folic Acid tablets are given on Monday in the schools and on every Thursday at AWC by AWW.

Buildings of 526 PHCs, 224 CHCs, 10 Swasthya Bhawans, 27 Drug Controller Offices, and 2,363 residential quarters at CHCS/PHCs have been constructed. Sanctions have also been issued for the construction of Maternal & Child Health (MCH) Units in districts.

At present 47,027 ASHA Sahyoginis are functional in Rajasthan.

(B) Child Health

A reduction of 14 points has been witnessed in IMR from 63 in SRS 2008 to 49 in SRS 2012. Following interventions have been witnessed in IMR from 63 in SRS 2008 to 49 in SRS 2012.

Thirty six Sick Newborn Care Units named as 'Priyadarshini Units' to provide curative services to neonates, 40 Malnutrition

Treatment Corners of management of severely malnourished children, 113 Newborn Stabilizing Units at selected CHCs to make the neonate stabilize and 1,201 Newborn Corners to resuscitate newborn have been established in the State. Efforts are being made to functionalize 107 MTCs (6 bedded) at selected CHCs.

ASHA Sahyoginis have been trained to provide Home Based Neonatal Care Services (HBNC). At present, 41,356 ASHA Sahyoginis are trained to provide HBNC services in the State. Mother and Child Health and Nutrition (MCHN) days have also been fixed to provide maternal, child and nutrition services.

The Annual Health Survey 2011-12 reported 69.2 per cent coverage of complete immunization in the State. Hepatitis-B vaccination has also been added as routine immunization since December 2011. No polio case has been identified in the State since December 2009. Pregnancy and Child Tracking System is being used to track left outs and drop outs.

To inform the beneficiary as well as the health worker regarding the schedule date of vaccination and due date of ANC in advance, a unique scheme has been initiated in the State named as 'Swasthya Sandesh Seva'. Under the scheme, the ANM and the beneficiary receive a free SMS regarding the due date of health services in advance sent from the State Headquarters.

The Government of Punjab is committed to upgrade infrastructure in terms of manpower, civil works and equipments in the hospitals for better health care. An outlay of Rs. 990.83 crore has been provided for the Annual Plan 2015-16.

Punjab has recorded an impressive performance with regard to vital health indicators. The Infant Mortality Rate (IMR) declined by 18 points from 44 in 2006 to 26 in 2013. The State has been awarded by the Government of India in each of the last 3 years on this account. The Maternal Mortality Rate (MMR) declined from 192 in 2004-06 to 141 in 2011-13. The child sex ratio has also improved from 798 in 2001 to 863 in SRS 2012.

Under the National Health Mission's progressive plan prepared by the State, it has been proposed to upgrade infrastructure and deploy additional manpower including 1,100 doctors. The dial 108 service initiative of the Government has been a huge success, Nearly 10.51 lakh lives have been saved so far due to this service, In another major initiative, the government has launched the 104 medical helpline to provide 24×7 medical advice, grievances redressal, and counselling services.

Primary Healthcare services in the rural areas of Punjab are provided through a network of medical institutions comprising of Sub-Centres (2,951), HCs/Dispensaries (1,322), PHCs (432) and CHCs (143). Out of 1,322 SHC/Rural Dispensaries had been transferred to the Panchayati Raj Institutions (Zila Parishads).

A comparative chart indicating the national norms and levels of achievement by the Government of Punjab is given below in Table 11:

Table 11: Health Indications: Achievement Level

Sl. No.	*Parameters/Indicators*	*National Norms*	*Level of Achievemen. by the State*
1.	Population served per doctor	3500	1100 (on the basis of registered doctors)
2.	Population served by Health Workers (M and F) (Rural)	M 5000 F 5000	M-5854 F-3474
3.	Ratio of HA (F) to HW (F)	1:06	1:06
4.	Population covered by Sub-Centre	3000-5000	5870
5.	Population covered by Primary Health Centre (Rural)	20,000-30,000	40600
6.	Population covered by Community Health Centre (Rural)	About 1 lakh	69327
7.	Number of Sub-Centres for each PHC	6 Sub Centres	7
8.	Number of PHCs for each Community Health Centre	4 PHCs	3

Source: Statistical Report, Department of Planning, Punjab.

Comparative current status regarding the Birth Rate, Death Rate, Infant Mortality Rate, etc. at the National and State level is given in Table 12.

Table 12: Health Indicators: Status

Sl. No.	*Indicator*	*Unit*	*Current Status*	
			India	*Punjab*
1.	Birth Rate (2014)	Per 1000 Population	21.7	15.7
2.	Death Rate (2014)	-do-	7.0	6.7
3.	Infant Mortality Rate (2014)	Per 1000 live births	40	26
4.	Maternal Mortality Rate	Per 1,00,000	167	141

Source: *Ibid.*

1

Haryana

SURINDER KUMAR AND SATISH KUMAR

SCOPE OF THE PAPER

[*Note*: Centre for Rural Studies (CRS) is a research centre under the National Institute of Administrative Research (NIAR), Mussoorie promoted by Lal Bahadur Shastri National Academy of Administration, Mussoorie (Uttarakhand). IAS Officer Trainees of Phase-II during their District Training Attachment are expected to conduct household survey and prepare village visit assignments.]

This State Paper is based on the 19 village study assignments of IAS Officer Trainees of Haryana cadre (Batches 2003-2010). The paper covers the following socio-economic aspects of villages in Haryana on which study assignments were based. The household survey covered the following six aspects:

1. Rural Infrastructure, Health and Education,
2. Agrarian Relations,
3. Social Structure,
4. Economic Activities,
5. Anti Poverty and other Rural Development Programmes, and
6. Panchayati Raj System.

This study has been divided into three Sections. In Section I, we have described the profile of rural Haryana based on available secondary data on above parametres. In Section II, we have examined the 19 village study based assignments and information therein and have tried to reconstruct a macro picture of Haryana. In Section III, we have tried to draw conclusions and suggest some policy measures which may be adopted by the government for further improvement in the socio-economic conditions of the people in rural Haryana.

SECTION I

I.1. Haryana—Land and People

Haryana, a small State spread over an area of 44,212 sq. km came into existence on November 1, 1966 as the seventeenth State of the Indian Union. The area of the State accounted for only 1.3 per cent of the total area, accommodating 2.54 crore population (Census 2011) comprising 2.10 per cent of the total population in the country. At the time of its formation, Haryana had only seven districts, namely Ambala, Karnal, Rohtak, Hisar, Jind, Gurgaon and Mahendergarh. Every district of the State had its boundary with some State or the other. The northernmost district of Ambala had Himachal Pradesh in the north, U.P. in its east and Punjab in the west. District Karnal had U.P. in its east and Punjab in the west. District Jind had Punjab in the north. Hisar was bounded by Punjab in the north, whereas on its west and north lied Rajasthan. Similarly, district Mahendergarh was bounded by Rajasthan. District Gurgaon had Rajasthan in its south and U.P. in the east. District Rohtak shared its boundary with the national capital Delhi and U.P. Various districts of Haryana were further reorganized into smaller administrative units from time to time and the total number of districts has now gone upto 21.

Geographically, though most of Haryana is plain, Shivalik hills in the north and Aravallis in its south-west provide it with some diversity. The only perennial river of the State, Yamuna, originates in the Uttrakhand and makes its boundary with U.P. in the east running from north to south. Ghaggar is another important river in its north making a natural boundary with Punjab. Markanda in the north and Sahibi and Indori in the south are the other important seasonal rivers.

The climate of Haryana is characterized as semi-desert. It is marked by extreme hot in summer to extreme cold in winter. Due to its closeness to mountains, the snowfall in the mountains has a direct impact here which brings down the winter temperature to 2.3 °C, whereas the summer temperature crosses 45 °C. A large part of

Haryana is in close proximity to western Rajasthan, where rainfall is about 25-30 cm, whereas the northern districts get about 200 cm of rainfall again due to its proximity to the mountains. The average annual rainfall is around 50 cm, most of which is during monsoon months of July-September. The winter months of December to February get some rainfall due to western disturbances.

As most of the area in the State is plain, there is very little area under forests which is limited to Shivaliks in the north and Aravallis in the south. In 1966-67 out of a total of 4,399 thousand hectares, only 91 thousand hectares, i.e., 2.07 per cent of the total area was under forests. 5.84 per cent of the total area was devoted to non-agricultural purposes and about 5.27 per cent of the total area was barren. Thus, about 11 per cent of the total area was unavailable for agriculture. Apart from this, about 6 per cent of the total area, mostly in western and central Haryana was marked by sand-dunes and uneven lands, which was used as pastures. Thus, about 77.81 per cent of the total area of the State was available for cultivation in 1966-67 (Table 1.1).

Table 1.1: Land-Use Pattern in Haryana

Land-Use Pattern	*1966-67*	*2009-10 (P)*
Total Area	4399	4371
Forests	91 (2.07)	40 (0.92)
Land put to non-agri uses	257 (5.84)	470 (10.75)
Barren & unculturable land	232 (5.27)	104 (2.38)
Permanent pastures & other grazing land	46 (1.05)	28 (0.64)
Culturable but barren land	87 (1.98)	29 (0.66)
Fallow land	259 (5.89)	133 (3.04)
Net area sown	3423 (77.81)	3550 (81.22)
Culturable area	3819 (86.82)	3756 (85.93)
Area sown more than once	1176 (34.36)*	2801 (78.90)*
Total cropped area	4599 (134.36)*	6351 (178.90)*

Note: Figures in brackets are percentages to total area of the State.
* Show percentage of Net Sown Area.
Source: *Statistical Abstract of Haryana*, 2010-11, pp. 225-27.

According to 2009-10 provisional figures, the area under forest had reduced to 0.92 per cent only. The areas under barren and uncultivable land and permanent pastures also came down. Area under fallow land also reduced from 5.89 to 3.04 per cent over the years. All this lead to an increase in net sown area from 77.81 per cent to

81.22 per cent of the total area. Area sown more than once increased substantially from 34.36 to 78.90 per cent of the net area sown. The total cropped area of the State also increased substantially from 134.36 per cent of the net area sown to 178.90 per cent in 2009-10 (Table 1.1).

In 1966, only 37.80 per cent of the net sown area of the State was under irrigation—mostly canal irrigation. On rest of the area agriculture was dependent upon rainfall, which was not only insufficient but was also quite uncertain. Coarse foodgrains like jowar, bajra, barley and gram were the major crops. Wheat, sugarcane and cotton were grown only on the irrigated land.

During the last 45 years or so, by 2009-10 the irrigational facilities in the State have increased substantially. Not only the area under canal irrigation increased, tubewells and pumpsets have emerged as major sources of irrigation. As a result about 86.40 per cent of the sown area has been brought under irrigation. With the increase in irrigation facilities, the cropping pattern of the State has changed quite substantially with wheat, rice, cotton and sugarcane replacing the traditional crops like jawar, bajra and gram.

Before the formation of the State, due to limited sources of irrigation, large parts of agricultural land were left fallow. Apart from the fallow land, large tracks around the villages were marked as pasture lands. Most of the villages had small forests, locally called *Bani*. All these served as pasture lands. It was because of poor agriculture and availability of pasture lands, animal husbandry played an important role in the local economy.

However, in the last five decades, the nature of animal husbandry has also changed. Whereas, the pasture lands have been converted into agricultural lands, the increased irrigation enhanced the availability of both green and dry fodder for the animals. Because of this the number of milch cattle and production of milk has increased substantially. Some of the scheduled castes have been engaged in pigs, goats and sheep rearing.

The rural artisans were engaged in leather tanning, making of shoes and other leather products, pottery, blacksmithy, carpentry, oil producing, etc. The modernization has had a negative impact on such traditional occupations. Most of the rural artisans have shifted to urban areas and have engaged themselves in modern industry and other occupations. A small section of these artisans is still engaged in their traditional occupations both in rural and urban areas.

I.2. People

In the medieval period of Indian history, like in most parts of the country, a section of population in Haryana region also converted into Islam. In 1600 A.D., the Haryana region fell under Delhi, Rewari, Hisar Feroza, Sirhind, Narnaul, Tijara and Sahar Sarkars (districts). There were 69 zamindaris under these Sarkars, out of which 48.75 (70.62%) zamindaris were that of Hindus and 20.25 (29.35%) of Muslims. In Narnaul and Sahar 100 per cent of the zamindaris belonged to Hindus, whereas in Tijara 95 per cent zamindaris belonged to Muslims. In other Sarkars, majority of zamindaris belonged to Hindus. Among the Hindus, maximum zamindaris belonged to Jats who had 100 per cent of the zamindaris in Sahar, 53.35 per cent in Delhi, 50 per cent in Narnaul and 45.39 per cent in Hisar Feroza. Next to Jats were Rajputs who had 50 per cent in Sirhind, 37.50 per cent in Hisar Feroza and 27.27 per cent in Rewari. Apart from them, Brahmin, Gujjars and Ahirs also had some zamindaris (Abul Fazal: *Ain-a-Akbari*).

At the time of first war of independence in 1857, a part of Haryana region was directly under the British Rule, whereas, another part was under the Sikh states of Patiala, Nabha and Jind. Ballabhgarh and Rewari were under Hindu rulers, whereas a part of the region was under Jhajjar, Pataudi, Dujana, Dadri, Farukhnagar and Loharu states which were ruled by Muslim nawabs. Thus from the medieval period to the independence of the country in 1947, Muslims have been an important part of the population of Haryana.

The partition of India and formation of Pakistan in 1947 changed the composition of population in Haryana. The Muslims of this region were forced to go to Pakistan, whereas Hindus and Sikhs came to this area in a large number from Pakistan. Though they were settled in almost all the districts of the State, the maximum allotments were made in districts Ambala, Karnal and Hisar.

The Mewat region of Haryana has been a Muslim dominated area since medieval period. At the time of partition, some of the Muslim population migrated to Pakistan, but they came back after some time, and thus this area is still Muslim majority area. This area was a part of Gurgaon district, but has been made a separate district on April 4, 2005. In 2001, the total number of Muslim population in Haryana was 12.2 lakh which formed 5.8 per cent of the total population of the State.

Sikhs are another important section of the population of Haryana constituting about 5.50 per cent of the total population. They are mostly settled in Sirsa, Hisar, Fatehabad, Jind, Kaithal, Kurukshetra, Ambala, Yamunanagar and Karnal districts.

The population of the State is further divided into various castes. Dalits, who are about 20 per cent of the total population, are spread all over the State, whereas different peasant castes are settled in different parts. The central districts of Rohtak, Sonepat, Panipat, Jind, Hisar, Bhiwani and Jhajar have Jats as the major peasant caste, though Brahmins and Rajputs also have significant presence. Brahmins and Rajputs are settled in other districts also. The special feature of Brahmins in Haryana is that they are also agriculturists.

The southern districts of Rewari, Mahendergarh and Gurgaon are dominated by Ahirs or Yadavs. This area is called Ahirwal. In Jhajjar district also their number is substantial. Whereas, Faridabad, Mewat and Panipat have a substantial population belonging to Gujjar caste, Rods are in good number in Karnal, Kurukshetra and Yamunanagar. The caste Saini is spread over in all parts of Haryana. Aggarwals, the trading caste is also spread over in all the districts.

The language-wise breakup of the population was last published in 1991 Census. At that time, 91 per cent of the total population was Hindi speaking, whereas Punjabi and Urdu was reported as their mother tongue by 7.11 per cent and 1.59 per cent of the State population. A distinct regional touch is found on the language/dialect of the people in different parts. Whereas, the influence of Punjabi can be clearly seen on Hindi/Haryanvi of the people living in the border districts towards Punjab, the influence of Rajasthani, Bagri and Shekhwati can be seen among the people of Hisar, Sirsa, Bhiwani, Mahendergarh and Gurgaon. Mewat, Faridabad and Palwal being close to Braj region of U.P., its influence is clearly felt among the people of this region.

I.3. Demographic Profile

The population of Haryana has increased at a very fast rate during the last six decades. In 1951, the population of Haryana was 56,59,487 persons, which increased to 2,53,53,081 persons in 2011, more than fourfold increase. However, the rate of growth of population has shown some decline over time but it has been very slow. The decadal rate of growth of population during 1951-61 was recorded at 33.79 per cent, which came down to 32.22, 28.75 and 27.41 per cent during 1961-71, 1971-81 and 1981-91 respectively. It increased during 1991-2001 to 28.43 per cent, The rate of growth of population reduced substantially during 2001-11 when it came down to 19.90 per cent, but it was still quite high, more than the national average growth rate of 17.65 per cent in Table 1.2.

Table 1.2: Growth of Population in Haryana

Year	*Population*	*Decennial percentage increase*
1951	56,73,597	—
1961	75,90,524	33.79
1971	1,00,36,431	32.22
1981	1,29,22,119	28.75
1991	1,64,63,648	27.41
2001	2,11,44,564	28.43
2011	2,53,53,081 (P)	19.90 (P)

Note: P—Provisional.
Source: *Statistical Abstract of Haryana* 2010-11, p. 32.

The district level figures for increase in population during 2001-2011 explain it to some extent. The fast emerging industrial and services hub of north India, district Gurgaon recorded a phenomenal increase of 73.93 per cent in its population. The other industrial district of the State, Faridabad recorded an increase of 31.75 per cent in its population. The other districts where increase in population was more than the State average were Mewat (34.94%), Palwal (25.49%) and Panipat (24.33%). District Jhajjar recorded the minimum growth rate of 8.73 per cent followed by Jind (11.95%).

The continuous increase in population in the State has increased the pressure on land. The density of population was 227 persons per sq. km in 1971, which had increased to 573 persons per sq. km in 2011, much above the national average density of 383 persons per sq. km. The highest density of population was recorded in district Faridabad at 2,298 persons per sq. km followed by Gurgaon at 1,241 and the lowest density was recorded in district Sirsa at 303. (Table 1.3)

Table 1.3: Density of Population by District in Haryana (P)

District	*Area in Sq. Kms. '(2001)*	*Population (2011)*	*Persons per Sq. Km*
Ambala	1574	11,36,784	722
Panchkula	898	5,58,890	622
Yamunanagar	1768	12,14,162	687
Kurukshetra	1530	9,64,231	630
Kaithal	2317	10,72,861	463
Karnal	2520	15,06,323	598
Panipat	1268	12,02,811	949
Sonepat	2122	14,80,080	697
Rohtak	1745	10,58,683	607
Jhajjar	1834	9,56,907	522
Faridabad	743	17,98,954	2298
Palwal	1368	10,40,493	761
Gurgaon	1254	15,14,085	1241
Mewat	1500	10,89,406	729
Rewari	1594	8,96,129	562
Mahendergarh	1899	9,21,680	485
Bhiwani	4778	16,29,109	341
Jind	2702	13,32,042	493
Hisar	3983	17,42,815	438
Fatehabad	2538	9,41,522	371
Sirsa	4277	12,95,114	303
Total (2011)	**44,212**	**2,53,53,081**	**573**
Total (2001)	**44,212**	**2,11,44,564**	**478**

Note: P—Provisional.
Source: *Statistical Abstract of Haryana,* 2010-11, p. 35.

Another feature of Haryana population which has attracted lot of attention in the whole country is its low sex ratio. Though the low sex ratio in Haryana has become a matter of serious concern only during the last about two decades when sex selected abortions were reported in the media, the fact about its low sex ratio is that it has remained so in the entire century since 1901. The lowest sex ratio in Haryana was recorded at 835 in 1911. The years 1921 and 1931 recorded the sex ratio at 844 females per 1000 males. After this it fluctuated between 871 in 1951 to 861 in 2001. The Census 2011 recorded the highest sex ratio at 877 female per 1000 male in its entire history since 1901, which was still much below the national average of 940. (Table 1.4)

Table 1.4: Sex Ratio in Haryana

Year	*Sex-Ratio*
1901	867
1911	835
1921	844
1931	844
1941	869
1951	871
1961	868
1971	867
1981	870
1991	865
2001	861
2011	877 (P)

Note: P—Provisional.
Source: *Statistical Abstract of Haryana,* 2010-11, p. 32.

The data on sex ratio at Birth as per Civil Registration Scheme is rather more alarming. It recorded its lowest at 709 in 1990. Further in rural areas it was recorded at 668 in the same year. The other years when it was lower than 800 were 1980, 1985, 1990 and 2000. The highest sex ratio at birth at 855 each were recorded in the years 2008 and 2009, after which it again came down to 840 in 2010 (Table 1.5).

Table 1.5: Sex-Ratio at Birth as per Civil Registration Scheme

Year	*Rural*	*Urban*	*Total*
1966	818	838	820
1970	821	839	826
1975	812	837	820
1980	766	861	787
1985	684	833	725
1990	668	799	709
1995	854	880	862
2000	797	784	794
2005	851	801	826
2008	882	829	855
2009	878	833	855
2010	863	820	840
Ambala	—	—	794
Panchkula	—	—	870
Kurukshetra	—	—	763

(*Contd.*)

Table 1.5 (*Contd.*)

Year	*Rural*	*Urban*	*Total*
Kaithal	—	—	826
Karnal	—	—	820
Panipat	—	—	862
Sonepat	—	—	800
Rohtak	—	—	826
Jhajjar	—	—	826
Faridabad	—	—	870
Palwal	—	—	893
Gurgaon	—	—	840
Mewat	—	—	901
Rewari	—	—	769
Mahendergarh	—	—	775
Bhiwani	—	—	833
Jind	—	—	870
Hisar	—	—	855
Fatehabad	—	—	855
Sirsa	—	—	877

Source: *Statistical Abstract of Haryana*, 2010-11, p. 109.

However, the rural-urban composition has changed on expected lines in Haryana. In 1971, 82.34 per cent of the State population lived in villages, which came down to 65.21 per cent in 2011. Districts Faridabad and Gurgaon, the most industrialized districts of the State recorded the lowest percentage of rural population with 20.56 and 31.18 per cent respectively. The other districts where percentage of rural population was lower than the State average were Panchkula (45.13%), Panipat (54.03%), Ambala (55.62%), Rohtak (57.96%) and Yamunanagar (61.06%). The maximum percentage of rural population was recorded in Mewat (88.62%) followed by Mahendergarh (85.57%) (Table 1.6).

Table 1.6: Rural-Urban Composition of Population in Haryana 2011 (P)

District	*Population*	
	Rural (%)	*Urban (%)*
Ambala	55.62	44.38
Panchkula	45.13	54.87
Yamunanagar	61.06	38.99
Kurukshetra	71.07	28.93
Kaithal	78.03	21.97

(*Contd.*)

Table 1.6 (*Contd.*)

District	Population	
	Rural (%)	Urban (%)
Karnal	69.73	30.27
Panipat	54.03	45.97
Sonepat	69.48	30.52
Rohtak	57.98	42.02
Jhajjar	74.61	25.39
Faridabad	20.56	79.44
Palwal	77.35	22.65
Gurgaon	31.18	68.82
Mewat	88.62	11.38
Rewari	74.18	25.82
Mahendergarh	85.57	14.43
Bhiwani	80.20	19.8C
Jind	77.18	22.82
Hisar	68.27	31.73
Fatehabad	80.96	19.04
Sirsa	75.25	24.75

Note: P—Provisional.
Source: *Statistical Abstract of Haryana,* 2010-11, p. 36.

According to 2001 Census, the scheduled castes constituted 19.35 per cent of the State population. The scheduled castes are not evenly distributed in various districts of the State. District Fatehabad recorded the maximum number of scheduled castes population, i.e., 27.43 per cent, followed closely by Sirsa (26.65%), Ambala (25.09%) and Yamunanagar (24.53%). Mewat district recorded the lowest percentage of scheduled caste population at only 7.93 per cent. This may be historically because of conversion to Islam in the region. The other districts where scheduled castes population was below the State average of 19.35 per cent were Gurgaon, Faridabad, Panchkula, Panipat, Mahendergarh, Jhajjar, Sonepat and Rohtak (Table 1.7).

1.4. Economic Profile of Haryana

Since its inception in 1966, Haryana's economic growth has been quite impressive, with an average annual growth rate of 6.4 per cent during the period from 1966-67 to 2004-05. Further, during the period of last 7 years (2005-06 to 2011-12), the State economy entered a

Table 1.7: Scheduled Castes by District 2001

District	*SCs as percentage to total population*
Ambala	25.09
Panchkula	15.51
Yamunanagar	24.53
Kurukshetra	20.52
Kaithal	21.55
Karnal	20.99
Panipat	15.79
Sonepat	18.09
Rohtak	19.10
Jhajjar	17.79
Faridabad	14.64
Gurgaon	14.75
Mewat	7.93
Rewari	18.87
Mahendergarh	16.31
Bhiwani	19.61
Jind	19.82
Hisar	21.99
Fatehabad	27.43
Sirsa	26.65
Total	**19.35**

Note: P—Provisional.
Source: *Statistical Abstract of Haryana,* 2010-11, p. 70.

higher growth trajectory and it grew at an average annual growth rate of 9.4 per cent, higher than the rate of growth of Indian economy at 8.4 per cent. Though, Haryana is geographically a small State but its contribution in the National Gross Domestic Product (at 2004-05 price) was 3.4 per cent in 2011-12. With per capita income of Rs. 94,680 at current prices during 2010-11, it occupies second position after Goa in the country (*Economic Survey of Haryana* 2011-12, p.1).

The growth story of Haryana has been phenomenal as this region of the erstwhile State of Punjab was very backward as compared to the part that stayed with the present day Punjab in 1966. In 1960-61, the net State domestic product of Haryana from all sources was Rs. 245 crore as compared to Rs. 404 crore for Punjab. Punjab was not only better developed in the field of agriculture, it was in a much better situation in areas like trade, transport and other services. This could be seen from the fact that in Punjab 30.36 per cent of its NSDP came from services as compared to only 21 per cent in Haryana. The contribution of secondary sector was a slightly higher in Haryana at 16.49 per cent, as compared to 15.62 per cent in Punjab. Though relatively backward, agriculture contributed 62.73 per cent in its total production as compared to 54.09 per cent in Punjab.

Agriculture was the mainstay of the population of Haryana and it was largely rainfed, as the irrigated facilities were very limited. In 1950-51 only about 25 per cent of the net sown area was under irrigation. Karnal was the only district of Haryana region, where 50 per cent of the net sown area was under irrigation. Districts Rohtak and Jind were also relatively better off with 38 per cent and 36 per cent of their net sown area under irrigation. District Hisar had only 17 per cent of its area under irrigation. District Ambala had only 1.3 per cent of its area under irrigation, whereas in district Mahendergarh, only 7 per cent of its area was under irrigation. With only 1.3 per cent of its area under irrigation, district Ambala was better off due to its annual average rainfall of about 200 cm, but district Mahendergarh was extremely backward because here as the rainfall was not sufficient. However after the planned development since 1952, more and more land was brought under irrigation in Haryana region and by 1966-67, the irrigated area of the region had also increased to 38 per cent of the net sown area.

After the formation of the State, the Government of Haryana devoted lot of attention to laying down of basic infrastructure. The Fourth Five Year Plan commenced in 1969 and till 1990, by the end of Seventh Five Year Plan, higher allocations were made for irrigation, flood control and power sectors. During the Fifth Five Year Plan (1975-79), as much as 75 per cent of the total plan expenditure was on Irrigation and Flood Control, Power and Agriculture and Allied Sectors. Apart from these, transport and social services were also given importance in various plans. It was only during the Tenth Five Year Plan that the priorities changed, when 42 per cent of the total expenditure was spent on social services sector alone.

Table 1.8: Net Area under Irrigation in Haryana

Year	*Net Irrigated Area as Percentage of Net Sown Area*	*By Govt. Canals (%age)*	*By Well/ Tubewells (%age)*
1966-67	37.80	70.57	23.43
1970-71	43.00	62.14	37.86
1975-76	48.40	59.06	40.94
1980-81	59.20	54.40	45.60
1985-86	62.20	52.98	47.02
1990-91	72.70	51.42	48.58
1995-96	77.00	49.82	50.18
2000-01	83.90	49.90	50.10
2005-06	82.30	45.33	54.67
2008-09	80.50	44.28	55.72
2009-10* Provisional	86.40	41.77	58.23

Source: *Statistical Abstract of Haryana*, 2010-11, p. 279.

Table 1.8 brings out that in 1966-67, only 37.80 per cent of net sown area was irrigated whereas it consistently increased to 86.40 per cent in 2009-10. It may further be noted that tubewell irrigation increased much faster than canals whereby the relative share of tubewell irrigation increased from 23.43 per cent in 1966-67 to 58.23 per cent in 2009-10 and that of canal irrigation decreased from 70.57 per cent to 41.77 per cent in the corresponding periods. This became possible due to fast electrification of villages and tubewells in Haryana.

In Kurukshetra, Kaithal, Karnal, Panipat, Sonepat and Fatehabad districts, almost 100 per cent area has irrigation facility. More than 90 per cent area in Sirsa, Jind, Hisar and Yamunanagar has irrigation facility. In Mewat, Bhiwani and Panchkula a large area still depends on rainfall as irrigation was available on 66.60 per cent, 54.40 per cent, and 66.7 per cent areas only (Table 1.9). This was so because in these areas, neither the canals could reach, nor the tubewells or pumpsets could be installed either because these areas had poor quality of underground water or the areas were hilly. In Panchkula, relatively higher rainfall compensates for less irrigation facility.

Table 1.9: District-wise Net Irrigated Area in Haryana 2009-10

Districts	*Percentage to Net Area sown*
Ambala	85.6
Panchkula	66.7
Yamunanagar	92.0
Kurukshetra	100.0
Kaithal	99.5
Karnal	100.0
Panipat	100.0
Sonepat	99.30
Rohtak	80.00
Jhajjar	74.20
Faridabad	97.30
Palwal	90.40
Gurgaon	84.50
Mewat	62.60
Rewari	86.50
Mahendergarh	83.40
Bhiwani	54.40
Jind	97.10
Hisar	80.40
Fatehabad	99.10
Sirsa	93.90

Source: *Statistical Abstract of Haryana* 2010-11, p. 279.

It is clear from above that electricity has played an important role in increasing irrigation facility in the State. Haryana was the first State in the country where electricity and roads reached each and every village of the State by mid seventies. In 1966-67, the total length of metalled roads was 5,032 kilometres, which increased to 26,888 kilometres by 2009-10 (Statistical Abstract of Haryana 2010-11, p. 483). Similarly, the power generation capacity of the State also increased substantially. In 1967-68, the total power generation capacity in Haryana was only 29.42 Megawatt, which increased to 3007 MW in 2008-09 (*Statistical Abstract of Haryana* 2010-11, p. 450). Apart from this Haryana has a share in the central agencies like NHPC and NTDP, etc. The consumption of electricity in 1966-67 was 4,343 lakh units, which increased to 1,92,903 lakh units in 2008-09. In 1966-67, the industrial sector was the major consumer of electricity, whereas agriculture sector consumed 23 per cent. The share of domestic consumption was only about 7 per cent. By the year 2001-02, agricultural sector had become the major sector consuming about 44 per cent of the total electricity consumed, whereas the consumption by industrial sector had come down to about 23 per cent. The share of domestic sector also went up from about 7 per cent in 1966-67 to about 21 per cent in 2010-11 (Table 1.10). During this period, the per capita consumption of electricity increased from 48 units to 521 units.

Table 1.10: Consumption of Electricity in Haryana

(Lakh KWH)

Year	Total consumption	Domestic percentage	Commercial percentage	Industrial percentage	Agriculture percentage
1966-67	4343.32	6.76	4.42	62.00	22.68
1970-71	9038.71	6.44	3.55	52.80	33.03
1975-76	16072.72	7.34	3.15	48.40	36.99
1980-81	25557.18	8.89	2.85	47.74	37.32
1985-86	33923.55	14.33	3.32	38.04	40.28
1990-91	60513.75	18.80	2.89	28.84	44.81
1995-96	83522.33	19.60	3.09	24.15	46.75
2000-01	101436.16	21.23	4.41	20.52	46.89
2005-06	152226.56	19.57	5.28	25.47	41.09
2009-10	228083.60	18.96	7.08	26.54	39.45
2010-11	240124.74	20.78	9.94	27.83	33.72

Source: *Statistical Abstract of Haryana* 2010-11, p. 444.

Along with this infrastructure of canals, power and roads, the banking infrastructure also expanded at an impressive rate. For the use of Green Revolution Package money was needed, which peasants of the State lacked. Tubewells have emerged as the major sources of irrigation in the State. This was not possible without the support of banks. Similarly, crop loans played an important role in purchasing HYVseeds, chemical fertilizers and pesticides. The increasing use of tractors and other agricultural implements was also not possible without the credit facilities from banks. In 1966-67, the total number of branches of commercial banks was 122, which increased to 1,549 in 2010-11. The number of Cooperative Banks and Post Office Saving Banks also increased from 36 and 969 to 348 and 2,650 respectively.

Because of the combined effect of the above factors, the increasing use of HYV of seeds led to an increase in demand for chemical fertilizers which increased from 13,347 metric tonnes in

1966-67 to 9,83,960 metric tonnes in 2010-11. The bullocks were replaced by tractors, whose number increased from 4,803 to 3,30,669 during the same period. Market committees were formed and new godowns were constructed for the timely purchase of agricultural produce at minimum support price.

Along with a phenomenal growth of agriculture, the basic infrastructure in the fields of education and health was also expanded, which had its direct impact on the industrial development of the State. Along with the increasing purchasing power in the agricultural sector, the laying down of basic infrastructure led to the expansion of trade in the State. Neighbourhood to the national capital provided some distinct benefits for the process of industrialization in the NCR region of the State. Thus, Haryana emerged as one of the leading States in terms of per capita income in the country.

I.4.1. Agriculture and Allied Sectors

Agriculture has remained the mainstay and leading occupation of the people of Haryana since its inception. This sector has always been an important contributor to the State Gross Domestic Product (GDP) and livelihood to majority of population. The growth rate of agriculture in the State picked up after independence as the government placed special emphasis on this sector in its Five Year Plans. Further the Green Revolution provided a major boost to the growth of agriculture sector. However, as a consequence of rapid structural transition of the State economy over the years, the contribution of agriculture and allied sectors at constant (2004-05) prices has come down to only 16.3 per cent in the State GDP during 2011-12. The economic growth of the State has, therefore, become more sensitive to the growth rate in industry and services sector during the past few years. But the recent experience suggests that high GDP growth without consistent and rapid agricultural growth is likely to accelerate inflation in the State, which may jeopardize the larger growth process. Therefore, the growth of agriculture and allied sectors continued to be a critical factor in the overall performance of the State economy (*Economic Survey of Haryana*, 2011-12, p. 17).

There could be four important factors to increase the agricultural production of a largely peasant proprietors ship based agriculture in the State: (1) to bring more cultivable land under cultivation, (2) to take more than one crop in a year on its area under cultivation, or increasing the intensity of agriculture, (3) to change the cropping pattern by bringing more areas under high yielding crops and (4) to improve irrigational facilities and other techniques to increase per acre yield and productivity. In Haryana, emphasis was given to all these factors as more and more uncultivable area was brought under cultivation, irrigation facilities were increased by expanding canal infrastructure and the increase in number of tubewells. This led to increased intensity of agriculture and more and more area under high productivity crops. The Green Revolution package was used to increase the productivity of land.

Table 1.11: Percentage Area under Principal Crops in Haryana

Year	*Wheat*	*Paddy*	*Total food-grains*	*Sugarcane*	*Cotton*	*Oilseeds*	*Gross area sown*
1966-67	16.16	4.17	76.54	3.26	3.98	4.61	4599
1970-71	22.78	5.43	78.03	3.15	3.89	2.88	4957
1980-81	27.08	8.86	72.56	2.07	5.79	5.69	5462
1990-91	31.26	11.17	68.91	2.50	8.30	8.26	5919
2000-01	38.51	17.24	70.97	2.24	9.08	6.77	6115
2005-06	35.38	16.09	66.23	1.98	8.97	11.31	6509
2006-07	37.08	16.26	67.86	2.20	8.23	9.71	6407
2007-08	38.11	16.61	69.32	2.17	8.16	7.91	6458
2008-09	37.88	18.63	71.09	1.40	7.02	8.12	6500
2009-10	39.17	18.99	71.52	1.24	7.95	8.23	6351

Source: *Statistical Abstract of Haryana* 2001-02 and 2010-11, pp. 240-48.

The gross area sown in 1966-67 was 45.99 lakh hectares which increased to 63.57 lakh hectares in 2010-11. The share of area under wheat and paddy crops in the gross area sown in the State was 59.15 per cent during 2010-11 (Table 1.11). This was about 80 per cent of the total area sown under foodgrain crops. This highlights a major change in the cropping pattern since the inception of Haryana in 1966-67. The area under wheat and paddy was 16.16 per cent and 4.17 per cent respectively of the gross area sown in 1966-67, which increased to 39.17 and 18.99 per cent respectively in 2009-10. Another important change in the cropping pattern of the State is that the area under sugarcane has come down whereas cotton and oilseeds have registered an increase in the area over the period. Table 1.12 presents district-wise percentage of area under major crops in Haryana for the year 2009-10. It shows that wheat has emerged as the main crop in almost all the districts. However dry crops like Gram, Bajra and Oilseeds still dominate the agricultural scene, especially in less irrigated districts of Mahendergarh, Rewari and Bhiwani. The highest percentage of area under wheat was registered in district Jhajjar (52.11%) in 2009-10, followed by Faridabad (50%). The lowest percentage of area under wheat was registered as 15.30 in district Mahendergarh. Districts Karnal, Kurukshetra, Kaithal, Panipat, Ambala and Yamunanagar the core region of Green Revolution have emerged as the major rice producing districts in the State. Other important rice producing districts are Sonepat, Jind, Fatehabad and Panchkula. The only district where rice has failed to make its entry was Mahendergarh. Districts Rewari, Bhiwani, Gurgaon and Mewat have little area under this crop.

Table 1.12: Percentage Area under Principal Crops in 2009-10 in Districts of Haryana

('000 hectares)

Sl. No.	*District*	*Wheat*	*Paddy*	*Total food-grains*	*Sugar-cane*	*Cotton*	*Oil-seeds*	*Total cropped area*
1.	Ambala	42.03	39.61	84.06	4.83	—	1.0	207
2.	Panchkula	41.03	20.51	84.62	—	—	7.69	39
3.	Yamunanagar	39.81	34.26	75.93	11.57	—	0.14	216
4.	Kurukshetra	40.28	41.70	82.33	4.95	—	2.12	283
5.	Kaithal	45.26	41.58	90.00	0.08	0.69	0.26	380
6.	Karnal	43.96	44.22	88.92	2.06	—	0.25	389
7.	Panipat	46.03	40.74	87.30	2.11	—	0.53	189
8.	Sonepat	47.47	30.30	87.54	1.35	0.12	1.01	297
9.	Rohtak	46.43	15.63	84.38	1.79	1.54	6.25	224
10.	Jhajjar	43.53	11.21	79.74	0.04	0.18	14.22	232
11.	Faridabad	50.00	14.71	73.53	1.47	—	1.47	68
12.	Palwal	52.11	16.32	76.84	1.05	0.06	1.58	190
13	Gurgaon	44.44	3.42	80.34	—	—	12.82	117
14.	Mewat	42.77	3.47	68.21	—	—	16.76	173
15.	Rewari	25.52	1.04	58.33	—	0.12	33.85	192
16.	Mahendergarh	15.30	—	55.22	—	0.18	35.07	268
17.	Bhiwani	21.99	2.66	60.08	0.01	6.50	19.47	714
18.	Jind	46.04	23.13	79.44	0.02	9.11	1.02	467
19.	Hisar	37.13	7.10	56.44	0.02	26.30	8.91	606
20.	Fatehabad	44.82	19.52	67.47	—	16.99	2.17	415
21.	Sirsa	40.67	8.89	52.77	—	38.22	6.41	686

Source: *Statistical Abstract of Haryana*, 2010-11, pp. 240-48.

Sugarcane has lost its importance as a commercial crop in Haryana over time, except in districts Yamunanagar (11.57%), Kurukshetra (4.95%) and Ambala (4.83%). Cotton has emerged as a major commercial crop in districts Sirsa, Hisar, Fatehabad, Jind and Bhiwani whereas oilseeds play an important role in the agriculture of Mahendergarh, Rewari, Bhiwani, Mewat, Rohtak and Gurgaon.

The cropping intensity in the State has reached 184 in 2010-11. The agricultural cropping pattern in the State is thus dominated by paddy-wheat rotation, causing degradation in soil fertility and fall in the underground water level.

Most of the area under major crops has been brought under high yielding varieties, recording 97.4, 64.6, 80.0 and 96.2 per cent respectively for wheat, paddy, maize and bajra in 2010-11. The foodgrain production, thus reached an impressive level of 166.29 lakh tonnes during 2010-11, as compared to a meagre production of 25.95 lakh tonnes in 1966-67, registering an increase of about 6 times. The production of wheat and rice in 2010-11 was 116.30 lakh tonnes and 2.23 lakh tonnes respectively as against 10.59 lakh tonnes and 2.23 lakh tonnes respectively during the year 1966-67, which amounts to eleven times increase in wheat and seventeen times increase in rice production (Table 1.13). Haryana is the second largest contributor of foodgrains to the central pool. More than 60 per cent export of Basmati Rice is taking place from Haryana alone. Whereas sugarcane production has been fluctuating in the State, the production of oilseeds and cotton have registered impressive growth.

Table 1.13: Agriculture Production of Major Crops in Haryana

('000 tonnes)

Year	Wheat	Rice	Total Food-grains	Oilseeds	Cotton	Sugar-cane
1966-67	1059	223	2592	63	288	5100
1970-71	2324	460	4771	92	373	7070
1980-81	3490	1259	6036	99	643	4600
1990-91	6436	1834	9559	188	1155	7800
2000-01	9669	2695	13295	638	1383	8170
2005-06	8853	3194	13006	563	1502	8310
2006-07	10059	3371	14759	830	1805	9651
2007-08	10232	3606	15294	837	1882	8850
2008-09	11360	3299	16405	617	1862	5206
2009-10	10488	3628	15345	911	1918	5707
2010-11	11630	3472	16629	862	1744	6042
2011-12	11861	3759	17205	942	2621	6745

Source: *Statistical Abstract of Haryana,* 2001-02, 2010-11, pp. 240-48.

The Green Revolution package was the most successful for wheat and paddy. The average yield of both wheat and rice have registered impressive growth in Haryana. The average yield of wheat which was only 1,425 kg per hectare in 1966-67 increased to 4,215 kg per hectare in 2009-10, much above the national average of 2,830 kg in the same year. Similarly, the average yield of rice increased from 1,161 kg per hectare in 1966-67 to 3,008 kg per hectare in 2009-10. The national average for rice was recorded at 2,130 kg per hectare which was much below the Haryana level (Table 1.14).

Table 1.14: Average Yield of Wheat and Rice in Haryana and at all India Level

(Kg per hectare)

Year	*Haryana*		*India*	
	Wheat	*Rice*	*Wheat*	*Rice*
1966-67	1425	1161	—	—
1970-71	2074	1697	—	—
1975-76	1980	2063	—	—
1980-81	2360	2606	—	—
1985-86	3094	2797	—	—
1990-91	3479	2775	2281	1740
2000-01	4106	2557	2708	1901
2005-06	3844	3051	2619	2102
2006-07	4232	3238	2708	2131
2007-08	4158	3361	2785	2203
2008-09	4614	2724	2907	2178
2009-10	4215	3008	2830	2130
2010-11	4624	2789	—	—
2011-12	4735	3044	—	—

Source: *Statistical Abstract of Haryana*, 2010-11, p. 268.

However, Table 1.15 brings out that out of 21 districts of Haryana, six districts namely Sirsa, Jind, Hisar, Fatehabad, Karnal and Kaithal produced more than 50 per cent of wheat in 2009-10. On the other hand Panchkula, Faridabad, Mahendergarh, Rewari, Gurgaon and Mewat districts together contributed about 10 per cent of the total production in the State. Similarly, seven districts Karnal, Kaithal, Kurukshetra, Ambala, Jind, Fatehabad and Yamunanagar contributed about 72 per cent of the total rice production in the State. District Mahendergarh is the only district of the State which does not produce any rice, whereas districts Rewari, Gurgaon, Mewat and Panchkula

Table 1.15: Percentage Production of Major Crops ('000 tonnes) in 2009-10 in districts of Haryana

Sl. No.	*District*	*Wheat*	*Rice*	*Total Foodgrains*	*Oilseeds*	*Cotton*	*Sugarcane*
1.	Ambala	3.30	8.43	4.29	0.34	—	12.43
2.	Panchkula	0.34	0.63	0.05	0.58	—	—
3.	Yamunanagar	3.38	7.36	4.08	0.58	—	31.70
4.	Kurukshetra	5.02	12.49	6.39	1.28	—	18.21
5.	Kaithal	7.36	12.73	8.18	—	0.62	4.03
6.	Karnal	7.37	14.36	8.47	0.23	—	11.21
7.	Panipat	3.69	5.65	3.86	0.23	—	5.43
8.	Sonepat	5.82	6.04	5.66	0.35	—	5.25
9.	Rohtak	4.02	1.38	3.43	2.55	0.90	4.20
10.	Jhajjar	3.98	1.30	3.57	6.03	—	1.23
11.	Faridabad	1.30	0.07	1.10	0.23	—	0.88
12.	Palwal	3.40	2.34	3.36	0.46	—	1.93
13.	Gurgaon	2.16	0.04	2.05	2.90	—	—
14.	Mewat	2.87	0.05	2.42	4.87	—	—
15.	Rewari	2.10	0.01	2.14	13.81	—	—
16.	Mahendergarh	1.52	—	2.25	16.82	—	—
17.	Bhiwani	5.35	0.12	5.67	24.83	4.59	1.40
18.	Jind	8.91	8.16	8.56	0.90	7.35	1.05
19.	Hisar	8.88	2.59	7.50	11.95	24.87	1.0
20.	Fatehabad	8.03	8.02	7.62	2.09	19.50	—
21.	Sirsa	10.70	5.62	8.93	8.93	41.76	—

Source: *Statistical Abstract of Haryana*, 2010-11, pp. 240-48.

together produce less than one per cent of the total rice production of the State.

About 98.5 per cent of the total production of cotton was contributed by just five districts namely Sirsa, Hisar, Fatehabad, Jind and Bhiwani in 2009-10. Sirsa district alone contributed about 42 per cent of the total production in the State. District Rohtak and Kaithal together contributed about 1.5 per cent.

The major producers of oilseeds in the State are Bhiwani, Mahendergarh, Rewari, Hisar, Sirsa and Mewat districts which produced about 81 per cent of the total oilseeds of the State in 2009-10.

District Yamunanagar and Kurukshetra are the major sugarcane producing districts of the State. In 2009-10 about 50 per cent of the total sugarcane production was recorded in these two districts. District Ambala and Karnal are the other two important sugarcane producing districts of the State.

The above story of the agricultural sector of Haryana paints a rosy picture, except the fact that the colour of rose is the brightest in wheat-paddy rotation districts of Karnal, Kurukshetra, Kaithal, Panipat and Jind districts and wheat-paddy-cotton districts of Fatehabad, Sirsa and Hissar and it starts fading away when we move towards central and southern districts of the State with districts Mewat and Mahendergarh as the most backward districts of the State.

Table 1.16: Percentage number and Area of Operational Holdings by Size-Groups in Haryana (2000-01) Provisional

	No.		*Area (in hectare)*	
Below 0-5	28.68	46.09	3.26	8.91
0.5 - 1.0	17.41		5.65	
1.0 - 2.0	19.25	30.28	11.88	23.29
2.0 - 3.0	11.03		11.41	
3.0 – 4.0	7.17	17.63	10.59	34.57
4.0 – 5.0	4.71		9.01	
5.0 – 7.5	5.75		14.97	
7.5 – 10.0	2.76	6.02	10.10	33.21
10.0 – 20.0	2.64		14.93	
20.0 & above	0.62		8.18	
Total	**15,27,774**		**2.32**	**Average size of holdings**
All India	**12,92,22,000**		**1.23**	**All India average size of holdings**
Percentage of Haryana	**(1.18)**			

Source: *Statistical Abstract of Haryana,* 2010-11, p. 235.

However, an analysis of the number and area of the size of landholdings in the State points towards emerging agrarian crisis. If we just compare the average size of landholdings with all India level, Haryana still looks better off with 2.32 hectares as against 1.23 hectares for the country as a whole. But the breakup of number and area of operational holdings shows that the agricultural land is very skewedly distributed in the State and so may be the gains of Green Revolution. Haryana had 15,27,774 operational landholdings in the State with 35,49,883 hectares of land in the year 2000-01. Out of these 46.09 per cent operational holdings were below the size of one hectare, covering a total area of only 8.91 per cent of the State. This group may be termed as marginal farmers. Another group with operational land holdings between one to three hectares and who may be called the small farmers constituted 30.28 per cent operating 23.29 per cent of the total land. Thus, the marginal and small farmers who constituted 76.29 per cent of the whole peasantry of the State operated only 32.2 per cent of the total land in Haryana. On the other hand the top 6.02 per cent of the landholdings with 7.5 hectares and above operated more than one-third of the total land in the state. In Table 1.17, we have presented district-wise average size of the land holdings in Haryana in 2000-01. It may be noted that only three districts namely Kaithal, Bhiwani and Sirsa had average holdings of more than 3 hectares size and in rest of the districts holding size varied between 1-3 hectares.

Table 1.17: District-wise Average Size of Landholdings in Haryana 2001-01 (Provisional)

Sl. No.	*Districts*	*Area in hectare*
1.	Ambala	1.74
2.	Panchkula	1.70
3.	Yamunanagar	2.15
4.	Kurukshetra	2.36
5.	Kaithal	3.02
6.	Karnal	2.12
7.	Panipat	1.47
8.	Sonepat	1.60
9.	Rohtak	2.29
10.	Jhajjar	2.07
11.	Faridabad	1.59
12.	Gurgaon	1.77
13.	Rewari	2.05
14.	Mahendergarh	2.01
15.	Bhiwani	3.16
16.	Jind	2.77
17.	Hisar	2.96
18.	Sirsa	3.38
19.	Fatehabad	2.62
	Total	**2.32**

Source: *Statistical Abstract of Haryana*, 2010-11, pp. 231-35.

ALLIED ACTIVITIES

After agriculture, Animal Husbandry is the next important sector which significantly supplements the income of rural people in Haryana. Presently, livestock population of the State is 90.50 lakh including 15.52 lakh cattle and 59.33 lakh buffaloes being catered by 2,790 veterinary institutions.

The milk production during the year 2010-11 was 62.67 lakh tonnes. The per capita per day milk availability in the same year was 680 grams in the State, which was the second highest in the country. Production of eggs was 39,644 lakh and that of wool 12.87 tonnes during the same year (*Economic Survey of Haryana*, 2012, p. 28).

I.4.2. Industrial Sector

Industrialization plays a vital role in the development of an economy. It accelerates economic growth and thereby increases the contribution of industrial sector in the State Domestic Product by way of increasing production and employment. Industrial sector is composed of mining, manufacturing, electricity, gas and water supply and construction sub-sectors as per the classification of Central Statistical Organisation, New Delhi for the purpose of compilation of Gross Domestic product (GDP). The Department of Economic and Statistical Analysis, Haryana prepares the estimates of GDP of industrial sector at current and constant prices on yearly basis to assess the growth of industry sector. Now industry is the second largest contributor to the State GDP after services sector. The relative contribution of this sector in the State GDP increased continuously before 2005-06. But thereafter, the share of this sector decreased considerably from 32.9 per cent in 2005-06 to 29.1 per cent in 2011-12 as the services sector has grown at the rate much higher than the growth rate of industrial sector. This eventually resulted in the decreased share of industry and increased share of services sector. The services sector, in fact, has become the growth engine of the State economy but the good growth of industry sector is also essential for the balanced and higher growth of the State economy on a sustainable basis.

The Gross Fixed Capital Formation (GFCF) in industry sector is also an important indicator of growth of this sector on a long term basis. The Department of Economic and Statistical Analysis, Haryana prepares estimates of GFCF on yearly basis to assess the growth of industry sector. The contribution of GFCF in industry sector was 55.4 per cent in 2004-05 which continued to increase to 59.3 per cent in 2009-10 with a slight decrease in 2007-08. The index of Industrial

Production is one of the prime indicators of Industrial Production with reference to a chosen base year. The general index of industrial production increased from 233.7 in 2009-10 to 241.4 in 2010-11 registering an increase of 7.9 per cent. The index of manufacturing sector which carries the highest weight in IIP rose from 218.0 in 2009-10 to 236.5 in 2010-11 (*Economic Survey of Haryana* 2012, p. 30).

The number of registered working factories increased from 1,168 in 1966 to 10,513 in 2010, about nine times increase. The process of industrialization in the State, however, was slow between 1966 and 1975. This number of factors increased from 1,791 in 1975 to 3,176 in 1980. Thereafter, the number of registered factories increased at a much faster rate. Similarly, the estimated number of workers employed in working factories of Haryana, increased from 71,016 in 1966 to 7,82,463 in 2010, an increase of more than eleven times. This increase was much faster after 1990 (Table 1.18).

Table 1.18: Number of Registered Working Factories and Workers Employed in Haryana

Year	*No. of registered factories*	*Estimated number of works employed in working factories*
1966	1168	71016
1970	1359	88675
1975	1791	109834
1980	3176	175025
1985	4484	226476
1990	4843	269411
1995	6498	391386
2000	8631	498656
2005	9282	574591
2009	10273	741411
2010	10513	782463

Source: *Statistical Abstract of Haryana*, 2010-11, through Labour Commissioner, Haryana.

However, the industrialization of the State is concentrated in two districts, namely, Faridabad and Gurgaon neighbouring Delhi, with Faridabad having 25.54 per cent of the total working factories in Haryana, whereas Gurgaon has 17.36 per cent of the total working factories of the State, thus together having about 43 per cent of the total working factories and about 59 per cent of the total estimated workers employed in the working factories of Haryana. Yamunanagar, Panipat, Sonepat, Jhajjar, Karnal, Ambala, Hisar and Rewari too have some industrial base. The other districts are quite backward in terms on industries (Table 1.19).

Table 1.19: Percentage No. of Registered Factories and Workers Employed in Haryana Districts

Sl. No.	Districts	Registered factories	Worker Employed
1.	Ambala	3.95	1.94
2.	Panchkula	1.49	1.57
3.	Yamunanagar	12.15	5.22
4.	Kurukshetra	1.60	0.50
5.	Kaithal	1.18	0.35
6.	Karnal	4.45	3.63
7.	Panipat	7.77	6.30
8.	Sonepat	6.06	5.26
9.	Rohtak	2.83	2.27
10.	Jhajjar	4.72	3.29
11.	Faridabad	25.54	26.79
12.	Palwal	0.18	0.58
13.	Gurgaon	17.36	31.98
14.	Mewat	0.03	0.02
15.	Rewari	1.89	3.36
16.	Mahendergarh	0.57	0.54
17.	Bhiwani	1.10	1.66
18.	Jind	1.52	1.68
19.	Hisar	3.30	1.70
20.	Fatehabad	1.13	0.49
21.	Sirsa	1.17	0.88

Source: *Ibid.*

The Haryana Agro Industries Corporation Ltd. has been engaged in trading activities such as sale of seeds, fertilizers, pesticides, tractors, spray and other agricultural machinery on economical prices to the farmers. The corporation has two manufacturing units, i.e., Cattle Feed Plant at Jind and Pesticide and Weedicide Plant at Shahabad. It has one Agricultural Engineering Workshop at Nilokheri. The corporation is also engaged in the procurement of wheat, paddy and bajra.

Most of the rural industries were promoted by KVIB. During the year 2011-12, the Khadi and Village Industry Board units produced goods worth Rs. 10,847 lakh and sold goods worth Rs. 17,790 lakh KVIB sells products of other States also and generated full time employment to 23,463 persons and part time employment to 29,873 persons. (*Economic Survey of Haryana* 2012, p. 33). Thus rural industrial sector still needs a strong rush.

Haryana is not known to have significant deposits of any major minerals and its mining operations are largely confined to minor minerals such as stone, boulders, gravels, sand, etc., which are largely used for construction industry.

I.4.3. Services Sector

The services sector in the State has grown at much faster rate than the other sectors of the economy, viz., agriculture and industry since its inception in 1966. The share of services sector in State Gross Domestic Product (GDP) at constant prices increased from 22.9 per cent in 1966-67 to 54.6 per cent in 2011-12. The rise in the services sector share in its GDP marks a structural shift in the State economy. During the period of last 11 years (1995-96 to 2006-07), the services sector grew at the average annual growth rate of 11.2 per cent. This growth rate was significantly faster than the annual growth recorded for combined agriculture and industry during the same period. The growth of services sector GDP has been continuously above the overall GDP growth during this period. It has also been more consistent than the growth of the other two sectors. The above trend of faster and comparatively stable growth of services sector as compared to the other two sectors remained on the same path throughout the period of the Eleventh Five Year Plan (2007-12). During the first three years, i.e., 2007-08, 2008-09 and 2009-10 of current Five Year Plan, the services sector recorded excellent growth of 13.6, 11.6 and 16.1 per cent as compared to the low and fluctuating growth of 0.0, 7.3 and 1.3 per cent achieved in agriculture and allied sectors and fluctuating growth of 6.6, 3.5 and 10.4 per cent in the industrial sector.

Among the four sub-sectors of services sector, Trade, Hotels and Restaurants was the largest group having the highest contribution to the State GDP. Finance, insurance and real estate was the second largest group followed by community, social and personal services

Table 1.20: Share of Different Sub-sectors of Services Sector in the State GDP (%)

Sub-sectors	*2007-08*	*2008-09*	*2009-10*	*2010-11 QE*	*2011-12 AE*
Trade, Hotels and Restaurants	18.4	19.2	20.8	21.9	21.9
Transport, Storage & Communication	9.2	9.0	9.0	9.0	9.2
Finance, Insurance, Real Estate and Business services	13.8	13.9	14.1	13.9	14.4
Communication, Social and Personal services.	7.4	8.3	8.7	8.7	9.1

QE—Quick Estimates, AE—Advance Estimates.
Source: *Ibid.*

and transport, storage and communication. The shares of all these four categories in the State GDP at constant (2004-05) prices during the period of Eleventh Five Year Plan is presented in Table 1.20.

Table 1.21: Sub-sector-wise Growth of Services Sector during Eleventh Five Year Plan

Sub-sectors	*2007-08*	*2008-09*	*2009-10*	*2010-11 QE*	*2011-12 AE*
Trade, Hotels and Restaurants	16.3	13.0	20.7	15.1	8.3
Transport, Storage and Communication	13.9	5.4	11.3	9.1	10.3
Finance, Insurance, Real Estate and Business services	13.3	8.8	13.0	8.1	11.6
Communication, Social and Personal services	7.7	20.9	16.1	10.4	12.6
Overall Services Sector	13.6	11.6	16.1	11.4	10.2

QE—Quick Estimates, AE—Advance Estimates.
Source: *Ibid.*

The review of growth in real GDP of sub-sectors of services sector during current Five Year Plan shows that trade, hotels and restaurants has registered two digits growth rates of 16.3, 13.0 and 20.7 per cent during 2007-08, 2008-09 and 2009-10 respectively (Table 1.21).

1.5. Social Sector: Education

Social Sector which consists of Education, Science and Technology, Health and Public Health, etc., plays an important role in a developing economy. The ultimate objective of development planning is human development or increased social welfare of the people. Increased social welfare of the people requires a more equitable distribution of development benefits along with better living environment. We have seen that the economy of the State has grown at an impressive rate. It was also noticed that though all the sectors of the economy recorded high rates of growth, the contributions of services and industrial sectors in the State GDP have increased and that of agricultural sector has gone down. This is generally believed to be a healthy sign in a developing economy. However, the increasing contributions of services and industrial sectors have not led to the desired change in the occupational structure of Haryana. The share of agriculture in GSDP has declined to 28.1 per cent and that of secondary and tertiary sectors increased to 71.9 per cent in 2001-02 whereas 51.3 per cent work force was still dependent on agriculture (Table 1.22). This implies that income distribution has become more skewed and disparities between rural and urban people have further widened. The share of services sector further increased to 54.6 per cent in 2011-12 and that of agriculture sector came down to 16.3 per cent with more than two-third of the population of the State still living in rural areas, majority of whom belong to either marginal and small farmers or landless agricultural workers and traditional artisan groups. These sections are at the lowest ladder of economic development in the state. Share of expenditure on social sectors has consistently increased over time. In the Fourth Five Year Plan, it was just 13.61 per cent and it has consistently increased to 47.71 per cent in Haryana (*Statistical Abstract of Haryana* 2010-11, pp. 619 to 622).

Table 1.22: Share in Gross State Domestic Product (GSDP)

(In percentage)

	1969-70	*2001-02*	*2011-12*
Agriculture	60.70	28.10	16.30
Industry	17.60	28.60	29.10
Service	21.70	43.30	54.60

Source: *Economic Survey of Haryana*, 2011-12, pp. 2-3.

Levels of Education and health are the two most important indicators of human development in any society. Haryana though boasts of second highest per capita income in the country was lagging behind in the field of education (Table 1.23). The literacy rate in the State was 76.64 per cent in 2011. Literacy levels were only marginally above the national average, 85.38 and 66.77 per cent for males and females as against 82.14 and 65.46 per cent for the country as a whole. However, it was much below Kerala with 96.02 per cent for males and 91.98 for females. Illiteracy is more widespread in rural areas than urban areas. Still improvement in litracy levels in 2011 in comparison to 2001 has been very impressive. Overall literacy rate recorded a growth of 8.73 per cent which is quite impressive. All the districts have shown a good improvement and performance over time.

Growth in the academic infrastructure has also been significant. The number of primary/junior basic schools has increased from 4,447 in 1966-67 to 13,073 in 2010-11. Similarly, the number of middle schools and High/Hr. Sec./schools also increased from 735 and 597 in 1966-67 to 3,439 and 6,771 respectively in 2010-11. The educational facilities are available in a radius of 1.52 km. There was just one

Table 1.23: District-wise Literacy in Haryana

(in percentage)

Districts	*2001 Census*			*2011 Census (P)*		
	Total	*Male*	*Female*	*Total*	*Male*	*Female*
Ambala	75.31	82.31	67.39	82.89	88.47	76.64
Panchkula	74.00	80.87	65.65	83.44	88.65	77.48
Yamunanagar	71.63	78.82	63.39	78.93	85.06	71.99
Kurukshetra	69.88	78.06	60.61	76.70	83.46	69.18
Kaithal	59.02	69.15	47.31	70.56	79.33	60.69
Karnal	67.74	76.29	57.97	76.44	83.73	68.29
Panipat	69.17	78.50	57.97	77.46	85.45	68.23
Sonepat	72.79	83.06	60.68	80.83	89.40	70.88
Rohtak	73.72	83.23	62.59	80.37	88.42	71.19
Jhajjar	72.38	83.27	59.65	80.83	89.44	70.96
Faridabad	76.29	85.14	65.53	83.04	89.94	75.17
Palwal	59.19	75.10	40.76	70.32	82.60	56.40
Gurgaon	78.51	87.97	67.49	84.44	90.27	77.64
Mewat	43.51	61.81	23.89	56.14	72.98	37.58
Rewari	75.25	88.45	60.83	82.23	92.92	70.54
Mahendergarh	69.89	84.72	54.08	78.87	91.28	65.25
Bhiwani	67.45	80.26	53.00	76.74	87.39	64.80
Jind	62.12	73.82	48.51	72.73	82.49	61.58
Hisar	64.83	76.57	51.08	73.24	82.79	62.31
Fatehabad	57.98	68.22	46.53	69.13	78.10	59.29
Sirsa	60.55	70.05	49.93	70.35	78.64	61.16
Haryana State	**67.91**	**78.49**	**55.73**	**76.64**	**85.38**	**66.77**

Source: *Statistical Abstract of Haryana*, 2010-11, p. 830.

University in 1966-67. This number had increased to 24 in 2010-11. However, quality of education remains a concern. A new Education Hub for higher learning is being developed in district Sonepat.

Table 1.24: Number of Recognized Institutes in Haryana

	1966-67	*2010-11*
Universities	1	24
Arts & Science colleges	40	190
Colleges for Physical Education	1	1
Teachers Training colleges	5	472
High/Hr. Secondary schools	597	6771
Middle/Senior Basic schools	735	3439
Primary/Junior Basic schools	4447	13073

Source: *Statistical Abstract of Haryana*, 2010-11, pp. 121-22.

Table 1.25: Number of Scholars in Recognized Colleges for General Education in Haryana (Arts, Science, and Home Science)

Year	*Total Scholars (including Scheduled Castes)*			*Scheduled Castes Scholars*		
	Total	*Boys (%)*	*Girls (%)*	*Total*	*Boys (%)*	*Girls (%)*
1966-67	27332	79.04	20.96	4.78	5.81	0.87
2000-01	196537	56.88	43.12	7.30	9.59	4.27
2005-06	192701	49.94	50.06	9.38	11.29	7.48
2009-10	250325	46.81	53.19	14.14	16.94	11.68
2010-11	241926	44.47	55.53	12.03	12.79	11.43

Source: *Statistical Abstract of Haryana*, 2010-11, p. 137.

Table 1.26: Number of Scholars in Recognized Schools in Haryana

	1966-67			*2009-10*		
	Total	*Boys (%)*	*Girls (%)*	*Total*	*Boys (%)*	*Girls (%)*
High/Hr. Sec./Navodaya	376080	76.17	23.83	2405479	54.22	45.78
Middle schools	250673	73.02	26.98	877767	54.41	45.59
Primary/Pre-Primary	534764	73.63	26.37	1694900	51.38	48.62
Grand Total	**1161517**	**74.32**	**25.68**	**4978146**	**53.29**	**46.71**

Source: *Statistical Abstract of Haryana,* 2010-11, p. 141.

However, it may be interesting to note that the male/female ratio in colleges has changed significantly in favour of females over time.

Table 1.27: Number of Scheduled Castes Scholars in Recognized Schools in Haryana

	1966-67			*2009-10*		
	Total	*Boys (%)*	*Girls (%)*	*Total*	*Boys (%)*	*Girls (%)*
High/Hr. Sec./Navodaya	30617	89.36	10.64	557433	53.93	46.07
Middle schools	22899	84.05	15.95	219469	52.04	47.96
Primary/Pre-Primary	62249	86.51	13.49	472123	51.64	48.36
Grand Total	**115765**	**76.78**	**23.22**	**1249025**	**52.73**	**47.23**

Source: *Statistical Abstract of Haryana* 2010-11, p. 143.

In 1966-67 the percentage of girl students was only 20.96 to the total students in 1966-69 which changed to 55.53 per cent in the year 2010-11 (Table 1.25). The share of scheduled caste students has also increased from 4.78 per cent of the total student strength to 12.03 per cent over the same period. The most significant fact is the share of SC girl students which was less than one per cent (0.87%) in 1966 increased to 11.43 per cent in 2010-11. It is a remarkable achievement which will have far reaching implications for the social transformation process in the Haryana society.

Table 1.26 shows the number of scholars in recognized schools in Haryana. It shows that the male-female ratio in the recognized schools in the State in 1966-67 was 74.32 and 25.68 which changed to 53.29 and 46.71. This clearly establishes that share of girl students in school education has shown a significant improvement and that of SC girl students increase is far more impressive.

The male/female ratio amongst the scheduled castes scholars was much lower in all the classes than that of the general category scholars. Of course the ratio came down further in high/higher secondary level where the percentage of girl students was only 10.64 in 1966-67. Over the years the percentage of girl students has phenomenally increased and now it was slightly lower than the boys, i.e., 47.23 (Table 1.27).

I.6. Health

The situation of health in Haryana also leaves much to be desired. As per India Human Development Report 2011, life expectancy in

Haryana was 67.1 years and in terms of human development index, among the major States in the country, it ranked at ninth place, first being Kerala. In the year 2000, the infant mortality rate (less than one year of age) in Haryana was 74.5 per thousand, which was worse than the national average of 71.1 per thousand. The data on inter-district gender-wise infant mortality rates for the year 2001 is more revealing. The Table 1.28 shows that in Haryana the infant mortality rate for the males was 60 as against 76 for females, a clear bias against the female infants. The female infant mortality rates were as high as 87 in Kaithal to 85, 84, 83 and 81 per thousand births in districts Gurgaon, Jind, Fatehabad and Hisar respectively. The lowest female infant mortality rates were recorded in Panchkula and Ambala at 67 and 68 respectively. These two districts recorded the lowest infant mortality rates for male infants also. The highest male infant mortality rate was recorded in district Fatehabad at 71 as against 60 for Haryana.

Table 1.28: Haryana's Inter-District Gender-wise Infant Mortality Rates, 2001

District	*Male*	*Rank*	*Female*	*Rank*
Ambala	49	1	68	2
Bhiwani	59	10	73	7
Faridabad	55	3	75	10
Fatehabad	71	19	83	16
Gurgaon	67	16	85	18
Hisar	56	5	81	15
Jhajjar	56	5	72	5
Jind	67	16	84	17
Kaithal	69	18	87	19
Karnal	60	12	78	14
Kurukshetra	62	15	70	3
Mahendergarh	60	12	76	13
Panchkula	50	2	67	1
Panipat	59	10	75	10
Rewari	60	12	70	3
Rohtak	55	3	72	5
Sirsa	58	7	73	7
Sonepat	58	7	73	7
Yamunanagar	58	7	75	10

Source: *Haryana's Human Development Report*, 2005, p. 50.

In 1968, the total number of health institutions in Haryana was 785 out of which 656 were in rural areas and 129 in urban areas. There were only 3 hospitals in rural areas whereas 58 hospitals were situated in urban areas (Table 1.29). Thus, the rural population had to visit urban centres for better health facilities or they had to depend upon Primary Health Centres, Dispensaries or Health Sub-Centres. It is important to note that about 84 per cent of the State population was living in 6,781 villages of the State. For these, there were only 73 Primary Health Centres, meaning thereby that there was one primary health centre for 93 villages. The numbers of total health sub-centres were 510 which meant one health sub-centre for 13.30 villages. This infrastructure was just not adequate. It is important to note that these sub-centres did not have qualified doctors. The role of health workers at these sub-centres was just to collect health statistics and family planning.

Table 1.29: Number of Health Institutions (Allopathic) in Haryana—Rural and Urban

Institution	*1968*			*2010-11*		
	Rural	*Urban*	*Total*	*Rural*	*Urban*	*Total*
Hospitals	3	58	61	6	63	69
Primary Health Centre	73	16	89	393	36	429
Community Health Centre	—	—	—	56	30	86
Dispensary	70	55	125	31	162	193
Health Sub-Centre	510	—	510	2465	—	2465
Total	**656**	**129**	**785**	**2951**	**291**	**3242**

Source: *Statistical Abstract of Haryana,* 2010-11, p. 162.

According to the National Health Policy 1984, one Health Sub-centre for a population of 5,000, one Primary Health Centre per 30,000 population, one Community Health Centre per lakh of population and one Hospital at every district were to be opened in the country.

The situation in Haryana was far behind these targets even in 2010-11. Since 1968, only 3 and 5 hospitals were added in rural and urban areas respectively. The total number of hospitals increased from 61 in 1968 to 69 in 2010-11. The population of Haryana had increased from 1.37 crore in 1971 to 2,53,53,081 persons in 2011. During this period the total number of health institutions increased from 785 to 3,242.

However, this increase in the number of health institutions was far behind the targets of National Health Policy. As per the norm of one Primary Health Centre on a population of 30,000, 845 PHCs were needed in the State. As against this, there were only 429 PHCs in Haryana in 2010-11, which was only about 50 per cent of the targeted numbers. Same was the case for other health institutions.

Similarly, the total medical staff was also much below the target set out in the National Health Policy. There were only 2.63 per cent doctors per institution, if we put together all the PHCs, CHCs and Hospitals, whereas it should be between 7 to 10 doctors in one Community Health Centre alone (Table 1.30).

Table 1.30: Medical Staff in Haryana (As on 31st December)

Year	*Medical Officers (I & II)*	*Nurse/ Matron*	*ANM's*	*Technicians/ Lab Astt.*	*Total*
1966	464	269	438	64	3312
1970	440	420	454	226	4388
1980	916	801	655	182	6836
1985	1225	1171	1326	278	10235
1990	1395	1448	2470	424	12723
1995	1519	1156	2380	487	13720
2000	1610	1442	2274	527	14159
2005	1839	1266	2100	527	13484
2009	1205	448	1756	333	9847
2010 Provisional	1538	485	2275	459	12937

Source: *Statistical Abstract of Haryana*, 2010-11, p. 163.

1.7. Public Health

All the villages of Haryana were provided with at least one safe source of drinking water by 31st March, 1992. Thereafter, the focus was shifted to augment/strengthen the drinking water supply infrastructure in the villages. But, a survey conducted in December 2004, found that out of 6,759 villages, as many as 1971 had slipped into the category of deficient villages where the water allowance had gone down below the approved norm of 40 litres per capita per day due to various reasons. By 31st March, 2011 drinking water supply facilities were improved in 1,844 villages, leaving a balance of 127 deficient villages (*Economic Survey of Haryana*, 2011-12, p. 59).

The above analysis clearly shows that though Haryana has

registered a remarkable overall growth in its economy, there are sharp differences among the various districts in terms of economic development. Further, the economic development in the State has not led to the desired increase in educational and health facilities. Also, there are sharp differences in the levels of achievements in these fields among the various districts and within the districts between males and females.

Haryana's Human Development Report-2005 was the first report of its kind in Haryana that determined inter-district ranking on the basis of various sub-indices relating to Health, Education and Income. Ambala district occupied the first position on the inter-district Human Development Index because of a clear picture of positive cumulative outcomes: first position on the Health sub-index, second position on the Education sub-index and third position on the Income sub-index. In contrast, Mahendergarh district occupied the last position on the Human Development Index by virtue of negative cumulative outcomes on the Health (14th position) and income (19th position) sub-indices.

The Human Poverty Index (HPI) represented the second stream based on the deprivational perspective where the absence of desirable outcomes on various sub-indices relating to Longevity, Education and Economic Status determined inter-district ranking. It was interesting to discover that Gurgaon district which included Mewat region had the highest value on the HPI and consequently, was the most deprived district in the State whereas Rewari had the lowest value and consequently, was the least deprived district. Gurgaon district (before the Mewat area was carved out as a new district) presented a unique scenario: the district ranked first in the State on Per Capita District GDP and yet occupied very low ranks on health and educational attainments. Its first rank on inter-district Per Capita Income was due to heavy doses of external capital investments in real estate and industry in the Gurgaon city and its immediate neighbourhood. The city is a classical example of "twin cities within the same city, the city of the rich and the city of the poor". The district as a whole represented an excellent example of 'the rural-urban divide' with the rural hinterland accommodating the Meos who had low attainments on health, educational and income indicators.

Another important aspect of this report was the Gender Equality Index (GEI). The GEI is an analytical instrument which seeks to analyse the attainments of females as a ratio of male attainments. The economically modest district of Jhajjar occupied the first position on the GEI by virtue of its fourth position on the Health sub-index, Sixth position on the Education sub-index and fifth position on the Work Participation Sub-Index. In contrast, the last position of Gurgaon district was due to its seventeenth position on both the Health and Work Participation sub-indices and nineteenth position on the Education sub-index (*Haryana's Human Development Report*-2005, Foreword).

I.8. Rural Development and Panchayati Raj Institutions

Rural Development and Panchayats Department, Haryana is primarily responsible to oversee the implementation of various development schemes in rural areas and also to regulate and coordinate various activities of the Panchayati Raj Institutions. Rural Development Fund Administration Board was constituted under Rural Development Act 1986. The amount collected under the fund is spent in the rural areas in connection with the development of roads, establishment of dispensaries, making arrangements for water supply, sanitation and other public facilities, and welfare of agricultural labour, etc.

The following schemes for development of rural people were in operation:

- Mahatma Gandhi Gramin Basti Yojana.
- Mukhya Mantri Anusuchit Jaati Nirmal Basti Yojana.
- Mukhya Mantri Sanitation Incentive Puruskar Yojana.
- Safai Karmis engaged under the Pavement of Streets Scheme.
- Mahila Choupal Scheme.
- Mahatma Gandhi National Rural Employment Guarantee.
- Swarnjayanti Gram Swarozgar Yojana (SGSY).
- Indira Aawas Yojana (IAY).
- Desert Development Programme (DDP).
- Integrated Watershed Development Programme (IWDP).

Mahatma Gandhi Gramin Basti Yojana is the flagship programme of the State government. Free residential plots of 100 sq. yards each are being allotted to eligible SCs, BCs (A) and BPL families. Sites on which these plots are located are developed with necessary infrastructural facilities including power supply, drinking water, streets. More than 6 lakh eligible families identified as on 31st October, 2008, were to benefit under this scheme. Out of these 3.80 lakh families have been allotted plots and the allotment process for the remaining eligible families is in progress where Panchayat land is available. The remaining villages where suitable Panchayat land is not available, land will be made available by way of exchange or acquisition. The development of internal roads and drains under the scheme has been converged with Mahatma Gandhi National Rural Employment Guarantee Scheme. Development works in more than 600 Villages sites are currently under progress.

The main objective of the scheme Mukhya Mantri Anusuchit Jaati Nirmal Basti Yojana is to provide basic infrastructure, like pavements of streets with drains, water supply pipelines, choupals, community centres, boundary wall of Shamshan Ghats in the villages having more than 50 per cent SC population.

To boost up total sanitation campaign in Haryana, the Mukhya Mantri Sanitation Incentive Puruskar Yojana has been launched to motivate and create an atmosphere of competition among the Gram Panchayats to promote accelerated sanitation coverage and to eliminate the practice of open defecation in rural areas.

In order to improve the sanitation environment in the villages more than 10,300 Safai Karmis have been engaged by the Gram Panchayats under the pavement of streets scheme, the government intends to cover all the 6,764 villages of the State by providing Rs. 10 lakh per village for pavements of main streets of the village. 98 selected villages are being developed on the line of modern township by providing urban like basic infrastructure facilities.

The primary objective of the construction of Mahila Choupal scheme is to provide a common platform to rural woman for social interaction and to take up social activities in the villages for women empowerment.

The Mahatma Gandhi National Rural Employment Guarantee Scheme is being implemented in the entire State since April 2008. The basic objective of the scheme is to enhance livelihood security in rural areas by providing at least 100 days of guaranteed wage employment in a financial year to every household whose adult members volunteer to do unskilled manual work. One-third jobs are reserved for women. The development works like canal irrigation, horticulture plantation, water conservation, water harvesting, drought proofing, forestation, tree plantation and land development facilities on private land of small and marginal farmers or scheduled castes or BPL families, etc., are covered in the scheme.

Self-employment scheme of Swarnajayanti Gram Swarojgar Yojana (SGSY) is being implemented in the rural areas of the State for the unemployed youth. This scheme covers different aspects of self employment such as organization of poor into self help groups, training, credit, technology, infrastructure, marketing, etc., the Ministry of Rural Development has restructured the SGSY into Aajeevika (National Rural Livelihood Mission) from the year 2011-12. This scheme will be implemented in I phase in all the districts of the State. In the first phase, 12 Blocks of districts Kaithal, Mewat, Bhiwani and Jhajjar (3 Blocks in each district) have been identified for the implementation during the year 2012-13.

The objective of Indira Aawas Yojana (IAY) is to help construction of dwelling units for members of scheduled castes and non-scheduled castes rural poor living below the poverty line. Districts Mahendergarh and Sirsa are covered under the 100 per cent centrally assisted scheme, namely, Backward Region Grant Fund (BRGF) from the year 2007-08. The objectives of the scheme are to fill up the critical infrastructural gaps in various sectors identified by the local bodies.

Area Development Programme, namely Desert Development Programme (DDP) and Integrated Watershed Development Programme (IWDP) are being implemented through the Panchayati Raj Institutions. The objective of these is to control severity of drought and desert conditions in the identified districts through watershed development approach (*Economic Survey of Haryana* 2011-12, pp. 61-64).

SECTION II

In this section we examine the profiles of 19 village studies conducted by IAS Trainees (Batches 2003-10) and reconstruct a macro level profile of Haryana State. On the basis of agro climatic conditions, the State has been divided into five broad regions and villages studied are located in their respective districts and regions for the purpose of analysis.

The sampling design for the assignment was a random sample of 40 households selected from the selected village having a population between 300 to 3,000 inhabitants from a district. The household survey covered the following six aspects: (i) Rural Infrastructure, Health and

Region	*Districts*	*No. of Villages*
I.	Kurukshetra	2 (Bir Amin & Adhon)
	Panipat	1 (Bhodwal Majari)
II.	Hissar	3 (Fransi, Ladwi & Neoli Khurd)
III.	Sonipat	1 (Nirthan)
	Rohtak	4 (Garhi Sampla, Masoodpur, Jindran Kalan and Gudhan)
IV.	Gurgaon	3 (Inchapuri, Gugana & Ghari Harsaru)
	Faridabad	3 (Mothuka, Bhainsravali & Sagarpur)
V.	Mahendergarh	1 (Mirzapur-Bachhod)
	Mewat	1 (Goela)
	Total	**19**

Source: Village Study Reports, 2003-10, LBS National Academy of Administration, Mussoorie.

Education, (ii) Agrarian Relations, (iii) Social Structure, (iv) Economic Activities, (v) Anti Poverty and Other Rural Development Programmes, and (vi) Panchayati Raj System. A detailed analysis of the data provided by the researchers and their observations in the assignments based on village studies have been presented in the subsequent sub-sections. Village-wise data provided by the researchers is sketchy and at times not in a comparable framework which constrains comparative analysis of the villages.

REGION I

District Kurukshetra

Kurukshetra district lies between latitude 29°50′ to 30°12′ and longitude 76°26′ to 77°04′ in the north-eastern part of Haryana. The district headquarters are located at Kurukshetra and is about 160 km north of Delhi, 39 km north of Karnal and 40 km south of Ambala. Kurukshetra town is located at a distance of about 6 km from Pipli, an important road junction on the National Highway No. 1, popularly known as Grand Trunk Road. Kurukshetra Railway Station, also called the Kurukshetra Junction is located on main Delhi-Ambala railway line. On the whole, the district is a plain which slopes from north-east to south and south-west. The plain is remarkably flat and within it are the narrow low-lying flood plains, known as Betre Khadar of Naili. Saraswati, Markanda and Ghaggar are the important rivers of the district. The soil is generally alluvial.

The district consists of 419 villages. The important towns of the district are Pehowa, Shahbad and Ladwa. The district is spread over 1530 sq. km with a population of 9.64 lakh implying a population density of 630 in comparison to the State average of 573 persons per sq. km. Kurukshetra is predominantly an agriculturally rich rural economy and 71 per cent of population lives in villages. Scheduled castes constituted 20.52 per cent of the population. Average size of landholding was 2.36 hectares against the State average holding of 2.32 hectares. All of its cultivated area was irrigated by a good network canals and tubewells. Cropping pattern was dominated by wheat and rice, covering more than 82 per cent of Gross Cropped Area. Literacy rate was 67.53 per cent and female literacy in rural areas was relatively low at 57.15 per cent. Kurukshetra University is the oldest university in the State established in early 1960s. Sex ratio was 763 in comparison to the State average of 877 which is very low. Kurukshetra's rank in terms of Male Infant Mortality Rate (IMR) was 15 and Female IMR rank was 3 (out of 18)

Two villages namely Adhon and Bir Amin were surveyed between 2008 and 2011.

Village Adhon

Village Adhon is located in the Thanesar sub-division. The village is situated on the Kurukshetra-Jhansa road at a distance of 16 km from the district headquarters.

Table 1.31: General Information about the village

Total Area	1000 acres
Area under cultivation	802.5 acres (80.25 %)
Total population	1783 (as per Census 2001)
Male	984 (55.19%)
Female	799 (44.81%)
SC Population	411 (23.05%)
OBC population	907 (50.87%)
Others	465 (26.08%)

Source: *Ibid.*

The population figures show that Adhon is an OBC dominated village. In the village case study, researcher has observed that the maximum decadal growth rate was reported in the decade 1981-91 after which it slowed down in the period 1991-2001. Imperatives of a growing population led to fragmentation of land, shrinking the size of landholdings. There was a pressure on the farmers to produce more and more from the small patch of land that he owned. This led to increase in land prices. Those who could not survive on small plots of land sold their land and became labourers. There also emerged a pressure on common resources. The greatest pressure was on water resources. Land hunger swallowed up *johads* (tanks). Groundwater levels plummeted as agricultural and domestic needs for water rose rapidly. The village is now faced with drinking water scarcity in peak summer season.

Agriculture was the primary occupation of the people. Other economic activities in the villages were:

(i) Poultry, (ii) Dairy, (iii) Workshops like cycle repair, TV repair etc., Petty shops, and (iv) General store.

The shrinking of green grazing areas and disappearance of waterbodies led to decreased cattle wealth. There was a time when every household owned some cattle. Now, only about 50 per cent of the households own cattle. The number of cattle has also come down.

The economically dominant caste in Adhon, the Jats own the maximum land (85%) of the village. The remaining 15 per cent was shared by OBCs (5.8%), Banias (4-5%) and SCs (1%) and others. Paddy and fodder were the main kharif crops whereas wheat and mustard were the major rabi crops. The productivity of land was quite high with paddy (29 quintals per acre), wheat (21 quintals per acre) and fodder (97 quintals per acre). The major source of irrigation is tubewell. The agriculture is highly mechanized. Use of HYV and chemical fertilizer is most common. The annual income of farmers ranged from Rs. 80,000 to Rs. 2,50,000 and above. About 63 per cent of the families were between 80,000-1,50,000 income group whereas 28 per cent had Rs. 2,50,000 or above as annual income. The wage rate was Rs. 180 per day, but during peak season it went upto Rs. 200-250 per day. Very few families would qualify for the category of the absolutely poor. However, above 70 people have BPL cards. Unemployment in the village is a chronic problem. There is one mobile PDS ration shop in the village which comes once in a week.

Infrastructure

The village thrives on its location. Road connectivity is excellent. The village is 100 per cent electrified. Telephone facility is available. Other infrastructure facilities in the village are:

> (i) Panchayat Ghar, (ii) Choupal, (iii) Primary and Middle school, (iv) Electricity Substation, (v) Temple, (vi) Anganwadi Centre, and (vii) Satya Bharti School of the Bharti Foundation.

The village has developed urban like infrastructural facilities. The major problems facing the people are inadequate provisioning of water and electricity. Though a new 132 KV substation has been installed in its premises, there are long power cuts in summers.

Market Access

The two nearest markets are at Thanesar (12 km) and Pipli (18 km). But the people of the village don't need to travel far to access markets. Most farmers sell their agricultural produce at the doorsteps because traders and middlemen give them the same price that they would get at the mandi and also because most of them lack the capacity to hold the stocks for long.

Status of Education

The literacy rate in Adhon as per 2001 Census was 70.91 per cent. The village has one Primary and one Middle school. Both the schools are co-educational. Mid-day meal is provided in the school. The male literacy rate in the village was 81.2 per cent as compared to the districts average of 78.06 per cent and the female literacy rate is 51.8 per cent as compared to districts average of 60.61 per cent. There has been a significant relationship between caste and literacy level in the village. Most of the people of upper castes are middle pass or above. The SC categories who were interviewed were economically poor and most of them were engaged in agricultural labour work. But, due to high awareness propagated amongst the people, all of them irrespective of caste and community were sending their children to school and there was no aversion to sending girls to school. In fact, most of the parents stated that the girls were more sincere than the boys and most of them wanted their girls to complete their education and take up job before marriage.

There were 417 students enrolled in the school and the students—teacher's ratio was one teacher to 42 students which compares well with Sarva Shiksha Abhiyan norms of 1:40. There was one dropout in classes 3rd and 5th each. It was found that more boys as compared to girls were enrolled in the school. The overall percentage of their presence was quite high which showed the level of keenness towards education in the village.

During the household survey all the forty households who were surveyed responded that it was necessary (realizing the significance of education) to send both girls and boys to the school. All the households ranked employment as the most important reason. There was only one instance, where a child of 12 years old was not going to school as he was engaged in wage labour.

Health and Sanitation

Issues of health and sanitation were not given much priority in the villages of this area. People of Adhon prefer to go to the district Hospital at Kurukshetra which was about 16 km from the village. They visited PHC only for minor ailments. There were 2 Registered Medical Practitioners (RMPs) who were first resource persons for the villagers. Most families have to spend at least 10 per cent of their income on health services. While most were able to pay from their savings, it was not uncommon to find people borrowing from friends, relatives and moneylenders too, if the sum was large. The disease pattern in the village was seasonal. Few TB cases were also reported. The increased use of fertilizers and pesticides in agriculture has led to common allergy attacks.

On the sanitation front, almost 85 per cent of the households had their own toilets, but the personal hygiene was still not satisfactory. Sweepers have been engaged by the village Panchayat under the Rural Sanitation Scheme.

Maternity and Child Care

The maternity and childcare services were mainly provided by the ANM and Anganwadi worker. One day each was fixed for maternal care by the ANM in the village. The pregnant women are given iron and folic acid tablets. The infants are administered DPT vaccine and polio drops, etc. As per records, no case of maternal mortality during childbirth was recorded in the village. All the people go in for institutional deliveries. The infant mortality rate was quite low at 12.12 per thousand. The incident of infant mortality was high in the labour class. The number of births in the last one year were 42 out of which there were 22 males and 20 females. The sex ratio at birth thus, was 909/1000. The birth rate was 24 per thousand, which was much higher than the national average of 17/1000. The death rate was 5.1 per thousand.

Poverty alleviation programme like Swarnajayanti Gram Swarojgar Yojana (SGSY) and MNREGA are there but their role is peripheral in the village.

Gram Panchayat

The village Panchayat consists of 9 members out of which four were females and it was headed by Ms Babli Devi (33 years), a scheduled caste woman as a sarpanch. The average age of Panchayat members was 41 years, quite a youthful composition in a traditional society. Women members were quite active. Panchayat meetings were held regularly. However, participation in Gram Sabha was poor and not that effective. As own income resources of Panchayat were limited, it mostly implemented government sponsored and financed schemes. Work was satisfactory.

Village Bir Amin

The village Bir Amin is also located in Thanesar sub-division and situated on Kurukshetra-Jhansa road at a distance of 12 km from the district headquarters.

(Description of the village studies of Adhon and Bir Amin were similar. In fact one study was by and large copied from the other, therefore, one is dropped for the purpose of analysis.) From the above analysis, it can be safely concluded that rural areas in Kurukshetra were agriculturally fairly developed. There were not many industries in the district, except for some agro-based industries. The district was educationally and socially relatively backward as reflected by the literacy rates and sex ratios, but was catching up fast.

District Panipat

District Panipat is situated on the bank of Yamuna, the only perennial river of the State. It lies almost in the central east of Haryana with river Yamuna making its natural boundary with U.P. The new district of Panipat was carved out of the old Karnal district on November 1, 1989. Panipat District has a geographical area of 1,268 sq.km with a population of 12 lakhs and a population density of 949 persons per sq. km. Its sex ratio is 862 females per thousand males. Its rural population is 54 per cent and SCs constitute 15.79 per cent. Whole of the cultivated area is irrigated and its cropping pattern is predominantly wheat and paddy, which covers 87.30 per cent of the cropped area. Average holding size is relatively smaller, 1.47 hectares in comparison to the State average of 2.72 hectares. Panipat town is famous for its handloom industry and after Faridabad, Gurgaon and Yamunanagar, it has largest number of registered factories (7.77%) and industrial workers (6.30%). Overall literacy rate is 66.57 per cent and 54.17 per cent of rural females. The district is well connected by roads and railways. In terms of IMR, it ranks at tenth place (out of 18). Thus, the district is agriculturally one of the most developed but its social indicators are not that satisfactory.

Village Bhodawal Majri

The village Bhodawal Majri is located about 25 km from the district headquarters and 11 km from Samalkha, the Block headquarters. It had 307 (71.1%) Gujjar and 35 (14.7%) Brahmin households and rest were other castes. The village had a population of 2,607 out of which 1,410 were Males and 1,193 were Females (2001 Census).

Table 1.32: Caste Composition of Households (HH) in Bhojdawal Majri

Sl. No.	Caste	No. of HH	% age of HH
1.	Gujjars	307	71.1
2.	Brahmin	35	14.7
3.	Baraygi	13	05.5
4.	Gadhariya	9	03.8
5.	Jeemar	14	05.9
6.	Badi	3	01.3
7.	Jogi	3	01.2
8.	Surav	2	00.8
9.	Scheduled Castes	17	07.2
	Total	**403**	**100**

Source: *Ibid.*

Rural Infrastructure

The village was considered one of the socially backward villages of the district and is located at a remote place in the river bed. However, it was connected by all-weather road to the Block headquarters, Samalkha. It had a regular bus service twice a day. The village was fully electrified with street lights. There was a STD/ISD booth in the village on the road and some people had mobiles as well. There was little problem of connectivity and communication. There was one primary school in the village. There was one adult literacy centre as a part of PLP which was follow up of the literacy programme of the NLM. There was a Primary Sub-Centre which functioned partially but people preferred to go to private practitioners. There were two anganwadis working in the village. PDS was reported to be functioning satisfactorily.

Education

Literacy rate in the village was low at 38.31 per cent for males and 24.14 per cent for females as per 2001 Census. This was primarily because the villagers migrate to the river bed with their children during the season for economic activities. A primary school was located in low lying area and was prone to water logging. The school had three teachers and 474 children out of which 246 were boys and 228 were girls. A total of 185 children, 74 boys and 111 girls were yet to be covered by the education system. Two rooms were constructed in the school and it also had a hand pump for drinking water and a sanitary toilet. Text books and uniforms were distributed free of cost under operation blackboard scheme. Under the mid-day meal programme, children were provided bulk quantity of cereals at the end of the month and not cooked food.

Health and Sanitation

Village being located near the river, it is vulnerable to water borne diseases. The prime sanitation issues in the area are waste water disposal, defecation place, safe drinking water and toilets. While the village has a health sub-centre, it is understaffed. The PHC is located at a distance of 8 km in Patti Kalyana. There were 53 births and 13 deaths during the year before the survey. There were 5 infant deaths, mostly due to malnutrition leading to premature babies. Most of the births took place at home itself. There were 356 women in reproductive age and 276 were couples. 112 women were adopting family planning methods and IUD was popular.

The above analysis of education and health facilities brings out the facilities were of poor quality, but State was making efforts to improve them.

Agriculture

The total area of the village is 708 acres out of which 624 acres are cultivable land, i.e., 85.8 per cent of the total land. The irrigation is primarily through tubewells. The village has 60 acres of community and panchayat land. The gram panchayat leases out the cultivable land through open auction. 18 families were allotted cattle sheds under 20-point programme to scheduled castes persons. The land is fertile with assured irrigation. Wheat and paddy are the main crops, though sugarcane and seasonal vegetables are also grown.

The average yield of wheat is nearly 28 quintals per acre, which gives a handsome remuneration to the farmers. Mustard is another important crop during rabi season. The average output of mustard is nearly Rs. 7,000 per acre after deducting the cost of seed and labour, etc. For the activities like sowing and harvesting, farmers engage labourers, who are generally paid in cash. The local labourers were given a wage of Rs. 2,430 per month.

The majority of farmers get credit from their respective private traders called Artias. Although a rural bank is available within 7 km from the village, but the farmers prefer Artias for different reasons.

Common Property Resources

The villagers are using common property resources like village pond, streets and common drinking water taps without any discrimination on the basis of caste. The other important property of the village is Panchayat land also known as Shamlat Deh. From time to time Panchayat has donated land to the people of lower strata to construct their houses. However, agricultural land of Shamlat Deh is leased out to the bidders for one year by the village Panchayat. In bidding 30 per cent of the land is reserved for the scheduled caste population of the village.

Poverty Alleviation Programme

The two schemes which provide employment are classified into self employed scheme, namely SGSY and the wage employment scheme, namely SGRY whose funds are directed straight to the Panchayats while the EAS goes through the Panchayat Samiti and Zila Parishad. There were 61 families in the village below the poverty line.

The Swrnajayanti Gram Swarojgar Yojana was started in the village on 1st April, 1999. The major activities are dairy farming and iron works workshop. The wage employment scheme that was running in the village was mostly under the SJRY scheme. No works was sanctioned for EAS which is allotted by Panchayat Samiti and Zila Parishad.

Under Indira Aawas Yojana, houses were generally constructed according to the requirements of the beneficiaries. Though there was a provision for latrines, they were not made properly as there was no way for water discharge. However, after the rural sanitation project was sanctioned in the district all the new houses were fitted with latrines with single soaking pit. In the village 14 houses were constructed or upgraded under IAY and PMGY. As a policy the houses were given in the name of women so that they had the right of property. Tau Devi Lal old age pension scheme, widow pension, handicap pension were also given to eligible persons in the village.

Gram Panchayat

The Sarpanch of the Panchayat was a 56 years old female named Bhateri Devi of the Gujjar caste, but the husband (Sarpanch Pati Jawan Singh) ran the Panchayat. There were 8 members including the Sarpanch.

The meetings of the Panchayat were reported to be held regularly and that of the Gram Sabha twice a year. In the village Panchayat there were 4 female members, but they hardly attend the meeting of the Panchayat. Their husbands instead enjoy all the respects and powers of the Panchayats. The division of the people on political lines affects the functioning of the Gram Sabha. It becomes very difficult to pass a resolution. The people belonging to the opposition party constantly complain about the discrepancies in the working of the Panchayat and that leads to various hurdles in the smooth functioning of the Panchayat. The village development committees are also there in the village.

REGION II

District Hisar

The district Hisar is located at a distance of 164 km west of New Delhi on the National Highway No. 10. It has borders with Fatehabad, Jind, Rohtak and Bhiwani districts of Haryana and also has borders with Rajasthan State. The Hisar district comprises of four tehsils—Hisar, Hansi, Narnaul and Adampur and 3 sub-tehsils Barwala, Uklana and Bass. The district comprises nine Blocks. They are Hisar-I, Hisar-II, Adampur, Agroha, Barwala, Uklana, Hansi I, Hansi II and Narnaund. Hisar is the westernmost district of Haryana.

The economy of the district is primarily agriculture. The major crops of the district are wheat, gram, barley, oilseeds, rice, bajra, cotton and sugarcane. 89.98 per cent of the area of the district is under agriculture and irrigation is done by canals and tubewells.

The city of Hisar is known as a city of steel as one of the biggest producers of stainless steel, i.e. M/s Jindal Stainless Steel Ltd. belongs to Hisar. There are many industrial estates in the district.

Village Neoli Khurd

Village Neoli Khurd is located at 17 km from the district headquarters and its Block headquarters is also at Hisar. There are 420 households in the village spread over four hamlets. A total of 40 households were surveyed out of which 5 families were beneficiary of NREGA, 5 were tenants, and 5 families having benefited from SGRY, 5 families benefited from IAY and the rest 20 were selected at random.

Demographic Features

It is a small village with a population of 1,739 (2001 Census). The sex ratio was 882, but the sex-ratio for the age group 0-6 years was 927. The SC population is around 9.4 per cent. The castes present in the village are Harijans (SC), Kumhar (BC), Nai (BC), Dudi, Kajla apart from Jats, the dominant caste.

Infrastructure

The village is well placed in terms of infrastructure. Besides all weather roads and electricity, the village has a high school, health sub-centre, 2 anganwadi centres, PDS shop, Panchayat Bhawan and public telephone facilities. The villagers have good access to market in the nearby tehsil town of Adampur, which has one of the biggest cotton markets in Haryana.

The Adampur town is 13 km from Neoli Khurd. The village has some of its males employed in military and paramilitary forces. There is one cooperative credit society in the village but it is almost non-functional. The nearest bank is the Haryana Grameen Bank which is 3 km from the village in Neoli Kalan village.

Land and Agriculture

The total area of the village is around 1,885 acres out of which land available for cultivation is around 1,727 acres. Usually two crops are grown, *rabi* and *kharif*. The important *Rabi* crops are wheat, mustard, gram and jowar while important *kharif* crops are jowar, bajra and cotton.

Nearly 43 per cent of the population is landless, who are generally wage labourers. Marginal farmers having landholdings of less than 3 acres constitute around 43 per cent of the total cultivators. The majority of farmers get credit from their respective private traders, to whom they sell their produce. Among the non-farm activities, dairy is the most common.

Education

Male literacy is 64 per cent and female literacy is a dismal 36 per cent. The total literacy in the village is 51.3 per cent. The village has a middle school. On the day of the visit the attendance was around 85 per cent. Cooked meal was served in the school. For the higher classes the students go to the nearby village Neoli Kalan at a distance of 3 km and for college education they go to Adampur and Hisar. There are 232 students in the primary level and 167 in the middle and high school classes. The number of girl's students are 185. The level of education is generally low. The village school committee is for name only.

Health Status

There is a Health Sub-Centre in the village, but in a bad shape. The nearest PHC is located at 4 km from the village. The infant mortality rate as per ANM register is one. There was no reported maternal death in the past one year. Immunization of children and pregnant women was claimed to be 100 per cent.

The normal maternal health care and child-birth is looked after by trained *dais* in the village. In case of a girl child, anganwadi certificate is necessary for a lump-sum grant of Rs. 500 for her nutrition. This amount is payable to maximum of two girl children per couple. The drinking water facility is not proper in the village.

Less than 5 families out of 40 surveyed had toilet facility in their houses. Rest use open field for the purpose. This was despite the fact that a Total Sanitation Campaign was going on in the village.

Poverty Alleviation Programmes

About 90 families in the village were classified as BPL families. The main projects/programmes were SGSY, NREGA, old age pension, widow pension and handicap pension. NREGA was implemented in 2008 and two ponds were dug and one road connecting another village was under construction. Wage employment was generated in the village under SGRY scheme since 2001. One of the work undertaken was earth filling in the school for which a cash payment of Rs. 53,624 and 3,379 kg of wheat were paid as wages. There were 8 beneficiaries of IAY in the village.

The panchayat consists of 7 members out of which 3 were females. Women members were usually represented by their husbands. It was reported that meeting of Gram Panchayat were being held twice a month and that of Gram Sabha twice a year. There was a complaint that Sarpanch in connivance with the Panchayat secretary avoided or bypassed Panchayat members opposed to him from meetings, and they usually came to know about the meetings later on. Gram Sabha meetings were also held on paper only. Panchayat had an income of about Rs. 57,000 per annum for leasing out Panchayat land of 26 acres. Functioning of Panchayat and Gram Sabha needs to be improved.

Village Franci

Village Franci is located 3 km from the Block headquarters Agroha. A total of 40 households were surveyed out of which 5 families belonged to SHG's, 5 were tenants, 5 families benefited from SGSY and 5 families benefited from IAY. It is a small village with a population of 2,109 (2001 Census). The sex ratio was 868. The SC population was 22.1 per cent of the total. Apart from Jats, the dominant caste, there were Harijans (SC), Kumhar (BC), Nai (BC), Dudi, and Kajla.

Infrastructure

Besides all-weather mettled roads, the village had a High School, Health Sub-Centre, 2 Anganwadi Centres, PDS Shops, Panchayat Ghar and Public Telephone facilities. The nearest bank is at Agroha, 3 km from the village.

Land and Agriculture

The total area of the village is 1,396 acre, out of which land available for cultivation was 1,230 acres. The important *Rabi* crops are wheat, mustard, gram, and jowar, while important *Kharif* crops are jowar, bajra and cotton. The watertable is going down due to continuous use of groundwater. Nearly 20 per cent of the population is landless, who are generally wage labourers. During the off season, they go to brick kilns as labourers.

Majority of farmers get credit for private traders called Arhtias. Dairying is the most common non-farm activity in the village.

Education

Male literacy is 71.4 per cent and female literacy a dismal 40.9 per cent. Literacy for the entire population was 57.3 per cent. The village has a middle school. The school did not have drinking water facility. However, it had adequate number of class rooms, playground and toilet. The attendance was 85 per cent on the day of the visit. Mid day meal of satisfactory quality was being regularly served to the students.

Health Status

There is a health sub-centre in the village looked after by an ANM. There is no private clinic. The nearest PHC is located at 4 km from the village. Vaccines for BCG, DPT and Hepatitis are given in the district civil hospital.

Maternal health care and child birth are looked after by trained *dais*. The major causes of ill health as perceived by the people are poor personal hygiene, no proper drainage and poor health facilities.

Poverty Alleviation Programmes

About 90 families have been classified as BPL families. The major schemes are SGRY and SGSY. There was one SHG functional in the village, who contributed Rs. 50 per month. There were 12 members in the group. The SHG was provided a loan of Rs. 3 lakh which was shared by all the members equally. Different pension schemes were operative in the village.

There were 9 members in the Panchayat out of which 3 were women. Women members were generally represented by their husbands. The Gram Sabha is not functional and it was on paper only.

Village Ladwi

Village Ladwi is located 25 km from the district headquarters and 14 km from the Block headquarters of Adampur. The village is well connected by roads. The nearest railway station is about 2 km at Jakhod Khera. The nearest market town is Adampur.

Demography

It is a medium size village with a population of 3,258 (2001 Census). The sex ratio is 795, much below the State average of 861. The scheduled castes population is around 17.56 per cent, while the OBC constitute 38.6 per cent of the total population. Apart from Jats, the dominant castes are Kumhar (BC), Chamar (SC), Nayaks, Dhanak, Lakhaar and Khati.

Education

The male literacy rate was 64 per cent and for females it was 51 per cent. This is reflective of gender bias in rural Haryana. The village has a government primary and high school with drinking water facilities, toilets, playground and adequate classrooms. Mid-day meal is served. The visit to the primary school provided a dismal account of the quality of education. Toilets were not cleaned. On the day of visit, the attendance in the classes was very poor. Most of the affluent families sent their children to a private school in the neighbouring village. The village education committee is non-functional.

Gender Issue

Sex ratio in Ladwi was 795 in 2001, which was very low. It is starkly conspicuous that the women folk do not have equal status in the society. The *pardah* system is in vogue. The dowry system is widely prevalent.

Health Status

The village does not have a health sub-centre. The ANM comes twice a week. The nearest CHC is at Siswal located 6 km from Ladwi. The infant mortality rate was 28.6 as per ANM register. There was no reported maternal death in the past one year. The common diseases prevalent in the village are skin diseases, malnutrition and diarrhoea in children, some cases of T.B. and anemia especially among women. Immunisation status of children and pregnant women was claimed to be 100 per cent. The normal maternal health care and the birth of children are looked after by private midwives. The average family size was 5-6 persons.

The village has adequate water supply, but sanitation was neglected.

Land and Agriculture

The total area of the village is around 2,999 acres out of which land available for cultivation is 2,512 acres. Net sown area is 2,500. Wheat, mustard, channa are sown in *Rabi* season, while cotton, bajra and paddy are the main crops of *Kharif* season. There is about 100 per cent land under irrigation. Canals and tubewells are the main sources of irrigation. Due to continuous use of groundwater, the water level in the village is going down.

About 25 acres of land was under tenancy, but that was not shown in records. About 45 per cent of the population is landless, who are wage labourers. The marginal farmers having landholdings of less than three acres constituted 15.3 per cent of the total population while cultivators having holdings greater than 3 acres constituted 38.8 per cent.

The nearest grain market where the farmers sell their produce is at mandi Adampur. They buy farm inputs like seeds, pesticides, etc., from the same place. There is a watershed development work going on in the village by the government, i.e., Haryali scheme. The scheme is being implemented on 1,250 acres. The majority of farmers get credit from their private traders called *arhtias*.

Dairy farming was the other important economic activity in the village. There were 367 cows, 1,802 buffaloes, 274 bulls, 490 sheep/goats and 116 other domesticated animals in the village.

Poverty Alleviation Programmes

There were 170 families in the BPL list of a total of 694 families. Most of them belonged to SC families. The SGSY was started in 1999. The major activities that are performed in the village include that of dairy farming. Individual loaning has been stopped in the village and only group loaning is taken up as that ensures the best recovery chances for the banks. However, the groups were not functioning in the true spirit of SHG. In fact in case of dairy farming, the group members distribute the money after the loans are sanctioned and repay the loans according to individual convenience. SGRY is the main wage employment scheme. There were 4 IAY beneficiaries in the village, out of which 3 were SC and 1 BC.

The Gram Panchayat of Ladwi consisted of 7 members of which three were women. Women are generally represented by their husbands/sons.

REGION III

District Rohtak

District Rohtak is located in the central part of Haryana. It is the only district of Haryana that does not touch the boundary of some other State. The district falls between latitude 28° 40′30″ N and 29° 5′35″ N and longitude 76° 13′22″ E and 76° 51′20″ E. The total area of the district is 1,668 sq. km. It is bounded by Sonepat district in the north and northeast, Jind district in the north, Hisar district in the northwest, Bhiwani in the west and Jhajjar district in the south. Due to its closeness to Delhi, the district is witnessing rapid urbanization, industrialization, diversification of agriculture and change in occupational structure.

According to 2001 Census, the population of the district was 9,40,000 comprising of 5,08,000 males and 4,31,000 females. The urban population in the district is 35 per cent. The population of Rohtak city, the district headquarters was 2,96,254, followed by Meham with 22,338 and Kalanaur 19,287.

The villages in the district have fairly large population. The rank-wise list is:

1. Mokhra — 16,156
2. Sunarian — 14,073
3. Madina — 12,992
4. Bahelbah — 12,857
5. Bohar — 12,807
6. Nindana — 11,553

According to the 2001 Census, the sex ratio in the district was 847, below the sex ratio of Haryana. The sex ratio for 0-6 age group was as low as 798.

The scheduled castes constituted 19.1 per cent of the total population. The sex ratio for SC population was 855. Village Katwara and Sampal has the highest 57 per cent SC population. The literacy rate of the district was 73.7 per cent in 2001. This was 83 per cent for males and 63 per cent for females. Literacy was 70 per cent in rural areas, whereas it was 81 per cent in urban areas. There were 191 associated primary schools and 19 independent primary schools in the district. A primary school was available within the average radius of 1.06 km. The enrolment ratio at primary level was 100 per cent.

There were 34 Middle schools, 58 Secondary schools and 118 Senior Secondary schools in the district. About 70 per cent villages in the district had Senior Secondary schools.

There are two universities in the district, namely Maharshi Dayanand University and Pt. B.D. Sharma University of Health Sciences. There are 13 degree colleges in the district. The admission for Indian Institute of Management has begun. There is one Medical and one Dental college in the district. A foreign language university is being established at Meham. The district lies in the National Capital Region. The distance from New Delhi is 70 km.

Village Jindran Kalan

Jindran Kalan is a small village located 3 km from Kalanaur, the Block and Sub-Tehsil headquarters. Before independence of India, Kalanaur was a Muslim dominated village. When Muslims migrated to Pakistan, the land was allotted to refugees coming from Jhang district of Pakistan. Kalanaur became Khatri dominated after independence. They sold their lands to Jats of neighbouring villages. The Jats came mostly from Bahebah and Rithal. They settled in a location outside Kalanaur. The habitation grew in size with time and in 1987 when the population crossed 1,500, a new village named Jindran Kalan was created.

While the Jats and Brahmins live in the centre of the village, the BC's and SC's live on the outer part. Jindran is located at 22 km from the district headquarters of Rohtak. It is well connected by-all-weather metalled roads. There are regular Jeep and Auto services to Kalanaur.

Demographic Features

It is a small village with a population of 2,049 (2001 Census). Two major communities were: Jats (1,680) and Brahmins (246) and the rest were from other communities in smaller numbers.

The sex ratio of the village was 844. The 0-6 year sex ratio (rough estimate) was around 860. The decadal population growth rate (1991-2001) was 16.42 per cent. The average landholding of the village was around 3.5 acres.

Infrastructure

The village is quite well placed in terms of infrastructure. Besides all-weather mettled roads joining it with the neighbouring villages, it has a high school, middle school, primary school, health sub-centre, 2 anganwadi centres, PDS shops, 2 Panchayat Ghar of course and 3 caste-wise baithaks. The village also has a waterworks. Of course all the villages of Haryana are electrified and Jindran Kalan is no exception. The Kalanaur market is quite close.

Education

There were 332 students in the primary level and 307 in the middle and high school classes. The number of girl students was 256 out of the total. On the day of the visit to the school, the attendance was around 85 per cent. The dropout rate is negligible in Primary school, but higher in High school. The dropout rate is higher for SC students. The village school committee was there but only in name.

Health and Sanitation

There is a primary health sub-centre having a female ANM and a male multipurpose health worker in the village. The Community Health Centre is there at Kalanaur, which is the first place of contract when there is an illness in the most families. There is an RMP in the village. The diseases pattern according to ANM register is high incidence of pneumonia and cough in winter, high incident of T.B. in summer and high incidence of diarrhoea in rainy season. The maternity care is provided by the ANM. However, most deliveries are conducted in the CHC pregnancy hut.

The birth rate of the village according to chowkidar register was 17 births per 1,000 population. The death rate was 5.4 per 1,000 population.

Land and Agriculture

The total area of the village is 1,957 acres. The land for cultivation forms the major chunk, around 1,840 acres, out of which net sown area is 1,804 acres, while 32 acres are under fallow-land. There is no land under forest. The pasture and grazing waste lands due to saline encrustation from brackish ground water are there.

The important *Rabi* crops are wheat, mustard and gram while the main crops of *Kharif* are rice, sugarcane and bajra. HYV seeds, chemical fertilizers like urea and DPAP and pesticides are common. The village has more than 150 tractors. Almost every farmer having land above 5 acres has a harrow, a tiller, a thresher and a trolley.

The surplus produce is sold to the *arhtias* in the market. These traders then auction their grains to the various Goverment agencies. The sugarcane is taken to Rohtak sugar mill at a distance of 15 km.

The agriculture labour in the village is classified as follows:

1. *Siri*—Fulltime agriculture labourers hired for complete one year. He is given a payment of Rs. 30,000 per annum along with daily and other festival benefits.
2. *Naukar*—Full time agriculture labourers of younger age. Paid Rs. 25,000 per annum.
3. *Hali/Pali/Baldi*—Young full time servant to take care of milch animals paid Rs. 22,000 per annum.
4. *Lamina*—Part time labourers engaged just during peak season such as harvesting and is paid Rs. 225 per day.

The village Panchayat owns 20 acres which has been given for annual rent of Rs. 66,900.

Around 90 per cent of the workforce is employed in farm activities. Small businessmen that own small shops in Jindran and Kalanaur constitute the biggest chunk of non-farm activities. Around 10 persons get their remuneration from poultry. Two families are involved in Bee Keeping. The Indian army, CRPF and Haryana government jobs are the main services sector for the villagers.

Poverty Alleviation Programmes

The poverty alleviation programmes carried out in the village are SGSY, NREGA, IAY, Pension schemes and Kanyadan Yojana. The population below the poverty line in the village was 18 per cent of the total population. Of this 70 per cent belonged to SC population and 17 per cent to BC's. There is just one SHC in the village. Out of 10 members in the group 4 were BC and 3 SC. The SHG got a loan from UCO bank to purchase 10 buffaloes, i.e., one each. There were 8 beneficiaries of IAY. The Panchayat has 9 members out of which

3 are women. The women members are usually represented by their husbands. No meetings of Gram Sabha are held.

Village Garhi Sampla

The village Garhi Sampla is located 32 km from the district headquarters on National Highway No. 10. The Block headquarters, Sampla is just 2 km from the village.

There are 372 households in the village situated in a single hamlet. A total of 40 households were surveyed out of which 23 families benefited from SGSY, 2 benefited from IAY.

Demographic Features

It is a medium size village with a population of 3,747 (2001 Census). The sex ratio was 827, much below the State average. The SC population is around 8.5 per cent while the OBC's dominate with 44 per cent of the population. Jats are the most influential caste in the village.

Infrastructure

Besides all-weather roads and electrification, the village has a middle school, primary health sub-centre, anganwadi centre, PDS shops, solar streetlight and telephone facilities. Villagers have good access to markets in Rohtak, Sonepat, Bahadurgarh and Delhi. In fact, the vegetables grown in the village are supplied to Delhi by Mother Dairy. The demand for power in the agriculture sector is met by diesel as electricity supply is very erratic.

Education

The male literacy was 70.37 per cent and female literacy only 54.65 per cent. There is a high school in the village with good infrastructure. However, the visit to the school provided a dismal account of the quality of education. The village school committee exists only in name.

Health Status

The village has a primary health sub-centre looked after by an ANM. The PHC is located at Sampla, about 2 km from the village. As per the ANM records the infant mortality rate was 12.5 in the village.

Immunization was 100 per cent. The village has 3 private midwives who conduct the deliveries. There is no focus on sanitation in the village. Less than 10 families, out of 40 surveyed had toilet facilities in their homes.

Land and Agriculture

The total area of the village is around 1,252 acres, out of which land available for cultivation is 990 acres. The important *Rabi* crops are wheat, mustard, channa and jowar, while important kharif crops are jowar, bajra and paddy. There is a problem of water logging in the village.

A good percentage of population is landless (48%), who are depended upon wage labour. Marginal farmers having land holdings less than 3 acres constitute around 39.8 per cent of the total peasantry, while cultivators having holdings greater than 3 acres are 16.6 per cent.

Poverty Alleviation Programmes

The common schemes like SGSY, SGRY, IAY and pension scheme are functional in the village. There were 4 SHG's in the village. There were 5 beneficiaries of IAY.

Village Gudhan

Village Gudhan is 3 km from the Block headquarters of Kalanaur. It is a well connected village by roads and has 100 per cent electrification. Village Gudhan was also a part of Kalanaur which was separated in 1989. The dominant caste of the village is Jat with 50 families of Brahmins. The backward classes consist of Bairagi, Lohar and Khati. The SC's include Chamar and Dhanak. The total population of the village was 4186 in 2001 with a sex ratio of 781 females per 1,000 males.

The village has a chaupal, separate chaupal for Harijans, Primary and Middle school, Secondary school, Private Middle school, health sub-centre, anganwadi centre and a PDS shop. The CHC is located at Kalanaur. The nearest market is also at Kalanaur.

The literacy rate in Gudhan as per 2001 Census was 73.8 per cent. The male literacy was 86.3 per cent and female literacy was 59.04 per cent. Issues of health and sanitation are not given much priority in the village of this area. The sub-centre at Gudhan is being looked after by an ANM and two multi-purpose health workers, one male and one female.

Apart from these, there are 4 Asha workers in the village. There are 3 RMP's in the village. Out of a total of 682 eligible couples, 312 have gone for tubectomy, 3 vasectomy, 45 have chosen copper tee. The birth rate in the village was 20.3 and death rate was 9 in the last one year. The village has been covered under total sanitation campaign, but the impact was not satisfactory. However, the toilets have provided much relief to the women.

The total land area in the village was 3,231 acres, out of which 3,001 was under cultivation. There were landless families in the village. About 80 per cent of the land was owned by Jats. Wheat, mustard and paddy are the main crops grown in the village. People use a combination of chemical fertilizers and organic manure.

Gram Panchayat

Gram Panchayat consists of 14 members out of which six members were females. Caste composition of Panchayat was: Jats (10), Chamar (2), one each from Khati and Dhanak communities. Four meetings of Gram Panchayat were held in last four months (2010). Gram Sabha had a poor response and participation.

Village Masoodpur

Masoodpur has a total area of 1,022 acres, out of which 1,000 acres are cultivated. Most of the farmers have land less than 3 acres. Paddy, jowar, bajra, cotton in *Kharif* and wheat and mustard are the main crops grown in Rabi season. The village is about 20 km from district headquarters. As per 2001 Census, the population of the village was 1,230. The village has a good infrastructure and was awarded Nirmal Gram Puruskar from the President of India. The literacy rate is about 70 per cent.

The Panchayat itself collected money from the villagers and laid the water pipeline in the village and provided water connections to all the houses in the village. A person is appointed by the Gram Panchayat on the tubewell for regular maintenance and supply and was paid Rs. 2,000 per month. The usual poverty alleviation schemes are functional in the village.

District Sonepat

Sonepat is located at latitude 28°59′ N and longitude 77°1′ E and lies in the South-East part of the State. District Sonepat has an area of 2,13,080 hectares. It lies north of Delhi and is bounded by the district of Rohtak, Jind and Panipat. The district shares an inter-State boundary with district Meerut of U.P. The river Yamuna runs along the eastern boundary of the district separates it from U.P.

Broadly speaking the entire district is a part of the Punjab plain. The soil over most of the district is fine loam of rich colour. However, some areas have sandy soil and others are of kallar. The plain has a gradual slope to the south and east. The economy of the district is primarily agricultural. District Sonepat comprising Sonepat, Gohana and Ganaur sub-division has 343 villages and covers an area of 2,13,080 hectares. Of the total agricultural land about 87 per cent is irrigated.

Village Nirthan

Village Nirthan was selected for the study. It is a small village in Block Kharkhoda. It is located at 12 km from the district headquarters Sonepat and 10 km from the Block headquarters. It is well connected by all-weather mettled road to Kharkhoda as well as Sonepat. It is primarily an agrarian village. The population of the village was 865 (2001 Census). The sex ratio was 1,034. The SC population was around 11 per cent. Jats were the dominated caste. There were a total of 42 BPL families, which included 14 SCs, 9 BCs and 19 others. A total of 40 households were surveyed out of which 5 families belonged to SHG's, 5 families having benefited from SGSY, 5 families benefited from IAY, 5 families benefited from surplus land and the balance of 20 households were selected randomly.

Village had a primary school, an anganwadi centre and a public distribution shop. Public telephone facilities are also present. There was no primary health sub-centre and veterinary dispensary. The nearest market was at Kharkhoda which is 10 km away. Nearest grain storage facility was also at Kharkhoda. The nearest bank branch was at Khanda which was 5 km away. Nearest post office was at Bhadane which is 7 km away. Nearest primary health sub-centre was at Bidhlan which is 4 km away. The village was fully electrified, however, the electricity supply was very erratic. The demand for power in the agricultural sector was met by diesel sets which were owned by the big or middle farmers and others hired on rent when needed.

Education

Literacy rate in the village was 75.25 per cent. For males this percentage was 88.50 whereas for females it was a dismal 59.34 per cent. The village primary school did not have drinking water facilities. On the day of the visit, the attendance was around 96 per cent. However, the total enrolment was very small. A total of 52 students were enrolled in 5 classes. The teacher-pupil ratio was 1:26. In rural Haryana, there is a huge proliferation in private schools. Families who were able to afford their fee send their children to these schools. This was due to the general perception that Government schools were not imparting quality education. The records of the past six months showed that cooked meals under the mid-day meal scheme were being served regularly in the school. The village committee has been constituted but it exists only in name. One of the few positive factors is that parents are sending girls also, at least upto high school level.

Health

A female Auxiliary Nursing Midwife (ANM) is the direct link of the village with the Government health agencies. Nearest Primary Health Centre was located at 4 km from the village in village Bidhlan. There was no private clinic. There were both trained and untrained *dais* (mid-wives) in the village. Nearest general hospital is at Sonepat. But the villagers normally go to private clinics at Block headquarters Kharkhoda or district headquarters Sonepat. Last year there were 17 births in the village. The infant mortality rate as per the ANM register was zero. There has been no maternal death in the past one year. The normal maternal health care and children is looked after by trained *dais* in the village. The ANM gives vaccines to the children. Children were regularly covered by the pulse polio programme. However, due to that the routine immunization had taken a back seat. Medicines for fever, malaria, common infections and diseases were available with the ANM. Iron tablets and calcium tablets were also available.

Fever is the commonest ailments in the village. Anemia is prevalent in woman. The average family size was reducing over the years. The major causes of ill health perceived by the people are poor hygiene, lack of proper sewerage system and poor health facilities.

Agriculture

The village has a total land of 754.41 acres, out of which 639.6 acres was available for agriculture (including current fallow) and 530 acres had canal irrigation. 44.5 acres had both canal as well as tubewell irrigation. 23.5 acres of land irrigated by tubewells only. Rest of the 41.6 acres can also be brought under tubewell irrigation with some effort. The Shamlat Deh (community land) was 128 acres out of which 45 acres were agricultural. The village has by and large self-cultivators, only about 8 acres were under tenancy. Out of 122 households, 40 households were landless. Five families have less than one acre of land. 21 households have 1-3 acres, 30 households have 3-5 acres, 25 households have 5-10 acres of land. Only one household has more than 10 acres of land.

Land by and large was very fertile. Hardly any land was left fallow. Due to irrigation facility, most of the cultivators go for multiple cropping. Usually two crops are grown by the farmers, *Rabi* and *Kharif*. Important Rabi crops are wheat and gram. The important *Kharif* crops are paddy and bajra. Another popular crop of this area was sugarcane. Farmers normally complained that agriculture was not viable.

Due to continuous use of ground water resources, the water level is going down. The cultivation was predominantly self-cultivation. Big farmers and people whose family members have outmigrated used hired labour. Few landlords leased out their land on *patta*. This tenancy was not recorded anywhere and was on year to year basis. The landlords were generally paid one-third of the produce as rent, whereas all the inputs are given by the tenant.

The surplus agricultural produce was marketed at the local *mandis*. It was mainly sold to the commission agents or the *artias*. The majority of farmers get credit from their *artias*, although a rural bank and other commercial banks are there at a little distance.

Poverty Alleviation Programme

A total of 42 families have been classified under BPL in the village, which was 37.5 per cent of the total population. The two major schemes implemented in the village are SGSY (Swarnajayanti Gram

Swarozgar Yojana) and SGRY (Sampooran Grameen Rozgar Yojana). The fund for SGSY goes through the Panchayat Samiti and Zila Parishads, whereas SGSY funds are directed both through the Panchayat Samitis and the Gram Panchayats.

Two Self-Help Groups are functioning in the village. Their monthly contribution is Rs. 200 per month for each member. Both were involved in Mini-Dairying and both are performing well. Akash group was granted a loan of Rs. 2.40 lakh and was repaying the instalment on time.

The main wage employment scheme operational in the village was the SGRY scheme. One Harijan choupal and one common path have been constructed under this scheme. A wage of Rs. 95 per day was provided, both in terms of wheat and money. This scheme was not working properly. Beneficiary selection was not proper. In practice all work was through contractors, although it is not so in the records. There were many beneficiaries of Indira Aawas Yojana in the village. Normally, the pattern of construction was 2 or 3 rooms with concrete ceiling, but without toilets.

Along with these developmental schemes, welfare schemes like old age pension, widow pension and handicap pension were also being implemented in the village.

Panchayati Raj

The elections for Panchayat bodies are hotly contested. The present Panchayat consists of 8 members of which 3 are women. The women members are usually represented or accompanied by their husbands—Panch Patis. But the women members are now slowly becoming aware of various activities carried out by the Panchayat.

Policy Recommendation

1. Considerable number of people were still defecating in open and a lot needs to be done in this area. An enthusiastic implementation of the total sanitation campaign is absolutely essential.
2. Quality of education is also an area of serious concern. Students tend to pass classes but are substandard in their actual level of understanding. It needs serious rethinking at the policy level.

3. In case of Panchayati Raj institution, lot of power was exercised by the Sarpanch alone. The institution of Gram Sabha was not working properly.
4. Women members refuse to remove their *pardah*, this directly shows that their mindset needs lot of change.
5. ANM is an infrequent visitor to the village. They should be made accountable to the Panchayats.
6. Agriculture department has abdicated from its responsibility. There is hardly any support that farmers get from them. Inputs are getting costlier. Output has stagnated and agriculture has become unprofitable.

REGION IV

District Gurgaon

The district is located in southern region of Haryana. On its north the district is bounded by Delhi, whereas district Faridabad lies on its east. On its south, the district shares its boundaries with Rajasthan and on its west lies district Rewari.

The district has an area of 1253.07 sq. km and a population of 8,30,539 as per 2001 Census. The population of the district is estimated to have increased to 15,14,085 in 2011. The district has witnessed a phenomenal growth in all spheres of development, particularly industrialization and urbanization. Its ideal location on the National Highway of Delhi-Jaipur, close proximity of Indira Gandhi International Airport and its well developed infrastructural base like existing roads and communications network throughout the district, total electrification environment has made Gurgaon the choicest location for the industry. High-tech and high value projects involving foreign collaborations with huge investments have come up in this area.

There are many prominent and prestigious industrial units involved in the manufacturing of cars, motor-cycles, automobile parts, telecommunications equipments, electric goods, software development, hardware, sports goods, rubber products, readymade garments, light engineering goods, pharmaceuticals, food items, air conditioners, shoes, pesticides and insecticides, etc.

The district has five tehsils namely Gurgaon, Sohna, Pataudi, Farukhnagar and Manesar and five Blocks namely, Gurgaon, Sohna,

Farukhnagar and Pataudi. There were a total of 210 Panchayats as on July 2010. The total cultivable area of the district is 79,896 hectares out of which 74,124 hectares have been brought under cultivation. The total cropped area was 1,19,561 hectares in 2009-10. Tubewells are the main source of irrigation as it was 1,034 and 70,397 hectares by canals and tubewells respectively. Wheat, barley and mustard are the main *Rabi* crops whereas bajra, paddy, jawar, guar and oilseeds are the main *Kharif* crops of the district.

The following special projects were in progress in the district— (a) Agriculture Technology Management Agency (ATMA) is working since 2007-08 to strengthen the present extension system; (b) the integrated scheme for oilseeds, pulses, oil palm and maize was going on since 2004-05; (c) since 2006-07, the macro management mode of agriculture is also being implemented to strengthen the mechanization in agriculture; (d) a small scheme, viz., front line demonstration on oilseeds and pulses and cotton is being implemented through ICAR in Krishi Kendra; and (e) National Horticulture Mission.

Village Garhi Harsaru

Village Garhi Harsaru is located on Gurgaon-Pataudi road at a distance of 15 km each from Gurgaon and Pataudi. The village is 100 per cent electrified, communication lines are good and so were the transport facilities.

Demography

It is a OBC dominated village, the communities living were Yadavs, Jats, Brahmins, Bairagi, Lohar and Khatris. The scheduled castes include Chamars and Dhanaks. The population according to 2001 Census was 10,033 with 5,510 males and 4,523 females, the sex ratio being 821.

Infrastructure

The village has 2 chaupals, one for general public and the other for scheduled castes. Primary, middle and secondary schools are there in the village. The village also has a sub-centre, anganwadi centre and a PDS shop. The peasants sell their surplus agriculture produce at

Gurgaon and Pataudi. The middlemen or *arhtias* also buy the produce from many farmers, directly at village.

Education

The literacy rate in the village was 73.8 per cent according to 2001 Census. Of this, male literacy was 86.3 per cent while female literacy was 59.04 per cent, higher than the State average. The enrolment of girls was also equal to boys, but the dropout rate of girls in higher classes was high. The well-to-do families tend to send their children especially boys to the private schools.

Health and Sanitation

Issues of health and sanitation were not given much priority in the villages. If one asked their main problems they would list electricity, water, employment and land. Issues of health and sanitation were rarely discussed.

There was one health sub-centre in the village. The nearest Community Health Centre was at Pataudi about 12 km from the village. The health sub-centre was looked after by an ANM and one Multi-Purpose Health Worker. One Asha worker was also there. There are 3 RMPs in the village. The disease pattern in the village was seasonal.

There were 92 births in the last one year out of which 49 were males and 43 females. As per the ANMs records, 2 children out of these 92 births died because of low weight. Both were from the scheduled castes. Although the village had been covered under total sanitation campaign, the impact was not satisfactory. All the houses had toilets, but many people still prefer to go in the open.

Land and Agriculture

The dominant caste in the village is Yadavs who own the maximum land (80%). The remaining 20 per cent is shared between Brahmins (8.9%), Banias (2.3%), SCs and BCs (8.9%). The main crops are wheat, mustard, jowar, bajra, guar, paddy and sugarcane. At least 400 people in the village are wage labourers.

Apart from agriculture, people are also engaged in poultry, pisciculture and dairy, workshops like cycle repair, T.V. repair, etc., petty shops, tent house, brick kilns, and auto drivers. About 120 people have BPL cards.

Gram Panchayats and Development Works

There are 14 members in the Panchayat with the dominance of Yadavs. There are 6 female members but they hardly participate in the activities of the Panchayat. Gram Sabha was not active. The works done under the Panchayat were cleaning of drains, construction of new drains, construction of roads, etc.

Village Gugana

Village Gugana is located 32 km from the district headquarters and 10 km from the Block headquarters at Farukhnagar. It is well connected with other villages by road with good transport facilities. The nearest railway station was about 20 km at Pataudi.

It is a small village with a population of 942 persons, out of which 522 were males and 420 females (2001 Census). The scheduled castes population was around 32 per cent, while the OBC dominate the population constituting about 66 per cent of the population. Rajputs, Prajapati, Saini, Brahmins, Khatris and Harijans were the other castes.

Infrastructure

The village is well placed in terms of infrastructure. Besides roads and electricity, the village has a Primary Health Centre, Anganwadi Centre, PDS shop and Panchayat Bhawan. Many people have Landline phones and majority have mobile phones. The nearest market is at Farukhnagar.

The village enjoys the privilege of being the first open defecation free village in the entire district of Gurgaon. The power supply in the village is very erratic. The demand for power in the agriculture sector is met by diesel sets.

Education

Male literacy in the village was 70 per cent, but female literacy rate was a dismal 35 per cent. These were a total of 78 students in the school with 100 per cent enrolment. Out of these 41 were boys and 37 girls.

Health

The nearest PHC is located 5 km from the village, but there is a Health Sub-Centre in the village with an ANM. There is no RMP in the village. The infant mortality rate in the village was 11.5 per cent as per the ANM records. There was no reported maternal death in the past one year. Immunisation status of children and pregnant women was claimed to be 100 per cent. The common diseases prevalent in the village were skin diseases, diarrhoea, especially in children, chicken pox and pneumonia.

Land and Agriculture

The village Gugana has a total 1,142 acres of land for cultivation, out of which 1,050 acres is the sown area. The land is mostly under ownership cultivation. Only 17 acres were under tenancy. The major crops sown during *Kharif* season are Bajra, Jowar and during *Rabi* season wheat, barley and mustard are the main crops. The land is mostly tubewell irrigated or rain-fed. There was no canal in the area.

The landless workers go to Hailimandi and Farukhnagar for wage labour during the non-farming seasons.

Poverty Alleviation Programmes

The poverty alleviation programmes that are in vogue in the village are SGRY and the IAY. There were no SHG's functioning under SGSY.

Gram Panchayat

The Panchayat consisted of seven members out of which four were the females. Except for the Sarpanch, other female members were usually represented by their husbands. However, there was lot of co-operation and functioning of Panchayat was smooth.

Village Inchapuri

Village Inchapuri is located 35 km from the district headquarters and 6 km from the Block headquarters at Pataudi. The village is well connected by roads with good transport facilities. It is a small village with a population of 1,540 (2001 Census). The sex-ratio is 994, much higher than the State average. The scheduled caste population is about 31 per cent. The castes present in the village are Ahirs, Valmikis, Brahmins, Chamars, Sainis and Kumhars. The dominant caste is Ahirs. A total of 40 families were studied out of which 5 were from OBC's and 9 from SC's. There were 12 BPL families and two IAY beneficiaries.

Infrastructure

Besides roads and electrification, the village has a Middle School, anganwadi Centre, Panchayat bhawan, an Old Age Home, Harijan Chaupal and public telephone facilities, apart from individual phones and mobiles. The nearest market is at Hailimandi (6 km). There is no Post Office and Health Sub-Centre in the village. The power supply is very erratic. The nearest bank branch is about 2 km from the village.

Education

Male literacy rate was good at 92.69 per cent but the female literacy rate was 63.4 per cent, but both were higher than the State average. Though there is a middle school in the village, it lacks in teachers. Mid-Day meal is served in the school. The visit to the school showed that there was little attention paid to the students. The village school committee was there but only in name.

Health Status

The village was very poor in terms of health facilities. The nearest PHC is at Muzaffra around 3.5 km from the village. There is one RMP in the village. No ANM was reported to have ever visited the village. There was no record of infant mortality rate in the village. There were two trained and three untrained *dais* in the village who took care of the pregnant women folk.

Land and Agriculture

The total area of the village is 750 acres, out of which land available for cultivation was 647 acres. Net sown area of the village was 645 acres. Usually two crops are grown by the farmers, *Rabi* and *Kharif.* Important *Rabi* crops are wheat, mustard, channa and jowar. The important kharif crops are bajra, jowar, paddy and oilseeds. Tubewells are the main source of irrigation. There are 26 acres of community land in the village out of which some land has been distributed to the lowest *strata* for construction of homes and the other is leased out for cultivation. A good percentage (28.17%) of the population is landless who are mostly agriculture labourers. During lean season they go to the towns for wage labour.

The nearest grain market is at Khod which is 2 km from the village. Most of the farmers are linked to one *arthia* or the other for credit and sale of their produce.

Poverty Alleviation Programmes

The village is quite unexposed to the benefits of various Rural Development Programmes. About 43 families are below the poverty line. There is no SHG in the village. There were beneficiaries of Indira Awas Yojana.

Gram Panchayat

Panchayat consisted of 9 members out of which three were women. Women were usually represented by their husbands in the meetings, but it has added to the prestige of the women in the village community. Panchayat suffered from petty politics. Gram Panchayat were not effective.

District Faridabad

Founded by Shaikh Frid, the treasure of Jahangir, Faridabad lies between latitude 27°35′ to 28°30′ and longitude 77°10′ and 77°33′. The district having an area of 2,151 sq. km, a share of 4.86 per cent of the total State land accommodates a population of 21,93,276 (2001), 10.40 per cent of the State population. It is surrounded by Gurgaon district on the west, Delhi on its north, Bulandshehar district of U.P. on its east. Only 55 sq. km area is under forest, which is 2.61 per cent of the total geographical area of the district. Its density according to 2001 population Census was 1,020 persons per sq. km against 372 in the State. It is the most densely populated district of the State.

The new township of Faridabad (NIT) was built after 1947 to settle the people who came here from Pakistan. Faridabad is well connected with other parts of the country by rail and road. The broad-gauge railway line of Central Railway passes through the district and most of the trains going to south and west of India pass through the district. Also Delhi-Mathura-Agra Road NH-2 passes through the middle of the district.

The Faridabad district was almost flat plain. The general slope is from west to south-west. In the north-western part of the district, a ridge starts from Harchandpur making an arch and runs towards Badarpur where it takes a north-west turn to continue into Delhi. The Badkal lake has been formed with the ridge which starts from Harchandpur.

The district has a semi-arid climate with extreme climatic conditions. The district comes under Yamuna flood plains. The soil is heavy textured and varies from sandy loam to clay loam. The watertable being high in the district, soil salinity has developed at some places.

The total geographical area of the district is 2,08,000 hectares. Out of this only 3,000 hectares are under forest and 37,000 hectares are put to non-agricultural uses. The cultivable land was 1.63 lakh hectares and the net sown area was 1.60 lakh during 2000-01. The gross irrigated area as percentage to total cropped area was 85.53 in 2000-01 and net area irrigated as percentage to net sown area was 86.01. The main food-crops in *Rabi* season are wheat, barley and gram. Paddy, bajra and jawar are main *Kharif* crops.

Faridabad is one of the major industrial hubs of the country. It is infact the 9th largest industrial estates of Asia. There are about 15000 small, medium and large industries in Faridabad providing direct and indirect employment to nearly half million people. Major industries of the district are Escort, Indian Drugs and Pharmaceuticals, Larson and Turbo, Asia Brown Boveri, Hyderabad Asbestos, Good Year Tyre, Bata, Eicher, Hindustan Wire Limited, Whirlpool of India Ltd. and Yamaha Escorts Motors Ltd. etc. The major industrial production of the district were: tractors, steel re-rolling, scientific instruments, power looms, agricultural implements and JCB cranes etc.

Village Bhainsravli

The Bhainsravli is located around 15 km from the district headquarters. It is situated about 3 km on link road from the Faridabad-Tigaon road. It is well connected by all-weather road to district headquarters and other villages. It is a small village of 565 households with a population of 2,983 as per Census 2001. The sex ratio of the village is 892. The scheduled caste population is around 2.1 per cent, while the other backward castes dominate the population and constitute around 54 per cent of the total population. The village is dominated by Brahmins and Gujjars. The other castes were Valmikis, Chamars (SC), Jats, Koli, Saini, Kumhar and Khatri.

The village has a good infrastructure. Besides all-weather approach road it is 100 per cent electrified. It has a primary/middle/high school, ICDS centre, PDS shop, old age house, Panchayat Bhawan, solar street light and public telephone facilities. The village also has a veterinary dispensary. There are more than 100 landline telephone connections. The villagers have good access to market in Faridabad.

The supply of electricity, however, is very erratic. The demand for power in the agriculture sector is met by diesel sets which the big and medium level farmers own and the others get on rent when needed. A number of villages were observed to be defaulter in payment of electricity bills. The nearest bank is in Tigaon about 3 km away from Bhainsravli.

A total of 40 households were surveyed, out of which 5 were tenants, 5 families having benefited from SGRY, 5 from IAY and the other 25 households were selected randomly. There was no household who benefited from SGSY or from distribution of surplus land from ceiling acts in the village.

Education Status

The literacy rate of the village was 57.05 per cent as per 2001 Census. The male literacy rate was 69.8 per cent while female literacy rate was 42.5 per cent. This shows the gender bias in rural Haryana. Apart from Government primary, middle and high school, there is one private school in the village with more strength than the Government primary school. On the day of the visit, the attendance in the Government school was around 83 per cent. The records of the past six months showed that cooked meals, under mid-day meal scheme were being served regularly in the school. The quality of education was observed to be very poor.

Gender Issues

It is a well known fact that Haryana has a low gender ratio, because the women do not have equal status in the society. The *pardah* system is very much prevalent. The girl child is discouraged from going to school. That is very much reflected in the overall percentage of girl children in the school. The percentage gets further dropped at senior secondary level as compared to that at primary level. It further dropped after twelfth class as girls were not encouraged to join college.

During interaction with educated women, it was learnt that the dowry system is one of the main reasons behind their lower status in the society. The parents borrow money to spend on wedding and dowry. The women have least say in major decisions.

No doubt the reservation of women in Panchayat has helped in raising the participation of women in the affairs of the village but it still requires major improvements.

Health Status

There is no primary health sub-centre in the village, but the villagers have access to nearest sub-centre at Tajpur which is around 3 km from the village. This sub-centre has a female ANM who has a charge of three sub-centres. There is one RMP in the village. The infant mortality rate is around 5 which is surprisingly low, there has been one maternal death in the past one year. The disease pattern in the village is seasonal. As per discussion with ANM and people, main reasons of such diseases were lack of personal hygiene, lack of education, malnutrition and lack of government dispensary.

In the last one year, there were a total of 37 births of which 21 were males and 16 females. Immunization coverage is 100 per cent. Tubectomy is the main source of sterilization.

Land and Agriculture

The total area of the village is 357 acres, out of which land available for cultivation is 280 acres. Usually two crops are grown by the farmers namely, *Rabi* and *Kharif.* The important *Rabi* crops are wheat, mustard and gram while the main *Kharif* crops are jawar, bajra and paddy. The average yield of wheat is 16 quintals per acre, which gives a low remuneration to the farmers. Mustard is more popular among the farmers as its inputs cost less. The average output of mustard is 6 quintals per acre and net profit is nearly Rs. 10,000 per acre after deducting the costs. Land is mostly tubewell irrigated or rainfed. Due to continuous use of groundwater, watertable is going down.

Only 3.5 per cent of the total households do not have land. The farmers having landholding of less than 3 acres constitute major chunk, around 80.5 per cent of the total cultivators, while cultivators having landholdings greater than 3 acres constitute around 16 per cent. During the offseason, people migrate to nearby areas to work in factories as skilled and unskilled labourers. At least 30 families in the village reportedly were wage labourers, most of them belong to scheduled castes.

The majority of farmers get credit from their respective private traders, called *artias*. Surplus agricultural produce of wheat, mustard and bajra was marketed in *mandis*. Some agricultural land of the Shamlat Deh is leased out.

Poverty Alleviation Programmes

The two schemes which provide employment are SGSY and SGRY. Apart from these, there are other schemes for improvement of quality of life like that of providing housing IAY or PMGY.

There are 25 families who have been categorized under BPL. Most of them belong to SC. No Self-Help Group was formed under SGSY. There are three SHGs made under ICDS scheme. Panchayat has taken up work of digging of ponds under SGRY. A total of 1,006 mandays of work was generated in the last financial year.

Gram Panchayat

The present Gram Panchayat consists of twelve members of which 4 were women. The Panchayat is dominated by Brahmins and Gujjars. Some women members were quite active. The meetings of Gram Sabha are held every six months and it approves the annual action plan of the Panchayat.

Village Sagarpur

Sagarpur is located in Ballabhgarh Block of Faridabad district. Its economy is predominantly based on primary activities like farming and animal husbandry. It is a medium sized village with an area of 862.5 acres and a population of 2,627 out of which 1,411 was males and 1,216 are females as per 2001 Census. The SC population was 741 and OBC is 827. The decennial rate of growth of population was 14.75. Situated at about 21 km from the district headquarters and around 13 km from Block headquarters, it comprises 4 hamlets. The sex-ratio of the village is 861.

Infrastructure

The village is well connected by roads. However, the public transport system was very weak. Private tempos were the main mode of transportation. Electricity was the major bottleneck since all the activities including running of tubewells was hampered due to long power cuts.

The nearest market was at Ballabhgarh, which is about 13 km from the village. There is a Gramin Bank in the village. This bank has helped the farmers in getting loans and the self help groups in maintaining their accounts and other professional activities.

Education

The literacy rate of Sagarpur as per government records was 68.74 per cent with male literacy of 83.9 per cent and female literacy of 51.21 per cent. The government school was not good, as most of the people prefer private school. The dropout rate was higher in government school as compared to private school. The dropout for girls was more than that of boys and especially so in case of SCs. Traditional mind-set that offers less freedom to girls was also found to be predominant. There was no high school in the village.

Health and Sanitation

Sagarpur village has a Primary Health Centre (PHC). However, the health infrastructure in the village was poor. Among the children, protein energy malnutrition (PEM), diarrhoea and bronchitis were the common ailments. Maternal mortality rate of the village was found to be around 4.5 deaths. It was more so in OBCs.

Land and Agriculture

Total land area of the village was 862.5 acres, out of which agriculture land was 755 acres. About 52 acres was fallow land. Tubewells are the main source of irrigation. Wheat and bajra are the main crops. For marketing farmers have to go to Ballabhgarh.

There were about 400 agricultural labourers. The number of landless agricultural labourers was 200. There were around 200 cultivators and about 75 were involved in household industry.

Poverty Alleviation Programme

The beneficiaries of SGSY were all below poverty line and were mostly women. Some of the activities of self help groups are dairy, embroidery and opening of cosmetics shop.

The scheme of SGSY was also functional. Various construction works have been done under the scheme. The National Rural Employment Guarantee Programme has proved to be a total failure in the village.

The National Old Age Pension Scheme provides pensions to 19 villagers. The Indira Aawas Yojana has helped BPL families to construct houses and work rooms.

Gram Panchayat

Gram Panchayat in the village was functional. It got a school up to Middle standard established and a hospital was reported to be its next priority.

Village Mothuka

Village Mothuka comes under Ballabhgarh Block and is situated on the bank of river Yamuna at a distance of about 17 km from the district headquarters. It comprises two hamlets namely Mothuka Nanglan and Mothuka Jogian. Although the village is well connected through roads, poverty was the special feature of this village because majority of inhabitants were landless. One medical and engineering college is coming up near the village which may provide some direct or indirect jobs to the villagers.

Demography

As per 2001 Census, the total population of the village was 2,422 out of these 1,068 were OBCs, 752 SCs and 602 were in general category. The sex ratio was 913. The main castes residing in the village are Gujjar (126 households), Jat (120 households), Bania (77 households), Kumhar (122 households), Brahmins (20 households) and scheduled castes (124 households). 94 families were covered under BPL category. The population growth rate in the decade 1981-91 was 21.04 per cent and in the decade 1991-2001 was 18.95 per cent.

There has been increasing number of cases of encroachment on common property like Shamlat Deh and Panchayat Deh. The waterbodies have also shrinked due to encroachment. One of the most worrying features was drastically reducing watertable.

Basic Infrastructure

Most the basic infrastructural facilities have been created in the village. It has all-weather road with a good public transport system. Village was 100 per cent electrified.

Education

The literacy rate in the village was 54 per cent much below the State and national average. The male literacy rate was about 64 per cent whereas female literacy rate was about 43 per cent. The literacy rate for the scheduled castes was significantly lower than other caste groups, i.e., 33 per cent.

There is one primary school in the village. There were 167 students enrolled in the school in 5 classes. The teacher student ratio was 1:40. The students in the village primary school generally belonged to scheduled castes, as others prefer to send their children to private schools in nearby areas. The dropouts rate was quite high in the village. It was more so among girls. There were more dropouts amongst scheduled castes as compared to general population.

Health and Sanitation

As per the ICDS centre's records, about 60 per cent of the children in age-groups 1-6 were underweight. Even the expecting and lactating mothers were anaemic. Sanitation is the most ignored part in the village. Defecation in open was the general practice. A community toilet has been constructed under total sanitation campaign, but its maintenance was very poor.

There is neither PHC nor sub-centre in the village. The RMPs are very common. A private medical college has come up near the village which was providing good health care to the villages. Fever, common cold, diarrhoea and malaria were the common diseases. A few were suffering from TB also. Malnutrition among children especially below the age of 6 years was very common.

Maternity and child care varies with the economical and awareness profile of the family. Expectant and lactating mothers were provided good care in well-to-do families. In the families of landless labourers they are not given adequate care basically due to economic problems and also due to lack of awareness. There was one Anganwadi in the village. But Anganwadi worker distributes only iron tablets. Malnutrition was one of the common problems among the children. This was mainly due to low protein calorie intake and diarrhoea due to poor sanitation conditions. There was 100 per cent immunization in the village.

Land and Agriculture

Majority of landholders belong to Gujjar and Jat communities. Scheduled castes and Kumhars were generally landless. The net sown area was about 99 per cent of the total cultivation area of the village. There was about 50 acres of Shamlat Deh which is mainly used for pasture and grazing land.

Wheat in *Rabi* and paddy in *Kharif* were the main crops. Agriculture productivity was generally good. About 95 per cent of rice was marketed as the staple food of the people was wheat. Surplus of wheat and maize were also marketed. Paddy and wheat were sold to different government agencies whereas mustard and maize are sold to private traders.

Poverty Alleviation Programmes

Out of 602 households in the village 43 households are BPL. There is a self employment programme in the village. There were 107 persons enjoying old age pension. 32 widows were getting pension under the scheme. Only two persons were getting handicapped pension. Three families were covered under Ladli Social Security Scheme.

12 families benefited from Rajiv Gandhi Family Insurance Scheme. 47 houses were built under Indira Awas Yojana.

Gram Panchayat

There were 8 members of Panchayat excluding Sarpanch. Sarpanch was a male and was from Gujjar caste. There were 4 female members, three BC members, 4 SC members and 2 general caste members. Very few people were interested in the functioning of Panchayat.

REGION V

District Mahendergarh

This is the only district in the State which has its headquarters at a town different from the one from which the district takes its name. Hence, the official name district Mahendergarh with its headquarter at Narnaul. The district lies between north latitude 27°48′ to 28°28′ and east longitude 75°56′ to 76°52′. It is bounded on the north by Bhiwani and Rohtak, on the east by Gurgaon and Alwar district of Rajasthan, on the south by Jaipur and Sikar districts and on the west by Sikar and Jhunjhunu district of Rajasthan. In fact, in terms of culture, language and topography of the district, it was closer to Rajasthan than to Haryana. The district has two subdivisions: Narnaul and Mahendergarh.

Population of the district was 8,12,521 in 2001 Census, with a sex ratio of 918 females per 1000 males, which was the highest amongst various districts in the State. It was the least urbanised district in the State with only 13.49 per cent of its population living in urban areas. The district exhibits typical dry land topography—inland streams, sandy plains, shifting sand-dunes devoid of vegetables, dissected upland tract and barren, rocky hilly ranges. The area of shifting sand is locally called *bagar*. Mahendergarh tehsils has the maximum number of sand-dunes.

Economy

The district is primarily agrarian. The main *Kharif* crops were bajra and guar. The main *Rabi* crops were wheat, gram and mustard. The area gives a good yield of mustard. The major problem here was the declining watertable coupled with scanty rainfall, absence of rivers and sandy soil. Because of dry land agriculture, family income was supplemented through animal husbandry. There were two chilling centres at Narnaul.

Agriculture was basically rain-fed. The years with a good rainfall were able to give a high productivity of most of the crops. The district is experimenting with crop diversification under the ongoing National Horticulture Mission. Certain varieties of citrus fruits have been taken up by the farmers with the support of the Mission.

The government is also trying to reach an agreement with the neighbouring States to enable it to complete the Hansi-Butana link canal. Once this link canal system becomes operational, it will boost the agriculture of the district. The district is one of the two districts of Haryana to get special assistance under the CSS Backward Region Grant Fund.

Not a single National Highway traverses through the district. The only roads worth mentioning are stretches of 5 State highways which pass through the district.

Village Mirzapur

Mirzapur is located on the main Narnaul-Rewari road of the district. It is about 10 km from the district headquarters and about 7 km from Ateli, the Block headquarters. The village is well connected by mettled roads with a good transport network. There is an airstrip at Bachhod, about 1 km from the village which is operational.

In fact Mirzapur and Bachhod is twin villages. Mirzapur PHC is located at Bachhod. The woman sanitary complex in Mirzapur is for both Mirzapur and Bachhod.

Demography

According to 2001 Census, the population of the village was 1,993, out of which 1,032 were males and 961 females, the sex-ratio being 931, higher than the district average of 918. Mirzapur is an OBC dominated village.

Infrastructure

Road connectivity is excellent. The village is 100 per cent electrified. Telephonic facility was also available. The village has the following infrastructure:

> (1) Panchayat Ghar, (2) Harijan Chaupal, (3) Primary and Middle school (Bachhod), (4) PHC (Bachhod), (5) Dharmashala and (6) Anganwadi centre.

There is a scarcity of water and electricity in the village. The two nearest markets are at Narnaul (10 km) and Ateli (7 km). There are two poultry farms in the village. Produce is sold through middlemen and *arhtias*.

Education

The literacy rate as per 2001 Census was 70.91 per cent, of this male literacy was 84.3 per cent and female literacy was 57.43 per cent, better than the State average. The village has two primary schools and two secondary schools. Mid-Day meal is served in the school.

Health and Sanitation

There is a PHC at Bachhod, but its building is in a poor shape. There is a delivery hut in the PHC. The general hospital at Narnaul is only about 15 km. People prefer using the facilities of the district hospital. They visit the PHC only for minor ailments. The PHC is located at Ateli at a distance of 8 km. There are 4-5 RMPs in the village who are quite popular.

In the past one year, there was a total of 29 births, of which 17 were male and 12 female children. The IMR as per ANM register was 27.2. There was 100 per cent immunisation in the village. The link between personal hygiene, community sanitation and health is not understood and incorporated. The village is called a Nirmal Gram also.

Land and Agriculture

The total area of the village is 1,119 acres. The dominant caste in Mirzapur, the Ahirs or Yadavs owns about 90 per cent of land. The remaining 10 per cent is shared between Brahmins (3.4%), Banias (1.2%), SCs and BCs (2%) and other castes. Of the total cultivable land of 864 acres, net sown area is 637 acres. Bajra and guar were the main *Kharif* crops, whereas wheat and mustard are the major *Rabi* crops.

Marketing of produce is done either at the doorstep or at *mandis* at Ateli and Narnaul. Most farmers sell their produce to middlemen. At least 150 families in Mirzapur are wage labourers, most of them are SC's. Mahendergarh is a drought prone district with extreme climatic conditions. Apart from agriculture, poultry, fish farming in Panchayat ponds, dairy, workshops like cycle repair, T.V. repair, etc., petty shops are the other occupations in the village. A large number of people go out for work.

Poverty Alleviation Programmes

About 70 people have BPL cards in the village. NREGA, IFC, IAY and Total Sanitation Campaign are the main projects going on in the village.

There are 10 members in the Panchayat with the dominance of Yadavs. The women members are not active. The Gram Sabha is not active.

District Mewat

Village Goela

The village Goela is situated around 9 km on a link road from the National Highway No. 8 and is about 3 km from the Block headquarters at Tauru. It is well connected by roads and has good transport facilities. It is a small village with a population of 1,123 (2001 Census). The sex-ratio was 994, much higher than the State average. It is a Meo-Muslim dominated village. The other castes are Valmikis, Chamars, Jat, Koli, Saini, Kahar, Khatri and Fakir.

Infrastructure

The village is well placed in terms of basic infrastructure. Apart from roads and electricity, the village has a Middle School, Health Sub-Centre, Anganwadi Centre, PDS shop, Panchayat Bhawan, solar street light and telephone facilities. There are three NGOs working in the village namely Sehegal Foundation, Deepalaya and World Vision. The vegetables grown in the village are supplied to Delhi by Mother Dairy. World Vision is active in the village in areas of water recharging and alternate sources of energy. The power supply is very erratic and people have to depend upon pump-sets for irrigation.

Education

The male literacy is 67 per cent but the female literacy is a dismal 25 per cent. This is reflective of gender discrimination in the village. The attendance in the middle school on the day of the visit was about

80 per cent. Mid-day meal was served in the school. For higher studies students have to go to Tauru, which is 3 km from the village. The village school committee is not functional. The number of teachers are less than the sanctioned posts.

Health Status

There is a Health Sub-Centre with an ANM. The nearest PHC is about 5 km from the village. There was no doctor or RMP in the village. The infant mortality rate was 12.5 as per ANM records. Immunization is 100 per cent. The ANM was not regular. The normal maternal health care and birth of children was looked after by trained *dais* (private midwives) in the village. The average family size was about 7-8, reflective of less adoption of family planning techniques. Less than 5 families out of 40 surveyed had toilet facilities in their homes.

Land and Agriculture

The total area of the village is around 330 acres out of which land available for cultivation was 292 acres. *Rabi* and *Kharif* are the two seasons. Important *Rabi* crops are wheat, mustard, channa and jowar while the important *Kharif* crops are jowar, bajra and paddy. The average yield of wheat is nearly 16 quintals per acre. Tubewells are the main source of irrigation. Some NGOs are promoting vermi-compost, especially for vegetables. A good percentage of population is landless (22%). The peasants depend upon *arhtias* for credit and sale of produce.

Poverty Alleviation Programme

No Self-Help group was formed in this village under SGSY, but Mewat development Authority, through NGO's Deepalaya and Sehegal foundation formed some Self-Help Groups. There were 5 beneficiaries of Indira Aawas Yojana.

The Gram Panchayat consisted of eight members out of which three were females. Woman members were usually represented by their husbands. They were also active and had enhanced their prestige. The village development committee in the village has further eroded the authority of the Panchayat, as these bodies are not elected by the people.

SECTION III

The general conclusions of the village reports are in conformity with the overall picture that emerges from the overall analysis of the socio-economic profile of the State. However, village studies provide us with insight into the weaknesses in the implementation of various schemes for socio-economic development.

Analysis of the secondary data in Section I brings out that Haryana achieved a very impressive growth rate since its formation in 1966. The State Government has adopted a number of schemes to develop and strengthen its rural infrastructure. All the villages have been connected by a metalled road, all the villages have been electrified, schemes are in operation for pavement of streets, drains, at least one source of drinking water, toilet at home, one Safai Karmi for cleaning the streets, construction of choupals, boundary wall of *Shamshan Ghats*, etc. For education, now educational facilities are available in almost all the villages. It is claimed that a high school is available in the radius of 1.52 km and a senior secondary school in a radius of 2.28 km. Government has enacted Right of Children to Free and Compulsory Education Act 2011. Every child of the age of 6-14 years, shall have a right to free and compulsory education in a neighbourhood school till the completion of elementary education.

The State Government has claimed to make a consistent endeavour to improve the health indicators of the people in the State. It has introduced free institutional delivery scheme and free transportation for child delivery whereby institutional delivery has increased to 77.2 per cent reducing mortality among pregnant women and new born children. With a view to reduce the infant mortality rate, new Home Based Neo Natel Care Programme (HBPNC) has been introduced through training of Accredited Social Health Activists (ASHA) and Auxiliary Nurse and Midwife (ANM).

The State has introduced a number of Anti Poverty and other Rural Development Programme which have already been discussed in the section in Rural Development and Panchayati Raj. After 73rd amendment of the Constitution, Panchayati Raj system is being strengthened and meetings of Gram Sabha, Panchayats have been made mandatory. Panchayats are expected to take up on themselves most of the developmental activities for which they have been delegated more and more economic and administrative powers.

Village studies bring out the emerging socio-economic state of villages in the light of various development programmes being implemented by the Central and State Governments. Study of 19 village studies clearly bring out that there was a significant improvement in the physical infrastructure in the villages of Haryana even in the remote places. All the villages in Haryana have been electrified, they are connected by metalled roads to the main roads connecting to the neighbouring towns. Almost all villages have a facility for school education in the periphery of 1.5 kilometres, which are quite impressive achievements.

However, quality of school education, health and drinking water, public health, etc., need a significant improvement. The quality of school education at primary, middle and secondary levels need a complete revamping in the rural areas. The average salary as well as qualifications of teachers in the government schools in rural areas was much higher than in the private schools, still most of families in the villages prefer to send their children in the neighbouring private schools, which is a matter of great concern. It indicates towards non-academic atmosphere in the schools which can be improved by addressing the underlying causes and improving the work culture in the schools. Health services need utmost attention as they were in the state of neglect in the villages. It appears many of them were on paper only or in a skeleton form just to meet the technical requirement than to provide a service with a genuine concern. It was noted that a number of rural development programmes, and schemes for self employment and wage employment have been implemented in the villages. But effort appears to be half hearted on the part of the State. For the success of these programmes, resource mapping of each village, micro planning and prioritizing the projects and their implementation with a social commitment was a precondition for the success of these programmes.

Discrimination against females continues to be a matter of serious concern, though a increasing number of girls were being admitted to the schools and colleges. There was a social tension in the villages which is reflected by frequent Khap Panchayat dictates. It requires a complementary social reforms movement to smoothen the social transformation process. All villages have village Panchayats but their functioning was not satisfactory. Gram Panchayats need to be devolved more finances to empower them to undertake projects of higher priority for upliftment and development of the villages.

Training programmes for capacity building of the elected representatives should be undertaken in Haryana in a big way, in fact, it should be undertaken as a social movement. Institution of Gram Sabha needs a special attention. They were the foundation of grass root democratic institutions and polity and need to be nurtured with care.

REFERENCES

Bishnoi, N.K. and Aneja, R. (2008): Regional Variations of Socio-Economic Development in Haryana: A District Level Analysis, *Indian Journal of Regional Science*, Vol. XL, No. 2, pp. 26-40.

Buddha Prakash (1970): Haryana Through The Ages, *Kurukshetra*, pp. 4-6.

Chaudhary, D.R. (2007): *Haryana at Crossroads: Problems and Prospects*, National Book Trust, New Delhi.

Dahiya, B.S., (2008): *Power Politics in Haryana: A View from the Bridge*, Gyan Publishing House, New Delhi.

Dhankar, J.S. (2003): *Haryana Past and Present*, Sanjay Prakashan, New Delhi.

Dubey, A. (2009): Intra-State Disparities in Gujarat, Haryana, Kerala, Orissa and Punjab, *Economic and Political Weekly*, Vol. 31, No. 2, pp. 475-505.

Government of Haryana (2006): *Haryana's Human Development Report* 2005, Panchkula, Haryana.

Government of Haryana, Department of Economic and Statistical Analysis (2012): *Statistical Abstract of Haryana* 2010-11, Panchkula, Haryana.

Government of Haryana, Department of Economic and Statistical Analysis (2012): *Economic Survey of Haryana* 2011-12, Panchkula, Haryana.

Government of India, Institute of Applied Manpower Research (2011): *India Human Development Report*, New Delhi.

Gupta, L.C. and Gupta M.C. (200): *Haryana on Road to Modernization*, Excel Books New Delhi.

Gupta, S.P. (1999): *Three Decades of Haryana: A Descriptive Study*, ESS PEE Publications, Chandigarh.

Gupta, S.P. (2001): *Haryana on Path of Progress*, S.P. Publications, Chandigarh.

Kumar, Satish (2005): *Haryana: Dasha aur Disha,* Sahar Prakashan, Rohtak.

Kumari, Rajesh and Sudesh Nangia (2007): Spatial Pattern of Scheduled Caste Literacy in Haryana (1991-2001), *Population Geography*, Vol. 29, No. 1&2, June-Dec., p. 55.

2

Socio-Economic Development of Rural Punjab

Two Decades of Lost Opportunities

SUCHA SINGH GILL

INTRODUCTION

The Census of India (2011) has brought out that majority of population of Punjab lives in the rural areas. A large proportion of them wholly or mainly are dependent on farm activity for their livelihood. The farm activity can be crop agriculture, horticulture, animal husbandry or fisheries or commercial forestry. But in the recent years there has been some shift of population from farm activities to non-farm activities within the rural Punjab. This is happening because labour absorption capacity of agriculture has declined due to high level of mechanization of agriculture. A large number of agricultural labourers and pauperized peasants are being forced out of agriculture to seek non-farm employment. At the same time, there is growing gap between the rural-urban incomes and amenities leading to shift of rural population to urban areas to seek employment and avail the benefit of the facilities such as health, education, sanitation. The growing gap in the income between farm and non-farm activities is also causing shift of wage employment from farm to nonfarm sector within the rural areas. The nonfarm activities especially in transport, production and repair of farm equipment, deepening of bore wells or construction activities require some skills based on education and training. With the spread of rural education, especially the elementary education, during the last two decades has added to the capacity the youth to acquire new skills and has created aspirations for higher standards of living. The network of the rural road, marketing of agricultural produce in the urban/semi-urban marketing places, purchase of agricultural inputs, access to mobiles and modern media both print and electronic have strengthened rural-urban connectivity and penetration of urban aspirations among the rural young population. This has filled the rural people with aspirations of craving for urban pattern of life. The rural Punjab has been enjoying global connectivity earlier in a small pocket which has extended now to the whole of Punjab. These developments have put Punjab on the fast path of structural change and the rural areas are integral part of this structural change. This change is initiated by the dynamism of a larger context of Indian economy and is affected by policy interventions. In this chapter attempt has been made to capture this change. This chapter is based on 23 reports of IAS probationers, secondary data available at the State level and research work of the scholars working on the regional economy of Punjab. This chapter has been organized into eight sections. Section I looks into evolution of conceptual framework and perspectives of rural development. Section II covers specific historical background of the rural development in the state. Section III deals with status of the rural development in the state in relation to all India level, specifically to that of Punjab's neighbours and also making inter-district comparisons within the state. Section IV examines the rural social structure of the state specifically the emerging religious and caste composition of the population and relations between different communities. Section V looks into livelihood and employment pattern in the rural Punjab and tries to capture the direction of change in the light of recent census and NSSO data. Section VI makes some observations on rural infrastructure, effectiveness of poverty alleviation programmes and PRIs. This is based on the village reports of IAS trainees between 2003-2009. Section VII tries to capture the emerging agrarian relations and agrarian crisis in the state. The last section makes concluding observations.

SECTION I
CONCEPTUAL EVOLUTION AND PERSPECTIVES ON RURAL DEVELOPMENT

Rural transformation is multidimensional phenomenon. It involves the entire rural society and the way it experiences the change over time. The rural transformation has historical context and reference period. The rural transformation has a dynamism based on the nature of the society in which the transformation takes place and its direction is shaped. The concept of rural change or transformation has undergone a change over a period of time. This change has been affected by evolution of economic theory. In 1950s when the ex-colonial countries embarked on the path of economic development, the focus of economic development was to increase gross domestic product through industrialization and modernization of agriculture. Basing on Lewis model (1954:139-91), industrialization was considered as the main vehicle of growth and transition of the economy. The urban industrial sector was seen as surplus producing sector and as a major source of accumulation and expansion of the economy. The rural areas represented subsistence economy and were dominated by agriculture. The agriculture was expected to increase food production and provide employment to majority of the growing population and supply surplus population, raw materials and foodgrains to urban industrial sector. In 1960s, therefore, major emphasis was on intensive agriculture through package of inputs including high yielding variety of seeds, irrigation, chemical fertilizers, pesticides and mechanical inputs. This led to growing inequality in rural areas as the major benefits of agricultural development accrued to large landholders and the small peasants and especially the landless labourers got the least benefits (Poudyal, 2007: 1-16). This led to paradigm shift in the concept of rural development towards redistribution of income. Apart from the poverty alleviation programmes, employment generation was given the high priority. At the same time, emphasis was also given to meeting minimum needs of all in the form of food, health, shelter, education, safe drinking water, sanitation, etc. This was given the name of Integrated Rural Development Programme (IRDP) in the late 1970s. The approach was to improve economic and social life of the rural poor. The four factors influenced the thrust of this programme: (i) concern for persistent and deepening rural poverty; (ii) changing concept of development; (iii) emerging diversified rural economy especially the rural non-farm sector; and (iv) need to reduce non-income dimensions of poverty to achieve sustainable improvement in the condition of the rural poor (Ravillion *et al.*, 2007: 667-701). The IRDP could not achieve expected results due to weak delivery service mechanism, corruption and incompetency of the staff involved, extent and depth of poverty and issues related to governance failure. With the arrival of agenda of neo-liberal reforms, the rural development was pushed to the margin. The whole emphasis was shifted to the rate of economic growth based on increased role of the market and private sector with reduced role of the government (UNESCO INRULED, 2012: 54).

In view of the Millennium Development Goals adopted in 2000, the term rural development began to be replaced by rural transformation. The rural transformation "does subsume the core ideas of rural development concerned with improving the well-being of rural people by enhancing their productive capacities, expanding their choices in life and reversing public policies that discriminate against the rural poor" (FAO, 2003:21). Thus, the rural development involves the agrarian change and integrated development without marginalizing rural people and rural economy. Further, it "recognizes the possibilities and opportunities in diversity and complexity of rural communities, sustainable livelihood and ecology, vulnerability with resilience, interdependence of development, and reshaping of socio-cultural organizations, leading to well-being and dignity of all including the rural people" (UNESCO INRULED, 2012: 55-56).

The changes in conceptual framework in theory and thinking within the international bodies especially dealing with the agriculture have been reflected in the policy framework in India. The policy framework in India has been translated into the programmes for rural development in different phases of post-independence period. Punjab has followed the national pattern of rural development.

SECTION II
HISTORICAL BACKGROUND OF RURAL DEVELOPMENT

The first phase of rural development started in Punjab in October 1952 with launching of Community Development Programme in India. The purpose of this programme was to bring change in mental outlook of the rural people and create a spirit of collective effort for change with involvement of the whole community in the village. The spirit of collective effort was supposed to be created by promoting feeling of cooperation among the people to improve rural infrastructure such as link roads, streets, buildings of school, health centre, veterinary clinic, stadium, etc. The improvement of the rural infrastructure created facilities/services to improve cleanliness, awareness and efficiency of the entire village community and produced favourable conditions for individual effort to improve economic and social life. This was accompanied by institutional reforms such as land reforms and network of cooperative societies for credit delivery and marketing of agricultural produce. The land reforms consisted of consolidation of landholdings, tenancy laws for protection of tenants, ceilings on landholdings and measures for better land management and improvements. Punjab introduced compulsory consolidation of land in 1949 and implemented it rigorously and completed the whole task by 1965-66. The occasion of consolidation of holdings was used to persuade the land owners to contribute to the pool of village common land in proportion to the land held by them. Punjab also did very well in land reclamation of waterlogged area by building network of drains in the State. Although, the State did not fair well in implementation of land ceiling and tenancy legislation yet enactment of the land reforms legislation turned Punjab into land of self cultivators (Gill, 2001). The establishment and strengthening of network of cooperative societies created provision of cheap credit for crop loans and investment in land improvement, purchase of agricultural machinery and irrigation equipment (Gill, 1993). The availability of common land, at the disposal of the village Panchayat on behalf of the whole community, created a base for development and consolidation of rural infrastructure where land was required. This created advantage for undertaking of programmes for collective rural development. The spirit of collective participation was further strengthened by the cooperative credit movement in the State. With the inauguration of Bhakra Canal, the irrigation facilities became available in the southern Punjab. The signing of Indus Water Treaty in 1960 increased availability of canal water in Majha region and also in the rest of Punjab. This gave a further fillip to rural development by raising productivity of various crops. The extension of canal irrigation also increased cropping intensity in the State.

The second phase of rural development began in Punjab in early 1960s. On the recommendations of Balwantrai Mehta Committee Report in 1958, the Government of India decided to introduce three tier Panchayati Raj Institutions (PRIs). Punjab introduced this scheme of three tier PRIs in 1961. This consisted of Gram Panchayat at village level, Block Samiti at Development Block level and Zila Parishad at District level. The task of rural development was handed over to these institutions. At village level, the government decided to appoint Gram Sewak or village level work (VLW) to coordinate the work of rural and agricultural development with officials at Block level. The VLW was expected to act as development secretary of the Panchayat or a circle (group of Panchayats) within the Panchayat Samiti. He was tasked to encourage village people in coordination with the village Panchayat to undertake construction of works of common benefits, from multipurpose cooperative societies for the village or group of villages and introduce modern agricultural practices to improve crop productivity. The establishment of Punjab Agricultural University (PAU) at Ludhiana in 1962 was a big milestone in the rural development. The efforts of PAU were supplemented by Agriculture Department of the State government in extension services for adoption of new technology and farm practices in agriculture.

Along with support in agricultural research and extension, the government played a significant role in development of irrigation. The massive public investment led to increase in the gross cropped area under irrigation from 55.90 per cent in 1960-61 to 74.0 per cent in 1970-71 and 85.48 in 1980-81. Irrigation and power remained priority under Five Year Plans in the State and accounted for 51.0 per cent of the total planned expenditure in period covering the First Five Year Plan to the Fifth Five Year Plan (1951-1978). During 1970s the State undertook to link every village with all-weather metalled roads so that connectivity could be ensured throughout the year with the market places. During this period the programme of rural electrification was launched and completed. The electricity became available in every village and a large number of farmers installed electricity operated tubewells as a means of assured irrigation. This also enabled farmers to instal electricity mechanized operated threshers for separating grain from chaff especially from wheat. The availability of electricity began to convert manual practices like threshing, irrigation, fodder cutting/preparing to machine operated practices. This along with the introduction of diesel operated tractors, increased the speed of agricultural operations raising cropping intensity. The construction of all-weather metalled roads allowed quick transport of agricultural produce to the regulated marketing yards for disposal/sale and acquisition of inputs from the market. The arrangement/availability of cooperative credit through the network of cooperative societies facilitated fast mechanization, increased in cropping intensity, introduced high yielding varieties of crops and commercialized agriculture of the State. The modern intensive agriculture led growth made Punjab a granary of India and the State with highest per capita income. This was reflected in rising consumption standards among all the sections of rural population though at higher rate among the well off sections of farmers. During 1970s the State witnessed a fast rate of reduction in the rural poverty (Chadha, 1986).

In the project of modernization of agriculture rural education is an important factor. The awareness about new technology, the skill of operating it and advantages of its introduction are connected with acquisition of knowledge of the rural population. Education especially the rural education is the best known method to create this awareness (Schultz, 1964; Chaudhary, 1979; Hendrix, 1981). The State Government took a keen interest in promotion of rural education. During 1970s, education accounted for a large share of the State budget. It stood above 20 per cent and the average of triennium ending 1981 (1978-81) the share of education in the State budget was 23.66 per cent. By the year 1980-81, almost every village had a primary school. By this time 92.02 per cent of primary schools, 91.21 per cent of the middle schools and 73.09 per cent of the High/Higher or Senior Secondary schools were located in the rural areas. Some villages got degree colleges especially after 1969 (Gill, Singh and Brar, 2010: 35-55). The rural literacy rate increased from 27.60 per cent in 1971 to 35.20 per cent in 1981. The male rural literacy improved from 34.55 per cent to 41.91 per cent and female rural literacy from 19.58 per cent to 27.63 per cent during this period (Gill, 2011: 37).

1970s is known as a period of green revolution and prosperity in the State. But at national level it began to be realized that the benefits of the green revolution was going to the large farmers. The small and marginal farmers and agricultural labourers could not benefit beyond the marginal gains of the green revolution. In order to protect their interests, Small Farmers Development Agency (SFDA) and Marginal Farmers and Agricultural Labourers Agency (MFALA) were created in 1970. Thus, a need began to be felt to protect the interests of the disadvantaged farmers and agricultural labourers. These agencies were started under centrally sponsored schemes and their offices were created at district levels in the States. The model village scheme was started in 1969-70 for improving civic amenities in the villages. Under this scheme 970 villages were selected initially with grant of rupees one lakh to the each village. The Jayanti Village Scheme was also started with one village selected from each development Block with grant of Rs. 50,000 for each of the village. The aim was to improve rural infrastructure under individual village approach for rural areas. The allotted amount was spent on pavement of streets, construction of drains and disposal of sullage water, etc. For improvement of physical infrastructure and environment, the grant was given on *ad hoc* basis which was insufficient to complete the works under the schemes.

The third phase of rural development was started in 1978-79 when it was realized that individual village approach was inadequate and it was replaced by Integrated Rural Development Programme. A large number of programmes have been started with the view to improve the condition of the rural poor, but these programmes did not cover the whole of the rural area in the country. They operated in some selected areas or in a number of Blocks. The territorial overlap and different finding patterns created many difficulties in effective monitoring. Consequently, they fell short of meeting their targets. But IRDP was started in Punjab to remove these weaknesses and also to tackle rural poverty seriously. The thrust of this programme was to provide the target groups the income generating assets, access to credit and inputs to empower to them to stay out of poverty in a sustained way. For this purpose investment in agriculture and allied activities by the beneficiaries was encouraged which suited their viability. The State finalized this programme in 1978 with objectives to (i) provide full and gainful employment; (ii) to achieve 50 per cent increase in agricultural production; (iii) to revive traditional industries and trades; (iv) to facilitate development of cottage and small scale agro based and ancillary industries; (v) to achieve full development of local resources; and (vi) to ensure participation of rural weaker sections in the development process. To achieve these objectives of IRDP the State government decided to adopt the strategy of focal points/growth centres in a planned way. Under this strategy no village in the State was to be more than 5 kilometres from the focal point. The State was divided into 500 units with an area of 100 sq. km for each unit. In the first instance, a cluster of five contiguous villages in each of the 117 Blocks were taken for development of focal points. The selection of the site was made on the basis of geographic location and capacity to generate development activities. The strategy of focal points was based on multi-sector investment by individuals and activities at the focal point was to create income and employment with spread effect in the surrounding villages. In fact, it was a strategy of decentralized development involving local people in the productive investment using local material and local market for the production of goods and services. The infrastructure was to be created by the State at focal point which included (i) banking and credit facilities; (ii) agro-service centre; (iii) retail outlet for essential commodities and agricultural inputs; (iv) marketing yard; (v) diesel/petrol pump; (vi) post office with telephone facilities; (vii) veterinary clinic/hospital; and (viii) civil hospital. At a later stage more facilities were to be created at the focal points such as godown and cold storage, research and training facilities and larger agro based industrial units. Public utilities like stadium, open air theatre/cinema, rural water supply, community centre-*cum*-library, etc., were also to be set up at the focal point. The focal points were expected to provide urban facilities in the rural areas, generate job opportunities for skilled, semi-skilled and unskilled rural workforce, ensure full utilization of local resources (Government of Punjab, 1978: 5-6). It was expected that over the period of 4-5 years, the entire rural Punjab was to be covered under this strategy. Unfortunately, the new government which came into existence after elections in 1980 abandoned the entire scheme and introduced a programme, which was aimed at poverty alleviation on the pattern of all-India programme. For implementation of the poverty alleviation programme a survey was organized to identify the poor in the State. A family with income of Rs. 3,600 from all sources per annum was identified as the poor and a yellow card was issued to them for availing facilities provided to weaker sections in the State. This survey while identifying the poor created many problems by excluding the deserving families and including the non-eligible families in this programme. Another survey was conducted in 1985-86 for the purpose of identifying the poor with almost the same consequences. In fact by that time, the Punjab fell deep into political crisis created by terrorist movement and Operation Bluestar. This made the task of identification of the poor more difficult. Many government officials were fearful of entering the rural areas and task of identifying the poor was left to the few who entered the rural areas. This resulted in improper identification of beneficiaries especially exclusion of the eligible and inclusion of the non-eligible households. Besides, improper assets were thrust upon the beneficiaries. This defeated the very purpose of the programme (Government of Punjab, 1987: 68).

In 1980, the National Rural Employment Programme (NREP) also became operational in the State. The three departments of the State Government, viz., Rural Development and Panchayats, Forest, and Irrigation were made responsible for its implementation. This programme was merged with Rural Landless Employment Guarantee Programme (RLEGP) in 1989 and named as Jawahar Rojgar Yojana. The Development of Women and Children in Rural Areas (DWACRA), a centrally sponsored programme, targeted at women and children has been operating in the State since 1982.

The main difficulty with the various development programmes in the State particularly with the operation, monitoring and implementation had been breakdown of law and order in the rural areas due to militancy. The prolonged insurgency led to long spell of President Rule during 1982-85 and 1987-1992. The main priority of the administration in the State was maintenance of law and order. The whole process of development and especially the rural development was relegated to the background. When other States made bold experiments with the decentralized development pattern in the rural areas, Punjab State was engulfed by the political turmoil and struggled with problems of establishment of peace. The States of Kerala, Karnataka and West Bengal moved very fast in creating machinery of decentralized development in 1980s and early 1990s. This is the period when Punjab faced breakdown of governance especially related to the rural development. Although the normalcy began to return in the State after the assembly elections of 1992 yet it took some time to restore it properly. In the meantime 73rd Amendment to the Constitution was passed by the Parliament in April 1993 bringing Panchayati Raj Institutions into the centre of socio-economic development in rural areas.

The fourth phase of rural development in Punjab began in 1994. In pursuance of the 73rd amendment, the State assembly passed the Punjab Panchayats Act 1994. The Governor of Punjab constituted a State Finance Commission in April 1994 to review the financial position of the Panchayats and municipalities and make recommendations. In this phase the rural development programmes in the country and in Punjab State are being operated through the involvement of the PRIs. In fact the formulation and operation of these programmes are increasingly through active participation of the PRIs and especially the village Panchayats. In the programmes where work is to be done at village level, the role of the Panchayats has been made crucial in the identification of work, its implementation and identification of the beneficiaries. In this phase the thrust have been changed from merely financial support to the weaker sections to capacity building and empowerment of them. After the 73rd and 74th Amendments to the Constitution, the third tier of the government has got legitimate mandated status. Elections to the PRIs and Urban Local Bodies (ULBs) are mandated after every five years. The States have been mandated to appoint State Finance Commissions to decide statutory allocation of funds for PRIs and ULBs. Twenty-nine line departments related to rural areas are expected to be transferred to the PRIs but in Punjab only seven[1] have been transferred. Under the 73rd Amendment, 33 per cent seats in elections are reserved for the women. This also applies to seats reserved for SCs and STs. In view of the shrinking job opportunities in the rural areas in the post-reform period, the Government of India enacted NREGA, 2005. This was subsequently named as Mahatma Gandhi National Rural Employment Guarantee Scheme (MGNREGS). It has been implemented in all the districts in the country since 2008. This is first right based programme of employment for rural population for maximum of 100 days work for job card holders from a family living in the village. No distinction is made on the basis of gender, ownership of land or caste in payment for work. In implementation of this programme adequate emphasis has been laid on PRIs. It has followed a three-tier structure of governance and planning is made at the village, Block and district levels. Along with providing employment to the needy families, NREGS intends to promote sustainable rural economy through creation of productive assets. In the project design apportion of material and labour costs have been fixed at 40:60. The State governments are required to meet one-fourth of the material cost including wages of skilled and semi-skilled workers while the rest of the material cost and the whole expenditure on the wages of unskilled labour are met by the Union Government. In case of failure to provide employment to the job card holders, the unemployment allowance is paid by the State Governments. The NREGS Act authorizes Gram Sabhas of the Panchayats to conduct social audit of the projects undertaken (Kannan and Jain, 2013: 33-34).

In Punjab NREGS has been implemented in all the districts following its launching in Hoshiarpur district in 2006. Although works under NREGS were picked up during 2008-09 to 2010-11, but the

State administration has not shown enough enthusiasm as brought out by various studies. The completed works have remained between 26.40 per cent during 2008-09 to 53.28 per cent during 2009-10. In the three years period between 2008-09 to 2010-11, there is *ad hoc* selection of projects, which are not based on comprehensive and systematic planning (Gill, *et al.* 2013: 470-71). In the social security schemes such as old age pension, financial assistance to widows and destitute women, enrolment under RSBY or issue of Blue Card for Dal-Atta Scheme, the village Panchayats are involved (Gill, *et al.*, 2013: 508-12).

Although in this phase there is greater involvement of PRIs in designing and implementation of the central schemes and programme yet in agricultural production planning everything is left to the market and judgment of the cultivators. The State agencies, banks, extension workers, State Agricultural Department or PAU deal with the farmers directly. The PRIs involvement is very less. Although District Planning Committees/Boards have been constituted yet their roles in agricultural planning and production is limited. It is only in the Backward Region Grant Fund (BRGF) districts that PRIs are involved in planning and implementation of various activities pertaining to the agriculture and related activities. The State has only one district under the scheme, i.e., Hoshiarpur district. In other districts involvement of the village Panchayats or Gram Sabha has very little role to play for agricultural development. Agriculture is still the main source of livelihood in the rural areas for the large majority of population directly and indirectly. But agriculture of the State has entered into a major crisis. This is manifested in the form of non-viability of farming for the marginal and small farmers, many among them are resorting to suicides. There is also emerging the situation of non-sustainability of farming due to environmental constraints reflected by depletion of groundwater resources and degradation of soil. There is also technological fatigue leading to nearly stagnation in the yield level of major crops. The State is increasingly moving towards mono-cropping system popularly known as wheat-rice rotation. There seems to be absence of major innovation in the technology, form of organization of agricultural production, marketing system and processing of agricultural produce. As a result the rate of growth of agricultural sector has become very low, below two per cent, in the recent years.

SECTION III
STATUS OF RURAL DEVELOPMENT

The status of rural development can be gauged through the secondary data collected after every decade by Census of India, reports of NSSO, other publications of various organizations of Government of India and Government of Punjab, studies by scholars and the reports of IAS probationers submitted to LBSNAA, Mussoorie. Census of India data bring out that the proportion of population of Punjab living in the rural areas has been falling continuously since 1951 especially 1981. In 1951, 78.30 per cent of population of the State was residing in the rural areas, which decreased to 76.90 per cent in 1961, further marginally decreased to 76.30 per cent in 1971. Between 1971 and 1981 the decline in proportion of the rural population was 4.0 per cent point and it decreased from 76.30 per cent in 1971 to 72.30 per cent in 1981. After 1981, the decline in the share of the rural population has been a regular phenomenon and Census 2011 has reported that the rural population of the State has come down to 62.52 per cent (Table 2.1). Although the proportion of the rural population is falling in the State but this change is not experienced by all the districts at the same rate. There are some districts where this proportion has fallen at a fast rate and majority of the population resides in the urban areas. In this category, the districts of Ludhiana, Amritsar, Jalandhar and Sahibzada Ajit Singh Nagar (SAS) Nagar (Mohali) fall where more than 50 per cent population has now (2011) become urban and less than 50 per cent live in the rural areas. The major cause of this is migration of population from the rural to urban areas both for employment and to enjoy better quality of life. The share of

Table 2.1: Distribution of Rural-Urban Population (1951-2011)

(In Percentage)

Year	*Rural*	*Urban*	*Total*
1951	78.30	21.70	100.00
1961	76.90	23.10	100.00
1971	76.30	23.70	100.00
1981	72.30	27.70	100.00
1991	70.50	29.50	100.00
2001	66.05	33.95	100.00
2011	62.52	37.48	100.00

Source: Census of India, various reports.

urban population in total population in Punjab is higher compared to the neighbouring States of Haryna, Himachal Pradesh, Jammu & Kashmir and Rajasthan and India as a whole. This is due to the early lead of the State in economic development and urbanization. The data pertaining to three latest census bring out that Punjab has been having high rate of urbanization among the States in the North-West region (Table 2.2).

Table 2.2: Distribution of Rural-Urban Population in India, Punjab and Neighbouring States

(In Percentage)

State/Country	*1991*		*2001*		*2011*	
	Rural	*Urban*	*Rural*	*Urban*	*Rural*	*Urban*
India	74.28	25.72	72.22	27.78	68.84	31.16
Punjab	70.50	29.50	66.05	33.95	62.51	37.49
Haryana	75.21	24.79	71.00	29.00	65.21	34.79
Himachal Pradesh	91.30	8.70	90.20	9.80	89.95	10.05
J&K	N A	N A	75.19	24.81	72.79	27.21
Rajasthan	77.12	22.88	76.61	23.99	75.11	24.89

Source: *Census of India*, various reports.

There is high concentration of the Scheduled Castes (SCs) population in the State. The share of the SCs population in total population was 28.85 per cent in 2001. This increased to 31.94 per cent in 2011. The proportion of SCs population in the rural areas was 33.04 per cent in 2001 which has increased to 37.41 per cent in 2011. The percentage of SCs population in the urban area was 22.74 per cent in 2011 (Table 2.3). The data indicate that the SCs in Punjab have high concentration in the rural areas. But in districts of Jalandhar,

Table 2.3: Share of Scheduled Castes Population in the Total Population in Punjab

(In Percentage)

Year	*Rural*	*Urban*	*Total*
1991	31.89	19.89	28.31
2001	33.04	20.70	28.85
2011	37.41	22.74	31.94

Source: *Census of India*, various reports.

SBS Nagar, Hoshiarpur, Faridkot, Muktsar, Moga, Mansa, Barnala and Fatehgarh Sahib, Bathinda, Taran Taran and Kapurthala, the proportion of the SCs population is higher than the State average. The SCs population in the rural areas is mostly engaged as agricultural labourers or unskilled labourers in other activities.

The literacy rate of the State has improved from 69.95 per cent in 2001 to 76.7 per cent in 2011 (Table 2.4). But the State has slipped its rank among the states and UTs from 16th in 2001 to 19th in 2011 (Tables 2.5 and 2.6). The States of Nagaland, Sikkim and West Bengal have overtaken Punjab in literacy rate. The literacy rate in the rural areas has remained far behind the overall literacy rate. The rural literacy rate has been 71.42 per cent compared to overall literacy rate of 76.7 per cent in 2011. In the rural area of the State literacy rate of the women is quite lower 66.47 per cent compared to the male literacy rate of 77.92 per cent in 2011. The literacy rate among the SCs population is lowest. Although 2011 literacy rate data of SCs is not available yet 2001 data are very clear on this count. The literacy rate among SCs was 56.22 per cent against overall literacy rate of 69.95 per cent in 2001. The female literacy rate in 2001 was 48.25 per cent against male SCs literacy rate of 63.38 per cent. In some of the districts the female literacy is very low. It was 29.78 per cent in Muktsar, 30.78 per cent in Ferozepur. In four districts of Mansa, Moga, Bathinda and Barnala, the female literacy among the Scheduled Castes was less than forty per cent in 2001 (Table 2.7). The low literacy rate reflects that a large proportion of the rural population is not empowered to access modern technology and lacks capacity to enhance knowledge. Among the literate population especially from the SCs, a large number of them have a very low level of education which enables them to just sign. They cannot read simple text in vernacular (Punjabi) and do not know how to make simple calculations. This speaks very poorly of the rural education/school system in the State. Pratham, an NGO, has been annually conducting surveys to show quality of rural education in the country since 2005. The latest data pertaining to the year 2012 about Punjab bring out that 71.3 per cent rural children studying in Standard V could read Standard II level text. Only 16.5 per cent of the rural student studying in government schools in Standard V could read Standard II level text. As per order of the government the students are not to be detained from going to next class, they go on to higher standards without acquiring capability to read. As English is being taught from the first

Table 2.4: Rural Literacy Rate in Punjab (1971-2011)

(In Percentage)

Year	Person	Male	Female
1971	27.60	34.55	19.58
1981	35.20	41.91	27.63
1991	52.77	60.73	43.85
2001	65.16	71.70	57.91
2011	71.42	77.92	66.47

Source: Census of India, various reports.

Table 2.5: States and UTs ranked by Literacy rate (2001)

Rank	State/UT	Literacy Rate (in percentage)
1.	Kerala	90.92
2.	Mizoram	88.49
3.	Lakshdeep	87.52
4.	Goa	82.32
5.	Delhi	81.82
6.	Chandigarh	81.76
7.	Puducherry	81.49
8.	Andaman Islands	81.18
9.	Daman & Diu	81.09
10.	Maharashtra	77.27
11.	Himachal Pradesh	77.13
12.	Tripura	73.66
13.	Tamil Nadu	73.47
14.	Uttarakhand	72.28
15.	Gujarat	69.97
16.	Punjab	69.95
17.	Sikkim	69.68
18.	West Bengal	69.22
19.	Manipur	68.87
20.	Haryana	68.59
21.	Nagaland	67.11
22.	Karnataka	67.04
23.	Chhattisgarh	65.18
24.	Assam	64.24
25.	Madhya Pradesh	64.11
26.	Meghalaya	63.31
27.	Orissa	63.11
28.	Andhra Pradesh	61.11
29.	Rajasthan	61.03
30.	Dadar & Nagar Haveli	60.03
31.	Uttar Pradesh	57.36
32.	Arunachal Pradesh	54.74
33.	Jammu & Kashmir	54.46
34.	Jharkhand	54.13
35.	Bihar	47.53
	India	65.38

Source: Director of Census Operation, Punjab, 2001, Chandigarh.

standard, it has been observed that 52.1 per cent rural students studying in Standard V could not read easy sentences of English and 28.4 per cent among them could read simple words. Though private schools are slightly better placed than government and aided schools yet difference is not very large. In government schools only 50 per cent rural students in Standard V could read text of Standard II in private schools this ratio stood at 68 per cent. Such a poor quality of education leads to high rate of dropout as and when examination based dropout system is adopted especially after the Standard VIII, the elementary education level. Thus, very few students go upto secondary level of education. It is further brought out that upto the age of 14 years only 2.2 per cent boys and 2.0 per cent girls were out of schools. But in the age group of 15-16 years 7.8 per cent of rural boys and 10.3 per cent of girls become out of schools. This shows quick dropout of the rural students once they cross elementary school level without any examination (Pratham, 2013: 183-84). One reason for the poor quality of education in the State is decline in the number of teachers in the elementary schools run/aided by government during 1991-2004. This situation continues even now (Gill, *et al.*, 2010: 45-47). At present (2013) it is reported that there is shortage of 29,000 more teachers in the schools of the State. There are many rural schools with two/three teachers for eight classes. It is difficult for two or three teachers to teach eight classes. There are several categories of teachers in the school. Some are employed under Parent-Teacher Association funds. Some are recruited under Sarva Shiksha Abhiyan (SSA). Secondly, teachers in the rural schools are asked to do non-academic work connected with data collection for census or other purposes, election duty for elections at every level, meetings at Block/tehsil headquarters. The poor infrastructure in the form of inadequate building, furniture, boundary wall, lack of safe drinking water, etc., and absence of inspection and monitoring machinery contribute to the poor quality of education among the government/aided schools. At the top of it the class divide in the school education is a big factor in deteriorating quality of education in the rural areas. The well off sections who dominate the rural power structure including the village Panchayats have withdrawn their wards from these schools and got them admitted in private schools in the villages, towns and cities. They do not take any interest in improving the infrastructure, ensure presence of teachers in the schools and improve quality of education. The government schools in the villages have turned out to be schools for

Table 2.6: States and UTs Ranked by Literacy Rate (2011)

(In percentage)

Rank	*State/UT*	*Literacy Rate (In percentage)*
1.	Kerala	93.9
2.	Lakshadeep	92.6
3.	Mizoram	91.6
4.	Tripura	87.8
5.	Goa	87.4
6.	Daman & Diu	87.1
7.	Puducherry	86.6
8.	Chandigarh	86.4
9.	Delhi	86.3
10.	Andaman Islands	86.3
11.	Himachal Pradesh	83.8
12.	Maharashtra	82.9
13.	Sikkim	82.2
14.	Tamil Nadu	80.3
15.	Nagaland	80.1
16.	Manipur	79.9
17.	Gujarat	79.3
18.	Dadra & Nagar Haveli	77.7
19.	West Bengal	77.1
20.	Punjab	76.7
21.	Haryana	76.6
22.	Karnataka	76.6
23.	Meghalaya	75.5
24.	Orissa	73.5
25.	Assam	73.2
26.	Uttarakhand	71.6
27.	Chhattisgarh	71.0
28.	Madhya Pradesh	70.6
29.	Uttar Pradesh	69.7
30.	Jammu & Kashmir	68.7
31.	Andhra Pradesh	67.7
32.	Jharkhand	67.6
33.	Rajasthan	67.1
34.	Arunachal Pradesh	67.0
35.	Bihar	63.8
	India	**74.0**

Source: *Census of India*, 2011.

have-nots. The children from scheduled castes, backward classes and pauperized peasants attend these schools and many times the mid-day meal is the main attraction. The private (unaided) schools charging high fees have gained strength in villages, towns and cities where children of haves from rural areas study. They travel long distances in buses and vans to attend these schools. In some of the cases the rural rich have shifted their residence partially or fully to towns and cities for education of their children. This class divide has created a situation where rural education is very difficult to improve.

The State government/universities defines the rural students for the purposes of reservation in admissions in the professional courses and institutions of higher education including universities who have completed their education upto Matric from schools located in the rural areas. Upto five per cent seats are reserved in these admissions for the rural students. The studies bring out that in many cases these seats remained vacant because many eligible students are not available. On the basis of this definition two studies conducted by scholars at Panjabi University, Patiala have brought out evidence which is eye opener. Both the studies are extensive and can be called census studies. The first study covers all campuses of the universities in the State. It brings out that the proportion of the rural students of the total students in the university campuses in 2005-06 was 4.07 per cent against 66.05 per cent of the share of the rural population in the total population in 2001. The share of rural boys and rural girls among total boys and girls in the universities of the State was respectively 4.96 per cent and 3.06 per cent. Panjabi University (Patiala) recorded highest proportion (8.16%) of the rural student while Punjab University (Chandigarh) showed the lowest proportion (2.20%). The Punjab Agricultural University (Ludhiana), which should have very high percentage of rural students, recorded this share at 4.73 per cent only (Ghuman, *et al.*, 2006: 67-68). Another study pertains to the student studying in the technical and professional courses. This study brings out the proportion of the rural students in all the professional courses stood at 3.71 per cent during 2007-08 against 66.05 per cent share of the rural population in the State in 2001. The highest proportion of the rural student was found in the Baba Farid University of Health Sciences, in its various affiliated colleges and stood at 8.88 per cent. This was due to a higher share of rural students in B.Sc. Nursing, which stood at 22.63 per cent. The lowest proportion of the rural students was found in Thapar University (Patiala), which was negligible at 0.30 per cent (Ghuman, *et al.*, 2008:97). Among the rural students the exclusion of the SC students was more glaring. There was nearly total exclusion of rural SC students from the university education. Their shares stood at 0.6 per cent of the total students. The share SCs rural boys among boys student stood at 0.91

Table 2.7: District-wise Literacy Rates of Scheduled Castes in 2001

(in percentage)

District	*Male*	*Female*	*Total*
Gurdaspur	71.67	55.67	64.03
Amritsar	56.70	42.70	50.10
Tarantaran	47.45	31.80	40.05
Kapurthala	71.02	56.16	63.96
Jalandhar	77.28	62.99	70.48
SBS Nagar	81.54	64.79	73.53
Hoshiarpur	85.25	69.62	77.66
Rupnagar	77.92	60.00	69.42
Sahibzada Ajit Singh Nagar	76.54	60.00	68.73
Ludhiana	72.25	56.91	65.07
Firozepur	48.48	30.78	40.12
Faridkot	49.17	34.39	42.17
Muktsar	45.51	29.78	38.11
Moga	48.00	35.65	42.22
Bathinda	47.90	34.25	41.45
Mansa	48.00	35.65	42.22
Sangrur	57.36	40.00	49.78
Barnala	49.01	35.00	42.44
Patiala	60.39	43.15	52.26
Fatehgarh Sahib	71.23	55.03	63.63
Punjab	**63.38**	**48.25**	**56.22**

Source: Director Census Operation, Punjab, Chandigarh, 2001.

per cent while the share of rural SCs girls stood at 0.23 per cent (Ghuman *et al.*, 2006: 22-23). In the technical courses the share of SCs rural boys was just 0.34 per cent and that of girls 0.93 per cent of the total boys and girls during 2007-08 (Ghuman, *et al.*, 2008: 40, 41, 60). The share of the scheduled castes population in the rural population in 2011 was 37.41 per cent and its share in total population was 31.94 per cent in 2001 (Table 2.3). The exclusion and especially that of SCs students in higher and technical education shows that the rural development process is facing serious difficulties. The rural population is excluded in development of its capacity to access modern occupations which are gaining importance in the growing dominance of the service economy of the country. The existing divide between the rural and urban economy expressed in the phrase of Bharat *vs.* India will grow further as the rural population and especially the rural

SCs population is being excluded from access to higher and technical education. At the root lies the collapse of the rural school education in the State. The fall of education to low priority in the budgetary exercises has contributed to this collapse. Education used to account for 23.0 per cent or more annually of the total government spending in early 1980s. This has continuously declined in the subsequent period. The share of public education in the budget was around 20 per cent during 1992-93 which has now stabilized around 12.5 per cent during the last five years ending 2009-10 (Table 2.8). The fall in the share of education expenditure has been at the annual rate of 6.64 per cent per year during 1992-96 and 5.25 per cent during 1997-2002 (Brar, 2008:341). The impact of relative fall in share in the public expenditure has adversely affected the education in State. The impact has been severe in the rural education and especially for the rural poor.

Table 2.8: Share of Public Expenditure in the Punjab Budget

(in percentage)

Year	*Share of Education*	*Share of Health and Family Welfare*
1992-93	19.85	5.79
1993-94	17.17	5.51
1994-95	11.86	3.74
1995-96	15.68	4.56
1996-97	14.73	4.55
1997-98	16.18	4.89
1998-99	19.19	6.15
1999-2000	16.86	5.34
2000-01	15.96	5.44
2001-02	13.92	4.86
2002-03	13.76	4.12
2003-04	13.25	3.88
2004-05	12.29	3.51
2005-06	12.57	3.82
2006-07	12.50	3.72
2007-08	11.60	3.28
2008-09	12.48	3.38
2009-10	13.30	3.56
2010-11	12.42	3.62

Source: ESA, *Statistical Abstract of Punjab*, various issues.

Along with the rural education, rural health has been one of the pillars of rural reconstruction and development in the State. Investment in rural health infrastructure was priority during 1970s and 1980s. During these decades health and family welfare accounted for 8-10 per cent of the total public spending (Singh and Gill, 2008: 354). This share has fallen to below four per cent during the last five years by 2009-10 (Table 2.8). Since 1981, there is no expansion of health infrastructure both urban as well as in the rural areas. The only initiative taken has been to reorganize the State health department with the establishment of Punjab Health Systems Corporation. This Corporation has taken over 154 hospitals covering District Hospitals, Sub Divisional Hospitals and Community Health Centres to improve secondary health care in 1995. The primary health care has been transferred to the PRIs since 2003. As the government has decided not to expand public health care in the State, the private sector has been allowed to open five star modern hospitals in the urban areas. There are also proposals to open some hospitals under public private partnership (PPP) mode. The decision to allow expansion of private health care is accompanied by deterioration in public health care in the State. This is reflected in the shortage of manpower in rural health services institutions. In rural health services there is a shortage of 58.6 doctors in Primary Health Centres (PHCs) and Community Health Centres (CHCs), 67.2 per cent shortage of health assistants/auxiliary nurses and 55.7 per cent shortage of laboratory technicians (Table 2.9).

In fact there is acute shortage of specialists such as Physicians, gynecologist, pediatricians and surgeons in the rural areas. The position of the staff has improved somewhat recently but shortage still continues due to low retention of the staff in the rural health sector. Although, the State has a very good rural health infrastructure but it remains non-functional. There are glaring deficiencies in machinery, equipment, appliances, buildings and residential accommodation. A large number of (70) rural subsidiary health centres do not have any beds for indoor treatment or have 2-4 beds. They are at the most consultation clinics and cannot provide hospitalization facilities.

Due to shortage of staff and poor delivery services the utilization of the rural health services is low. It has been found that bed occupancy rate in the PHCs ranged between 13.5 per cent to 22.3 per cent during 1990-95 (Singh and Gill, 2008: 361-63). With the poor quality of

Table 2.9: Manpower Requirement, Availability and shortage in Rural Health Institutions in Punjab (March, 2008)

(In numbers)

S. No.	Type of Manpower	Required	Available	Shortage
1.	Health Workers (SCs)	5716	4336	1380 (24.1)
2.	Health Asst./ANMs (PHCs)	968	318	650 (67.2)
3.	Nurses/Staff Nurses (PHC and CHCs)	1366	1024	342 (25)
4.	Lab Technicians (PHCs and CHCs)	610	270	340 (55.7)
5.	Radiographers (CHCs)	126	61	65 (51.6)
6.	Doctors (PHCs and CHCs)	988	421	577 (58.6)

Note: Figures in parenthesis are in percentage.
Source: Director of Health and Family Welfare, Punjab, *Rural Health Statistics, 2009,* Chandigarh, 2009.

rural public health services rural people are forced to consult private doctors to get treatment in the private clinics or hospitals. The private health care is very costly. As a result many poor people lack access to health care and those access it pay very heavily for it. It has been brought out in a study of two districts (Amritsar and Gurdaspur) of Punjab that 20.00 per cent to 23.2 per cent credit acquired respectively by small and marginal famers was on account of health reasons (Singh, 2010:23).

The fallout of the relative decline in the rural health services is that in vital statistics like birth rate, death rate and infant mortality rate, the rural areas continue to lag behind the urban areas. The rate of decline of the vital ratios has slowed down after 1990 for the two decades (Table 2.10). At the same time, the achievements in immunization which earlier used to be more than the targets have fallen in several components, viz., T.T. for expectant mothers, D.P.T. for infants (0.2 years) and D.T. for children between 3-8 years (Table 2.11). When slackness comes the worst effects are found in weak link of the chain. In this case the weak link is found in the rural areas because of large number of vacancies and poor supervision and monitoring mechanism in healthcare.

Table 2.10: Rural-Urban Birth Rate, Death Rate and Infant Mortality Rate in Punjab (Per thousand per annum)

Year	*Birth Rate*			*Death Rate*			*Infant Mortality Rate*		
	Rural	*Urban*	*Combined*	*Rural*	*Urban*	*Combined*	*Rural*	*Urban*	*Combined*
1980	30.3	28.3	29.9	9.2	6.6	8.7	96	58	89
1990	28.4	25.6	27.6	8.5	5.8	7.8	66	45	61
2000	22.7	18.6	21.6	7.9	5.9	7.4	56	38	52
2005	18.8	17.0	18.1	7.2	5.8	6.7	49	37	44
2007	18.3	16.4	17.6	7.7	5.9	7.0	47	35	43

Source: Director, Health and Family Welfare, Chandigarh, Punjab.

Table 2.11: Progress of Immunization in Punjab

(in percentage)

Year	*Expectant Mother (T.T.) Achievement Target Ratio*	*Infant (D.P.T.) (0-2 Years) Achievement/ Target Ratio*	*Children D.T. (3-8 years) Achievement/ Target Ratio*
1980-81	107.0	46.72s	100.48
1990-91	101.1	120.25	125.94
2000-01	97.7	113.43	100.63
2009-10	81.9	98.2	87.9

ESA, Statistical Abstract of Punjab 2010.

In physical infrastructure such as all-weather metalled roads, rural electrification, rural schools and network of health centres, Punjab is still leader in the rural development. But the rural areas of the State have lagged behind in literacy rate, availability of clean drinking water, gender ratio especially in the age group of 0-6. In child sex ratio it is among the two bottom States and ranks above Haryana only. It must be noted that compared to 2001 Census, the State has recorded a visible improvement in 2012 in child sex ratio. This shows that there is a large scope of rural development provided that the government has the will to do it.

SECTION IV
SOCIAL STRUCTURE OF RURAL PUNJAB

Rural structure of Punjab is undergoing change over period of time. The proportion of the scheduled castes population has improved more in the rural areas. It has jumped from 31.89 per cent in 1991 to 37.41 per cent of the total population of the rural areas. This jump is nearly 5.50 per cent point compared to rise in its share in urban areas by 2.65 per cent point and a rise of 3.63 per cent point in the total population share of the State (Table 2.13). This is indicative of two things, one, it shows that growth rate of SCs population is higher than that of non-SCs population in the State, Second, the non-SCs or Upper Caste population is shifting to urban areas at a higher rate because of their higher literacy and education to access modern occupations. They have better economic resources to ensure upward mobility. The rising share of SCs population in the rural areas at higher rate shows that SCs population lacks both material and intellectual resources to access the new opportunities created by fast rate of economic growth during the last two decades. In some of the villages the SCs population now outnumber the non-SCs population. Using their numerical strength they have started asserting their position both in electoral process and control over religious places. With increased mechanization of agricultural operations, the dependence of SCs population on land owners has declined considerably. The *jajmani* system is considerably weakened. The SCs population was earlier largely employed as casual and regular agricultural labourers is now compelled to seek employment outside agriculture and also outside the villages.

The reports of IAS trainees in Punjab bring out that there is large variation in the share of scheduled castes population across villages in different districts of Punjab. It is as low as 9.0 per cent in one village and as high as 62.2 per cent in another village. Even in one district variation is very large. In Gurdaspur district in one village the share of the SCs population was 9.0 per cent while in another village this share stood at 60.7 per cent. Of the 23 village reports by the trainees in three villages the share of the SCs population was more than 50 per cent showing high SCs population concentration, another nine villages with SCs population share ranging between 38.9 per cent out of 45.0, i.e., above the State average for share of SCs population. These villages can be called villages with substantial concentration of the SCs population. It is evident that 12 villages out of the 23 villages demonstrate that there is high or substantial presence of the SCs population (Table 2.12). Such a large presence of the SCs population have implications for decisive electoral outcomes in the local, State and parliamentary elections.

Table 2.12: Share of SCs Population in Selected Villages of Punjab

Sl. No.	*Village*	*District*	*SCs*
1.	Manga Rode	Kapurthala	39.6
2.	Mishriwala	Faridkot	27.8
3.	Shamaspur	Patiala	40.1
4.	Bakhopir	Sangrur	44.9
5.	Kakkar	Amritsar	33.6
6.	Chakromwala	Ferozepur	23.5
7.	Anial	Gurdaspur	60.7
8.	Bejechak	Gurdaspur	9.0
9.	Bir Behman	Bathinda	39.0
10.	Ghasitpur	Hoshiarpur	38.9
11.	Warring	Mukatsar	45.0
12.	Khusroopur	Kapurthala	31.1
13.	Mugal Chak	Kapurthala	11.5
14.	Channu	Mukatsar	56.1
15.	Naya Shahar	SAS Nagar	N.A.
16.	Burj Dalla	Bathinda	N.A.
17.	Chaminda	Ludhiana	36.5
18.	Nahianwala	Bathinda	N.A.
19.	Barapind	Ropar	62.2
20.	Attari	Ferozepur	47.2
21.	Chak Romwala	Ferozepur	23.5
22.	Charhewan	Mukatsar	43.5
23.	Chima	Ludhiana	40.3

Source: Compiled from the Reports of IAS Trainees in Punjab (2003-09).

The trainees reports also bring out village-wise growing differential in access to the school education. It is reported that the children from SCs families join government schools. The children from the land owners families especially the well off among them attend the private schools. The division on class lines for access to education is becoming very sharp. The have not (SCs, BCs and poor peasants) send their children to government schools but have sent their children to private schools. Apart from the fee structure which differ between these schools, the differences in the monitoring are very sharp. The reports bring out SCs population does not own land nor they are cultivating land by leasing in. Their main occupation is labour both in agriculture or in non-agricultural activities. As most of them are uneducated and lack skills, they survive on the wage employment. The case studies of the poorest of the poor and agricultural labourers conducted by the trainees bring out very clearly that they belong to the SCs. Their main occupation is that of agricultural labour. Due to mechanization of most of agricultural operations employment opportunities are shrinking for SCs in the rural areas. As they have no other source of income with them, they are poor and vulnerable sections of the society. Self-Help groups are formed by the poor in some villages. They cannot afford costly education in the private schools. The poor quality of education in the government schools is not empowering them to access jobs in the modern and urban sectors of the economy. The process of modern development in the rural areas, unless corrected, will further widen the divide between have and have nots.

The religious composition of the state bring out that Sikhs continue to dominate in number in the rural areas. They constituted 71.25 per cent of the total rural population of the State in 2001. They are followed by Hindus who constitute 25.25 per cent of the rural population. The Muslims and Christians account for respectively 1.34 per cent and 1.31 per cent of the rural population. A change has taken place during the last two decades between 1981 and 2001 which is worth noting. Between 1981 and 1991 a period of terrorism, the proportion of the Hindu population declined and that of Sikh increased in the rural areas as Hindus faced threats from the terrorists. As the normalcy returned to the State, the proportion of Hindu population increased and that of the Sikh population decreased and both reached 1981 level. This shows that the communal harmony has been restored in the decade of 1991-2001 (Table 2.13). Although data related to religious composition is not available for 2011 yet it is hoped that

Table 2.13: Religious Composition of Rural Population of Punjab

Sl. No.	*Year*	*Hindu*	*Sikh*	*Muslim*	*Christian*	*Others*	*Total*
1.	1981	25.51	71.30	8.8	1.25	0.06	100
2.	1991	23.56	73.97	1.01	1.25	0.21	100
3.	2001	25.25	71.24	1.34	1.31	0.24	100

Note: ESA, *Statistical Abstract of Punjab*, 1992, 2002 and 2010.

there is not much change in decade of 2001-2011. This decade has been free from any conflict leading to communal polarization. However, the polarization within the religious groups on class and caste lines especially among the Sikhs has been sharpened. Jat Sikhs have been dominating the rural areas. They own and cultivate land and employ SCs and BCs persons as agricultural labourers.[2] There are sharp decline in the number of SCs operational holdings from 54,000 in 1990-91 to 37,000 in 2005-06. Jat Sikhs also control common property resources such as Shamlat Land, Panchayati Land, land of the religious places such as the *Gurudwaras* (Sikh temples). They have been able to establish political hegemony along with economic dominance. They dominate legislative assembly and parliamentary seats, Shiromani Gurudwara Prabandhak Committee seats and also the PRIs and cooperative societies. They have been discriminating against the SC Sikhs at religious places at the time of religious ceremony or social ceremonies requiring holy book, *Guru Granth Sahib*. Consequently, in many villages the Sikh SCs have built their separate Gurudwaras (Puri, 2009: 31-63). In some of the places there has been strong struggle over control Gurudwaras especially in the Doaba region of the State. This struggle culminated into violence creating further rift among the Jat Sikhs and SC Sikhs in the State (Jodhka and Luis, 2003).

The SCs are no longer as much dependent on Jat Sikh farmers for employment as earlier due to mechanization of agricultural operations. Many of them are now seeking employment outside the agriculture and sometimes outside the village. They have started assertion of their position in religious matters now. Some of them have started going to the *Deras* (religious centres) exclusively headed by persons from SCs background which have come up during the last decade and half. Several of them are joining congregations in the *Deras* dominated by SCs following and especially the ones not liked by the dominant Jat Sikhs.[3] This is a pointer to Dera Sacha Sauda with headquarters at Sirsa (Haryana) and several branches in the Southern Punjab. There has been many conflicts between the *Dera* followers and Akalis (Jat Sikhs) during 2008-10.

Although, this conflict is under control yet the divide between upper caste Sikhs/Jats and SCs Sikhs is persisting and has widened over time. The growing inequality in the society, shrinking employment in agriculture and dominance of commercial ties undermining *jajmani* system has contributed to this process. The attempt by certain political parties (BSP) and groups to mobilize SCs exclusively on caste lines has also played some role in creating differentiation and encouraging their assertion against the Jat Sikh dominance and discrimination in religious matters.

SECTION V
LIVELIHOOD AND EMPLOYMENT PATTERN

Agriculture continues to be the main source of livelihood in Punjab especially in the rural areas. It accounts for 61.8 per cent of the total rural workers. They are employed either as cultivators or agricultural labourers and agriculture is the dominant source of income. Compared to 1999-2000 when 62.7 per cent of the total rural workers were engaged in agriculture, there is marginal decline in 2009-10 in the share of agriculture to 61.8 per cent. The share of agriculture employment has declined by 0.9 per cent point (Table 2.14). The decline in the share of agriculture in the net State Domestic Products has been more than 11 per cent point. It is down from 27.33 per cent in 2000-01 to 15.93 per cent in 2009-10. This shows that employment in agriculture brings less per worker income compared to the income in other occupations. The second major source of employment in the rural Punjab has emerged in construction activities which employs 13.4 per cent of the total work force in the rural areas. The construction activities in the rural areas have gained a momentum during the last one decade and overtaken the rank of manufacturing and trade, hotel and restaurant. In 2009-10, manufacturing engaged 7.4 per cent of the total work force followed by trade and repairs (3.7%), education (2.0%), public administration (1.9%) and other community services (1.6%). The other sectors account for the rest of 9.2 per cent of the rural workforce (Table 2.14). Although the agriculture employs more than three-fifth of the work force yet 38.2 per cent of the total rural work force of the State is engaged in non-agricultural activities. This indicates that diversification of rural employment in Punjab is going on and has achieved a notable level. But most of the diversified employment is as yet in the informal sector. The quality of this employment is poor and needs improvement through State intervention. The structure of the rural workforce in the State shows that 58.1 per cent are self employed, 11.8 per cent are regular wage and salaried employees and 30.1 per cent are casual labourers (NSSO, 2011:65). It is the last category of workers which is most vulnerable

Table 2.14: Percentage Distribution of Rural Workers (Male & Female) According to usual Status (PS & SS) by National Industrial Classification (2004) in 2009-10

Sl. No.	*Sector*	*Share in Percentage*
1.	Agriculture	61.8
2.	Mining and Quarrying	0.2
3.	Manufacturing	7.4
4.	Electricity, Gas and Water Supply	0.5
5.	Construction	13.4
6.	Wholesale Trade and Repairs	5.3
7.	Hotels, and Restaurants	0.4
8.	Transport Storage and Communications	3.7
9.	Financial Intermediation	0.2
10.	Real Estate, Renting and Business Activity	0.4
11.	Public Administration and Defence	1.9
12.	Education	2.1
13.	Health and Social Work	0.7
14.	Other Community, Social and Personal Service Activities	1.6
15.	Activities of Private Household as Employers and Undifferentiated Production Activities	0.5
	Total of All	**100**

Source: NSSO (2011) 66th Round, Key Indicators of Employment and Unemployment in India 2009-10, Ministry of Statistics and Programme Implementation, GOI, New Delhi, 2011, p. 75.

both in terms of income as well as employment. Due to high mechanization of agricultural operations the harvesting and sowing seasons have been shortened to few weeks making casual labourers unemployed for longer number of days during the year. They seek employment outside agriculture but lack proper protection of social security. Leaving a small proportion of population, a large majority of the rural population is poor and vulnerable.

The structural change in the rural employment pattern has taken place from agriculture to non-agricultural activities in Punjab. Agriculture employed 75.7 per cent of the rural workforce in 1983. This declined to 67.7 per cent in 1993-94 and 62.7 per cent in 1999-2000 and 61.8 per cent in 2009-10. The major shift has taken place from agriculture towards construction, trade, hotel, commerce, transport and communication sectors. In fact there has been decline in the share of other services such as financial intermediation, public administration, education, health and social services and private households as employers. The share of such activities stood at 10.5 per cent in 1993-94 which has declined to 7.7 per cent in 1999-2000 (Singh, 2008:156) and further to 7.4 per cent in 2009-10 (NSSO, 2011:75). There would have been faster change in the structure of employment in the rural Punjab had there been less influx of migratory labour both in the rural and urban areas. With introduction of MNREGA in the country, there has been reduction in migration of labour to Punjab from the eastern India. This is likely to accelerate this process in the future.

The structural change in rural employment, as shown by census data, manifest a turning point between 2001 and 2011. During this decade there has been decline in absolute number of cultivators and agriculture labourers in the State. The decline in the absolute number of cultivators has been recorded at 2,61,207 and that of agricultural labourers at 3,21,840. The decline in the number of cultivators in 2011 over 2001 has been 12.65 per cent. The decline of agricultural labourers has been much faster during this decade which has been recorded at 21.60 per cent. While the share of these two categories of the workers has recorded a decline, the total number of rural workers in the State has increased by 8.43 per cent during the last decade (Table 2.15). This indicates that both cultivators and agricultural labourers are shifting to non-agricultural activities as agriculture is not able to provide them gainful employment. This has happened for the first time in the rural Punjab after independence. This is happening under the pressure of market forces in the era of neo-liberal policy. Those who are experiencing upward mobility, they can manage this change. But those who have been experiencing downward mobility, this change has been a traumatic experience. The cultivators who have become labourers after losing their identity as peasants lose economically, face loss of social status and suffer psychologically. None of the IAS trainee has been able to capture this change. In fact this change has been responsible for the unfortunate phenomenon of suicides by cultivators and agricultural labourers in the State.

A study conducted by experts at PAU (Singh *et al.*, 2009) has brought out the directions of this change especially related to the cultivators. This change is induced both by distress related push factors as well as prosperity related pull factors. The marginal and small cultivators are facing distress induced non-viability of farming. The income from all sources of distressed cultivators is less than

Table 2.15: Changes in Number and Proportion of Cultivators and Agricultural Labourers in Punjab between 2001-2011

Sl. No.	Cultivators	2001	2011	Change in 2011 over 2001
1.	Cultivators	20,65,067 (22.62)	18,03,860 (19.14)	–2,61,207 (12.65)
2.	Agricultural Labourers	14,89,861 (16.32)	11,68,021 (11.80)	–3,21,840 (21.60)
3.	Total Workforce in the State	91,27,474 (100.00)	98,97,362 (100.00)	+7,68,888 (8.43)

Note: Figures in Parenthesis are in percentage.
Source: Director Census Operations, Chandigarh 2001 and 2011, Punjab.

expenditure of all types. They borrow every year to finance their annual consumption expenditure and ultimately are involved in debt trap. This makes them vulnerable to crop failure or to sudden health expenditure due to illness of a family member or expenditure related to social ceremonies around birth, marriage and death. In most of the cases this leads to the depeasantisation of the cultivators. The comprehensive study by experts covering 40 villages from all the cultural regions of Punjab, viz., Majha, Doaba and Malwa and all agro-climatic regions, viz., sub-mountainous region, central and south-western Punjab shows that the process of depeasantisation had begun in the second half of 1980s and gained momentum in the mid 1990s. This process had begun among the small and marginal cultivators and had engulfed some middle cultivators also. But this phenomenon largely has been concentrated among the small and marginal farmers. Table 2.16 shows a clear divide between the distressed cultivators and non-distressed cultivators. The table shows occupation distribution of the farmers after leaving cultivation. The study shows that 28.1 per cent of the marginal farmers and 20.8 per cent of the small farmers have become casual labourers in agriculture, factory or construction or labourers with other farmers. But none of the large farmers, who left cultivation, joined this category of labourers. This, distressed induced shift in occupation is prevalent among the marginal and small family households cultivating land up to 2.0 hectares or farmers cultivating up to 5 acres of land. But occasionally some medium farmers are also found in distress. But in case of large farmers it is the prosperity induced pull factors which are operating and they are shifting to occupations which are more profitable. Among the large farmers who left cultivation, 28.3 per cent of them stated that

Table 2.16: Occupational Distribution of Farmers after Leaving Farming in Punjab

Activity after	Before	Marginal (N=217)	Small (n=192)	Medium (n=134)	Sub-Total (n=543)	Large (n=46)
Labourers	(i) Agriculture	6.9	4.1	1.4	4.6	—
	(ii) Factory	3.7	4.2	1.5	3.3	—
	(iii) Construction	1.4	0.5	—	0.7	—
	(iv) Unspecified	16.1	12	9.8	13.1	—
N = 118	**Sub-Total**	**28.1**	**20.8**	**12.7**	**21.7**	—
Milkmen (n = 53)		10.1	8.8	10.4	9.8	6.6
Distress-rentiers	(i) Capital interest	0.5	0.5	0.7	0.6	8.7
	(ii) Land rent	1.8	13.0	15.7	9.2	28.3
(n = 53)	**Sub-Total**	**2.3**	**13.5**	**16.4**	**9.8**	**37.0**
Trader/ dealer	(i) Livestock	0.9	0.5	0.7	0.7	—
	(ii) Vehicle	—	0.5	1.5	0.6	—
(n = 4)	**Sub-Total**	**0.9**	**1**	**2.2**	**1.3**	**6.6**
Abroad (n = 37)		6.9	6.8	6.7	6.8	8.7
Service	Government	6.9	10.9	9.7	9.0	10.9
	Private	16.1	11.5	15.7	14.4	2.2
(n=127)	**Sub-Total**	**23.0**	**22.4**	**25.4**	**23.4**	**13.0**
Entrepreneur	(i) Flour Mill	2.3	2.6	1.5	2.2	—
	(ii) Operator (truck, taxi, auto, van)	6.9	7.3	3.0	6.1	2.2
	(iii) Repair shop	5.1	4.2	1.5	3.9	—
	(iv) Mason	2.8	2.6	0.7	2.2	—
	(v) Grocery shop	2.8	4.7	1.5	3.1	1.9
	(vi) Miscellaneous	7.4	5.2	17.2	9.0	—
(n = 144)	**Sub-Total**	**27.2**	**26.6**	**25.4**	**26.5**	**13.1**
Others (n=4)		1.4	—	0.7	0.7	4.4
	Total	**100.0**	**100.0**	**100.0**	**100.0**	**100.0**

Source: Singh, Karam, Sukhpal Singh and H.S. Kingra (2009), Agrarian Crisis and Depeasantisation in Punjab: Status of Small/Marginal Farmers who left Agriculture, *Indian Journal of Agricultural Economics,* Vol. 64, No. 4.

the higher rent of land was the reason for shifting out of cultivation. Among the large farmers leaving cultivation, 11 per cent became commission agents whereas none of the small and marginal farmers pushed out became a commission agent. Among the distressed farmers 36.2 per cent (45.2% among the marginal operators) sold out their entire land but this proportion was 8.7 among the large farmers shifting out of cultivation. It is evident from Table 2.16 that the majority (75.3%) of the cultivators leaving agriculture belong to small and marginal class of the cultivators. Thus, the land is shifting from the small and marginal holders towards the relatively well off farmers both through, land lease and land sale processes. This is further sharpening the class differences in the rural areas. There is no specific study available on agricultural labourers who are leaving agriculture. It is obvious that they are resource poor and uneducated, therefore, have no means to experience upward mobility. They have been converted into circular labourers undertaking any type of wage employment available within the village or outside.

SECTION VI
RURAL INFRASTRUCTURE, EFFECTIVENESS OF POVERTY ALLEVIATION PROGRAMMES AND PRI'S: OBSERVATION BASED ON TRAINEES REPORTS

There are 23 village reports prepared by IAS trainees for 22 villages. One village (Chakromwala, Ferozepur district) has been studied twice, viz., First time in 2005 and second time in 2009. These reports in many cases are not comparable as trainees have collected information casually and on many specific issues information is not available. From descriptive reporting we have constructed three tables to gather idea about quantitative assessment of rural development. One (Table 2.12) have also been constructed from these reports indicating the share of SCs population in the villages of the state. The three Tables (2.17, 2.18, 2.19) in this section provide village-wise data on three different aspects. They are:

- Village Infrastructure,
- Poverty Alleviation Programme, and
- Effectiveness of Panchayati Raj Institutions.

The rural infrastructure helps in the increase of productivity especially agricultural productivity and is critical factor in human capital formation. These reports provide useful information on five variables, the number of schools in villages, existence of mid-day meal scheme, shortage of teachers in the (government) schools, availability of health centres and visit of ANM/ASHA. Although the information of Public distribution system especially on the operation of *dal-atta* scheme is available yet it has not been collected. At the same time, data on post offices and bank branches in villages has not been collected. It is well known from the secondary data that each village is covered by PDS, post office and bank branch. Each village is linked with metalled road and has access to electricity. The trainees reports bring out that each village in the State has at least one school. But in nine villages out of 22 there are two or more schools. In these villages, in addition to the government schools, private schools have come up during the last two decades. In some villages along with the elementary schools, high or secondary level schools have been established by the State government. There is provision of drinking water and separate toilets facilities for boys and girls in the several

Table 2.17: Village Infrastructure

Sl. No.	*Name of Village*	*District*	*No. of Schools*	*Mid Day Meal*	*Shortage of number of teachers in Govt. School*	*Health Centre*	*ASHA/ ANM*
1.	Manga Roda	Kapurthala	1	Yes	3	No	Yes
2.	Mishriwala	Faridkot	3	Yes	N.A	No	Yes
3.	Shamaspur	Pawala	1	Yes	1	No	Yes
4.	Bakhopir	Sangrur	1	Yes	4	No	Yes
5.	Kakkar	Amritsar	1	Yes	N.A	Yes	Yes
6.	Chakromwala	Ferozepur	2	Yes	1	Yes	Yes
7.	Anial	Gurdaspur	2	Yes	N.A	No	No
8.	Bajechak	Gurdaspur	1	Yes	N.A	No	Yes
9.	Bir Behman	Bathinda	2	Yes	Nil	Yes	Yes
10.	Ghasitpur	Hoshiarpur	1	N.A	N.A	No	No
11.	Warring	Mukatsar	2	Yes	5	Yes	Yes
12.	Khusroopur	Kapurthala	2	Yes	1	Yes	Yes
13.	Mugal Chak	Kapurthala	1	Yes	N.A	No	Yes
14.	Channu	Mukatsar	2	Yes	N.A	No	Yes
15.	Naya Shahar Badala	S.A.S. Nagar	2	Yes	N.A	No	Yes
16.	Burj Dalla	Bathinda	N.A	N.A	N.A	N.A	N.A
17.	Chaminda	Ludhiana	1	Yes	N.A	N.A	N.A
18.	Nahianwala	Bathinda	1	N.A	N.A	N.A	N.A
19.	Barapind	Ropar	1	Yes	N.A	N.A	Yes
20.	Attari	Ferozepur	2	Yes	N.A	Yes	N.A
21.	Ckakromwala	Ferozepur	2	Yes	1	Yes	Yes
22.	Charhewan	Mukatsar	2	Yes	Nil	No	Yes
23.	Chima	Ludhiana	1	Yes	N.A	No	N.A

Note: N.A. means not available/not collected.
Source: Reports of IAS Trainees.

Box-1: Best Practices

Among the best practices the village Chakromwala can be reported as a case study. Teachers are regular in these schools and students from neighbouring villages also attend classes. Mid-day meal is cooked and served properly. Students also turn up in the school regularly. There are proper buildings for the schools and playground is also available. The village has a health centre and people avail the services. The working of the Primary Health Centre is satisfactory. The doctors are regularly available, so is the case with the para medical staff. The health of people of the village is satisfactory. Deliveries take place with the help of a trained mid wife. The health centre has also its own building.

Box-2: Worst Practices

The village Anial in Gurdaspur district present a worst practice. There are two schools in the village: one government and another private. The Government Primary School shares two rooms accommodation with Aganwadi Centre. The rooms' roofs are leaking. Toilet in the school is not functional. There has been fall in the enrolment and students have begun to shift to private school. This was because there were no teachers in the school (2004-05). Although two teachers have been appointed by Zila Parishad and Mid-Day Meal has been started yet situation has not improved. The village has no health centre. Even ANM sub-centre is not there. The nearby one mini PHC has no doctor. The general health condition of the people is very poor and 30 per cent among them suffer from asthma. Water diseases are very common. The connectivity is very poor. The road condition is also bad.

schools. In all the schools, except one where the trainee has not collected the information, mid-day meal scheme is in operation. In seven villages the shortage of the school teachers have been reported while in 14 schools such information has not been collected by the trainees. Only in two schools no shortages of teachers have been reported. Although, the trainees have not applied any measure of quality of teachings in the schools yet several of them have pointed out towards the needs to improve quality of teaching and health in the rural areas. In some of the cases it is reported that teaching and health services have reached the point of complete breakage.

Absenteeism among teachers, lack of monitoring, absence of motivation to teach and shortage of teachers have been reported as the major factors. Out of the 23 village reports only seven points to the existence of health centres or government clinics. The availability of ANM/ASHA is reported in the 15 villages and data are not reported from 7 villages and no availability is reported in only one case.

Thus, it is brought that infrastructure especially related to education and health is available but delivery of services is poor.

On the issue of poverty alleviation, Punjab has not evolved its own programme but has adopted central programmes. These programmes have been designed at central level specifically to eradicate poverty in the poor States. Punjab does not belong to this category of States. The incidence of poverty is considerably lower compared to the poorer States. The incidence of rural poverty has been 22.1 per cent compared to 41.8 per cent at all India Level (Tendulkar Committee 2009). The trainees have generally suggested modification of criterion taking into consideration the specific needs of the State. Generally speaking the State seems to be less enthusiastic on poverty alleviation programmes. These programmes are implemented by the Department of Rural Development and Panchayati Raj Institution. The officials are generally apathetic towards these programmes. Most of these programmes are implemented through the involvement of village Panchayats where the power structure is in the hands of the well off sections. They operate in factional manner generally ignoring the needs of the rural poor. It has been found that in the 12 case studies out 23 that Indira Awas Yojana (IAY) was not in operation in the villages. This is a central sponsored scheme which provides Rs. 25,000 in two instalments for construction of pucca house for the rural poor. This scheme is not operational in the majority of the villages where several new poor families need support. Similarly in the 12 village reports SGSY (Swarnajayanti Gram Swarojgår Yojana) is not in operation. MNREGA has been implemented in seven villages. As we know that MNREGA has been started after 2006 and we can leave the 9 case studies before that. The studies carried out after 2005 are 14 and 7 villages (50%) could start MNREGA. This programme is right based approach to manual employment up to maximum of 100 days for a family holding job card. The story is not different in the case of Self-Help Groups (SHG). This has been implemented in 11 villages out of the 22 villages studied by the trainees. It is evident that nearly half the Punjab villages have been deprived of the poverty alleviation programmes in one or the other ways (Table 2.18). This is a sad commentary on the commitment of the State Government on implementation of poverty alleviation programmes on one hand displays the nature of power structure in the villages which operates against the poor on the other hand. One hears voices of people who matter that implementation of MNREGA has led to rise in the wage rate of unskilled labour adding to the cost of production of crops and industrial production. This has generated a tendency among the village leaders heading the village Panchayats to remain indifferent to the implementation of these programmes. Wherever the Sarpanchs take lead and District Commissioners take interest the programme takes off (Gill *et al.* 2013).

Table 2.18: Status of Poverty Alleviation Programme in the Village

Sl. No.	*Name of Village*	*District*	*IAY*	*SGSY*	*SGRY*	*MNREGA*	*SHG*
1.	Manga Roda	Kapurthala	No	Yes	Yes	No	Yes
2.	Mishriwala	Faridkot	Yes	No	Yes	No	No
3.	Shamaspur	Patiala	Yes	No	Yes	No	No
4.	Bakhopir	Sangrur	Yes	No	Yes	No	Yes
5.	Kakkar	Amritsar	No	No	Yes	No	No
6.	Chakromwala	Ferozepur	No	Yes	Yes	No	Yes
7.	Anial	Gurdaspur	No	Yes	Yes	No	Yes
8.	Bajechak	Gurdaspur	Yes	Yes	No	No	Yes
9.	Bir Behman	Bathinda	No	No	Yes	No	No
10.	Ghasitpur	Hoshiarpur	No	Yes	No	Yes	Yes
11.	Warring	Mukatsar	Yes	No	Yes	No	No
12.	Khusroopur	Kapurthala	Yes	No	Yes	No	No
13.	Mugal Chak	Kapurthala	Yes	No	Yes	No	No
14.	Channu	Mukatsar	Yes	Yes	Yes	Yes	Yes
15.	Naya Shahar Badala	S.A.S. Nagar (Ajitgarh)	No	No	Yes	Yes	No
16.	Burj Dalla	Bathinda	No	Yes	No	No	Yes
17.	Chaminda	Ludhiana	No	Yes	No	Yes	Yes
18.	Nahianwala	Bathinda	No	No	No	No	No
19.	Barapind	Ropar	Yes	No	Yes	Yes	No
20.	Attari	Ferozepur	No	Yes	Yes	No	Yes
21.	Ckakromwala	Ferozepur	No	Yes	Yes	No	Yes
22.	Charhewan	Mukatsar	Yes	No	No	Yes	No
23.	Chima	Ludhiana	Yes	Yes	No	Yes	Yes

Source: Reports of IAS Trainees.

The thrust of rural development programme including poverty alleviation schemes is to implement them through the third tier of the government. In the villages this tier is represented by the village Panchayats. The village Panchayats have become highly contested centres of power for political parties. The elections are contested on party lines and candidates generally make huge expenditure to woe the voters. This makes Panchayat contest among the rich sections of the society. Even when seats are reserved for the SCs/STs and women, the poorest sections remain out of contest. The expensive Panchayat

Table 2.19: Effectiveness of Panchayati Raj System

Sl. No.	Name of Village	District	Regularity in Gram Sabha Meeting	Awareness among Sarpanches	Awareness of lady member Sarpanches	Division among members
1.	Manga Roda	Kapurthala	No	N.A	Poor	N.A
2.	Mishriwala	Faridkot	No	Poor	Poor	N.A
3.	Shamaspur	Pawala	No	Poor	Poor	Yes
4.	Bakhopir	Sangrur	No	Poor	Poor	N.A
5.	Kakkar	Amritsar	N.A	Aware	Poor	Yes
6.	Chakromwala	Ferozepur	N.A	Poor	Poor	N.A
7.	Anial	Gurdaspur	No	Poor	Poor	N.A
8.	Bajechak	Gurdaspur	N.A	Poor	Poor	N.A
9.	Bir Behman	Bathinda	N.A	Poor	Poor	N.A
10.	Ghasitpur	Hoshiarpur	N.A	Aware	Aware	No
11.	Warring	Mukatsar	N.A	Aware	Aware	N.A
12.	Khusroopur	Kapurthala	N.A	N.A	N.A	N.A
13.	Mugal Chak	Kapurthala	No	Poor	Poor	N.A
14.	Channu	Mukatsar	No	Aware	Poor	N.A
15.	Naya Shahar Badala	S.A.S. Nagar (Ajitgarh)	N.A	N.A	N.A	N.A
16.	Burj Dalla	Bathinda	N.A	Aware	Aware	N.A
17.	Chaminda	Ludhiana	No	N.A	Partly Aware	Yes
18.	Nahianwala	Bathinda	N.A	N.A	Aware	N.A
19.	Barapind	Ropar	No	Less	Aware	N.A
20.	Attari	Ferozepur	N.A	Poor	Poor	Yes
21.	Ckakromwala	Ferozepur	N.A	Poor	Poor	N.A
22.	Charhewan	Mukatsar	No	N.A	Partly Aware	Yes
23.	Chima	Ludhiana	No	Aware	Aware	Yes

Note: N.A. means Not Available/Not Collected.
Source: Reports of I.A.S. Trainees.

elections generally crowd out the poor from the local power structure. The way PRIs have evolved in the State, this has led to factionalism in the villages. Except for one village, the trainees reports either point towards division among the elected members or have not collected data on this count. In fact, it has been taken for granted by the IAS trainees that there is division among the village Panchayat members. Gram Sabhas which are very crucial for involvement of the voters in decision making are not held properly and regularly. Two mandatory meetings are not held but are managed on technical grounds by showing the lack of quorum on papers and later on shown to be held without quorum. This had made Gram Sabhas as non-functional and put village Panchayat in the hands of a few influential persons. At present it is in the hands of the persons who do not have knowledge of the potentials of the PRIs. Out of 23 village reports only 6 Sarpanches have been found to be aware. The encouraging aspect has been growing awareness among the women Sarpanches and Panches. In 8 cases, the women members/Panches of the village Panchayats are reported as partly or fully aware. It is very sad that PRIs which are supposed to lead rural development and poverty alleviation programmes are ailing themselves. The party politics is injected division at local level, rich sections have hijacked it, Gram Sabhas have been made non-functional by manipulations and lack of awareness among the PRI leadership who have made them poor, sick and non-functional. The training of the elected representatives of PRIs has been suggested by the IAS trainees. This has been put into practice by the Department of Rural Development and Panchayats in the State. This is creating awareness about the rights, duties, functions and procedures among the elected representatives. This helps in improving the functioning and effectiveness of PRIs but issues of factionalism and non-working of Gram Sabhas need immediate attention to fully harness the potentials of the Panchayats.

SECTION VII
AGRARIAN RELATIONS AND AGRARIAN CRISIS

Punjab was a pioneer in ushering green revolution and intensive cultivation. With maturing of green revolution agriculture became capital intensive. In order to save labour cost, to avoid problems connected with labour management, and fasten harvesting and sowing to reduce weather risks, the farmers invested heavily in farm machinery. The massive expansion in production, productivity and productive forces have led to change in agrarian relations. The change in agrarian relations can be viewed in terms of relations of the agricultural workforce to means of production such as land, agricultural implements and other productive resources. At the same time change in agrarian relations involves changes in relations between owners of the productive resources and workers who work with the resources. The growth in the productive resources increases the speed of the work through mechanization or revolutionisation of technology. These changes have been drastic in the State during the last 50 years of agrarian change. The cultivation in the State is mainly by owner cultivators. But some cultivators especially the medium or large resort to leasing in land from the small owners who cannot afford to own or arrange costly machinery for cultivation. This is known as reverse tenancy (Gill, 1989: A 79-85, Singh, 1989: A 86-92, Singh and Grewal, 2001: 203-14, Brar and Gill, 2001: 215-37). This pattern of tenancy is allowing relatively big and richer farmers to make greater use of their machinery and organise agriculture on capitalist lines. This has also led to development of land lease market in the State. The small operators have been crowded out in the lease market because of competition from the rich farmers with greater financial capacity and ownership of the modern machinery and other agriculture equipment. Thus, land and capital is under the ownership and control of farmers especially the rich. Private investment in agriculture has been facilitated by public investment in irrigation electrification and other infrastructure, agricultural research and credit by cooperative societies and banks (Chadha, 1986). The data of operational holdings for the State for the last 40 years from 1970-71 to 2010-11 bring out that the proportion of marginal holdings of the total holdings has declined from 37.63 per cent in 1970-71 to just 12.31 per cent in 2000-01but rose to 15.61 per cent in 2010-11. The proportion of the small holdings has remained stable around 18-19 per cent while the share of semi-medium and medium holdings has increased respectively from 20.44 per cent and 18.01 per cent in 1970-71 to 31.83 per cent and 28.35 per cent in 2010-11. The share of large holdings has also increase marginally. The proportion of marginal and small holdings was 56.54 per cent in 1970-71 which declined to 34.19 per cent in 2010-11. This has led to concentration of operational area and number of operational holdings to relatively of large size holdings (Table 2.20). The share of operated area jointly by the marginal small farmers in 2010-11 was 9.33 per cent against their 34.1 per cent share in number of holdings.

Table 2.20: Size Class Distribution of Operational Holdings in Punjab (1970-71 to 2005-06)

Size Class	*1970-71*	*1980-81*	*1990-91*	*2000-01*	*2010-11*
Marginal	51756	197323	295668	122760	164431
(0-1 below hectare)	(37.63)	(19.21)	(26.47)	(12.31)	(15.62)
Small	260083	199368	203842	173071	195439
(1-2 hectares)	(18.91)	(19.41)	(18.25)	(17.35)	(18.57)
Semi-medium	281103	287403	288788	328237	324515
(2-4 hectares)	(20.44)	(27.98)	(25.86)	(32.91)	(30.83)
Medium	247755	269072	261481	300954	298451
(4-10 hectares)	(18.01)	(26.20)	(23.41)	(30.18)	(25.35)
Large	68883	73941	67172	72356	69718
(10 hectares and above)	(5.01)	(7.20)	(6.01)	(7.25)	(6.63)
All holdings	**1375392**	**1027127**	**1116951**	**997372**	**1052554**
	(100.00)	**(100.00)**	**(100.00)**	**(100.00)**	**(100.00)**

Source: *Statistical Abstract of Punjab 2011*, Government of Punjab, Chandigarh.

SECTION VIII
AGRICULTURE CENSUS OF PUNJAB, DEPARTMENT OF AGRICULTURE, GOVERNMENT OF PUNJAB, CHANDIGARH

The area operated by the medium and large holdings was 90.67 per cent while their share in number was 63.81 per cent in 2010-11. The concentration of operational holdings in the semi-medium, medium and large categories has made landholders as supervisors and managers with major part of the labour being performed by hired wage labourers. The hired wage labourers operate the various agriculture instruments and machinery owned by landholders. These labourers get wages in cash on daily, six monthly or yearly contracts. It has been observed by the IAS trainees that this has created a culture among the landholders to get the physical work done from hired workers. Even the small and marginal landholders avoid physical labour. This trend is quite visible among younger generation/children of farmers. They either want government jobs or want to go abroad rather than working on their own farms. This has made small and marginal holdings unviable. A high level of mechanisation (Bhalla and Singh, 2012) has reduced days in the harvesting and sowing seasons reducing the work for hired labour also. Consequently, the number of persons leaving agriculture (especially poor farmers) and agricultural labourers has increased very much. The number of cultivators declined by 2,61,207 (12.56%) and agricultural labourers by 3,21,840 (21.60%) between 2001 and 2011 (Table 2.15). This indicates that agriculture of the State is following capitalist pattern and following intensive commercial farming. The cropping intensity has reached 189 in 2010-11 from 140 in 1970-71 (Table 2.21). This shows that State agriculture has become nearly two crops a year. Three main crops, viz., wheat, paddy and cotton account for 87.0 per cent of the total gross cropped area. All other crops such as pulses, sugarcane, vegetables and fruits and fodder account for 13 per cent of the gross cropped area. The State agriculture has become highly mechanized, specialized, commercialized capitalist agriculture and not sown area has also saturated.

This pattern of agriculture development based on individualised intensive and commercial agriculture has produced crisis of serious proportion in the State. This crisis has been manifest in some specific forms. One such form has been viability crisis for small and marginal cultivators. In their case annual income from all sources has been less than annual expenditure of all types making them deficit cultivators and resorting to debt for financing their consumption (Bhalla, 2007). Such farmers have been involved in debt trap and several among them have committed suicides (Singh, *et al.*, 2012, 12-14; Singh 2009, 261-84). Second form of the agrarian crisis has been related to sustainability of a agriculture in the state. This is related to environment degradation especially concerned with depletion of ground water resources, declining fertility of soil due to degradation of quality of soil and poisoning soil and ground water resources. The present cropping pattern is considered ecologically non-sustainable (Johl Committee, 1986; Johl Committee, 2002; Kalkat Committee 2013). Thirdly, from of this crisis is reflected in market clearance especially for commodities other than wheat, paddy and cotton. A bumper crop of vegetables, fruits or other crops create marketing crisis. Occasionally, this is also found in the case of wheat and paddy clearance. The market clearance is highly dependent on minimum support price declared by the Union Government, purchase support by the FCI/CCI. In the recent years FCI has been showing reluctance to buy paddy from the State as eastern and southern States are fast emerging as surplus States. The three committees appointed by the

Table 2.21: Net Sown Area and Cropping Intensity in Punjab

Year	*Net Sown Area (hectares)*	*Cropping Intensity (in percentage)*
1970-71	4053	140
1980-81	4191	161
1990-91	4218	178
2000-01	4264	186
2010-11	4158	189

Source: *Statistical Abstract of Punjab*, 2002 and 2011.

State Government (1986, 2002 and 2013) have suggested diversification of agriculture towards high value crops and diversification of economy away from agriculture especially promotion of agro-processing industries to absorb surplus workforce released from agriculture. These committees have recommended package of policy measures to achieve diversification to save farmers and farming but concretely speaking as yet State agriculture is unable to show any achievement in this direction. One of the principal factors has been lack of financial resources to implement the suggested measure on it own. State has been demanding special package from the Union Government and has also been expecting that private corporate sector of the country will be involved in agro-processing and provide assured market clearance at remunerative prices to the farmers. As yet the Union Government has not shown any interest nor the corporate industrial houses have shown interest in the agro-processing on noticeable scale. The agriculture and farmers of the State continue to be entrapped in the crisis.

CONCLUSION

Rural society in Punjab is in the process of fast rate of transition. It is showing a fast rate of structural change both in terms of income generation as well as in the employment pattern. Recently, there has been a large shift of population from agriculture both of the cultivators and agricultural labourers towards non-agricultural activities. In fact differentiation in the farming community is becoming very sharp between the capitalist farmers, pauperised farmers and agricultural labourers. The latter two categories are being crowded out of agriculture.

The concept of rural development has undergone change from being segment of the economy providing foodgrains, raw materials and surplus work force to modern sector/industrial sector towards rural transformation which subsumes the core ideas of rural development but goes beyond it. This includes well-being of rural people by enhancing their productive capabilities, expanding their choices in life and reversing policies which discriminate against the rural poor. This involves agrarian change and integrated development without marginalizing rural people and rural economy. The possibilities and opportunities in diversity and complexity of rural communities, sustainable livelihood and ecology are recognized for reshaping of development leading to well-being of rural people. This framework in India is being translated into the programmes for rural development.

Punjab economy has been very well integrated into Indian economy both through backward and forward linkages. The State has been following the overall Indian pattern of rural development through the process of planned development. But the State achieved a remarkable development in agriculture by becoming pioneer in initiating green revolution. The intensive cultivation based on exploitation of surface and ground water and using modern technology based on mechanized machinery and chemical inputs have created both positive and negative implications. On positive side it brought a lot of economic prosperity, high level of yield and production making the country self-sufficient in foodgrains. On the negative side it has brought a lot of differentiation and polarization in the rural areas to the extent of separate schools and health care for the rich and the poor. It has also led to distortion in the ecology especially depletion of the ground water resources, a non-sustainable cropping pattern, damage to soil productivity and pollution of ground water resources. It has also brought out severe distress for pauperised peasants and poor labourers who have been resorting to suicides. In the recent years this pattern of agriculture development has crowded out a large number of poor peasants out of the land lease market and also out of agriculture. From structural point of view it may seem positive development but from human angle it is bringing a lot of hardship for the workforce released out of agriculture which lacks education, skills and resources to participate in non-agriculture labour market where employment opportunities are very less. Many of them are facing downward mobility.

The examination of rural health and rural education provides very dismal picture. The rural health facilities have crumbled in the State due to apathy of the government which have been facing financial crisis for more than two and a half decades. The public funded rural schools are not performing and the rural rich are withdrawing their wards from such schools. A parallel structure of unaided private schools have come up for the rich. A class divide is visible in the rural education and rural health. The rural students are not reaching higher/university and technical education. The rural urban divide in income, education and health has widened at higher rate during the last two or three decades. The rural population is being left out bordering discrimination in the division of gains of economic and social development.

The rural power structure especially in the third tier of the government is in the grip of the landed rich class. They are using it to promote their own interests. They are not showing any keenness to implement poverty alleviation programmes mostly sponsored by the Union Government. This has made the task of rural transformation very difficult in the State.

In view of the emerging crisis in the State agriculture the government has been appointing committees to suggest measures to make agriculture remunerative, sustainable and integrated with the agro-processing industries. But as yet these recommendations have not been implemented for want of financial resources with the State government and lack of interest among the industrialists to promote agro processing industries in the State. The State government has been approaching the Union Government for the last one decade for special package without getting positive and concrete response. Consequently, the State which was a success story both in agriculture and rural development has been gone astray. The agriculture is facing stagnation and overall growth rate has slowed down. In order to overcome the stagnation in agricultural production and productivity, the State government must make a bold initiative to strengthen agricultural research and extension services. The breakthrough in agricultural productivity is possible only through introduction of new varieties of seeds of the crops which can give yield levels which are very high. As area under cultivation cannot be increased, the future of agriculture will depend on technological breakthrough. New technology can save the agriculture but in order to save the peasantry especially the poor (small and marginal) the present form of organisation of agriculture on individual ownership of agriculture machinery and cultivation of land with it or through custom hiring of machinery from the private owners, is making farming non-viable. There is urgent need to develop co-operative structure in the rural areas for joint ownership of machinery for cultivation by pooling of resources. At the same time the present method of marketing of produce of the individual farmer through commission agents is highly exploitative. The place of marketing co-operatives of farmers needs to be involved. The marketing co-operatives can provide the credit to the farmers both for productive and consumption needs. They can replace commission agents both for marketing and credit activities. At the same time, the co-operatives can be helped by the State government to involve in processing of agricultural produce and co-operative quality brands on the pattern of Verka or Markfed can be developed to generate massive employment both for farmers and other workers which are being released from the agriculture.

To achieve the transition from individual to co-operative forms of organisation, the State must make massive investment in improvement of quality of rural education. The quality of rural education must be raised to be at par with urban education. The success of measures of improvement in the rural education will be raising the share of rural students in university and technical education in proportion to its share in the total population which at present is above 60 per cent. In addition to raising quality of rural education, the quality of health services needs massive improvement. The schemes like NRHM, poverty alleviation programmes, social security measures like old age pension, widow pension and subsidized food to the weaker sections and above all serious implementation of MNREGA need attention of the State government. This would require change in the orientation and outlook of the political leadership in the rural areas, at State level and also change in the orientation of the State bureaucracy. At present the State is faltering in implementation of rural development not only because of shortage of financial resources but also because of its weak political commitments towards the needs of the rural poor. It is because of this the State government is not in the position to convert rural development into rural transformation in which ecologically sustainable, equitable and non-discriminatory progress takes place and choices of the people are widened for improvement in quality of life. Given the natural resources (land, water and quality of human material) there is lot of scope achieving rural transformation by involving the rural people provided the leadership in the State change its vision and commitments to the cause of the rural people especially the poor. The shift from individualized economic, social and political activities towards co-operatives can be extremely useful in correction of distortions in the process of rural development/transformation. This avoids the massive tragedy of rural suicides in Punjab. This would require visionary and committed leadership in politics and bureaucracy of the level, which Punjab experienced in 1950s.

NOTES

1. The following seven Departments have been transferred to the PRIs in Punjab:
   (a) Social Security, Women and Child Development;
   (b) Welfare of Scheduled Castes and Backward Classes;
   (c) Public Health;
   (d) Rural Development and Panchayati Raj Institution;
   (e) Health and Family Welfare;
   (f) School Education; and
   (g) Veterinary Services.
2. The share of SCs operational holdings in the total operational holdings in the State was 4.82 per cent in 1990-91 which has declined to 3.68 per cent in 2005-06. The average size of SC operational holdings was 1.76 hectares compared to average size of overall holdings of 3.8 hectares. In case of SCs operational holdings the average size has fallen to 1.6 hectares whereas it increased in case of overall holdings to 3.9 hectares. There are sharp decline in the SCs number of operational holdings from 54,000 in 1990-91 to 37,000 in 2005-06.
3. This is a pointer to Dera Sacha Sauda with headquarters at Sirsa (Haryana) and several branches in Southern Punjab. There has been many conflicts between the Dera followers and Akalis (Jat Sikhs) during 2008-10.

REFERENCES

Bhalla, G.S. (2007), *Condition of Indian Peasantry*, National Book Trust, New Delhi.

Bhalla, G.S. and Singh, Gurmail (2012), *Economic Liberalisation and Indian Agriculture: A District Level Study*, Sage Publications, New Delhi.

Brar, Jaswinder Singh (2008), "Public Expenditure on Education: As Evaluation", in A.S. Dhesi and Gurmail Singh (Eds.), *Rural Development in Punjab: A Success Story Going Astray*, Routledge, New Delhi.

Brar, Jaswinder Singh and Gill Sucha Singh (2001), "Tenancy Reversal and Operational Enclosures: A Study of Doaba Region" in Sucha Singh Gill (Ed.) *Land Reforms in India, Vol. 6: Intervention for Agrarian Capitalist Transformation in Punjab and Haryana*, Sage Publications, New Delhi.

Chadha, G.K. (1986), *The State and Rural Economic Transformation: Case of Punjab (1950-85)*, Sage Publications, New Delhi.

Chief Minister's Advisory Committee on Agriculture Policy and Restructuring, (Johl Committee II, 2002), *Agricultural Production Pattern Adjustment Programme in Punjab for Productivity Growth: A Report,* Submitted to the Government of Punjab, Chandigarh.

Committee for Formulation of Agriculture Policy for Punjab State (Kalkat Committee, 2013), *Agriculture Policy for Punjab,* Submitted to Government of Punjab, Chandigarh.

Expert Committee on Diversification of Agriculture in Punjab (Johl Committee I, 1986), *Report of the Expert Committee on Diversification of Agriculture in Punjab*, Submitted to Government of Punjab, Chandigarh.

FAO (2003), *Best Practices for Education and Training of Rural Youth: Lessons from Asia*, Bangkok.

Ghuman, Ranjit; Singh, Sukhwinder, Brar; Jaswinder Singh (2008), *Professional Education in Punjab: Exclusion of Rural Students*, Publication Bureau, Panjabi University, Patiala.

Ghuman, Ranjit Singh; Singh, Sukhwinder; Brar, Jaswinder Singh (2006), *Rural Students in Universities of Punjab*, Publication Bureau, Panjabi University, Patiala.

Gill, Manohar Singh (1993), *An Indian Success Story: Agriculture and Co-operatives*, Somaiya Publications, Bombay.

Gill, Sucha Singh (1989), "Changing Agrarian Relations and Implication for land Reforms", *Economic and Political Weekly*, Vol. 24, No. 25.

Gill, Sucha Singh (2001), Land Reforms in India, Vol. 6, *Intervention for Capitalist Transformation in Punjab and Haryana*, Sage Publications, New Delhi.

Gill, Sucha Singh (2011), "Punjab" in *Socio-Economic Profile of Rural India (Series II), Vol. 5, North and Central India*, (Ed.) Raj Mohini Sethi, Concept Publishing Compancy (P) Ltd., New Delhi.

Gill, Sucha Singh, Sukhwinder Singh and Jaswinder Singh Brar (2010), *Globalization and Indian State: Education, Health and Agriculture Extension Services in Punjab*, Aakar Books, Delhi.

Gill, Sucha Singh; Sukhwinder Singh and Jaswinder Singh Brar (2013), "Functioning of NREGA in a Prosperous State: A Study of Punjab", in K.P. Kannan and Jan Breman (Eds), *The Long Road to Social Security: Assessing the Implementation of National Social Security Initiatives for the Working Poor in India*, Oxford University Press, New Delhi.

Gill, Sucha Singh; Sukhwinder Singh and Jaswinder Singh Brar (2013), Social Security in Punjab: A Blend of State and Central Schemes, In K.P. Kannan and and Jan Breman (Eds), *Long Road to Social Security: Assessing the Implementation of National Social Security Initiatives for the Working Poor in India*, Oxford University Press, New Delhi.

Government of Punjab (1978), *Integrated Rural Development, Punjab*, Planning Department, Chandigarh.

Government of Punjab (1980), *Integrated Rural Development Programme*, Publication No. 544, The Economic Advisor to Government of Punjab, Chandigarh.

Jodhka, Surinder and Luis, Prakash (2003), "Caste Tensions in Punjab: Talhan and Beyond", *Economic and Political Weekly*, Vol. 38, No. 26.

Lewis, W.A. (1954), "Economic Development with Unlimited Supply of Labour", *Manchester School of Economic and Social Studies*, Vol. 22, pp. 139-91.

NSSO (2011), *Key Indicators of Employment and Unemployment in India 2009-10*, NSS 66th Round, Ministry of Statistical and Programme Implementation, GoI, New Delhi.

Poudyal, D.P. (2007), "An Overview of Rural Development in Asia", *Asia Pacific Journal of Rural Development*, Vol. 17, No. I.

Pratham (2013), *Annual Status of Education Reports 2012,* ASER Centre, New Delhi.

Puri, H.K. (2009), "The Scheduled Castes in the Sikh Community: A Historical Perspective", in Kira Hall (Eds.) *Studies in Inequality and Social Justice: Essays in Honour of Ved Prakash Vatuk*, Archana Publications, Meerut.

Ravillion, M., Shaohua, C. and Sangraula, P. (2007), "New Evidence on Urbanization of Global Poverty", *Population and Development Review*, Vol. 33, No. 4.

Singh Gurmail (2008), "Agricultural Modernization and Rural Transformation" in A.S. Dhesi and Gurmail Singh (Eds.), *Rural Development in Punjab: A Success Story Going Astray*, Routledge, New Delhi.

Singh, Sukhwinder and Sucha Singh Gill (2008) "Health Services in Punjab: A Rural Perspective", in A.S. Dhesi and Gurmail Singh (Eds.), *Rural Development in Punjab: A Success Story Going Astray,* Routledge, New Delhi.

Singh, Iqbal (1989), "Reverse Tenancy in Punjab Agriculture: Impact of Technological Change", *Economic and Political Weekly*, Vol. 24, No. 25.

Singh, Karam (209), "Agrarian Crisis in Punjab: High Indebtedness, Low Returns and Farmers Suicides", in D. Nirasimha Reddy and Srijit Mishra (Eds.), *Agrarian Crisis in India,* Oxford University Press, New Delhi.

Singh, Narinder Deep (2010), "Rural Health Care and Indebtedness in Punjab", *Economic and Political Weekly*, Vol XLV, No. 11, March 13.

Singh, R.P. and Grewal S.S. (2001), "Tenancy Pattern in Post-Green Revolution in Punjab" in Sucha Singh Gill (Ed.) *Land Reforms in India, Vol. 6: Intervention for Agrarian Capitalist Transformation in Punjab and Haryana*, Sage Publications, New Delhi.

Singh, Sukhpal, R.S. Sidhu, K. Simran, H.S. Kingra, and Sidhu, M.S. (2012), *Farmers, and Agricultural Labourers Suicides: A Study of Mansa, Sangrur, Barnal and Ludhiana*, Submitted to Government of Punjab, Chandigarh.

Tendulkar Committee (2009), *Report of the Expert Group to Review the Methodology for Estimation of Poverty*, Planning Commission, GOI, New Delhi.

UNESCO/INRULED (2012), *Education and Training for Rural Transformation: Skills, Jobs, Food and Green Future to Combat Poverty*, Beijing.

List of Unpublished Village Study Reports by IAS Trainees

1. Agarwal, Rajat (2003), *Socio-Economic Report,* Village Manga Roda, Kapurthala District.
2. Roojam, Verum (2004), *Village Study Report on Mishriwala*, Faridkot District.
3. Chauhan, Kavita (2004), *Village Study Report,* Village Shamaspur, Patiala District.

4. Singh, Arshdeep (2004), *Village Study Assignment*, Village Bakhopir, Sangrur District.
5. Garg, Basant (2005), *Village Study Assignment*, Village Kakkar, Amritsar District.
6. Sibin, C. (2005), *Socio-Economic Report*, Village Chakromwala, Ferozepur district.
7. Lakra, Diparwa (2005) *Village Study Report*, Village Anial, Gurdaspur District.
8. Abhinav (2006), *Village Study*, Village Bajechak, Gurdaspur District.
9. Dhaka, Amit (2006), *Socio-Economic Report*, Bir Behman, Bathinda District.
10. Agarwal, Pradeep (2006), *Village Study Report*, Village Ghasitpur, Hoshiarpur District.
11. Bhagat, Ravi (2006), *Village Study*, Village Warring, Mukatsar District.
12. Kashyap, Tanu (2006), *Village Study Assignment*, Village Khusroopur, Kapurthala, District.
13. Mitra, Anindita (2007), *Village Study Report,* Village Mugal Chak Kapurthala District.
14. Tayyab, Mohammad (2007), *Village Study Assignment*, Village Channu, Mukatsar District.
15. Thind, Parveen (2007), *Village Study Report: Land/Agriculture Report*, Village Burj Dalla, Bathinda District.
16. Goel, Khushboo (2008), *Village Report*, Village Naya Shahar Badala, SAS Nagar District.
17. Gulati, Supreet Singh (2008), *Village Study Assignment*, Village Chaminda, Ludhiana District.
18. Beda, Joram (2008), *Village Study Report: Land and Agriculture Report*, Village Nahiawala, Bathinda District.
19. Rupanjali (2008), *Village Study Report*, Village Bara Pind, Rupnagar District.
20. Kumar, Amit (2008), *Village Report*, Village Attari, Ferozepur District.
21. Ramvir (2009), *Assignment on Village Study*, Village Chakromwala, Ferozepur District.
22. Sharma, Varinder Kumar (2009), *Village Study Assignment*, village Charhewan, Mukatsar District.
23. Ujwal, Vipal (2009), *Village Study Report*, Village Chima, Ludhiana District.

3

Socio-Economic Profile of Rural J&K State

DR. BASHIR AHMAD DABLA

SECTION I

Introduction of the State

(i) Origin and Nature of the State

The State of Jammu & Kashmir was founded by the British rulers in the eighteenth century. The three regions of Jammu, Kashmir and Ladakh became a single political entity by the Treaty of Amritsar, signed by Maharaja Gulab Singh with the British government on March 16, 1846. J&K, being a native state governed by a local ruler, was allowed to retain the existing system of political control, economic and social arrangements, but was subject to the paramountcy of the British Crown. The State acceded to India in 1947 through Instrument of Accession Treaty signed by Maharaja Hari Singh and became an integral part of India.

The State occupies a strategic place on the country's map with its borders touching Pakistan, China and Afghanistan. The three distinct regions have their specific resource base. Except for Jammu and Kathua districts, the entire State is mountainous. The plateau of Ladakh, flanking the State on the east with lowest population density, is separated from rest of the State by high mountain ranges, which offers peculiar problems of development, communication and integration. In actuality, State with its varied and diversified geographic, agri-climatic and topographic feature and connectivity and other such features characterize development challenges.

The land of the State is highly fertile and water resources are in abundance. Rice, maize and wheat are the major cereals of J&K. The State stands as the largest producer of apples, walnut, almond and many other temperate dry and fresh fruits. It has also widespread occupational network of handicrafts. So, it stands as the major exporter of superior quality of carpets, wooden articles, embroidered clothes and many other valuable crafts. The State has a distinction in having maximum number of tourist sports and destinations and horticultural-floricultural activities.

(ii) Area, Population and Demography

The State of J&K, located between latitudes 32°15′ north and 37°5′ north longitude, 72°35′ east and 28°26′ east, has a geographical spread of 2,22,236 sq. km (including an area of 1,20,849 sq. km under the occupation of Pakistan and China) accounting for 7.02 per cent of the total area of India, making it the sixth largest State in the country. The forest area of the State is 20,230 sq. km which constituted 19.95 per cent of its geographical area.

According to the latest Census 20111, the State had the following total (male-female and rural-urban) population:

	Persons	*Males*	*Females*
Total	12548926	6665561	5883365
Rural	9134820	4809619	4325201
Urban	3414106	1855942	1558164

The population growth rate (2001-2011) was 23.71 (rural 19.77 and urban 35.66) and percentage of rural-urban population was 72.79 per cent (72.16% and 73.56%) and 27.21 per cent (27.84% and 26.48%). The density of population (persons per sq. km of area) was 124. The percentage of child population to total population was 16.01 (rural 17.47 and urban 12.08). The sex ratio (females per 1000 males) was 859 (rural 860 and urban 854). The sex ratio (females per 1000 males) was 883 (rural 899 and urban 840). The decadal percentage growth rate was 23.71. The population in previous decades was as under:

Census year	1981	1991	2001
Population	5987389	7837051	10143700

Source: Census of India.

Among the districts, Jammu stands at number 1 in terms of population and Leh is the least populated district. District Leh has the largest area of 45,100 sq. kms., while as Shopian is the smallest district having an area of 312 sq. km.

The State had combined birth rate (per million) in 2010 was 18.3 (rural 19.5 and urban 13.5) and death rate (per million) in 2010 was 5.7 (rural 5.9 and urban 4.7). The annual birth rate (per million) was 18.3 (rural 19.5 and urban 13.5 and death rate (per million) was 5.7 (rural 5.9 and urban 4.7) in 2010. The natural growth rate (per million) in the State in 2008 was 13.1 (rural 14.2 and urban 9.1) and 17.6 (rural 18.8 and urban 12.6) in 2009 and 12.6 (rural 13.6 and urban 8.8) in 2010. The infant mortality rate in 2010 was 43 (rural 45 and urban 32). The expectation of life at birth during 2006-10 was 65.0 years (male) and 67.0 years (female).

(iii) The Administrative Set-Up

For the purpose of administration, the J&K State has been divided in two divisions of Jammu & Kashmir. Ladakh forms a region of the Kashmir Division. There are three regions and 22 districts in the State as mentioned below:

Kashmir Region	Jammu Region	Ladakh Region
1. Kupwara	1. Poonch	1. Leh
2. Budgam	2. Rajouri	2. Kargil
3. Baramulla	3. Kathua	
4. Bandipora	4. Doda	
5. Srinagar	5. Ramban	
6. Ganderbal	6. Kishtwar	
7. Pulwama	7. Udhampur	
8. Shopian	8. Reasi	
9. Anantnag	9. Jammu	
10. Kulgam	10. Samba	

Source: Census of India.

The State has the following administrative units:

No. of Tehsils	82
No. of C.D. Blocks	142
No. of Towns	75
No. of Panchayats	4136
No. of Patwar Halqas	1720
No. of villages	6652
No. of inhabited villages	6417
No. of Legislative Assembly segments	87
No. of police stations	1477
No. of parliamentary constituencies	06

(iv) Scope of the Study

This chapter is meant to make a presentation of socio-economic profile of J&K State with focus on the rural situation. In this context, a particular thematic framework was devised which was (theoretically and methodologically) proper, relevant, and scientific. The information and data collected for this study was from authentic, primary and official, and non-official and secondary sources. The whole chapter is divided into four main sections as follows:

Section A: It dealt with origin, nature, establishment, of the J&K State with its area, population, demographic and administrative features. Moreover, the scope of this chapter and methodology was also explained.

Section B: It was devoted to the explanation of region-wise and district-wise socio-economic profile of the State.

Section C: This section presented specific socio-economic profile of rural J&K which was suggested by the sponsors. This profile was explained in terms of six following features:

(a) Rural Infrastructure,
(b) Agrarian Relations,
(c) Social Structure,
(d) Economic Activities,
(e) Anti-poverty/Rural Development Programmes, and
(f) Panchayati Raj System.

Section D: This section is composed of the case studies of eight particular villages in Jammu region of the State. The surveys of these villages was carried out by IAS officers during their probation, the written reports of which became the source of information for this chapter.

(v) Methodology

The universe of this study/chapter is the J&K State which has three regions of Jammu, Kashmir and Ladakh and 22 (10 + 10 + 2) districts. In addition, 8 villages of Jammu and Ladakh regions provided the base-level information.

The main sources of information/data were as follows:

- Official documents of J&K government;
- Reports of 8 particular villages in Jammu and Ladakh regions prepared by IAS officers; and
- Non-official documents like books, research papers, yearbooks and so on.

The method of content analysis and simple statistical methods were used in identifying features through deductive and inductive logic.

The variables and features of socio-economic profile of rural J&K were determined mainly by scientific, realistic and sociological criteria.

The degree of reliability of the official information and data was not questioned but was presented in rational order and logical arguments.

The conclusions were arrived at through main stages of scientific method.

SECTION II
REGION-WISE AND DISTRICT-WISE SOCIO-ECONOMIC PROFILE OF RURAL J&K STATE

As mentioned earlier, the J&K State is composed of three distinct regions of Jammu, Kashmir and Ladakh. The population of these regions in 2011 was as follows:

Region	*Total*	*Male*	*Female*	*% of Total*
Jammu	5350811	2844397	2506414	42.68
Kashmir	6907623	3647466	3260157	55.03
Ladakh	290492	173698	116794	02.31

Source: Census, 2011.

Here we present the socio-economic profile of these three regions.

1. The Jammu Region

The Jammu region has been referred in ancient religious documents such as *Mahabharata*. The remains and artifacts added new dimension to its ancient character. *Gulabnama* and *Raj Darshini* are two principal chronicles of Jammu. It is upheld that the city was founded by Raja Jambu Lochan, the fourteenth century BC ruler. In the twelfth century AD, Rajputs took refuge in the mountainous tracts of Jammu and carved out separate estates. Raja Ranjit Dev ruled over Jammu from 1733 to 1982 and consolidated the kingdom around 22 principalities. Maharaja Ranjit Singh annexed Jammu in his kingdom in 1808. But, the Mughal rulers did not allow the kingdom to maintain its independence.

The Jammu region is dominantly on one side, while Muslims are in majority on the other side. Among Hindus, there are Rajputs, Brahmins, Shudras, further divided among thousands of castes and sub-castes. The *Harijans* present in this region are in significant numbers and they have undergone a radical change and have also occupied some high and higher positions in the public and local administration. They are also included among the beneficiaries of the revolutionary land reforms implemented successfully in the State in 1950s. Many of them carry on the trades and occupations of their ancestors. Rajputs, Brahmins, Vaish, Muslims, Sikhs and Christians are found in all and diverse occupations.

The Jammu region adjoins Pakistan and Indian States of Punjab and Himachal Pradesh. It has both plain areas as well as mountainous regions, though these mountains are over 5,000 feet heights. In the *Kandi* or dry areas, water is very scarce and even availability of drinking water is a serious problem. Pir Panjal mountains divide two provinces of the State and begin from south-east at the Chinab river and ending on the north-west. Towards north, these ranges gradually attain greater heights extending up to 15,000 feet and rise like a wall to embrace the Kashmir valley from its southern end.

The Jammu region has broadly two types of climates. Plain areas of Jammu region, which are continuous with Punjab, have the tropical heat and share with it the periodical rainfall. Average annual rainfall of Jammu and Kathua districts is about 1,143 mm. Temperature in these districts in summer season is almost the same as that of Punjab, though in winter it may fall even up to 5 degrees. Other parts of Jammu region, which are comparatively on higher elevation, have a cooler climate. The climate zone can be classified as intermediate zone between the sub-tropical zone of Jammu and temperate zone of Kashmir valley. In this lie the districts of Doda, Udhampur, Poonch and Rajouri. High peaks and higher elevated areas of this zone experience snowfall during winter and the average annual rainfall is 1464-1708 mm, though in Rajouri district, it experiences lower than that level.

(a) The Doda District

The total population of Doda district (which includes the former tehsils and newly-formed districts of Kishtwar and Ramban) was as follows:

District	*1981*	*1991*	*2001*	*2011*
Doda (Ramban+Kishtwar)	425262	545527	691929	409576+283313+231037

Source: Census, 2011.

The district derived its name of one utensil maker, Duda, a migrant from Multan and settled permanently in this territory and set-up there a utensil factory. The entire area of this district was initially divided into two States of Kishtwar (now a district) and Bhadewah. The erstwhile Kishtwar State was divided into 11 parganas. The present district Doda consisted of all these areas including Allaqa Deng Battal.

The Doda district has 655 villages, 3 of these uninhabited and has been divided into four sub-divisions, viz., Doda, Ramban, Bhaderwah and Kishtwar. In 2001, it had seven tehsils as under:

Doda	Bhhaderwah	Banihal
Ghat	Gandoh	Kishtwar
Ramban.		

In the same year, the district had following 14 C.D. Blocks:

Aseer	Bhagwa	Bhaderwah
Banihal	Gandoh	Inderwal
Kishtwar	Marwah	Padder
Ramban	Ramsoo	Thathri
Warwan	Ghat.	

The Doda district stands as third largest in terms of area after Leh and Kargil lying in the outer Himalayan range in J&K. It falls between 32° 53′ and 34° 21′ north latitude and 75° 1′ and 766° 47′ east longitude. On its north is Anantnag district, while south-west and south are bordered by Udhampur and Kathua districts and Chamba area of Himachal Pradesh. On the east and south-east is Leh district.

The district is endowed with vast wealth of natural beauty and resources. The altitude varies from 8,000 to 15,000 feet. Owing to varying physical features, the climate is varied. While the areas like Bhaderwah, Banihal and Kishtwar have a temperate climate, the climate of areas like Ramban and Doda is sub-tropical. The average rainfall is 35 inches per annum that is lowest as compared to other districts of the division. The Chenab river flowing through the district is commercially very vital for the transportation of timber from forests and power generation. The district has good potential for tourism including pilgrim and adventure tourism to its scenic splendour and other tourist centres and lofty mountain peaks. Places of archeological importance in the district include fort at Bhaderwah, Bhanharkot fort in Kishtwar and Ghajpot Qila at Ramban.

(b) The Jammu District

This district had following population:

District	*1981*	*1991*	*2001*	*2011*
Jammu	943395	1231553	1588772	1526406
(+ Samba)				318611

Source: Census 2011.

Administratively, the district has been divided into five following tehsils:

Akhnoor	Bishnah	Jammu
Samba	R.S. Pura	

The popular legend says that Raja Jamboo Lochan founded the Jammu city in fourteenth century BC. During one of his huntings, he reached near Tawi where he saw a goat and a lion drinking water together at the same river. He decided to stay there and set up a town which was named after him. With the passage of time, the town came to be known as Jammu. This name also figured in *Mahabharata* and in the memories of Timor. It is also considered as a part of Harrapan civilization on the evidence near Akhnoor.

Jammu, known as the city of temples, had a number of principalities but the kingdom of Jammu always remained a leading place. Maldev and Ranjitdev were among the eminent rulers. At present, it stands as the winter capital of J&K State and has attracted many people from surrounding areas. It is located 74° 24' and 75° 18′ east longitude and 32° 50′ and 33° 30′ north latitude. It is surrounded by Udhampur district in the north and north-east, Kathua district in the east and south-east, Sialkot (Pakistan) in the west and POK (Pak occupied Kashmir) and Rajouri district in the north-west.

(c) The Kathua District

The Kathua district had the following population:

District	*1981*	*1991*	*2001*	*2011*
Kathua	369123	452739	550084	615711

Source: Census 2011.

The district has been divided into four tehsils which are:

Kathua	Hiranagar	Basohli
Billawar		

Administratively, the distrct has eight C.D. Blocks as under:

Kathua	Barnoti	Hiranagar
Gaghwal	Billawar	Basohli
Bani	Lohri Malhar	

The district comprises three distinct zones as under:

— *Border Zone*: It has areas falling south of Pathankot-Jammu National Highway in four Blocks of Kathua, Barmoti, Hiranagar and Gaghwal.

— *Kandi Zone*: It composes areas to the north of National Highway and up to the foothills in Billawar and Basohli Blocks.

— Hilly Zone: Further areas of Bani and Lohri Malhar Blocks and partly Basohli and Billawar Block areas.

The district has 586 villages, among which 32 are uninhabited, 183 Panchayats and equal number of Patwar Haqas. The six major towns of the district are as under:

Kathua	Basohli	Lakhanpur
Hiranagar	Billawar	Pasola

As the official records reveal, *there is mention of three* villages, namely, Taraf Tajwal, Taraf Manjali and Taraf Bhajwal. The conglomeration of these villages was called Kathai in folk language in earlier times. Later on, this name turned in to Kathua. Starbo described Katjhaioi as a mighty republic of the area located in the foothills along the river Ravi.

The Kathua town is also known as 'gateway of J&K' because it is situated in south-east of the State. It is surrounding by Chamba district of Himachal Pradesh on the east and by Shakergarh tehsil of Pakistan and Gurdaspur district of Punjab on the south. Ramnagar tehsil of Udhampur district and Bhaderwah of Doda district falls on its north, while Samba tehsil of Jammu district is on its north-west. On the south-west lies the international Indo-Pak border. It is located at 32° 17′–32° 55′ north latitude and 75° 32′–76° 16′ east longitude. The border areas are mostly irrigated and economic condition of people is better than that of people in Kandi and hilly areas.

Due to altitudinal variations, there is difference between the temperature of two plain tehsils of Kathua and Hiranagar and that of hilly tehsils of Basohli and Billawar. The temperature rises up to 48° in the plains and goes down below 1.5° in upper hilly areas. Most of these areas experience snowfall during winter and average rainfall ranges between 200 mm and 1200 mm. Two main rivers of the district are Ravi and Ujh, which are major contributors to the prestigious "Ravi-Tawi Irrigation Complex". Alum exists in Serai Nallah near Ramkot and Ujh river. Clay of various colours and varieties were also found at many places in the district.

(d) The Poonch District

The population of district Poonch was as follows:

District	*1981*	*1991*	*2001*	*2011*
Poonch	224197	290727	372613	476820

Source: Census 2011.

The district had three tehsil units as under:

Haweli	Mendhar	Surankot

It had five C.D. Blocks mentioned below:

Poonch	Mendhar	Mandi
Surankot	Haveli	

It has 178 villages of which 168 are inhabited, 115 Panchayats and one town. Poonch and Kashmir valley are separated by the gigantic Pir Panjal mountain range, whose highest peak Tatakuti (15,560 feet) fall in this district and is considered a virgin peak, throwing challenge to trekkers and mountaineers. There are several Alpine lakes, viz., Sukhsarr, Neelsar, Bhagsar, Kaldachinsar and Nansar, which all are surrounded by glaciers and snow-capped peaks. In winter, these lakes freeze. There are many tourist attraction spots and beautiful places which include Girjam, Panjtari, Isanwali, Nainsukh, Dharamarg, Pirmarg and Sarimaster.

(e) The Rajouri District

The district Rajouri had following population:

District	*1981*	*1991*	*2001*	*2011*
Rajouri	302500	384435	483284	619266 (124 density)

Source: Census 2011.

It is divided into six tehsils of:

Nowshera	Kotranka	Thanamandi
Budhal	Kalakot	Sunderbani

The district is composed of seven Blocks as under:

Rajouri	Budhal	Kalakote
Nowshera	Sunderbani	Manjakot
Darhal		

It has 381 villages and 160 Panchayats and the town is located at 154 km from Jammu.

Rajouri remained the area of importance in ancient times. In *Mahabharata*, there was a kingdom as Panchel Desa. It finds its mention in the travelogue of Hiuen Tsang who visited the town in the seventh century AD and described it as a part of Kashmiri dominion. During the Buddhist period, it formed a part of Gandhar territory and later was included in the dominion called Daarabhisanga. At the time of Alexander's invasion, Rajouri was at the height of its glory. It became a great trading centre in the Mauryan period. In the eleventh century, Rajouri was ruled by Chiefs of the Pala dynasty under the Suzerainty of Kashmir. Alboruni visited Rajouri in 1036 during Sultan Masud's reign and wrote about Raja Vari. The writer of *Rajatarangini* also referred to this area as Raja Vari. With the passage of time, the name changed from Rajaver to Rajpuri to Rajvara to Rajour to Rajouri. It emerged as main principality in the eleventh century and its first ruler was Raja Prithvi Paul.

Rajouri district is located between 74.3° east longitude and 33.38° north latitude. It is flanked by Poonch district in the north, Jammu district in the south, Udhampur district in the east and POK in the West. This district has an area of 2,639 sq. km. The Dhaula Dhar range across the north-eastern part of the district and topography of Rajouri, Budhal and part of Kalakote tehsils consists of numerous hills and small valley of meandering brooks. The tehsils of Sunderbani, Naushera and Kalakote mostly plain and Kandi lie in the south and hilly Budhal tehsil is in the north-east of the district.

The climate of the district varies from semi-tropical in the southern part comprising Naushera, Sunderbani and Kalakote to temperate in the mountainous northern part encompassing the areas of Rajouri, Budhal and Darhal Blocks. The sub-tropical region receives regular monsoon while as the northern part is prone to hailstorms experiences excessive rains. The average rainfall is 500 mm and average temperature varies from 7.4 to 37.4°C. The Sukh Taawi, the Khandli, the Ans and the Jamola are famous places in the district. The remnants of fortified Mughal inns at Nadhpur, Chingus, Rajouri, Fatehpur and Thanamandi are a pleasant reflection of the past glorious days of the place when it was used to be a camping site for the Mughal entourage towards Kashmir valley. But it also recasts a negative picture of the dark days of the partition in 1947.

(f) The Udhampur District

The population of district Udhampur was as under:

District	*1981*	*1991*	*2001*	*2014*
Udhampur [Reasi]	453636	584051	743509	555357 +314714

Source: Census 2011.

The district has five tehsils as under:

Ramnagar	Udhampur	Reasi
Goll Gulah Garh	Chenani	

It has 12 C.D. Blocks as mentioned below:

Udhampur	Ramnagar	Chinani
Majalta	Arnas	Pancharri
Mahore	Gooll	Duda-Basantgarh
Ghordi	Reasi	Ponrie

The district has six main towns as follows:

Udhampur	Ramnagar	Rehenble
Reasi	Chinani	Reasi

It has 624 villages including 6 uninhabited and 215 Panchayats.

Udhampur is the fifth largest district of J&K and is situated in the southern part of the State bounded by Rajouri district in the north, Anantnag in the north-east, Doda in south-east and Jammu in the south-west. It has been named after Raja Udham Singh, eldest son of Maharaja Gulab Singh. The town was built in place of the total provisional area to which Singh went on hunting trips till he developed love for the spot and chose it as the site for township.

The district lies between 72°-34′ to 39°-30′ north latitude and 74°-16′ to 75°-38′ east longitude. It has an area of 4550 sq. km which accounts for 2.05 per cent of the total provisional area of the State. It is situated 66 km from Jammu on Srinagar-Jammu national highway. Due to altitudinal variation from 600 to 3,000 metres, there is wide variation in temperature in the district. The temperature rises as high as 42°C and very seldom goes below 15° in low altitude areas. Most of the rainfall takes place during July-September in summer and January-February in winter.

It stands rich in minerals like coal, bauxite, magnesite, gypsum, limestone, etc. Coal and bauxite deposits occur in Jangalgali and Sukhalgali and magnesite deposits are located in Katra-Panthal area. Gulabgarh area is rich in gypsum. Palaeozi clay is found in Thakkursui, and Tikri. Though Udhampur is drained by major rivers Chenab, Ans, and Ujh yet due to mountainous and undulating topography, much utilization of water is not possible. The district is mainly drought prone and only small area has been brought under irrigation. The famous Mansar lake lies in the south-east of the district. It provides drinking water and also stands as beautiful tourist spot.

2. The Kashmir Province

The history of Kashmir can be traced to ancient times as per *Rajatarangini* and *Nilmat Purana*. Ashoka, the great Buddhist monarch, annexed Kashmir to his kingdom in about 250 BC. Among other reforms, he introduced improved versions of agriculture, especially saffron. Kashmir presents a unique homogeneity of population with two broad divisions of Muslims and Pandits who live together in the same folk cultural, social and economic situation for centuries. It was only due to exogenous factors that Kashmir Pandits (KPs) made mass migration to places outside Kashmir. According to a legend, Kashmir valley was a vast lake and Kashyapa Rishi drained this water out making it worth living. According to archaeological research, earliest inhabitants of the valley came here in about 2000 BC and subsequently tremendous progress was made till the regime of Avantivarman (855-883 AD). In the entire history of Kashmir, King Zain-ul-Abidin (1417-1469 AD) was the towering figure who proved most popular and most illustrious ruler. During his time, basic efforts were made for rural development, canals, bridges, irrigation, handicrafts and so on. More important, he strengthened and legitimized the composite character (unique synthesization between Hindu and Islamic cultures in folk tradition) and its absolute tolerance.

The Kashmir province is generally mountainous and varies in height from 5,200 to 10,000 feet. The average height of the valley above sea level is about 6,000 feet and is 84 miles in length and 20-25 miles in breadth approximately. The Jhelum, the Sindh and the Lidder are three main rivers of the province. There are number of large and beautiful lakes like Dal and Wullar lakes. While Dal stands one of the most beautiful lakes in the world, Wullar is the largest fresh water lake in Asia. Due to its scenic beauty and tourist resorts, tourists from all over world are attracted to this part of the State. The valley remains free from the extremes of heat. However, it has temperate salubrious climate. The temperature ranges between 31°C during summer and minus 3-7°C during winter, though sometimes temperature falls to minus 10-12°C. The whole valley, especially the mountainous hilly areas, experience heavy snowfall making the people's life more hectic and difficult as there is acute shortage of electricity and shortage of daily-use items. The Kashmir winter is considered severely very cold, spring is pleasantly cold, summers are not so warm and autumn is entertaining cool and sometimes wet. Rains in this part of the State are expected during the months of March-April. Average rainfall ranges between 732 to 854 mm.

The Kashmir province has the following 6 (and now 10) districts:

(a) The Anantnag District

The population of the district was as follows:

District	*1981*	*1991*	*2001*	*2011*
Anantnag	656351	883043	1172434	1069749
[Kulgam]				423181

Source: Census 2011.

The district has five tehsils as follows:

Pahalgam	Anantnag	Doru
Kulgam	Bijbihara	

It had 10 C.D. Blocks as under:

Sahab	Achabal	Kulgam
Shangus	Damhal Hanjipora	Qaimoh
Brehg	Qazigund	Khoverpora
Dachnipora		

District Anantnag has 8 towns, 645 villages and 309 Panchayats.

The Anantnag district has inherited its name from the name of spring or ananth (countless springs) situated in the south of town. This name has been mentioned in *Nilmat Purana* as a sacred place for the Hindus. This town also got prominence during the medieval period when it was named as Islamabad by the Mughal rulers. However, the Dogra rulers revived the old name as Anantnag. The majestic Martand temples in the district stand as important archeological sites of the entire country. Its impressive architecture reflects the glorious past of the area. These temples also convey the glory of Kashmir's old civilization.

The area of Anantnag is spread over 3,934 sq. km and is situated at about 55 km. In the south-east of Srinagar, it is bounded by Srinagar district in the north, Pulwama in the north-west and Kargil district in the north-east. It is flanked by Doda and Udhampur districts in the east and south-east respectively and by Rajouri district in the south-west.

Anantnag has enjoyed the status of the second largest city of the valley after Srinagar. The travellers who visited the town during the eighteenth and nineteenth century found it with glory. However, during Dogra period, it was made a part of the Srinagar district.

(b) The Budgam District

The Budgam district had the following population in the past:

District	*1981*	*1991*	*2001*	*2011*
Budgam	367262	483698	629309	755331

Source: Census 2011.

The district has three tehsils of Budgam, Chdoora and Beerwah and has 496 villages. It is surrounded by three districts of Srinagar, Baramulla and Pulwama. The total geographical area of the district is 1371 sq. km of which 482 sq. km are under forests. There are 8 C.D. Blocks as follows:

Budgam	B. K. Pora	Beerawah
Khag	Chadoora	Khemouch
Nagam	Narbal	

There are 19 Panchayats in the district. Since significant part of this district is urban or suburban, there are more than 15 notified area committees at present.

Earlier this district was known by the names of Sri Pratap and Pargana Deesu. It has a long history. According to a chronicle, the present town of Budgam was known as Deedmarbag and it was densely populated. Some people believe that the name of Budgam is related to this dense population of the town (because Budgam means 'big village' in Kashmiri). Famous Chinese traveller, Hiuen-Tsang, passed through this town while going to Poonch town.

The most popular folk-cultural Kashmiri personality, Sheikh Nooruddin Noorani (popularly known as Nundu Resh and Alamdare Kashmir—the flag-bearer of Kashmir) has travelled, meditated and stayed most in the places in present Budgam district. His resting place where he was buried is also situated in the same district. The present district was extracted from District Srinagar and came into existence in 1979-80. This bifurcation was in tune with the efforts of the State government to make to corner/areas in the State the fruits of speedy development. Consequently, this new district, alongwith Kupwara and Pulwama, was elevated to the status of district. After the re-organization, the Budgam district became a hub of horticulture activities and place of pilgrim tourism.

Budgam district has both mountainous and plain geographical areas. The south and south-western parts are mostly hilly whereas eastern and northern parts are plain. The climate in the entire district remains temperate. The average rainfall in the district has been 588 mm. The winter experiences extreme snowfall during the months of December-February.

(c) The Baramulla District

The district Baramulla had the population as follows:

District	*1981*	*1991*	*2001*	*2011*
Baramulla [Bandipora]	670142	891044	11699780	1015503 [385099]

Source: Census 2011.

It had 8 tehsils whose names are as under:

Bandipora	Sonawari	Sopore
Baramulla	Gulmarg	Uri
Gurez	Pattan	

The district has 14 C.D. Blocks as mentioned below:

Gurez	Boniyar	Baramulla
Rohama	Uri	Rafiabad

Sopore	Zaingir	Pattan
Wagoora	Singhpora	Kunzar
Tangmarg		

The district has 660 villages and 276 Panchayats. It occupies the geographical area of 4,588 sq. km.

The district was known as the gateway of Kashmir valley. This route attracted several kings and queens, travellers and trekkers, and preachers and raiders and they left some signs of their stay on this road. In fact, of history of Baramulla dates back to the time when the entire Kashmir valley was a vast lake known as Satisar. Its oldest name Varamul finds its mention in a legend, according to which, thousands of years back, there lived a gang of demons and their chief was one Jaldev. These demons used to cause a lot of destruction and harass the common people. After some time, a saint Kashyapa, who was considered the great grandson of Lord Brahma, visited this place and saw all this misery here. Due to prayers and penance, Lord Shiva, Vishnu and Shiva came to his help. All of them with Indra fought these demons and got success over them. They were also in search of *Jalodbhava*, who alongwith his companions had taken refuge under the depth of water. As per this legend, Lord Shiva chased demons for thousands of years in the depth of water and finally killed them. After this, he cut the mountain by his tail, giving way to the water to exit. Thus water of the lake was drained and the Kashmir valley became worth inhabitance.

Kalhana recorded in *Rajatarangani* that in memory of *Varaha Avtara*—Lord Vishnu, the first *teeratha* of Kashmir valley was built near the place where the mountain was cut and place was named Varahamulla. According to another version, since the river Jehlum flows down after getting a bend at this place, i.e., why it has been named as Varamulla, *var* means a bend and *mull* means a place in Kashmiri. The popular view is also that the water of Satisar lake was drained off by a volcanic eruption at 12 places in the close vicinity of Baramulla. The place was thus named as Baramulla meaning 12 bores.

The city of Baramulla, founded by Raja Bhimsina in 2306 B.C., has a hoary past. There was a watch station known as Drang (presently known as Drangabal village) where there used to be strong guard. The visitors were received at this station. Raja Darlabdurana received the famous Chinese visitor Hieun Tsang here in 631 A.D. This watch station existed up to the nineteenth century. The English historian, Moorecraft, visited this station in 1823.

During the Buddhist period, Baramulla was at the top of glory and was described as the most prosperous trading centre of Kashmir. The Mughal kings and queens had a particular fascination for this area and they have left several material signs like buildings and gardens on this famous route. It has also religious importance because several Hindu *teeraths*, Buddhist *vihars*, Sikh *gurudwaras* and Muslim shrines and mosques made this district more sacred for all religious communities in the State. It was in the context of this communal harmony that the area resisted the tribal raiders in 1947.

Baramulla district has also been named as 'Panipat of Kashmir'. It is because the residents of this place have becomc the victims of internal and external invasions from medieval times up to 1947. In a way, it was a regular battlefield for the kings of Kashmir and later amongst the princes who fought among themseives. The internal disturbances affected the trade of the town and retarded the economic status of the people.

(d) Kupwara District

The Kupwara district had the population as follows:

District	*1981*	*1991*	*2001*	*2011*
Kupwara	328743	465948	650393	875564

Source: Census 2011.

The district has three tehsils as follows:

Kupwara	Handwara	Karnah

It has 10 C.D. Blocks as mentioned below:

Sogam	Vavoora	Kalsaroos
Kupwara	Trehgam	Rajwara
Langate	Ramhal	Kralpora
Tangdar	Teetwal	

The district is comprised of 369 villages, out of which 4 are uninhabited. There are 115 patwari halqas, 23 girdawari circles, 17 niabats, and 224 Panchayats. Handwara tehsil is the largest having 183 villages and 3 C.D. Blocks followed by Kupwara tehsil with 137 villages and 4 C.D. Blocks. The Karnah tehsil has only 49 villages and one C.D. Block. There are two Notified Area Committees for Kupwara and Handwara towns and has five Legislative constituencies as follows:

Karnah	Trehgam	Kupwara
Handwara	Langate.	

The district Kupwara created in 1979 has the geographical area of 2,379 sq. km and is flanked in the east and south by Baramulla district and in the west and north by LOC (Line of Control). It is located about 90 km from Srinagar in the north-west corner of Kashmir valley. It is situated at an altitude of 5,300 feet above sea level with varied topography. The western, northern, and eastern areas of the district are plains. A Himalayan spur goes down from Zozila to west separating the Kishanganga valley from the main Kashmir valley. The main Srinagar-Gilgit route near a high pass called Rajdahani pass, joining Gurez valley with Bandipora, crosses the spur. This southern extension is known as Kazinag range, the home of Markhore goat. The Zozila-Kazinag spur is crossed by some famous passes like Tatmar Gali, Nastachun Gali, Farkyan Gali and Jar Gali connecting Leepa Valley POK (Pakistan Occupied Kashmir), Karnah, Keran, Machil areas with Kupwara.

Kishanganga is the main river in the district, originating from Himalayan range that flows through outer north-west areas from east to west. It passes through Keran-Teetwal and finally joins the Jhelum at Domel. There are other streams also flowing in the district. Famous among these are Kahmal Nallah (Chowkibal), Batamaji Nallah (Karnah), Mawar Nallah (Mawar), and Lolab Nallah (Lolab town). All these streams finally merge with Porhi Nallah, which in turn joins river Jhelum at Doabgah, Sore in Baramulla district.

The hilly areas of Karnah, Keran and Machil are situated on the LOC. These areas generally remain cut off from rest of the district during winter for about 4-5 months. Some other areas like Bodnambal, Jumagand, Kumkari and Lashdutt fall in the hilly belt of the district.

The climate of the district is pleasant in spring, moderate in summer and coldest in winter. During summer, mercury goes up to 27°C and in the winter it falls down to –6°C. However, Karnah experiences moderate climate during winter and is little hot during summer months. Lashdutt also falls in the same category. The average rainfall in the district is 100 centimetres.

(e) The Pulwama District

The Pulwama district had the population as mentioned below:

District	*1981*	*1991*	*2001*	*2011*
Pulwama [Shopian]	404078	516350	652607	570060 [265960]

Source: Census 2011.

The Pulwama district had four tehsils as follows:

Pulwama	Shopian	Tral
Pampore		

It had six C.D. Blocks a s mentioned below:

Pulwama	Pampore	Shopian
Tral	Awantipora	Khrew.

The district has the geographical area of 1,398 sq. km of which 729 sq. km area is covered by forests. It has 561 villages, out of which three are uninhabited. While 219 fall in Pulwama tehsil, 29 are Pampore, 82 in Tral and 124 in Shopian. It is situated 32 km from Srinagar and lies in south of Kashmir. It is surrounded by Srinagar in the north, Poonch and Budgam in the west and Anantnag in the south-east.

The original name of Pulwama was Punwangam which included four local areas of Dulipora, Chatpora, Dangerpora and Malikpora. These areas and their names still survive. The district has a rich cultural historical background with legendary people having born and brought up in the area. Some ancient kings have chosen this area as their capital city. The ninth century ruler, Awanti Verma, founded Awantipora as his kingdom's capital. The remains of this city are still located in the preserved form in the Awantipore area, which is 25 km away from Srinagar on the Srinagar-Jammu National Highway. Archaeological monuments and ruins in the preserved form at Awantipora, Jawbrari, Kakapora, Norastan and other places signify the rich history of this district. Awantiverman (who ruled Kashmir from 854-883 A.D.) was a great patron of art and culture. Besides Awanti Swami temple, he built another great temple at Jawbrari. These temples were surrounded by artificial lakes, which added to their beauty. His son too continued with this capital town and also extended areas of kingdom. His army consisted of the local people.

(f) The Srinagar District

The district Srinagar had the population in recent decades as follows:

District	*1981*	*1991*	*2001*	*2011*
Srinagar [Ganderbal]	708328	928526	1202447	1250173 [297003]

Source: Census 2011.

This district has three tehsils as follows:

Srinagar Khas Ganderbal Kangan

It has four C.D. Blocks ass mentioned below:

Srinagar

The five other districts surround this district. It is flanked by Kargil in the north, Pulwama in the south, and Budgam in the west. The capital city of Srinagar is located 1,730 metres above sea level. It has an area of 2,228 sq. km and has 175 villages.

The history of Srinagar is, in fact, the history of Kashmir. It has always retained the capital city character. It has been at the centre of all economic, political, cultural, social and other developments in Kashmir. This city has a chequered history which dates back to 600 B.C. when Emperor Ashoka built this capital city. This city was at the site of Pandrethan, 5 km away from Srinagar at present and named it Srinagari. Hieun Tsang defines the boundaries of Pandrethan extent along Zabarwan hills from Harwan to Zewan or Sempur. King Ashoka brought Buddhism to Kashmir and was strengthened by Kanishka. In the sixth century A.D., Huns came to rule Kashmir. Though the areas under Kashmir attained freedom but it was short lived.

The city of Srinagar was also known by many other names such as Praverpora and Praversenpur. It has retained the status of seat of power ever since, with different kings shifting their capital from one portion of the capital territory to the other. In the sixth century A.D., Raja Praversena founded a new city at the present site near Hariparbhat hill which came to be known as Praverpora. After various developments through centuries, the old name was revived as Srinagar.

Travellers and chroniclers have praised the beauty and grandeur of Srinagar. Kalhana in the eleventh century gave a glowing picture of the beauties of this city. It was not only the principal city of Kashmir, but also excelled in beauty over all other cities in the surrounding kingdoms. Under the Mughal rule, Srinagar was a splendid city of the standard of time. According to Abul Fazl, Srinagar is a great city and has long been peopled.

3. The Ladakh Region

Ladakh is situated on the eastern mountain range of Kashmir. This is one of the highest mountain ranges throughout the world. Ladakh is the land of ancient Buddha, and now the followers of Dalai Lama. They are believed to be descendants of a blended race of the Mons of north India, the Dards of Baltistan and the Mongols of Central Asia. Ladakhis are divided into four principal castes which are as follows:

- (i) Gyalpo or Raja,
- (ii) Jinak or officials,
- (iii) Mungrik or cultivators, and
- (iv) Rugan or menials.

The Ladakh region covers an area of 1,17,000 sq. km and is subjected to intense difficult weather conditions. It is cold desert under rain shadow, receiving very little precipitation, temperature remains below freezing point during most of the year due to its high altitude. This area is situated at heights varying from 7,000 to 15,000 feet and due to unique topography and mountainous nature, the cultivating area is very limited. Only one crop a year is possible and that too on irrigated land. The two main occupations of the people here are agriculture and animal husbandry. The river Indus and its tributaries flow in the region.

With mending ranges of rocks, Ladakh region has become a world known spot of rock beauty. Accordingly, the tourist traffic to Ladakh has increased considerably in the recent decades. This region falls in the arid zone. It has warm summers but because of arctic cold conditions, the temperature may fall even up to minus 23°C. The average rainfall of this region is about 97.6 mm.

This region has two districts. Its total population was 65,992 (1981), 89,334 (1991), and 1,19,307 (2001). The district-wise population was as follows:

(a) The Leh District

The Leh district has the following population:

District	*1981*	*1991*	*2001*	*2011*
Leh	68380	90076	117232	147104

Source: Census 2011.

The district has one tehsil only and 9 following C.D. Blocks:

Leh	Chwhot	Khalsati
Saspol	Nyoma	Dushbak
Kharu	Panuime	Deskit

On the other hand, the Kargil district has the population as mentioned below:

District	*1981*	*1991*	*2001*	*2011*
Kargil	57675	78052	107138	143388

Source: Census 2011.

This district has two tehsils of Kargil and Zanaskar. It has also 9 C.D. Blocks as under:

Kargil	G.M. Pora	Sankoo
Shaker	Chaktan	Shergol
Taippuru	Zanaskar	Lungnak

The Ladakh region about 3,000 years back was perhaps a wilderness surrounded by Tibet, Gilgit, Turkistan and Pamir and areas of present Himachal Pradesh. With the increasing population and shrinking cultural land and pastures in these countries, some people drifted to Tibet and uninhabited areas of Zanaskar, Puric and Baltistan. Some of them advanced to Ladakh proper and settled down there. The ancient inhabitants of Ladakh were Dards. But, immigration from Tibet largely overwhelmed the culture of Dards and moped up their racial characters. In northern and central Ladakh, today's population seems to be mostly of Tibetan origin. Buddhism reached Tibet from India *via* Ladakh where the area was stronghold of this religion before the arrival of Islam. Missionaries carried out a peaceful conversion to Islam in the early sixteenth century whose success was guaranteed by the conversion of sub-rulers of Drass, Kargil and Suru valley. Today Muslims constitute over 20 per cent of the population of Leh district.

Caravans carrying textiles spices, raw milk, carpets, dyestuffs and narcotics traversed the rugged terrain for centuries. This route was considered as the best trade route between Punjab and Central Asia. On this long route, Leh was the halfway destination and developed into a bustling entry point with merchants from all countries thronging its bazaars. The famous Pashmina also came from the western Tibet where it was carried *via* Leh to Srinagar for its end product like world famous Pashmina shawl. It was this lucrative trade that attracted Maharaja Gulab Singh to invade Ladakh and Baltistan and were incorporated by him in the newly created State of J&K.

In the post-1947 preriod, Pakistan and China occupied 78,114 sq. km and 37,555 sq. km of land respectively, while the remaining part of the State was acceded to India. Later on, Pakistan gifted 5,180 sq. km area to China. In 1979, the Ladakh district was divided in two districts of Leh and Kargil. Ladakh is situated between 30° to 36° east latitude and 76° to 79° north longitude. The area of this region is 96,701 sq. km. It remains normally land locked between November to April because of heavy snowfall. Ladakh-Srinagar and

Ladakh-Manali highways remain closed during this winter season. Ladakh is also known as the land of lakes and springs, famous among these are sulphur springs of Nobra, Chumathang and Puga springs and mineral springs in remote areas. People of the region use these varieties of water as medicine to cure themselves from many diseases.

SECTION III
SOCIO-ECONOMIC PROFILE OF RURAL JAMMU & KASHMIR

1. Rural Economic Sectors

The major sectors/fields of economy in rural areas of J&K State and their assessment are follows:

(i) Agriculture

Agriculture sector has a vital place in the overall economy of the State, despite its consistent decline in its contribution. With a natural agriculture resource base, out of quantum of 11,33,935 hectares gross area sown, only 4,63,179 hectares (40.85%) are irrigated during the year 2007-08. The net area sown is 7,34,003 hectares, out of which 3,08,044 hectares (41.97%) are irrigated. The average holding size is 0.67 hectare as per agriculture census of 2000-01. The production eked out of agricultural land is 16,508 thousand quintals which include 15,707 thousand quintals of foodgrains and 80 thousand quintals of diversified crops like oilseeds, spices and vegetables for the year 2007-08. The fourth advance estimates put the foodgrains production in the State to be 16,275 thousand quintals for the year 2008-09, recording an increase of 3.62 per cent over the previous year.

J&K has basically an agrarian economy. The dependence of rural labour force on agriculture and allied activities is substantial as it directly or indirectly supports about 70 per cent of population. As per Census 2001, 18.38 lakh persons (cultivators and agricultural labourers) depend on agriculture for their livelihood forming about 49 per cent of the total working force. However, despite concerted efforts for amelioration of agricultural sector, the State had to import 7.50 lakh tonnes of foodgrains during 2007-08 for supplementing the domestic demand.

In order to transform the socio-economic status of farming community, the State has won the distinction of having introduced reform legislation of considerable magnitude by articulation of land reforms through vesting ownership rights of the State land to the farmers. There is second major agrarian reform which has an exception of non-payment of compensation for acquisition of surplus land with the condition that the beneficiers under the scheme shall stylize the land for *bona fide* purposes underlying the Act popular as Roshni Act. The response has inbuilt spirit of inclusive growth of agriculture sector aimed at increasing the production and productivity on the one hand and removal of poverty, employment generation and self-reliance on the other hand.

Agriculture has a significant contribution in the export of rare agriculture produce like saffron, honey and basmati rice from the State and remain an important source of raw material demanded by many industries. The agriculture and allied sectors have contributed to the State economy 27 per cent of the Gross State Domestic Product (GSDD) in 2007-08. The individual share of agriculture has been estimated to the range of 8-9 per cent in 2007-08.

As per the land-use statistics in 2007-08, the total reporting area of the State is 24.16 lakh hectares which is distributed in the following way:

Net area sown	—	30.38%
Under forests	—	27.23%
Land put to non-agriculture uses	—	12.12%
Under barren and uncultivable land	—	11.98%
Other categories, i.e., land under tree crops and groves.	—	18.29%

The total cropped area in 2007-08 was 11.34 lakh hectares. Out of net sown area of 7.34 lakh hectares, 4.00 lakh hectares is the area sown more than once determining the extent of double cropping to be 54.50 per cent for 2007-08.

The cropping intensity, i.e., the percentage of gross cropped area to net area sown for the year 2007-08 stands at 154.49 per cent which is higher than national level cropping intensity of 135.88 per cent during 2005-06.

The 2001 Census recorded 14,42,984 landholdings, the corresponding figure in 1995-96 Census was 13,35,779, showing the increase of 1,07,115 holdings. The holding size of an average in the State was 0.76 hectares in 1995-96 in comparison to 0.67 in 2000-01. Thus, there was the decline of 0.09 hectares in the size of average landholdings. The agriculture insurance has been decentralized from district to tehsil level from *kharif* 2007 for rice, maize and potatoes.

The annual average growth rate was worked out at 1.79 per cent in 2007-08 in the agriculture and allied sectors from the previous year. The State government spent an amount of Rs. 288.70 crore of its annual plan outlay for 2009-10 in agriculture and allied sectors.

The banks have issued 65,350 Kisan Credit Cards in the State till March 2007. The production of honey in the State was reported as 443 tonnes in 2008-09. The mushroom production reached to 6,156 quintals in 2008-09. Saffron, mostly cultivated in Pulwama, Budgam, and Kishtwar-Doda districts was cultivated in 3,110 hectares and production was 5,000 quintals in 2008-09.

(ii) Horticulture

J&K is well known for its horticulture products, particularly variety of temperate fruits like apples, pears, peacles, plum, apricot, almonds, cherry and sub-tropical fruits like saffron and zeera. Nearly all these products fall in the rural sector. Its contribution to the State's economy was estimated as 7-8 per cent. Almost 45 per cent economic returns in agriculture sector is accounted for by horticulture produce. About 5 lakh families in the entire State are involved in horticulture production and trade. In the year 2008-09, it was reported 3.06 lakh hectares of land was under horticulture.

The production of fruits was reported as 16.91 lakh tonnes in 2008-09. Out of this, 90.53 per cent constituted fresh fruits and 9.47 per cent were dry fruits. Among the fresh fruits, apples and walnuts were of 78.82 per cent and 8.73 per cent respectively.

A careful assessment reveals that 46 per cent of the fruit production is exported from the State. However, the export has remained stagnant in previous few years. While the highest quantity of 8.70 lakh metric tonnes of fruits were exported in 2005-06, this export increased to 11.17 lakh tonnes in 2008-09, out of which 11.01 lakh tonnes were fresh fruits. Dry fruits are generally to foreign countries and fetch a good amount of foreign exchange for the country. In the year 2007-08, the export of dry fruits (almond and walnut) was 6,889.11 metric tonnes (197.11 metric tonnes almond and 6,692 metric tonnes walnut) and foreign exchange earnings increased up to 34.71 per cent.

The horticulture growers face numerous problems and, among other formal and informal actions, 261 fruit-growers co-operative societies with 19,194 individual members have been established and several fruit and vegetable *mandis* were developed. At present, three main fruit and vegetable markets have been operating at Nowpora, Sopore, Parimpora-Srinagar and Narwal-Jammu.

(iii) Floriculture

Various floriculture nurseries have been developed in J&K State because of its growing demand in domestic and foreign markets. The Directorate of Floriculture has produced more than 40 lakh seedlings of different kinds of flowers and ornamental plants not only for its own requirement but also sells in the inside and outside markets in cash terms. On an average, it earns rupees 8 lakh on this account annually.

The landmark achievement in J&K floriculture was the establishment of Tulip Garden, first of its kind in Kashmir. It is situated on the foothills of mighty Zabarwan mountains. This garden has the distinction of being considered as the largest Tulip Garden in Asia and stands next only to Tulip Gardens in Canada in the world. This garden remains in full bloom for more than a month during March-April. In the recent years, it witnessed highest inflow and visit of tourists and attracted many film makers and producers for shooting songs, etc., in the background of this most beautiful garden. In this way, this garden has emerged as a permanent source of income for the Directorate of Floriculture. It has also given rise to some local private initiatives in this unconventional sector with the financial support of the State government.

(iv) Livestock and Poultry

As the sub-sector of agriculture, livestock makes deep inroads in the rural economy in the J&K State and provides gainful employment to marginal and small and landless farmers. It is considered as the booming eco-friendly sector and so, besides covering domestic biodiversity, it is a means of producing food in dry lands without depleting ground water resources. This sub-sector contributes about 11 per cent to the State economy.

There were 98.993 lakh livestock in the stock in 2003 which makes their density 98 animals per sq. km of area. There were 926 animals per 1000 population in J&K and average livestock was 6 animals for 44 in the year 2001. An integrated sample survey (ISS) in 2007-08 gave the following figures of livestock in the State:

Number of cattle	—	29.416 lakhs
Number of buffaloes	—	6.192 lakhs
Number of sheep	—	37,380 lakhs
Number of goats	—	13.559 lakhs

This survey also revealed the number of 61.36 lakh poultry birds with 55.66 lakh fowls and 5.70 lakh ducks. The production of milk for that year was estimated at 1515.29 thousand metric tonnes and net production was 275.42 lakh kilograms. This survey also recorded wool and egg production as 70.83 lakh kg and 6667.74 lakh numbers respectively. In this way, the per capita meat and egg production was 2260 grams and 55 eggs per annum. Similarly, per capita milk production was 341 grams per day.

The livestock sector stands as a fast growing sector in the State. In order to promote and develop this sector on large scale, various centrally-sponsored schemes are in operation in the State to achieve the following objectives:

- Genetic improvement of the livestock;
- to introduce hi-tech commercial poultry development;
- adequate health cover to the livestock on priority basis;
- to provide in all districts various para-veterinary services in about 1,400 centres in the entire State during the period of five years; and
- introduction of Dorpor so as to receive improved quality animals to increase mutton and wool production. The main developments related to animal and sheep husbandry can be summarized as under:

— increase of 21 per cent in milk production, 207 per cent increase in poultry meat production achieved during 2002-08.

— 244 dairy cooperative societies were formally organized and registered.

— 19 per cent increase in mutton production and 26 per cent increase in wool production during 2002-08.

— 341 grams of milk are available per person per day in the State, as was confirmed by ISS report of 2007-08.

The poultry production has assumed tremendous amount of significance in J&K as this sub-sector provides some earning to the youth, especially in rural and suburban areas, and also provides highly nutritious and quality poultry meat and eggs to the consumers in the State throughout the year. The number of poultry cooperatives in the State was 450 with 10,500 individuals engaged in 2007-08. Four new poultry projects, one each in Udhampur, Doda, Achhabal and Ranbir Bagh, stand sanctioned. According to the Animal Husbandry Department, the egg production increased to 566.00 million in 2008 from 462.05 million in 2002. At the same time, poultry meat has increased to 431.70 lakh kg from 140.69 lakh kg in the same period.

(v) Forests

The State has 20,230 sq. km area under forests constituting about 10.95 per cent of the total geographical area. Division-wise distribution of forest cover was as under:

Kashmir region	—	8128 sq. km (50.97%)
Jammu region	—	12066 sq. km (45.98%)
Ladakh region	—	36 sq. km (00.06%)

Per capita forest area accounts for 0.17 hectares. In addition, the State has following forest features:

- Spice-wise forest area reveals 90.68 per cent Indian coniferous with 5.32 per cent, deodar 9.02 per cent, chir 9.70 per cent, kail 16.81 per cent and other varieties 49.80 per cent. 9.32 per cent forest cover is claimed by non-coniferous uncommercial resources.

- The outturn for the year 2007-08 was 101.16 thousand cubic metres with 68.27 ('000 cubic metres) timber and 32.89 ('000 cubic metres) fuel wood.
- The export of timber was 30.70 ('000 cubic metres) and deodar 10.17 ('000 cubic metres) and chir 15.35 ('000 cubic metres) during 2007-08.
- The State has four national parks, 16 sanctuaries and 35 conservation reserves covering an area of 15,912 sq. km. Important protected habitat include those of leopard, chiru, hangul and musk deer.
- There have been several international and national schemes—programmes implemented to stop deterioration and restore the purity of world famous Dal Lake in the capital of the State. The beauty of the Dal still remains the lifeline for tourism in Kashmir.
- Under afforestation programme of the Central Government, the State has been provided a huge amount for managing properly 42,797 hectares of degraded forests with people's participation. It will nurture the forest areas on which local populations are dependent for their needs. The Twelfth Finance Commission has also provided a grant for maintenance of forests in the State.

(vi) Fisheries

The State of J&K has plethora of stream, lakes and hilly torrents, reservoirs, and has the potential to grow all types of fisheries. While Kashmir valley offers potential for development of cold water fisheries, Jammu region offers potential for warm water fisheries and Ladakh region is bestowed with the atmosphere suitable for production of cold water fisheries and for brackish fisheries. The famous 'Trout' fish is known world over.

According to Livestock Census of 2003, there was 0.31 lakh fishermen population in the State. The length of 27,781 km of rivers/streams facilitate farming of more than 40 million tonnes of fish catch. The number of fishing licence holders was 13,026 in 2009. Moreover, there are fishing communities spread over the whole valley and very less number of them have got licences for fishing. They practice it as the hereditary and family occupation.

The fish catch during 2008-09 was 1.927 lakh quintals. In the following year, this figure has increased significantly. Simultaneously, the production of 'trout' fish has increased to 112.12 per cent between 2000-01 and 2008-09.

The development of fisheries attained importance in the background of its employment opportunities for youth in the State. Under Prime Minister's Package, 481 units have been completed up to 31 March, 2009 with most of them harvesting the crops.

Since the fishermen population is prone to natural calamities, two insurance and housing schemes are under operation as a welfare measure for the last 10 years.

(vii) Co-operatives

The details about co-operatives in the rural context of J&K are follows:

1,558 cooperative societies were registered in the State during 2001-02 to 2007-08. Out of these, 450 societies (i.e., 28.88%) were involved in poultry, 438 societies (i.e., 28.11%) in agriculture and 366 societies (23.49%) in dairy and remaining societies were associated with housing, floriculture, women credit co-operatives, and others.

The rural credit co-operative structure has 3 levels with State Co-operative Bank at district level and followed by Primary Agricultural Credit Societies at village level. The co-operative banks have a network of 204 branches employing 1,673 persons. The deposits of the co-operative banks were Rupees 1582.72 crore and loan outstanding amounts to Rupees 659.88 crore up to 31 March, 2008.

There are 109 district co-operative societies with a membership of 32,000 undertaking procurement of agricultural produce to enable the agriculturists to get the minimum administered price for their produce in the market.

The number of Primary Agricultural Credit Societies in the State was 765 in 2008, out of which 215 were made credit worthy.

The 'Integrated Cooperative Development (ICDP)' and 'Housing Co-operatives' have also been introduced in the State. While the former projects were meant for Anantnag and Kathua districts, the latter have developed many colonies in all regions of the State.

(viii) Irrigation

Irrigations stand as an essential requirement for agriculture. A major constraint in the development of agriculture in J&K is that ultimate irrigation potential has been assessed at 1,358 thousand hectares, which includes 250 thousand hectares to be developed through major and medium irrigation and 1108 thousand hectares through minor irrigation. Till the end of Tenth Plan, the State has been able to create a total potential of 677.66 thousand hectares only, out of which 580.61 thousand hectares (i.e., 85.70%) of potential is being utilized.

It has been reported that 25 major or minor irrigation schemes are under implementation in the State during 2008-09, 13 of which are funded by AIBP, 7 in the State sector and 5 under loan received from NABARD. The total estimated cost of these schemes was Rupees 194.5 crore and 50 schemes for Ladakh region on an estimated cost of Rupees 46.84 crore have been sanctioned by the Centre during 2007-08.

The net area sown in the State during 2007-08 was 734 thousand hectares whereas the gross area sown was 1,134 thousand hectares. The mode of irrigating the crops mainly used is by canals. About 90 per cent of the net area sown is irrigated through canals, while tanks, tube wells and other means are also used.

(ix) Handicrafts and Handlooms

J&K has specialized in many fields of handicrafts, which have maintained upward trend continuously in exports as well as in the national market. Production of handicraft goods for the year 2008-09 stood at rupees 1100.00 crore approximately.

Keeping in view the market importance of handicrafts, handlooms and other related traditional sectors in the State economy, the State government is going to develop the International Trade Centre (ITC) in order to promote trade facilities and to boost the export-oriented sectors. The Centre is coming up at Pampore, Srinagar at the cost of Rupees 115.84 crore.

In order to give boost to the labour-intensive cottage industry, the State government is laying focus on product design and diversification, providing credit facilities, enhancing workers' productivity through upgradation of skills and efficient use of looms. Market areas to handloom products is being extended through marketing incentives and wide publicity.

Ending March 2009, Handloom Department has recorded a number of 598 handloom units in the State providing employment to 2334 persons. In the co-operative sector, approximately 7.045 million metres of handloom fabrics valuing Rupees 36.61 crore were produced in 2008-09.

During Eleventh Five Year Plan, the Central government introduced an Integrated Handloom Development Scheme (IHDS) to facilitate the sustainable development of handloom weavers located in and out of identified handloom cluster into a cohesive, self and competing socio-economic units. An expenditure of Rupees 15.94 lakh has been incurred during the year 2008-09.

(x) Sericulture

The sericulture activities are carried out in 2,421 villages, almost 35 per cent of the total in the State and about 2,000 families are engaged. The number of mulberry trees has increased to 81.00 lakh in 2008-09. The production of cocoons has been recorded as 7.38 lakh kg. during 2008-09 resulting in an income generation of Rupees 522.00 lakh. Seeds production and seeds imported were 23 thousand ozs and 6,060 ozs. Production of raw silk was recorded as 8,200 metres in 2008-09. The number of reeling units has gone up to 31.25 cacoon markets were organized throughout the State in 2008-09 in order to provide better returns to the rearing farmers.

(xi) Tourism

J&K is an important tourist destination and has been a place of attraction for tourists for centuries. As a result, the tourist inflow to the State increases continuously from 69.12 lakh in 2004 to 77.18 lakh in 2008. The percentage increase in pilgrim visitors to Amarnathji shrine in Kashmir has been to the extent to 24.51 per cent, Mata Vaishno Devi by 7.80 per cent, domestic tourists by 58.79 per cent and foreign tourists by 34.15 per cent in the same period. During 2009, 32.49 lakh tourists visited the State. It may be mentioned here that the flow of foreign tourists shifted from Jammu & Kashmir to Ladakh due to disturbances in the former regions.

Tourism generates employment and there is more scope for more revenue generation. The revenue earnings made under the public sector during the last 4 years was about Rupees 102.63 crore. There has been substantial increase in the earnings from Rupees 20,72.26 lakh in 2004-05 to Rupees 2,916.93 lakh in 2007-08. Out of 36 projects at the total cost of 74.02 crore under various centrally-sponsored schemes related to development/promotion of leisure, pilgrim, adventure and heritage tourism, an expenditure of Rupees 30.32 crore has been registered as against the availability of Rupees 49.34 crore during 2003-04 to 2008-09. 19 Tourist Development Centres (TDCs) have been created in the State, 8 in Jammu region, 8 in Kashmir region and 3 in Ladakh region. Their main function was to create the tourist assets at the prime tourist destinations.

Under Twelfth Finance Commission, an amount of Rupees 100.00 crore has been earmarked for the State, out of which Rupees 90.00 crore were earmarked for need specific projects and Rupees 6.00 crore for heritage tourism.

The State government has made recommendations to the Thirteenth Finance Commission for an amount of Rupees 289.00 crore for further development of infrastructure and allied services in leisure, pilgrim, heritage and adventure tourism.

(xii) Health

The number of health institutions has made an expansion to 4,804 in March 2009 gaining about 40 times increase since 1950-51. Still the Government institutions are overloaded heavily as 91 per cent of in-patients are dependent on public sector medical institutions. The State had the following health institutions in 2008-09:

S.K. Institute of Medical Sciences (Deemed University)	— 01
Medical colleges in the State	— 04
Associated hospitals	— 12
Ayurvedic hospitals	— 01
Dental colleges (including 01 in private sector)	— 03
District level hospitals (14 old and 08 new hospitals)	— 22
Sub-District level hospitals/CHCs	— 78

Primary Health Care Services

■ P.H.C.s	375
■ Allopathic Dispensaries	238
■ Sub-Centres/MACs	2253
■ ISM Dispensaries	417
■ Area Specific Health Centres/Control Units/ STD/VD Clinics/TB Cenres/Laprosy Sub-Centres/Trachoma Units/Anochi Units	302

Total number of personnel (doctors, para-medical staff and other ministerial staff)		— 35000 (approx.)
Ambulances available at primary, secondary and Tertiary level		— 483
Bed strength in health institutions:	Primary level	— 1046
	Secondary level	— 6977
	Tertiary level	— 4863
	Total	12886

Under teaching institutions, two medical colleges (one in Srinagar and another in Jammu) have intake capacity of 100 seats each for MBBS course. The intake capacity for Post-Graduate degree in GMC, Srinagar is 61 and in GMC, Jammu 68. While 22 P.G. Diploma seats are available in GMC, Srinagar, and 34 seats are provided in GMC, Jammu. The Government Dental College (GDC) Srinagar has 54 seats, while GDC, Jammu has 50 seats. The P.G. courses (MS and MD) in critical categories of Gynaecology, Obstetric, Anaesthesia and Paediatrics are provided in GMC, Srinagar and Jammu and ASCOMS in Jammu and SKIMS in Srinagar.

The mortality, fertility and growth rates in J&K in 2007 were as mentioned below:

Birth rate	— 19.0 per million
Death rate	— 5.8 per million
Infant Mortality Rate (IMR)	— 51/'000 live births
Natural Growth Rate	— 13.2 per million

Life expectancy at birth:

Males	— 65.0 years
Females	— 67.0 years

An increasing trend of expenditure on social services by the government was observed clearly. Expenditure on health sector increased from 3.13 per cent of the J&K State Plan to 6.80 per cent of the State Plan. The outlay for the year 2008-09 has been estimated at 3.96 per cent only. The corresponding percentage of health expenditure in the social sector increased from 20.22 per cent to 24.00 per cent during the same period.

In GMC, Srinagar, the Institute of Traumatology is being established under a new project sponsored by the Central government with nine following super specialities:

- Neuro Surgery
- Cardio-Vascular Thoracic Surgery
- Urology
- Neurology
- Plastic surgery
- Paediatric surgery
- Gastroenterology
- Cardiology
- Nephrology

These super specialities are being created at GMC, Jammu. More specialities to be introduced in both colleges are as follows:

- Surgical Oncology
- Endocrinology
- Pulmonary Medicine
- Clinical Haematology
- Medical Oncology

The following health-related provisions have been made formally and action either been taken or to be initiated soon:

- 15 additional PHCs will be made functional for 24x7 services. 14 additional First Referral Units (FRU) shall be created and 70 additional CHCs and sub-district hospitals for upgradation to IPHS norms shall be taken up.
- Establishment of 8 new district hospitals in newly created districts by upgrading of CHCs will be catered to during the Eleventh Plan period of 2007-2012.
- In order to bridge the infrastructural gap and enable access to enhanced diagnostic care by specialists, J&K has made a beginning with Indian Space Research Organization (ISRO) connecting 12 district hospitals and medical colleges to its telemedicine network including AIIMS.

(xiii) Education

In order to enhance the level of literacy, several initiatives in the form of interventions were introduced to develop this core indicator of Human Development. With the help of these target oriented interventions, the number of educational institutions has increased which resulted in maximum area coverage and decreased the area per school covered. Despite a phenomenal decrease in average area per school from 9.87 sq. km in 1980-81 to 3.90 sq. km in 2008-09, the State still lags behind all-India average of area coverage of 2.65 sq. km of 2004-05. At the State level, the students per lakh of population have increased from 14,602 students in 1980-81 to 15,836 students in 2008-09 which indicates that people's participation in education has increased from 14.06 per cent to 15.83 per cent.

The literacy rate at State level has increased from 26.67 per cent (36.29% males and 15.88 females) as per Census 1981 to 55.52 per cent (66.60% males and 43.00% females) as per Census 2001, showing an increase of 28.85 per cent points over last two decades. This literacy rate has further increased to 65.67 per cent (73.30% males and 57.11% females) as per the survey in 2008, showing a growth rate of 18.32 per cent (10.15% points). Thus literacy in the State has registered growth rate of 2.126 per cent per annum. The highest literacy rate was exhibited by districts Jammu (83.73%) and Samba (81.91%) while as the lowest literacy rate was in districts Rajouri (48.38%) and Kupwara (50.05%). With the expansion in educational facilities, the number of literates has increased but has not been able to keep pace with the increasing population. Thus the number of literates has increased from

3.93 lakh in 1961 to 45.16 lakh in 2001 and further to 61.65 lakh in 2008. It has been observed that the number of literates has exceeded the number of illiterates for the first time in 2001.

The large disparity between sexes continues in literacy situation. While about three-fourth of the males in the State are literate in 2008, the landmark of 50 per cent has recently been achieved for females. The gap in literacy has increased from 12.70 per cent points in 1961 to 23.60 per cent points in 2001. This is an indication of improvement of female literacy. The female literacy at both rural and urban has shown higher growth in literacy than males.

At present, 14,820 (13,516 government and 1,304 private) primary schools 8,300 (6,264 government and 2,036 private) middle schools, 1901 (1,156 government and 745 private) high schools and 786 (597 government and 189 private) higher secondary schools are functioning in the State, besides two Sainik Schools, 39 Kendriya Vidyalayas and 14 Jawahar Navodayas Vidyalayas in the government sector. The estimated child population from 6-14 years stood at 21.64 lakh, out of which 19.30 lakh is enrolled in Primary and Middle schools run by the government and private sector, 8.01 lakh children are enrolled in High and Higher Secondary schools. The drop out rate at Primary and Upper Primary level is 1.13 per çent and 2.94 per cent respectively. The number of 'out of school children' stands at 0.40 lakh as on March 2009. The education system is manned by 200 zonal education officers, 877 headmasters, 10,284 masters, 51,890 teachers, 7,000 third teachers, besides 30,570 RET teachers working under SSA, out of which 4789 teachers completed the tenure of 5 years. The pass percentage at Matric and Plus 2 was 33.74 per cent and 34.37 per cent respectively, while the same percentage of Graduate and Post-Graduate courses was 83.66 to 87.12 per cent and 77.90 to 86.30 per cent.

Three new universities have been established in recent years making a total of 8 universities in J&K with main and off campuses. 22 new degree colleges have been set-up during the Tenth FY Plan. 18 Degree colleges under State Plan have also been made functional. The Post-Graduate courses have been introduced in 19 Government colleges of the State. Professional courses such as BCA, BBA, BIT, and MCA have been started in 15 colleges of the State. EDUCAST facility has been provided in government women colleges in Srinagar and Jammu with the assistance of ISRO. The GGM Science College of Jammu and S.P. College Srinagar have been declared as heritage colleges.

The department of Technical Education, established in 1981 has unified the administrative control of Polytechnics and it is of the State for imparting technical and vocational training to the youth. A centrally sponsored scheme for establishment of 18 new polytechnics has been conceived for skill development in a phased manner. Skill development through vocationalization in a Mission Mode for National and International placement is the recent initiative and targets are to be achieved in phased manner for increasing the technical procedure for employability up to 2022.

(xiv) Women Empowerment and Child Development

Female population of J&K rose very marginally from 47.1 per cent in 1981 to 47.2 per cent in 2001 with an increase of 19.60 lakh. At 69.44 per cent growth rate of female population for 1981-2001 was slightly higher than the male population growth rate of 69.40 per cent. However, the life expectancy for women was 68.1 years than men of 65.8 years. The sex ratio as per Census 2001 is 892 which is unfavourable to the women in J&K. Although a recent official survey in 2006 showed sex ratio of 925 (819 in urban areas and 917 in rural areas). However, the position improved with 919 in urban areas and 925 in rural areas.

As per 2001 Census, the literacy rate in J&K was 55.52 per cent and for females it was 43 per cent with rural and urban level of 36.74 per cent and 61.98 per cent respectively. The gender gap in literacy is 23.6 per cent in rural and urban areas. The literacy rate at State level has further increased to 65.67 per cent (males 73.30% and females 57.11%) in 2008. The gender gap in the literacy was 16.19 per cent in favour of males. However, the female literacy in both rural and urban areas has shown higher growth in literacy than males. 12 Nari Niketans are functioning in the State with total capacity of 400 inmates to provide free boarding, lodging, and healthcare to the destitute. 546 beneficiers were covered with a financial assistance of 3.20 crore in 2008. At present, there are 141 ICDS projects with 25,483 Aaganwadi centres providing services to 6.19 lakh beneficiaries comprising of 4.98 lakh children and 1.21 lakh pregnant and lactating mothers under ICDS.

(xv) Poverty and Poverty Alleviation Schemes

The total BPL estimated population rate of J&K has been arrived at 21.63 per cent (24.21 lakh persons) with a dispersion of 26.14 per cent (22.00 lakh persons) from rural areas and 7.96 per cent (2.21 lakh persons) living in urban areas. This shows that a fifth of State's population fell below the poverty line. Out of every five persons, one stands below poverty.

At the regional level in Kashmir, the total BPL population ratio has been worked out at 21.37 per cent (12.91 lakh persons) with a dispersion of 26.34 per cent (11.63 lakh persons) in rural areas and 7.87 per cent (1.28 lakh persons) in urban areas.

In Ladakh region, estimated BPL population was worked out 27.3 per cent (0.71 lakh persons) with 31.29 per cent (0.68 lakh persons) in rural areas and 5.63 per cent (0.03 lakh persons) in urban areas.

As regards Kashmir and Ladakh regions, the total BPL estimated population ratio has been worked out 21.60 per cent (13.62 lakh persons) with a dispersion of 26.58 per cent (12.31 lakh persons) in rural areas and 7.81 per cent (1.3 lakh persons) in urban areas.

At the rural level, the Kashmir division (26.58%) have more BPL population percentage as compared to Jammu division (25.61%) while as Jammu division (8.19%) has more urban poverty percentage as compared to that of Kashmir division (7.81%).

In Jammu division, the total estimated BPL population percentage was arrived at 21.67 per cent (10.59 lakh persons) with a dispersion of 25.61 per cent (9.69 lakh persons) in rural areas and 8.19 per cent (0.90 lakh persons) in urban areas.

The survey results show that in rural areas, out of the total 387 villages, 8.00 per cent of the villages have been recorded in the poverty slab of '50 per cent and above' BPL population which include 3.36 per cent villages having about 70 per cent incidence of poverty. 24.55 per cent of the villages have been recorded in 30-50 per cent band. 55.56 per cent have been recorded in 10-30 per cent band while only 11.89 per cent fall in the 0-10 per cent poverty group.

The total BPL estimated population (absolute poverty) of J&K has been arrived at 24.21 lakh persons of the total population with a dispersion of 22.00 lakh persons from rural areas and 2.21 lakh persons living in urban areas.

At rural level, the highest BPL population percentage have been observed in District Raesi (40.15%) followed by District Kishtwar with (40.10%) while as District Srinagar (8.16%) recorded lowest BPL population percentage followed by District Kathua (12.66%).

In rural Kashmir region, District Kupwara (2.30 lakh persons) had the highest number of estimated BPL population followed by District Baramulla (2.23 lakh persons), Budgam (1.70 lakh persons), Pulwama (1.19 lakh persons) and Bandipora (1.14 lakh persons). In Rural Jammu region, District Poonch (1.35 lakh persons) had the highest number of BPL population followed by District Rajouri (1.30 lakh persons), Jammu (1.20 lakh persons), Udhampur (1.18 lakh persons) and Doda (1.01 lakh persons).

The J&K government has initiated a number of poverty alleviation schemes to mitigate rural poverty as well as urban poverty, which are being implemented in the State with full financial and technical support of the Central government. These schemes serve the dual purpose of poverty alleviation as well as employment generation. These schemes in the J&K State are explained below:

(a) Swarna Jayanti Gram Swarozgar Yojana (SGSY)

The SGSY is one of the centrally sponsored programme aimed at to bring the poor families above poverty line in three years by providing them income generating assets through a mix of bank credit and government subsidy. During 2006-07, financial outlay under this scheme was rupees 10.68 crore, out of which 8.65 crore (80%) have been spent by providing employment to 8,219 persons and 3,808 self help groups during the year. The following activities were carried out during 2008-09 under this scheme in the State of J&K:

No. of SHGs assisted for economic activity	— 4123
No. of individuals assisted for economic activity	— 6155
Total No. of units helped	— 10278
Credit disbursed	— 30.98
Subsidy disbursed	— 7.23
Availability of funds	— 16.27 crore
Expenditure	— 10.42 crore
Expenditure percentage	— 64

(b) Sampoorna Grameen Rozgar Yojana (SGRY)

Under this scheme, employment in the form of cash and foodgrains is provided in rural areas by giving preference to poorest among the poor and SC/ST families. Part of the wages is to be made in the shape of foodgrains allocated by the Central government free of cost. The financial outlay during 2006-07 was Rupees 39.65 crore, out of which 37.46 crore had been spent. 13,601 numbers of works have been completed by generating 29.18 lakh mandays employment during the year. The following activities were performed under this scheme during 2007-08:

Number of works taken up	— 13061
Number of works completed	— 12083
Number of mandays generated	— 21.08 lakh
Total availability of funds	— 38.35 crore
Total expenditure	— 33.66 crore
Expenditure percentage	— 88

(c) National Rural Employment Guarantee Scheme (NREGS)

This flagship scheme has been launched in J&K from 2006 in 9 districts at present. Its main objective is to provide 100 days of guaranteed unskilled wage employment to each rural household opting for it. The financial outlay during 2006-07 was Rupees 41.54 crore, out of which 36.70 crore had been spent. 1,79,133 number of households were issued job cards and 32.89 lakh mandays were generated. This scheme performed the following activities during 2008-09 in the State:

Number of employment generated	— 79.25 lakh
Number of household issued job cards	— 498022
Total availability of funds	— 146.52 crore
Total expenditure	— 86.89 crore
Expenditure percentage	— 59

(d) Indira Awas Yojana (IAY)

It is a centrally sponsored scheme whereunder funds in the ratio of 75:25 are being allocated by the Central and State government respectively. The target groups for housing under IAY are households below poverty line living in rural areas, particularly those belonging to SC/ST and freed bonded labourers. During 2006-07, 9,939 houses were constructed with the financial expenditure of Rupees 23.81 crore. The scheme made the following achievements during 2008-09:

Number of construction	— 19794
Number of upgradation units	— 7010
Total number of constructions/upgradations	— 26804
Constructions completed	— 13700
Upgradations completed	— 5310
Total number completed	— 19010
Percentage achievement	— 70.92
Expenditure incurred	— 53.54 crore

(e) Drought Prone Area Programme (DPAP)

This scheme is in operation in the districts of Doda and 8 Blocks of Udhampur. It is aimed at to tackle the special problems faced by the areas constantly affected by drought conditions. There are 560 projects under implementation in these two districts at an estimated cost of Rupees 168.00 crore for an area of 280 lakh hectares. Achievements under this programme during 2008-09 are as follows:

Item	*Expenditure*	
	Udhampur	*Doda*
Availability of funds	7.37	12.27
Expenditure	1.07	6.40
Percentage expenditure	15	52

Source: Annual Plan, 2014-15, Planning & Development Dept., J&K.

(f) Desert Development Programme (DDP)

It was launched in 1977-78 to mitigate the adverse effects of desertification. The basis of implementation of the programme has been shifted from sectoral to watershed basis from April 1995. It was launched to mitigate the adverse effects of desertification. The programme is in operation in Leh and Kargil districts, where

729 projects have been sanctioned for treating an area of 3.64 lakh hectares at an estimated cost of Rupees 218.70 crore.

(xvi) Panchayati Raj System

Historically, the Panchayats did exist in J&K even before 1947. It may be interested to note that responsibility of establishing Panchayats in the State were given to the Revenue department under which the relevant Acts of 1935 and 1941 were prepared and implemented. The first Panchayat in the State was established in 1934. In the following year, the government provided an assistance of Rs. 40,000 which was increased to Rs. 3,85,000 in 1945-46.

After Independence, the land reform legislation and its successful implementation was a watershed in the history of J&K. Not any other State in the country was so successful in 'land to the tiller' revolutionary measure as this State was. The statutory recognition of proprietary rights on the tillers over the lands titled by them changed the whole socio-political and economc landscape of Kashmir. In this background, there was a great opportunity for the Panchayati Raj system to play its role effectively and meaningfully. These and other enactments, especially the Act of 1958, revealed that there has not been much difference in the functioning and powers of the Panchayats.

It was in this backdrop of Panchayati Raj in the State that J&K Panchayati Raj Act 1989 appeared on the socio-political scenario, raising new hopes for the participation of people in the economic and democratic processes at the grass root level. This Act aimed at introducing the Panchayati Raj system in realistic framework. It envisages avenues of people's participation in the decision-making and decision-implementing processes. It proposes to involve the common people in policy planning and thereby ensuring their participation at grass root level. The rationale of the Act is "to promote and develop Panchaytati Raj in the State as an instrument of vigorous local self-government to seek the effective participation of the people in the implementation of development programmes." This Act provdes for the establishment and constitution of the following authorities:

(i) Halqa Panchayats,
(ii) Block Development Councils,
(iii) District Planning and Development Boards, and
(iv) Panchayat Adalats.

The Halqa Panchayat is of the basic and of pivotal importance. It is considered as 'soul of the system', around which the planning, developmental and political activities of the people at grass root level would revolve. Its main features were as mentioned below:

- It must be under a legal duty to prepare plans for the development of the area and undertake measures for implementation of the development plans;
- It is required to deal with problems like soil conservation, water management, social forestry, rural electrification, overall improvement and progress in agriculture, animal husbandry, health, sanitation and infrastructure;
- It is also required to frame regulations relating to construction of buildings, shops and entertainment houses, to check offensive and dangerous trades, to maintain the ecological balance and protect the environment;
- It is required to formulate regulations for consumer protection and for evolving the plans for poverty alleviation and creating avenues for employment for educated youth;
- It shall be involved in the implementation of schemes related to universalization of elementary education;
- It shall have a fund which will be raised for the comprehensive and totalistic development;
- It shall comprise of seven members including the Sarpanch. Two members may be nominated by the government in order to give representation to women, SCs and STs;
- It has the obligation to develop an area and to implement development plans; and
- It will ensure decentralization of power at the top and at every level.

The Act envisages Block Development Council (BDC), which shall have the functions of construction, maintenance and supervision of inter-Halqa Panchayat communication system. It will provide administrative and technical guidance to the Halqa Panchayat and review its work. The establishment of BDC is a continuum of the efforts to create a new power structure under this Act.

The Act also envisages the constitution of District Planning and Development Board (DPDB) and a cabinet minister will be its chairman.

Finally, the Act envisages the establishing of the District Planning Board (DPB) which will monitor the flow of funds as per district Plans. The DPB has the power to guide to formulate the development programmes for the district and undertake priorities for various schemes to consider issues relating to speedy development and economic upliftment for the district. The board shall formulate and finalize the Plan and Non-Plan budget, lay down the policy guidelines for BDC and HP, coordinate poverty alleviation and employment generation of programmes and extend assistance to HP in this regard.

Despite developing such a comprehensive and multi-layer system of decentralization in J&K, the Panchayati Raj could not be initiated in the State due to onset of militancy in Kashmir and some parts of Jammu region in 1989. The disturbed conditions did not allow any major or minor actor related to Panchayati Raj system to start any activity in this regard. It is now in recent years, when militancy has nearly died down, that election for Panchayats were held. Subsequently, the Gram Panchayats have started working for overall development of the people in the State.

SECTION IV
VILLAGE SOCIO-ECONOMIC PROFILES—EIGHT CASE STUDIES IN J&K STATE

In three preceding sections, we presented details about socio-economic profile of rural J&K at the state, division-region, and district levels. In this section, we will present the socio-economic profile of rural J&K at the village level. In other words, the basic source of information of this section will be reports of eight village studies in the State carried out by I.A.S. officers during their probation and part of their training during the period 2005-2011. The details of the village studies are as follows:

Sl. No.	Year of District	Name of village	Tehsil/Block	District	Name of the Tehsil Officers Trainees, IAS
1.	2005-07	Fatehpur	Rajouri	Rajouri	M. Raju
2.	2006-08	Bhalwal Bharath	Khour/Akhnoor	Jammu	Sheetal Nanda
3.	2007-09	Poria	Reasi	Reasi	Yasha Mudgal
4.	2007-09	Rangpur Maulana	R.S. Pora	Jammu	Simrandeep Singh
5.	2008-10	Babbar Brahamana	Reasi	Reasi	S.V. Meena
6.	2008-10	Maan	Dusbrok	Leh	J.K. Singh
7.	2009-11	Hartaryan	—	Udhampur	Shahid Iqbal Chowdhry
8.	2009-11	Laroka	Nowshera	Rajouri	Sushma Chander

Source: Annual Plan 2014-15.

Though these studies have been carried out in the same/uniform thematic framework at large, some different and extra details were also included in the reports. These aspects will be taken care of while explaining the village studies as follows:

1. Village Fatehpur (Block Rajouri, District Rajouri)

(a) *Population and Demography*: This village is located around 10 kms from the district headquarters of Rajouri. Its population in 2001 was 5,529 (males 3,265 and females 2,264). The community-wise population is STs 2,316, OBCs 1,214 and others 1999 and no SCs. While the sex ratio in the village is 922, the growth rate in 1,081 was 29.65 per cent.

(b) *Education*: The village had the literacy rate of 58 per cent for males and 35 per cent for females in 2001. It has the schools as follows:

Government Schools

— AWC

— Primary School

— Middle School

— Higher Secondary School

Private Schools

— Primary School

— Middle School

— Higher Secondary School

There is no college facility and villagers have to go to Rajouri headquarters. While primary schools perform better than government schools, more number of girls is in government schools because of poverty condition. Most of the village households in the village send their children to school regularly. The mid-day meals scheme is effective in government schools benefiting about 83 students. There is not good educational infrastructure in both types of schools in the village. The classrooms are practically in dilapidated condition and children sit in the open air. In the private schools, the condition is better and they have better classrooms.

(c) *Health*: The health facilities in the village revolve around ANM sub-centre and Sub PHC. The hospital buildings too are in dilapidated condition. There is only one nurse and two attendants and doctor rarely visit the village centre. There are no beds in the centre. Though TB is most common in the village, no proper medicine is provided to the patients. There are some local meditioners who treat fever, cold like diseases from the local available plants. The villagers first approach them for cure and if it does not work, they turn to PHC. But, most of them are referred to the district hospital for treatment. The infrastructure of health system is in shambles. There is no maternal death found in the village. It is because complicated cases are referred to the district. In many cases, the delivery takes place in their houses. The most common diseases found in the village were TB, dysentery, scabies, pneumonia and fever. The centre possesses medicines only for these diseases. The reasons for these diseases identified by villagers include lack of sanitation, lack of good dispensary, malnutrition and superstitions.

(d) *Agriculture and Land*: The total area of village is 2,579 acres, out of which 1,290 is cultivable and only 20-25 per cent of area lies in plain area. The land in the village is of following types:

Land under forest cover	— 23.6 acres
Fallow land	— 70.0 acres
Wasteland	— 202.3 acres
Pasture and grazing land	— 127.7 acres
Land for homestead	— 12.0 acres
Net sown area	— 430.0 acres
Community lands	— 5.0 acres

For irrigation, canals were used near the river Tawi. The pumps are also used. Most of the cropped area comes under rainfed farming, so maize is the most dominant crop in the village. Most of the lands are cultivated by land owners themselves. Out of 1,290 acres of land, 1,073 acres are cultivated by the owners themselves. Most of the households have an average of 1-3 acres of land. After famous land reforms in the State, all landless people have got land of 1 acre in general. The pattern of land ownership in the village was as under:

less than 1 acre	— 153
1-3 acres	— 623
3-5 acres	— 152
5-10 acres	— 14
20 acres and above	— Nil

Nearly 70-80 per cent of the crop comes under double cropping, paddy during June-October and wheat during October-May. The agricultural productivity of the crops is also average. In the case of maize, the total cost of inputs come to Rupees 8,000. While most of these crops are for self-consumption, small number of villagers go for commercial purpose. The villagers have no grain marketing facility in the village. The technology of cultivation stands very obsolete. Overall, the agricultural scene in the village is not satisfactory.

(e) *Occupational Pattern*: Nearly 90 per cent of the households in the village are involved in cultivation. The other occupational groups are household industry 3 per cent, agricultural labourers 2 per cent, government service 3 per cent and cultivators 92 per cent. Non-farm activities involve 4-5 STD booths and some shops. 2-3 households depend on fishing also. Financial assistance is taken from money lenders on 8-10 per cent interest rate. Migration is not a regular phenomenon in the village. The role played by Panchayats is seen in the schemes like SGRY and development activities in the village.

(f) *Property Resources*: The common property resources in the village include all varieties of land except the following:

(i) Land belonging to individuals in the revenue records;
(ii) Land acquired under any law; and
(iii) Residential areas and land earmarked for such purpose.

(g) *Wage Rate*: The general wage rate in the village stand around Rupees 80 to 100 per day for skilled labourers. In the peak season, the rate goes up to Rupees 200 per day. Since most of the villagers are agriculturists, the availability of labour is less. High demand increases the wage rate.

(h) *Poverty Alleviation Programmes*: While the BPL families in the village is 72 in 2002, the following centrally-sponsored poverty alleviation programmes are implemented here.

Sampoorna Grameen Rozgar Yojana (SGRY): This programme started in the village in 2000-01 and the works done are as mentioned below:

Construction of pucca road	— 2003-04
Tractor road	— 2003-04
Repair of primary school	— 2003-04
Construction of *khul*	— 2002-03
Pond at Panowali	— 2004-05
Bowlie at Lahran	— 2004-05
Tractor road	— 2005-06
Panchayat Ghar	— 2005-06

Indira Awas Yojana: There are 12 beneficiaries under this scheme in the village who were provided Rupees 27,500 in two instalments.

Swarnajayanti Gram Swarozgar Yojana (SGSY): The beneficiars in the village under this scheme have undertaken retail trade as key activity. It has two training centres which train regularly girls of the village in carpet weaving and other handloom works. There are 5 individual beneficiars under the scheme to whom Rs. 2.5 lakh have been disbursed who all live under BPL.

2. Village Bhalwal Bharath (Block Khour, Tehsil Akhnoor, District Jammu)

(i) *The Village*: The village Bhalwal Bharath is located on the south-western side of tehsil Akhnoor. It forms part of the well irrigated and more fertile belt of the district. It is at a distance of 2 km from Niabat headquarters at village Pargwal. The village has a total area of 8,386 acres and lies at a distance of 42 km from district headquarters and 54 km from the Block headquarters. The nearest railway station is

Jammu at a distance of 49 km. It has river Chenab flowing through its north which has changed its life over the years. The village was inhabited by Rajput, SC and Muslim families before 1947. But after 1947, Muslim families migrated to Pakistan and refugees came from that country and settled here. The village has often been flooded by Chenab. Additional land was claimed when a dam was constructed there in 2001. Rice has become the main crop with wheat and maize.

(ii) *Population and Demography*: As per 2001 Census, this village has population of 1,021 (males 520 and females 501 and all rural) with a sex ratio of 963. There is 56.5 per cent SC population in the village. The literacy rate is 48 per cent and number of households is 223 in 2001. The village is comprised of three hamlets of (a) Bhalwal Bharath, (b) Madh Kullian and (c) Chanda. All these hamlets are a mix of castes and classes. Bhalwal Bharath has majority of Rajputs and stand well off economically. The other hamlets have more SC and poor households.

(iii) *Education*: While the village has one primary and one middle schools, the high and higher secondary schools are available at 2 km distance. The schools have least infrastructure. The service of mid-day meals is not regular. The middle school has a building, functioning hand pump, 7 class rooms, blackboard in each class, 5 teachers and one headmistress. While there is no sanitation, toilets are dysfunctional. Mid-Day Meal is served to students regularly, but without checking quality and quantity. 4 out of 5 teachers are locals and they attend school regularly. In the case of girl child, her education can be sacrificed for family purposes.

(iv) *Health*: There is no proper health facility, government or private, is available in the village. The nearest health facility is PHC at Pargwal which has been upgraded to 24 hour service under NRHM. It has two allopathic doctors (male and female), one ayurvedic doctor. 3 pharmacists, 2 safai karamcharies, two ambulances and one X-ray technician. 24 hour service is available on the duty day of the male doctor but the lady doctor leaves at 5.00 pm. The laboratory Technician is always available.

Two females have been appointed as ASHA. There are two ICDS centres but are not functional except providing food for children. There is sanitation and open defecation is a norm. Children are seen bare foot and females undernourished and anemic. Common diseases in the village are fever and malaria.

(v) *Agriculture and Land*: The total land area of this village is 8,386 acres, out of which 5,604 acres is cultivated area. The average ownership holding size is 3-5 acres, while as average operational holding size is 8-10 acres. There are 7 families without any land and depend on non-farm activities. 6 families have more than 10 acres of land. Under the prevalent system of share cropping, the one who rents out the land takes half of the produce as share.

There are 6 tractors and are hired by others at certain cost. Entire land is under two crop a year, wheat and rice and fodder. Maize, pulses, sugarcane and vegetables are grown by some households for self and commercial purposes. Rice is sown in July-August and harvested in October, while wheat is sown in November-December and harvested in April.

There is no water storage and agriculture produce market facilities. Only 6-7 households have substantial good quality basmati rice surplus which is picked up by traders from Jammu and Akhnoor. As regards wheat, 99 per cent households keep it for self consumption. The average farmer in the village is caught in vicious circle of credit. They keep on taking credit from local shopkeepers and then barter entire surplus against their dues which average around Rupees 5,000 for six months.

(vi) *Economic Activities*: Agriculture is the main stay of the village with 100 per cent households engaged in cultivation. There are 38 retired military men, 3 police officers and 19 (8 female) government employees working in different departments. There are 19 following shopkeepers in the village:

Kiryana	—9	Barber	—1	Tailor	—1	Vegetables	—2
Atta Chakki	—1	Poultry	—1	Fishery	—1	Sheep farm	—1
Livestock	—2						

While there is rising immigration of labour in the village from Punjab, Bihar, U.P., and West Bengal. There is migration from the village to Jammu, Akhnoor, Katra and Pathankot for seasonal labour.

At large, the village has following amenities in the nearby village Pargwal:

PDS Ration Depot	—2	PHC	—2
Veterinary Dispensary	—2	Niabat	—2
Agri. Store & Sale Centre	—2	Bus Stand	—2
High School	—2	H.S.S. School	—2
Post Office	—2	Bank Branch	—2

(vii) *Socio-Economic Set-up*: The village society is mix of Rajputs, Brahmins and SCs. There was an established system of '*kamin*' and '*jagirdar*' relationship which has now faded away. But, Bawalas are still not allowed to sit alongwith upper castes, but this pattern is undergoing slow change. Out of 223 households, 98 are BPL, out of which 20 are *antyodaya* families. Landlessness or inadequacy of holdings are major reasons for poverty. Though *purdah* is observed by women, they are not married before 18 years. The general age of marriage for boys is 25-27 years.

(viii) *Poverty Alleviation Programmes*: The only successful scheme in the village is 'Indira Awas Yojana' under which 2.5 cases every year are sanctioned for the village. The houses were provided to the villagers. The job cards under NREGA have been issued to 90 per cent of the households without any registration. No unemployment allowance is paid to those who have applied for jobs. There are no self-help groups in the village but two individuals have benefited by various schemes.

3. Village Poria, Tehsil/Block Reasi, District Reasi

The village Poria is one of the small village of this district and is located at 35 km distance from district headquarters. Except for very poor families, the houses of others are of pucca or semi-pucca construction. It is self-sufficient in education till eighth standard. It is well connected from the city by a metalled road and bus service. The main occupations in the village are agriculture, orchards and business. Though some women have got jobs with the government, most of them prefer to stay at homes.

(ii) *Population and Demography*: The total population of the village is 371 and the average size of a household is seven. While the family planning programmes are not effective, preference for male child is dominant. Since the population is increasing, there is a trend to break away from joint family. It has resulted in higher burden of maintaining a separate kitchen.

(iii) *Village Infrastructure*: The village has the following items of infrastructure:

Middle School	—1	Veterinary Dispensary	—1
Community Hall	—1	Community Latrines	—4
Medical Sub-centre	—1	Aganwadi Centres	—2
S.S. Abhiyana Units	—1	Playground	—1
Public Wells	—5		

(iv) *Education*: The overall literacy in the village is 55 per cent (males 35% and females 20%). But, the present trend is to send children, especially boys, to school is increasing. While rich people have higher level of education, the poor have lower level. Girls are not encouraged to go for education. The perception of unemployment is very high in the village. The conditions of SSA with 45 students and 2 teachers are not good. The middle school, established in 1955, is spacious but face dearth of furniture. No mid-day meals are served in this school and no cleanliness of toilets is maintained. In 2006, few TLC centres were established in the village but were later closed.

(v) *Health and Sanitation*: The health conditions in the village are not satisfactory. It has one Health Sub-Centre which has two workers; one who attends patients and assist with small ailments (FMHW) and other who assists in dressing, etc. The people in the village have not a positive image about facilities provided by the centre. The Allopathic dispensary which is at a distance of 35 km away provide these minimum facilities. There is no private medical agency or service in the village except a medicine shop run by a villager. The health sub-centre stands far from NRHM mandated IPHS standards. In place of two prescribed FMPHW's there is only one. The common diseases identified were as follows:

- Gastroentitis in summers
- Typhoid
- Hypertension
- Migraine
- Measles
- Upper respiratory tract infection
- Jaundice

The common ailments with women in the village are:

- Reproductive tract infection
- Leucorrhoea
- Moderate Anaemia

Maternity and child care is supposed to take care of by sub-centre level FMPHW, the AWW and ASHA in joint manner stand poor in the village. Village health and sanitation is not celebrated in the village. The ASHAs have failed due to late arrival of funds. So, they have lost the confidence of the villagers. For immunization, the villagers go to the district hospital. There is no exclusively centre where women can entertain.

In the village, there is least consciousness about family planning. The average spacing is 1 to 1.5 years between children. The most preferred contraceptive is IUCD followed by 'multiload' and MALA-D and condom ranks last, which is less preferred by men.

Three cases of maternal mortality in last 6 years have been reported and one delivery at home, and patients suffered from infection, loss of blood and other complications. There was one case of infant mortality in a year due to pneumonia and two such cases with polio were reported last year. It was found that infant deaths were generally caused by anaemia, polio, pneumonia, diphtheria and still births.

(vi) *Agriculture and Land*: Agriculture is the mainstay of the people in the village. While share cropping is practiced, main products are rice, maize and wheat. Maximum area in the village is unirrigated and there are some orchards also. A survey in the village found that Rajputs, Brahmins and Baniyas held larger shares of land whereas Lohars had lesser landholdings.

The total land available for cultivation is 148 acres and 161 acres are left uncultivated. Only 78 acres are irrigated by *khul*. While the total land under ownership cultivation stands at 146 acres, only 2 acres is cultivated under tenancy. The cropping pattern and agricultural productivity is as follows:

Sl. No.	*Crop*	*Sowing*	*Harvesting*
1.	Rice	April-May	First to last week of September
2.	Maize	April-May	August to September
3.	Wheat	September-October	Last week of May

Source: Annual Plan, 2014-15.

The agricultural productivity of rice is 12 quintals per acre, maize 1 quintals per acre and wheat 4 quintals per acre. The usage of HYV seeds is not popular, only big landholders or orchard owners go for progressive experimentation. While the tractorization is 40-50 per cent, 5 tractors are available on rent in the village. Surplus agricultural produce is sold in the local, Reasi and Jammu markets.

Villagers who are landless or having small land practicc agricultural labour in other's fields and are paid in cash and food. The labour rate varies from 101 to 160 per day. There is common property land 12.5 acres as grazing land. Some encroachment of this land has been observed.

(vii) *Occupation and Unemployment:* As mentioned earlier, agriculture is the most dominant occupation in the village. But, at the same time, educated villagers are employed. Many landless villagers work as agricultural and non-agricultural labourers. Some households are engaged in petty retail business while as there is one barber and one blacksmith's shop in the village.

There is lot of unemployment in the village and it has given rise to out-migration. The girls are mostly unemployed and they get education in order to reduce the dowry demand on the part of the boy's family. There is no skill training institute in or around the village.

(viii) *Poverty Alleviation Programmes*: The programmes of IAY, SGRY, TSC, NREGA, CDS, and MPLADS are in operation in the village. As per the reports, though there are 8 IAY and 9 SGRY schemes running, there is the least effect felt in the village. The main reasons identified are political interference and non-payment of bank loans.

(ix) *Gram Panchayat*: The Gram Panchayat in the traditional form exists in the village. It has not adopted new Panchayat Act, so its members cannot exercise any power. The substantial function lies in the consultation for formulation of the village plan. Only 10-20 people of the village attend the Panchayat meeting. Presently, there are 7 members of the village Panchayat with one big landlord (having 100 acres of land) happens to be its Sarpanch. There is no woman member in the Panchayat.

4. Village Rangpur Maulana Tehsil/Block R.S. Pora, District Jammu

(i) ***General Features:*** This village has the following common features:

Nearest Bus Stop	—	Baspur	5 km
Nearest Bus Stand	—	R.S. Pora	11 km
Nearest Railway Station	—	Jammu	30 km
Nearest Market	—	R.S. Pora	11 km
Nearest J&K Bank Branch	—	Baspur	5 km
Nearest Post Office	—	R.S. Pora	11 km
Nearest PHC	—	Baspur	5 km
Nearest Grain Storage Facility	—	R.S. Pora	11 km

(ii) ***Population and Demography***: The total population of the village is 1,373 (males 698 and females 675). While the sex ratio stands at 967, the number of households is 299. SCs compose 244 persons and STs nil. The OBCs, Hindus and Sikhs have 34, 492 and 630 persons respectively. The literacy rate in the village is 64 per cent and number of literates is 892. While the dominant castes are Brahmins, Rajputs and Jats, the SCs include Bhagats, Ramdasias and Nai, and OBCs include Labanas and Tarkhans. A clear co-relation is visible between caste and prosperity. So, the SCs in the village live in worst poverty conditions.

All SC households are landless, illiterate and unemployed and live in Indira Awas houses or J&K government housing scheme. These people are locals and non-refugees and did not receive the benefit of land allocations as in the case of refugees. On the other hand, Jat Sikh and Brahmins are prosperous, live in pucca houses, have electricity and drinking water facilities. Almost all of them have land which stands most productive and one member in a family at least in government job.

(iii) ***Village Infrastructure***: The village has the following infrastructure:

- A middle School
- An aganwadi centre
- A sewing teaching centre
- A community hall (made under BADP)
- A computer centre (under MPLAD)
- A sub-centre

For irrigation purpose, there is a well cemented Ranbir canal that waters the entire R.S. Pora. There is no grain storage facility. They sell their produce to local intermediaries after harvest.

(iv) ***Education***: The village has got a Government Middle School from 2001. It caters to the needs of surrounding villages too. There are 8 teachers, headmistress and 84 per cent of students for Higher Secondary schooling, the village children need to go to neighbouring R.S. Pora. As per a survey, all 40 households in the village send their children to school and gave equal importance to both sexes. There are different reasons quoted by villagers for giving education to their children. While majority wanted to enhance good matrimonial chances, the minority of them wanted to enhance their job chances. A little minority did not give education to their children because they feel it is useless to study when there are no jobs. The village has one doctorate, two master degree holders, and one Manager of J&K Bank. There is an aganwadi centre in the village, but the villagers did not find it too beneficial. There are 47 registered children, but not all children were attending it. While all services of the scheme were not in operation here, villagers too avoided to send their children to this centre.

(v) ***Health and Sanitation***: The village has got a PHC at Baspur at 5 km distance and a sub-centre that is not functional because of absence of the doctor there. People prefer to go to the PHC and sub-district hospital which are well connected with village. Serving or retired army personnel go to the military hospital at Satwari. For deliveries, women go to R.S. Pora and Jammu and prosperous families engage trained *dais*. In last two years, there have been 36 births in village and 29 institutional deliveries in various hospitals. Out of 36 births, 5 children died before their first birthday. There was no case of maternal mortality reported.

(vi) The state of sanitation in the village is not satisfactory. No OBC/SC household has a latrine. Even some good houses have no sanitation facility. It is mainly due to lack of health. Some efforts were carried out to start proper sanitation but were not successful.

(vii) ***Agriculture and Land***: The total area of the village is 331.75 acres, out of which 302.39 acres are for cultivation, 3.18 acres for homestead, 300 acres sown area and 0.68 acres as community land. Out of the total cultivable area of 302.39 acres, 11.8 acres is under ownership cultivation, while 290.59 acres are under Custodian Department. The caste-wise distribution of land was as follows:

Jat Sikhs	— 166.1 acres	General Hindus	— 90.6 acres
SCs	— 9.6 acres	OBCs	— 36.24 acres

The class-wise land ownership pattern was as follows:

Landless households	— 40	HHs with 0-3 acre	—238
HHs with 3-5 acre	— 21	HHs with 5 and above acre	—Nil

The cropping pattern in the village was as under:

- 91 per cent of the village area is cultivable. Entire land comes in ABI soil type-irrigated land. The area agro-climatic conditions are most appropriate for a double cropping of wheat and paddy. The Ranbir Canal irrigates the whole area. There are hardly one or two tube wells in the village.

The region performs well in terms of yield per acre (productivity) because technology is fully utilized. HYV of wheat and rice are sown. Surplus agricultural produce is sold to private dealers. Only 2-3 households have the storage facility. The common property resources include the ponds, cremation ground, canal, roads, lanes and temple and gurudwara. Almost entire area under CPR stands encroached.

(viii) ***Occupational Pattern and Employment***: In the village, there are 218 cultivating households. About 24 households are agri-labourers and 20 households are landless. The other occupational trends are as follows:

Army	— 46	J&K Police	—11
PHE Department	— 07	Education Department	—08
Health Department	— 05	Pvt. shops and business	—11
Ad hoc daily-wagers	— 33		

(ix) *Poverty Alleviation Programmes*: As per BPL survey, the village has 313 BPL population in 2002. All relevant Central and

State schemes are being implemented in the village. The SGSY, which is functional in the village, has both self help groups and individual cases. The details follow:

- The Kisan group has 5 SC members engaged in minor irrigation and has grade passed since 2010.
- The 'future pack' has 10 women, engaged in dairy 04, provision store, 03 and box making 03, have grade passed since 2010.

There are two works sanctioned for FY 2009-10, *viz*., construction of *khal* and renovation of traditional pond. The wages were raised to Rs. 110 per day which influenced the people's life. 32 men and women, mostly SC and OBC, were engaged in the construction of *khul* in which total man days created were 1,848.

11 households in the village have been benefited by IAY and RHS, both of which are related to rural housing.

Rangpur Maulana falls under Korotana Panchayat. While the Sarpanch is Jat, the Panchs belong to Jat and SC communities. There is no woman Panchayat member. According to the report, the involvement of Panchayat in development activities and PAP is nil. This is mainly because of extreme form of political interferance in the Panchayat affairs. It was reported that it is MLA/MP who decide the list of IAY and refer it to the BDO, so much, so that, villagers approach the MLA/MP for SGSY benefits.

5. Village Babbar Brahamana (BB) Tehsil/Block Reasi District Reasi

(i) This village has two hamlets and its location from different points is as follows:

District headquarters:	Reasi	—20 km	Block headquarters:	Reasi	—20 km
Nearest bus stop:	Dera Baba	—3.5 km	Railway station:	Udhampur	—80 km
Nearest town:	Reasi	—20 km	Market	Reasi	—20 km
Nearest Bank branch:	Reasi	—20 km	Post Office:	Dera Baba	—3.5 km
Nearest PHC:	Reasi	—20 km	Grain Storage:	Jammu	—86 km

It stands as the average village in the district. While the dominant households are poor, a few rich household are in pucca houses. It is well connected with a road from the city. The women in the village generally do not prefer to work outside.

(ii) ***Population and Demography***: The total population of the village, as per 2001 Census, was 573 (males 272 and females 301) and total number of households was 86. The SCs numbered 145 and ST 61. The sex ratio in the village was 1,107. The number of literates was 295 (males 165 and females 130) and number of agricultural labourers was 50. The language spoken in the village is Dogri. The number of migrants to urban areas was 50. In addition to having positive sex ratio, the population is increasing with a moderate decennial growth rate of 28 per cent during 1981-1991, 26 per cent during 1991-2001 and 25 per cent during 2001-2010. The average size of the household is seven. Until recently, did not figure significantly in the village. But, it has been now progressively. Preference for male child is still prevalent. As a result of increase in population, there is increasing pressure on existing resources in the village. Urge to break away from joint family system has been observed quite often. This has led to lower income from agriculture and higher expenditure on separate kitchen. The population pressure has also been seen affecting the available resources.

(iii) ***Village Infrastructure***: This village has the following potential infrastructure:

High School	1	Panchayat Ghar	1
Veterinary dispensary	1	Community hall	—
Passenger sheds	—	Primary school-private	1
Aaganwadi centre	1	S.S. Abhiyan centre	1
Playground	1	Public wells	3
Stone crusher	1	Flouring machine	1
Tractors	1	Private medical practitioner	1

(iv) ***Educational Status***: The educational status of the village has been characterized as "average". It follows that the literacy in the village was 51.48 per cent (males 60% and females 43%). The present trend reveals that more children are going to the school. Boys are preferred in private than government school. The better off families have graduates and post graduates but less in number. The drop out was found due to poverty, health fall and family compulsions. Girls education is mostly up to Matric. The perception of unemployment is very high in the village. Since it lacks job generation in private and public sector, the required skills for jobs are not met merely by High School pass literates.

The position of SSA is bad. It is run from two rented rooms of a broken and unsafe house. There are 45 students and RET teachers in this school. Teaching here is neither effective nor productive. The Middle school upgraded in 2008 but lacks very basic facilities like drinking water, toilet, and playground. There are no furnishing, furnitures, blackboards and charts. There are no rooms for cooking and serving mid-day meals which is poor in service. There is no sweeper in this school. The TLC programme was started in the village but continued for three months only due to administrative reasons.

(v) ***Health and Sanitation***: The health conditions in this village are far from satisfaction. While the prosperous families are enough, the poor and unlettered have nothing. The village does not have a Health Sub-centre. The nearest sub-centre is 3.5 km away which has one doctor and 2 health workers. The people in the village do not report positively about the facilities available woth the sub-centre. The village does not have the next grade of health facilities, i.e., Allopathic Dispensary. There is a private health service in the village which performs some medical functions. The villagers have faith in this centre and get the medicines for day to day ailments like fever and headache. The village health sub-centre is far from the NRHM mandated IPHS standards. In place of two FMPHEWs, there is only one, thereby giving less time than required to the patients.

The disease pattern of the village is as follows:

- Gastroenteritis in summer
- Typhoid
- Hypertension in males
- Migraine
- Measles
- URTI in winter
- Jaundice

The common ailments with women are RTI, Leucorrhoea and moderate anaemia. A common ailment in the village is head and body ache. The operational interlinking between aaganwadi worker, ASHA and sub-centre is very poor related to maternity and child care. While people have lost faith in the role of ASHA, the latter too has lost confidence in her. For immunization, people visit the sub-centre or district hospital. There is no source of entertainment in the village. The village lacks the facilities needed at the time of delivery. There is no concept of family planning among women in the village. The preferred contraceptive is the IUCD followed by 'Multiload' and Mala-D. Condom ranks the last. Three cases of maternal mortality have been reported during last 6 years. There was one case of infant mortality in this year and the child died due to pneumonia. Last year, two children died, one because of polio.

(vi) ***Agriculture and Land***: Agriculture is the mainstay of the people of the village. Double cropping is practiced and main produce is rice, maize and wheat. While maximum land is unirrigated, many orchard owners are in the village. According to a survey, while Rajputs and Brahmins were holding larger shares of land, lohars, etc., had lesser landholdings.

The total land in the village is 530 acres and net sown area is 477 acres. 53.5 acres of land is left uncultivated. 208 acres comes under ownership cultivation and 90 acres is cultivated under tenancy. The cropping pattern is as follows:

Rice	— sowing: 20 April to 15 May	Harvesting —	1 to Last week Sept.
Maize	— 1 April to 15 May	—	15 August to 15 Sept.
Wheat	— mid-Sept. to October	—	1 to last week May

The agricultural productivity of rice is 12 quintals per acre, maize one quintals per acre, and wheat 4 quintals per acre. The usage of HYV seeds is not so popular. There is one tractor in the village which is available at rupees 150 per kanal. Surplus agricultural produce is sold in local markets and in Jammu. There is also the practice of remunerative and swapping labour. The labour wages are 110-160 per day. There is common property land of 1.25 acres demarcated as grazing ground.

(vii) ***Occupational Pattern and Employment***: Agriculture is main occupation of the villagers. Though many young are educated but not employed, particularly in the government service. Many landless work as agricultural and other labour. There is one blacksmith, one barber and some people in business and petty retail. The most unemployment period is December to March but villagers had gone for out-migration. Girls are slow in opting for jobs. There is lack of skilled personnel in the village. There is not a single SHG in or around the village.

(viii) ***Poverty Alleviation Programmes***: Several such programmes are in operation in the village under the Rural Development Department such as IAY, SGRY, TSC, NREGA, CDF, MPLADS, KCC, etc. There are 5 IAY cases and 35 individual beneficiaries in SGSY schemes running in the village. The MNREGA job card holders are 64 but all of them do not work. It was reported that in all PASs there is some amount of political interference in the identification of the beneficiaries.

(ix) ***Gram Panchayat***: This system exists in the village in the traditional form. Though the Panchayat Act has been passed, the new Panchayat body is pending since last few years. The old members are continuing as 'dummy members' and do not exercise any power. If they have some power, it is because of their traditional leadership. They hear disputes within the village, provide consultation in the plan, and facilitate mate selection. There is certainly some political influence on it functioning. The present Sarpanch is a marginal farmer with 1.5 acres of land.

6. Village Maan, Block/Tehsil Durbuk, District Leh

In the past, people of this region procured medicines from this village area. So, it was given the name of 'Maan' means medicines. It is situated 170 km from the district headquarters and 55 km from Block headquarters. It is 1 km in length and 0.5 km in width; this area provides the village with 1,000 kanals of land. The people mainly depend on livestock and agriculture for livelihood. It is situated near important river and lake Pangong lake and important mountain Manmopundun.

(i) ***Population and Demography***: The village consists of 23 households with a population of 148 people (males 71 and females 77). While 92 persons are literate, 63 persons are aged between 15-44 years. Out of the total people of 148, 63 are 15-44 years, 17 are 60+years, and 49 are 0-49 years. Bodhi is local language and Hindi is known by all. Everyone in the village has got the ST status. People have completely traditional lifestyle and 5 per cent among them live BPL. The overall literacy is 30 per cent.

(ii) ***Infrastructure***: This village has following infrastructural facilities at present:

P. D. S. Unit	—1	Primary school	—1
Middle School	—1	High·school	—1
H. S. School	—0	Metalled/dirt road	—1
Bus service	—1	Amchi	—1
Health institutions	—3	Community hall	—1
Panchayat Ghar	—1	Handicraft centre	—1
Cooperative store	—1	Television	—1
Animal feed bank	—1	Hand pump	—1
Water tap	—1	Plantation by forest	—1

The main problems identified by the villagers included bad condition of road, no telephone facility, no electricity, no television, and so on.

(iii) ***Education***: A primary school exists at centre of the village with 5 class rooms and a class house. It is situated about 100 metres from households. After primary schooling, Tharuk residential school lies at a distance of 60 km away with facilities of teachers, learning material, library, laboratory, playground, toilet and drinking water. Three teachers are there for 16 students. The pre-school and mid-day lunch facilities are available there. While there is high enrolment of female students, but their drop out rate is higher because they get engage in household work. The interventions needed are from government, NGOs, SHGs and VECs. The educational problems identified by the villagers are lack of drinking water in educational institutions, and no higher educational institute available in the village.

(iv) ***Health***: There is one M.Sc. and two medical persons in the village but lack of ambulance. These persons provide treatment to minor diseases. For major diseases, the villagers have to travel to hospital in Leh or Tangste, the nearest big centre. The villagers, especially the elder ones, also get treatment from local Amchi practitioners who do not charge but accept whatever is offered by patients. Health records in the village show the occurrence of diseases as follows:

Disease	Diagnosed on			No cases treated by	
	Up to 14 years	14-60 yrs	60+ year	Amchi	Doctor
Cold & cough [champa]	Yes	Yes	Yes	50%	50%
Joint pain	—	—	Yes	—	—
Diarrhoea	Yes	Yes	Yes	—	—

Source: Annual Plan, 2014-15.

Some of the problems reported by villagers regarding their health included the following:

- Lack of facilities at the health centre;
- Shortage of medicines at health centre;
- Staff do their duty irregularly; and
- No ambulance.

The sources of drinking water facilities are as under:

Glacier	—15	Taps	—6	Hand pump	—3
Springs	—6	Streams	—22	Kanal	—3

However, the villagers feel that shortage of pure drinking water.

(v) ***Agriculture and Land***: The agriculture is the major contributor towards livelihood. The land available in the village is of following types:

% of cultivated land	—20	% plantation	—10
% of mass meadow	—05	% of Pasture	—40
% cultivable barren land	—10	% of waste land	—15

There are 200 kanals of cultivated land which produces barley, pea and vegetables. As per land ownership pattern, out of total land of 1,000 kanals, 400 kanals are pasture owned and about 900 kanals are owned/used by villagers. Other report says that 90 per cent of the land is owned by villagers and 10 per cent occupied by government. Most of the land is barren. Since villagers live a traditional life, they do not have land disputes. If there is any, that is resolved by arbitration.

Due to extreme cold, the sowing season is very short and crop is very limited. People have no knowledge of mechanization of agriculture and girdawari is still not prepared in some areas. The major crops in the village are: barley (from 200 canals of land), pea (from 40 canals of land), and vegetables (from 5 kanals of land). The major problems related to agriculture have been identified as lack of seeds, lack of training in vegetable cultivation, floods which wash away the fertile land, insufficient water, lack of tools and lack of fencing around land.

The details about livestock in the village are as follows:

Type of animal	*No. of animals*	*No. of hh[h]*	*No. of hh[l]*	*Average holding*	
Sheep	161	14	2	22	1
Goat	1013	3	1	104	1
Yak	104	14	1	15.5	1
Cow	64	11	3	5.5	2
Horse	59	7	1	4.5	1
Donkey	5	22	1	2.5	1

Source: Annual Plan, 2014-15.

The village has the following animal products:

- Wool: 0.375 kg per sheep from 121 sheep (i.e., 45.37 kg. In a year);
- Pashmina: 142 gm per year;
- Khulu: 104 kg per year; and
- Dairy products: 100 lit of milk per day, 6.25 kg butter per day.

Handicrafts too contribute to villagers' income in a minor way.

(vi) ***Poverty Alleviation Programmes***: There are several SHGs active in the area for this purpose. In the year 2004-05, there was the strength of 17 (11 + 6) women members working for this cause. The 'Edches Yarges Tsogpa' group related to the activities of carpet, pure woollen cloth, socks, gloves and sweaters. Upto 2007, it sold 22 carpets at the rate of Rs. 1,500 per piece. The group has Rs. 1,00,000 in its savings account. The second SHG, 'Samtun Thundel Tsogpa', established in 2005, is also related to the activity of carpet weaving. The products of this group included carpets 6, sweaters, gloves 10, and socks 12. This area of activity is growing and main problems faced by the villagers are no training centre, no marketing facilities, no furnitures, lack of space and financial support.

(vii) ***Gram Panchayat***: The report says that the Panchayat do the developmental work. The members do have regular meetings and the work is satisfactory. The village has the Panchayat Ghar and a Community Hall. The report gives no statistical details.

7. Village Hartaryan, Tehsil/Block Udhampur, District Udhampur

The village is located at 17 km from district and Block/tehsil headquarters. While the nearest bus stop is 2 km away, the nearest railway station is 17 km away. Udhampur is the nearest town apart from nearby market Rehmbal. The village has hilly and plain areas and is composed of 8 hamlets. Villagers speak Gojri and Dogri languages. The village have Brahmin, SC, ST, and other inhabitants.

(i) ***Population and Demography***: The total population of the village was 1,650 in 1981, 1970 in 1991, and 2,688 (males 52.64% and females 47.36%) in 2001. The decadal growth rate was 20 in 1991 and 30 in 2001. The major groups of population composed of Brahmins-Rajputs 1895, Chamars-Meghs 286, Gujjars-Bakerwalls 120 and other castes 387. With the increase in population, there has been increasing pressure on resources, the proactive approach of various departments, and people's own initiative that resources are utilized in a sustainable manner.

(ii) ***Education***: The literacy rate in the village stands higher than the average rate of the district. While the village literacy rate is 75.25 per cent, that of the Udhampur district is 54 per cent. Female literacy is 69.99 per cent with 891 literate women and male literacy stands 80 per cent with 1,132 literate men. The village has 4 primary, 3 middle, one high schools, but no higher secondary school. The teacher-taught ratio is 1 to 25 and has lowest drop out rate of 2.5 per cent for primary and 3.9 per cent for middle standards. The SSA has made massive positive impact in creating infrastructure and employment in the village. The Adult Literacy Campaign has also picked up well in the village and many villagers were benefited by this.

Since Gujjars live in this village, migratory schools have been provided to them, in the plains during winter and in the mountains during summer. These schools accompany the migrating Gujjar community and impart education to their children. The village has also been benefited by RET scheme in which recruitment of local teachers on payment of limited honorarium is made for providing education to the local communities. Thus village has been benefited significantly in the field of education.

(iii) ***Health and Sanitation***: The village has one sub-centre and nearest PHC is at 7 km distance. There is no ambulance attached with this centre. The sub-centre has one doctor and 5 para-medicos. While doctor visits 2 or 3 times a week, the para-medicos are regular. The ASHA report to the centre and through them an effective health care delivery system has been established in the village. The public health service delivery system is quite effective. It is because people have proactive approach towards health and hygiene. Sanitation in the village has received impetus from various agencies. Most common diseases in the village are related to bacterial infections or those arising due to malnutrition, especially among children and women.

Childcare is mostly the domain of families themselves. In the anganwadi centre, 7 neonates of 0-6 months were registered and 5 have been enrolled as beneficiers; out of 59 children of 6 months to 6 years age, 40 have availed the anganwadi services; and 3 out of 20 adolescent girls have also been benefited. The village records reveal that out of 273 cases of eliveries in past two years not a single case of maternal mortality has been reported. The last maternal death was reported 12 years back. The village has also not reported any infant mortality for last 965 cases of child birth. In the year 2010, 72 births and 9 deaths were recorded in the village. Immunization for various diseases have been successful campaign in the village. The system of medicine, the Ayurveda has been serving as a vital cure for many diseases. Traditional medicine is something on which some still rely on. Different practices of family planning are in vogue in the village. In 2010, there were 32 cases of vasectomy and tubectomy reported.

(iv) ***Agriculture and Land***: The village has the land whose details are as follows:

Land under cultivation	—702 acres	Two cropping seasons
Under forest cover	—666 acres	Moderate to dense forest
Fallow land	—49 acres	Needs soil improvement
Pasture and grazing land	—103 acres	Common village land

Wasteland	—85 acres	Heavy slope
Homestead	—69 acres	Eight hamlets
Net sown area	—462 acres	Paddy, wheat, mustard, maize
Community land	—63 acres	Under plantation, community hall
Misc.	—48 acres	Pathways, canals, pond, etc.

The dominant case owns maximum one prime land in the village. The working class owns the land next to the dominant caste. The artisans and other social castes own more than the average size. Employed people have also the same pattern of ownership. Crops are grown in *rabi* and *kharif* seasons, i.e., two crops a year. Productivity of land ranges from medium to high, depending on the input, cropping pattern and practices. Since the village is on a slopy terrain and upper reaches of village are hilly areas, lifting of water to fields is very easy. So, creation of canals has taken this natural advantage. The canals in the village irrigate most of the village fields. HVY of seeds of various crops is made available to the farmers on subsidized rates. The State Agriculture Department has one agriculture sub-centre in the village, which houses a seed centre. The village has barter system in practice wherein crop produce is exchanged between households, for crops, vegetables and so on. 20-25 per cent of the produce go to the market. There is no presence of agricultural labourers. The common property resources in the village include grasslands, community forestry, minor forest produce, etc.

(v) ***Occupations and Employment*:** The major occupation in the village is agriculture and allied practices. There are about 36 government employees and about 20 in military and paramilitary forces. Entrepreneurship involves about 100 people. But, at the same time, the village has more than 150 unemployed youth. There are 12 graduates, 5 post-graduates, only 3 of them are employed. In addition to agricultural activities, animal husbandry is a common practice. The Gujjars usually are involved in sheep and goat rearing. The milk is collected and sent to Rahmbal and Udhampur towns. About 120 households are involved in petty trades and work through NGOs. Six households are engaged in poultry husbandry and 47 households in fishery.

The villagers do not involve themselves in long term and far off migration, but they do work outside village in the off season. Gujjars are constantly move from plains to the mountains and back.

(vi) ***Poverty Alleviation Programmes*:** The village has been benefited a lot from various PASs. During the year 2009-10, there were 5 beneficiers under SGSY, 2 under IAY and 259 MGNREGA. Several SHGs like Jai Mata Di, Amar Jyoti, Satya Narayan Organisation, are actively involved in PA programmes. 72 women (16 SCs and 1 ST) are involved in these groups. Dairy remains the largest enterprise being taken up by these groups.

18 per cent of village population live BPL and RDD is providing them land cultivable through development scheme under Mahatma Gandhi National Rural Employment Guarantee Scheme (MGNREGS). The DSW runs a number of schemes for overall welfare of old-aged, women, children, SCs and STs.

(vii) ***Gram Panchayat*:** There is no Panchyat in the village because no elections were held in the village.

8. Village Laroka, Block/Tehsil, Nowshera, District, Rajouri

(i) Laroka stands as one of the larger villages of Nowshera Block with a population of about 2,000 persons. It is a border village, only 3 km away from Pakistan and is situated 26 km from Nowshera and 45 km from Rajouri. Before 1947, this village was Muslim dominated. But, after migration of Hindus and Sikhs, called refugees and came from PAK, dominated the village. At present, 15 per cent population of this village is Muslim who migrated here after 1982. Like other villages in the area, this village is well connected by metallic roads. Autos are main source of transportation. Being a hilly area, there are different hamlets, called '*mohras*' in the village. The populated *mohras* are bus stand, Patrari, Said Bagla, Toori Mohalla, and Naka Mohalla.

(ii) ***Population and Demography*:** As per 2001 Census, the village population is 2,096 (males 1,180 and females 916). While general castes are 1,300, SCs and STs are 186 and 610 respectively. The religious composition in the village is 1,296. 610 Hindus and 190 Sikhs. While all Muslims are locals, all non-Muslims are refugees. The sex ratio is below 900 Gujjars and Bakerwals live in migratory lifestyle. Now, one of the two members of every Gujjar household has started staying back in order to take care of their immovable property in the village.

(iii) ***Infrastructure***: The common village infrastructure available is as follows:

- One high school
- Three primary schools
- Three aganwadi centres
- One community centre
- Village shopping centre
- One bus stand
- One water works unit
- Roads under BADP
- two middle schools
- one PHC with ISM
- one Panchayat Ghar
- one Shamshan Ghat
- two private middle schools
- one sericulture extension centre
- two ration-kerosene depots

The village seems a well of standard. Most of the houses are pucca. There are many who possess cars, bikes and tractors. Almost every one has a mobile. It is because of refugees who possess vast land which was allocated to them as rehabilitation. Even SCs have got land allocated to them. Thus, the village has institutions for all basic services. There is good village market that caters to the needs of villagers.

(iv) ***Education***: The literacy rate in the village (2001) is 54 per cent (males 64% and females 45%). While Jats and Brahmin have 74 per cent, SCs and STs have 45 per cent and 39 per cent respectively. The educational infrastructure in the village is fairly good. There are one high school, two middle schools (two more private) and three primary schools. While upper castes dominate in these schools, the lower castes have a decent share. The Sadbhavana initiative of the army has also contributed to the educational infrastructure. The teacher-student ratio in the village is 1: 25 (high school 1:44 and middle school 1:20). The drop-out rate has come down considerably. As per teachers information, 2-4 students drop out of schools every year. Rehbar-e-Taleem scheme has bennefited all except the SCs in the village. There prevails wider consciousness for education. The village education committee (VEC) is working for this cause. The SSA and mid-day meal schemes have also made an impact in the village.

(v) ***Health and Sanitation***: The village has a well built PHC with ISM component but no doctor. There is ISM doctor and one pharmacist apart from other employees. There is another centre of availing health service—Army doctor. People often go to this centre. There is private clinic-*cum*-chemist who is known as private doctor'.

While ANM register refers to cough and cold, fever, diarrhoea and arthritis as disease pattern, anaemia is the common disease among the females. Lot of polio case was noticed in 2004. Some people suffer from hypertension and diabetes. The impact of ASHAs and JSY is visible. The CHC at neighbouring Sunderbani tehsil; is most preferred destination in case of delivery. The migratory Gujjar women are least aware about health practices. No maternal death has taken place in past one year and there was no case of malnutrition. The immunization of children and women is 100 per cent. This programme includes BCG, DPT, OPV, Measles and TT. The birth rate in the village is 17 births per 1000 and death rate is 5.6 deaths per 1,000.

The sanitation is not satisfactory in the village. No SC/ST house has a modern latrine. Defacation outside is common. So, the poor sanitation is related to lack of health consciousness.

(vi) ***Agriculture and Land***: The village has the total area of 4,496 acres and it has the following types:

Land for cultivation	—856 acres	land under forest cover	—2404 acres
Land net sown	—774 acres	pasture and grazing land	—411 acres
Wasteland	—781 acres		

The houses in the village are constructed mostly in wasteland and forest land. The Jat community have the maximum land followed by SCs and STs. The details of class-wise distribution of land is as follows:

Landless	—nil	less than 1 acre	—02	1-3 acres	—111
3.5 acres	—187	5-10 acres	—118		

Just 20 per cent of the total area of the village is put to cultivation. Usually two crops are grown by the farmers, *rabi* and *kharif*. Wheat is a major crop of rabi season. It is sown in November and harvested in April. People cultivate vegetables also for self consumption. 90 per cent farmers used HYV seed which is purely rainfed cultivation. The farmers used chemical fertilizers like DAP, urea and organic fertilizers. Only 26 per cent of households have their own tractors.

While the farmers produce for self consumption, only 25 per cent farmers go to Nowshera to sell their excessive produce. Agricultural labourers are hired during harvest season. They are brought from Nowshera on daily wage rate. The common property of the village included 411 acres of Kahcharai, one pond, and village street.

(vii) ***Occupational Patterns*:** Most of the villagers are engaged in agriculture and allied activities. 8 per cent of people are government employees. Here is the occupational pattern of the village:

Indian Army	—66	Police personnel	—20
Education department	—19	Health department	—9
P.H.E.	—11	P.W.D.	—8
Forest department	—4	Others	—6

The Bakerwal community remains moving for the whole year in search of pastures. About 70 people in the village are involved in this activity. Their annual migration is as follows:

Laroka — Rajouri — Dera ki Gali — Bafliaz — Shopian — Laroka

(viii) ***Seasonal Unemployment*:** The major types of unemployment in the village are the structural unemployment and disguised employment. In some families, 4-5 young men are doing farming over 2-3 acres of land which only one person can do. The unemployment is more among SCs and it is minimized through NREGA.

(ix) ***Poverty Alleviation Programmes*:** The following PAPs are carried out by:

— RDD	— MGNRERA	SWD	— Old age pension
—	— SGSY		— SC/ST scholarships
—	— IAY		— Widow pensions
—	— TSC		—Handicap pensions
—	— BADP		

There are varying estimates of poverty prevailing in the village. One estimate puts BPL population at 189 while other puts it at 233.

Out of the 8 SHGs in the Laroka Panchayat, 5 arc in this village. The activity taken by all groups is dairy. The details follows:

Khatana group	— 10 men/women	ST
Bright group	— 10 women	General
Jat group	— 10 men/women	Mixed
Modern group	— 10 women	Mixed
Raza group	— 10 women	ST

NREGA has got the impact as 11.96 lakh which have been spent in the FY 2010-11. 328 job cards were issued out of which 26 were SCs and 145 STs. The works performed included land levelling, pond work, tractor road, pathways and drain channels. Sufficient infrastructure such as buildings, computers, internet connectivity, reporting formats, master sheets, job cards, etc., are in place. All functioners have been imparted necessary training. Payment to the workers is made in time and in a transparent manner through bank account. Works are measured and SOR applied. No unemployment allowance was paid. 34 beneficiers, mostly SCs and STs, have been covered by IAY. The poorest of the poor have been preferred in this process. There has been great impact of Cluster Programme of Central Silk Board (CSB). Laroka and two other villages form one of the three clusters for creating additional income for the rural people. A total of 150 beneficiers have been chosen in this cluster out of which 40 are from Laroka. The government provides for everything, including a separate room (@90,000 per beneficiary), trays and racks to keep the silkworm and also mulberry leaves and trees. An average worker earns Rs. 15,000 in one season. Some earn up to Rs. 40,000.

(x) ***Gram Panchayat***: Though the last Panchayat in the village was elected in 2002, it expired in 2007. The present Panchayat consists of one Sarpanch and 8 Panches. While the former is from Jat community, rest of the members are from Brahmin, SC and ST communities. There are 3 female and 5 male members.

4

Socio-Economic Profile of Rural Rajasthan Village Study

S.N. SINGH

The village has been a basic and important unit in the organisation of Indian social, economic and political life. It is the basic unit of study for understanding the Indian socio-economic situation and development needs. A scientific study of village real life situation is the prerequisite for developmental planning and decentralisation. From time immemorial the village satisfies all their needs and has a sense of unity and a feeling of togetherness towards each other. The development of India can only be achieved by the development of the village. In this way the village is the primary institution and focal point for any development process and planning. Therefore, in the training of Indian Administrative Service (I.A.S.) village study is an important part of field study and each trainee is assigned in-depth study of a particular village.

The present study is based on the village study report of the 26 I.A.S. officers of the 2003-2009 batches of Rajasthan. Every probationer was assigned particular village. He collected data from the village and wrote about its factual situation based on his observation, interaction with the villagers, local leaders and officials. The probationers also submitted a detailed description of the village along with the two case studies. The case studies were of similar nature related with the women representatives of Gram Panchayat, the story of the poorest of the poor in the village, impact of the land reforms based on the study of beneficiaries of distribution of ceiling surplus land, benefit from the agricultural activities and health hazards of the village and study of maternity deaths in the village.

This study report of the trainees used analysed and explained Rajasthan for the grass root facts and observation. But all these data correlated with the latest situation during 2013-14 the village level facts has been presented in the context of Rajasthan and different government sponsored schemes going on in Rajasthan. The report includes the study report of the following I.A.S. trainees of Rajasthan cadre from 2003-2009 (see Table 4.1).

Table 4.1: Socio-economic Profile of Rural Rajasthan: Name of Village and Officer Trainees

State: Rajasthan

Sl. No.	Name of Officer Trainee	District	Village	Batch
1.	Niraj Kumar Pawan	Pali	Baniyawas	2003
2.	Bhanu Prakash Yeturu	Udaipur	Dhar	
3.	Preetam Yashvant	Jhalawar	Uni	
4.	Krishna Kunal	Kota	Nonera	
5.	Ravi Kumar Syroyr	Ajmer	Devanagar	2004
6.	A. Sreenivas	Alwar	Nathusar	
7.	Samit Sharma	Jhalawar	Khanpuriya	
8.	Ravi Jain	Kota	Kotra	
9.	Ambrısh Kumar	Udaipur	Kharpeena	
10.	Punam	Ajmer	Narvar	2005
11.	Purna Chandra Kishan	Ajmer	Narvar	
12.	Arushi Choudhary Malik	Alwar	Jatiyana	
13.	Joga Ram	Jhalawar Shorti	Shorti	
14.	Pallakonda Ramesh	Udaipur	Bhanda	
15.	Arti Dogra (Ms.)	Gogunda	Not Applicable	2006
16.	Gaurav Goyal	Jodhpur	Udaniyon-Ki-Dhani	
17.	Rohit Gupta	Jhalawar	Ratlai	
18.	Saravana Kumar V.	Kota	Thailyakhedi	
19.	Shilpa Ramesh Begar	Ajmer	Ghoogra	
20.	Arushi Malik (Ms.) (2005 Batch)	Alwar	Jatiyana	
21.	Anandhi	Ajmer	Ajaysar	2007
22.	Bishnu Charan Mallick	Jhalawar	Todri, Jagannath	
23.	Tina Soni	Jodhpur	Man Chitiya	
24.	Parameswaran B.	Jodhpur	—	2008
25.	Muktanand Agrawal	Ajmer	—	
26.	Sharandeep Kaur Brar (Ms.)	Ajmer	Ardaka	2009

Source: Village Study Assignments, CRS, LBS National Academy of Administration, Mussoori.

Dr. D.N. Mazumdar, Prof. N.K. Bose, Prof. S.C. Dube and Prof. M.N. Srinivas are the pioneers among those who worked a lot at village level. The Planning Commission has introduced several projects for Rural Development: Community Development Project, Land Reforms, Co-operative Movement, Five Year Plans, Panchayati Raj, National Extension Service and so on and have contributed a lot towards the development of rural study in India.

Now-a-days Rural study is a compulsory subject at the undergraduate level for B.Sc. (Agricultural Engineering), B.Sc. (Home Economics or Home Science), B.Sc. (Veterinary Science) and B.Sc. (Agriculture) students in all agricultural for colleges and universities and it is a major field of specialisation at Post-Graduate level in some of the universities in India however, the Development of rural study of India has not yet attained a scientific level. It is to be hoped that there will be development in this direction in the future.

I. IMPORTANCE OF THE STUDY CONDITION

The importance of the study of rural conditions can be evaluated properly only when one realizes the importance of rural society. village presents a picture of rural life. Villages are important because they are the springs which feed urban areas. The importance of rural study can be put under following heads as administration. Man has an urge to know human life, its relationship change on its situation, innovation, development and this can be fulfilled through the rural study in the following scenario:

(a) In almost all the countries of the world majority of the population resides in villages. It is true that over 65 per cent population of India resides in villages.

(b) It gives complete knowledge of Village Life: Rural study gives us complete knowledge of village life. Village is the first unit of development in a country.

(c) **Rural Reformation:** Rural reformation is the primary aim of rural study. In this context it helps in the following direction.

   (i) ***Organization***: Village units which are disorganized can be organized through rural study. It improves the co-ordination of various units and helps in bringing an improvement in economic, social and health conditions.

(ii) ***Economic Betterment*:** Through detailed study of village problems and observations, rural sociology gives stress on the importance of increasing the quantity and quality of production. This results in raising the standard of living.

(iii) ***Systematic knowledge of progress and reforms in village*:** The Main occupation of nearly 80 per cent population in villages is agriculture.

(iv) ***Solutions of Pathological Social Problems*:** Rural study examines the social pathological problems and it suggests ways for solving this problem.

(v) ***Education*:** The improvement and development of any community depends on its education. Rural study lays stress on education to eradicate rural problems.

(vi) ***Planning for Development*:** Rural study encourages the development of various plans for any rural development programme with the active enrolment of rural people. The work must be carried out according to the plans prepared and executed for the progress in rural society.

The Rural Society of India is extremely backward. Its backwardness is very much due to the several problems that haunt the rural society. The process of change is very slow and so the problems are more or less age old. In recent years, the process of change has been accelerated and so new problems are also cropping up.

The major problems are to do with agriculture, the ownership of land, lack of cottage industries, lack of education, social evils, death of cattle and so on. These problems are the result of traditionalism and conservatism of the Rural Society. The problems of the villages may be studied under the following heads:

(1) The problems concerning agriculture;

(2) The problems of small and cottage industries;

(3) The problems of population growth and Family Planning, animal wealth and animal husbandry;

(4) The problems of rural health and education;

(5) The problem of the status of women;

(6) The problem of child marriage and elderly people;
(7) The problem of traditionalism and conservatism;
(8) The problem of unemployment;
(9) The problem of landless labour;
(10) Rural indebtedness;
(11) Problem of nutrition in villages; and
(12) Problem of housing. Apart from it there are also the problems of untouchability and casteism.

The burden of indebtedness in rural India is great, and falls mainly on the households of rural working people. The exploitation of this group in the credit market is one of the most pervasive and persistent features of rural life in India, and despite major structural changes in credit institutions and forms of rural credit in the post-Independence period, Darling's statement (1925), that "the Indian peasant is born in debt, lives in debt and bequeaths debt", still remains true for the great majority of working households in the countryside. Rural households need credit for a variety of reasons. They need it to meet short-term requirements for working capital and for long-term investment in agriculture and other income-bearing activities. Agricultural and non-agricultural activity in rural areas is typically seasonal, and households need credit to smooth out seasonal fluctuations in earnings and expenditure. Rural households, particularly those vulnerable to what appear to others to be minor shocks with respect to income and expenditure, need credit as an insurance against risk. In a society that has no free, compulsory and universal education or health care, and very few general social security programmes; rural households credit for different types of consumption. These include expenditure on food, housing, health marriage, rituals and education. In Rajasthan, another important purpose of borrowing is to meet expenses for a variety of social obligations and rituals.

About 75 per cent of the Indian population lives in rural areas and about 80 per cent of this population is dependent on agriculture for its livelihood. According to NSSO 68th rural summary, employment and unemployment in India in 2011-12 nearly 48.9 per cent workforce were working in agriculture. Agriculture accounts for about 37 per cent of the national income. The development of the rural areas and of agriculture and its allied activities thus becomes vital for the rapid development of the economy as a whole. In this regard, India has succeeded in developing one of the largest rural banking systems in the world. Various regulatory measures have been taken enabling the banking system to play an important role in the economic development of the rural areas. The two most prominent measures are rural commercial bank branch expansion, thus moving from class banking to mass banking and secondly, priority sector.

Rajasthan—Socio-Economic Profile

Rajasthan is the largest State in the country having an area of 3.42 lakh square km. The State is extremely deficient in water resources and has erratic rainfall. It accounts for 89 per cent of the total desert in the country. Geophysical disadvantages faced by the State constitute major constraints in achieving the desired pace of rural development and delivering of public service to the widely dispersed population and habitations of the State. The State accounts for 5.67 per cent of country's population and 10.4 per cent of country's area, but it has barely 1.1 per cent of the country's surface water and 1.7 per cent of ground water. Per capita availability of water of the State is only 640 cubic metres against the national average of 1,700 cubic metres. The State is also faced with the problems of quality of the ground water. The State also has large tribal tracts in the south and south-east of the State (Table 4.2).

The low density and scattered settlement pattern in the desert around their farm holdings and isolated hills in tribal areas raises the unit cost of delivery of services enormously, almost for all the services delivered, like education, drinking water, medical and health care services, power supply, revenue and general administration.

In Rajasthan the contribution of the Agriculture sector has decreased from 25.62 per cent in the year 2004-05 to 21.41 per cent only in the year 2011-12, while the share of agriculture in national economy has reduced from 19 per cent to 14 per cent. The contribution of industrial sector during the period 2004-05 to 2011-12 has remained at around 31 per cent. The services are growing at a much slower rate than national average. The contribution of the services sector has increased from 43.82 per cent in the year 2004-05 to 47.53 per cent in the year 2011-12, but it is still much below the national average of 58.39 per cent.

Table 4.2: Key Indicators of Rajasthan *vis-à-vis* India

Indicators	*Year*	*Unit*	*Rajasthan*	*India*
Geographical Area	2011	Lakh sq. km.	3.42	32.87
Population	2011	In crore	6.85	121.06
Decadal Growth	2011	Percentage	21.3	17.7
Density of Population	2011	Per sq. km.	200	382
Urban Population to total Population	2011	Percentage	24.9	31.2
Sex Ratio	2011	Per '000 Male	928	943
SC Population to total Population	2011	Percentage	17.8	16.6
ST Population to total Population	2011	Percentage	13.5	8.6
Human Development Index	2011	Value	0.537	0.653
Literacy	2011	Percentage	66.1	73.0
Female	2011	Percentage	52.1	64.6
Male	2011	Percentage	79.2	80.9
Birth Rate	2011	Per '000 Population	26.2	21.8
Infant Mortality Rate	2012	Per '000 Live Birth	49	42
Maternal Mortality Rate	2007-09	Per Lakh	318	212
Life expectancy at Birth –	2006-10 (P)	Years		
Male			66.1	65.8
Female			69.2	68.1
Gross Domestic Product at constant prices (base year 2004-05 (A)	2012-13	Rs. in crore	239913	5503476
Per-capta income at constant prices (base year 2004-05) (A)	2012-13	Rs.	29917	39143
Road Length per 100 sq. km of Area	March, 2011	Km.	71	115
Railway Route Length per 1000 sq. km of Area	March, 2011	Km.	16.90	19.61
Percentage of Forest Area to Reporting Area	2008-09	Percentage	7.96	22.8

(A) Denotes Advanced Estimates

(P) Denotes Projected

Source: Memorandum to the (Fourteenth) Finance Commission Government of Rajasthan, Jaipur, February 2014, p. 62.

The slow annual growth at 5.56 per cent highlights the fact that Rajasthan has not been able to keep pace with growth trends in other parts of the country. In terms of per capita income Rajasthan stands at thirteenth rank amongst the non-special category States. Unless we address the primary reasons for this lower per capita income, i.e. dependence on agriculture, largely traditional methods of cultivation, frequent droughts, limited accessibility to road and rail network in many parts and its typical geographical characteristics, the State's population will remain trapped in low growth and low per capita income cycle. Rajasthan's economic development has many hindrances. But the faulty priority of different plane failed to provide safe drinking water in many rural areas, but constructed metro in Jaipur. The geophysical disadvantage, water deficient agriculture, low industrial base, higher cost of developing infrastructure and delivery of socio-economic and governance services has inhibited the development of the State.

Rajasthan in the last few years has been making all its efforts to develop its economy. Rural development got much attention of the State government. Earlier Rajasthan was regarded as a backward region in a backward economy of India. In the 80's it was grouped as 'BIMARU' State, which includes Bihar, Madhya Pradesh, Rajasthan and Uttar Pradesh on the basis of their demographic indicators and socio-economic backwardness. At present Odisha has similar economic indicators and it also falls in this group and now these States are called 'BIMARU'. These States are lagging behind in socio-economic development compared to advanced States such as Punjab, Haryana, Maharashtra, Tamil Nadu, etc. In 1969, Government of India (GOI) introduced the concept of Special Category State (SCS) during the Fifth Finance Commission to allocate more central assistance to certain disadvantaged States. Three States Assam, Nagaland and Jammu & Kashmir were granted Special Category States (SCS). After this on political consideration eight more Himalayan and North Eastern States were included in SCS. Rajasthan being a desert State was continuously demanding SCS status but has denied by GOI. In May 2013, GoI of India constituted an expert Committee headed by Raghuram G. Rajan (Presently RBI Governor) to consider the demand of SCS, which submitted its report on September 2, 2013. It evolved an underdevelopment index/need index based on ten indicators— monthly per capita consumption, education, health, household amenities, poverty rate, female literacy, percentage of SC/ST population, urbanisation rate, financial inclusion and connectivity. The committee categorised 10 States that scored below 0.6 and above 0.4 as less developed. These include Arunachal Pradesh, Assam, Bihar, Chhattisgarh, Jharkhand, Madhya Pradesh, Meghalaya, Odisha,

Table 4.3: Rajasthan amongst States Ranking by Financial Performance 2011-2012 (Budget Estimates)

Sl. No	States	Tax revenue	Non-tax revenue	Total revenue	Expenditure on general services	Expenditure on social & community services	Expenditure on economic services	Total expenditure
	1	2	3	4	5	6	7	8
1.	Andhra Pradesh	10	16	14	20	17	12	16
2.	Arunachal Pradesh	12	2	2	6	5	1	4
3.	Assam	23	12	19	15	19	21	19
4.	Bihar	28	27	28	28	28	27	27
5.	Chhattisgarh	15	13	20	26	18	14	20
6.	Goa	1	7	4	3	1	3	3
7.	Gujarat	13	20	21	18	20	17	21
8.	Haryana	7	15	13	16	9	10	11
9.	Himachal Pradesh	6	9	9	7	4	9	5
10.	Jammu & Kashmir	16	6	7	4	11	8	8
11.	Jharkhand	26	14	23	27	25	18	24
12.	Karnataka	5	24	17	19	18	11	17
13.	Kerala	4	25	15	10	15	24	13
14.	Madhya Pradesh	21	19	24	23	26	25	25
15.	Maharashtra	11	22	18	17	14	22	18
16.	Manipur	18	5	6	8	8	6	7
17.	Meghalaya	17	8	8	14	6	5	9
18.	Mizoram	8	3	3	2	3	4	2
19.	Nagaland	27	4	5	5	12	7	6
20.	Odisha	19	17	22	21	23	19	22
21.	Punjab	9	18	16	9	22	13	14
22.	Rajasthan	22	21	25	25	24	23	23
23.	Sikkim	2	1	1	1	2	2	1
24.	Tamil Nadu	3	26	12	13	13	15	15
25.	Tripura	20	10	10	11	10	20	12
26.	Uttarakhand	14	11	11	12	7	16	10
27.	Uttar Pradesh	25	28	27	24	27	28	26
28.	West Bengal	24	23	26	22	21	26	28

Source: *A Comparative Study of State's Finance 2011-12* Directorate of Economics & Statistics, Government of Rajasthan, Jaipur, 2013, p. 48.

Rajasthan and Uttar Pradesh. Rajasthan scored 0.626 points and it is demanding for SCS status in 14th Finance Commission. If included in SCS list the State will get much more central assistance for its development activities, including much needed rural development. Next table explains Rajasthan's 23rd rank economic condition in 2011-12 among the 28 states in India in terms of per capita expenditure, and the table supports its dormant for SCS states (See Table 4.3).

Comparison of Rajasthan with the all-India average and the highest level achieved among the non-special category States clearly indicates the alarming gap between the level of development in the State and rest of the country. It is due to generation of own tax revenue and very limited support for the State governments various projects. By December 2013, State had borrowed Rs. 1,31,742 crore loan and in last six months again borrowed Rs. 8,151 crore from various sources.

Poverty in Rajasthan is due to the long history of feudal rule, extremely hostile geographical conditions, the demographic factor, slow economic growth and inadequate budget allocation for the social sector. In 1951, Rajasthan was one of the most economically backward States in India, lacking infrastructure and institutional support for its all-round development. Spread over an area of 3.42 lakh square kilometres it is the largest State in the country. The Aravali hills diagonally divide the State into two parts, South-West to North-East. The region North and North-West which comprises 11 (out of 33) districts and about 61 per cent of the total area of the State is inhabited by 40 per cent of population and this area is known as the famous desert—"The Thar". The population is spread over distant parts of the State and basic facilities such as drinking water, communication, social services and education are not properly available to rural folk. The State's population has been growing at a rate much faster than the national average witnessed during 1931 to 2011 Census. In 1931, its population was only 1.1 crore and 2011 it was 6.85 crore.

***Population Growth*:** The increasing trend in population is continuing the decadal growth rate has declined during 2001-2011 from 28.41 per cent to 21.39 per cent. Despite this deceleration, there are social, economic and ecological imbalances coming up. In the 90's, the government of Rajasthan and a few non-government organisations (NGO) took interest in two children norms, Ever after this initiative in 2011 Census population growth in Rajasthan is more than the national average of 17.70 per cent. The higher decadal growth in population also witnessed higher rise in the number of people under categories of non-worker landless people and BPL. The bakes of nature is getting worsened it creating resource problem. Faster growth of population is also creating degradation, drought, famine and crisis of drinking water along with malnutrition, mass poverty and under-development economically impoverished State. The population growth rate in Rajasthan is much faster than the national average. In 1951, the population of Rajasthan was 160 lakh and rose to 685 lakh in 2011. The growth rate of 3.2 per cent in Rajasthan in 1981 was highest amongst all the States except J&K and North Eastern States. The rapid pace of population growth is also creating tremendous pressure on environment, labour market and social institutions like schools, hospitals and communication. In terms of population it ranks at the ninth position amongst the States of India. The increasing population has also put more pressure on land and other facilities.

***Poverty Rated*:** The greater availability of the NSS data sets has promoted a flurry of studies of poverty in India. NSS data of July 1999 and June 2000 survey estimates only 26.10 per cent of people as BPL. It means a substantial drop of nearly 10 per cent from the estimates for 1993-97 which was earlier at 37 per cent. In 2011-12 total poverty ratio in Rajasthan declined to 14.70 per cent. In the same period national poverty was 21.90 per cent (Table 4.4).

Table 4.4: Rural-Urban Poverty Ratio in India and Rajasthan

(in percentage)

Year	*Rural*			*Urban*			*Total*		
	2004-05	*2009-10*	*2011-12*	*2004-05*	*2009-10*	*2011-12*	*2004-05*	*2009-10*	*2011-12*
Rajasthan	38.80	26.40	16.10	19.90	10.70	34.40	34.40	24.80	14.70
All India	42.00	33.80	25.70	25.50	20.90	13.70	37.20	29.80	21.90

Source: *A Comparative Study of State's Finance 2011-12* Directorate of Economics & Statistics, Government of Rajasthan, Jaipur, 2013, p. 48.

In the context of poverty in rural areas poverty ratio is only 16.10 per cent in Rajasthan and this is 25.50 per cent in all-India. The major causes of rural poverty are concentration of land in a small section of society, primitive agricultural techniques, insufficient irrigation system, drought and famine.

The BPL family constitutes only 14.70 per cent of the families in Rajasthan in 2011-12. But in Tribal areas in the districts of Banswara, Dungarpur, Udaipur, Rajsamand and Chittorgarh it happens to be larger respectively. Banswara and Dungarpur are predominantly tribal and they constitute more than 70 per cent of the total population in the districts respectively. It is also true in the context of the SCs. In the Indian context lower castes are traditionally in a disadvantageous position in the overall socio-economic structure and they have lived for long in perpetual poverty. They continue to face unequal access to public services such as education, decent work, access to equal justice before law. The India Exclusion Resent 2013-14 explains the extent of exclusion of marginalised groups from access to public goods and facilities. In 2011 the Scheduled Castes (SC) constituted above 17.8 per cent and the Scheduled Tribes (ST) 13.5 per cent of the State population. The high percentage of SC and ST category-31.3 per cent put special responsibility on the State Government for their development. A large percentage of them are living below the poverty line. During different Five Year Plans several special strategies for social and economic mobilisation were adopted to eradicate poverty among SC and ST.

The PAP programmes have not brought much changes in their economic and social situation. Inspite of constitutional safeguards, several incentives in educational and economic field, reserved posts and seats in jobs, educational institutions and legislatures, their socio-economic condition remained intact in terms of the percentage of population.

Rajasthan is backward in terms of educational development. The literacy rate in 1937 was only 8.50 per cent as compared to 18.33 per cent in all India. Female literacy rate was only 2.66 per cent. In 2011 Census 66.10 is the overall per cent literacy rate and the female literacy rate is 52.51. It is seven per cent less than all India average.

Table 4.5: Comparative Sectoral Composition of the Economy of Rajasthan *vis-à-vis* All India

(In percentage)

Sector	*All-India*				*Rajasthan*			
	2004-05	*2009-10*	*2010-11*	*2011-12*	*2004-05*	*2009-10*	*2010-11*	*2011-12*
Agriculture	19.03	14.64	14.45	14.10	25.62	19.53	22.60	21.41
Industry	27.92	28.27	28.23	27.51	30.56	32.57	30.93	31.06
Services	53.05	57.09	57.32	58.39	43.82	47.90	46.47	47.53

According to 2011 concentration 75.1 per cent population lives in rural areas. In the last 60 years (1991-2011), the rural population came down to only 75.1 per cent from 84.43 per cent. It also reflects the slow pace of urbanisation in Rajasthan in comparison to other Indian States. In rural areas, agriculture is the major source of livelihood that is why 70 per cent working force in Rajasthan is engaged in agricultural activities. A comparison of the occupation-wise data of the census in 1981 with that of the census in 2011 indicates that the work force has increased from 36.61 per cent to 43.6 per cent. There has been an appreciable increase in the number of female workers in 2011 over 1981 Census; the percentage of female workers (rural) has increased from 24.99 in 1981 to 42.7 in 2011.

II. LAND REFORMS

Soon after Independence, the Government of India and State governments announced land reforms to bring structural changes in rural areas to give land to the tillers to improve the economic situation of the rural poor. Greater emphasis was given to redistribution of land and improving the plight of the landless tenants by tenancy reforms and imposing ceiling on large landholdings. In feudal Rajasthan, Jagir system was in vogue to collect land revenue. In 16,780 villages, the Jagir system, and in 16,834 villages Khalsa land was prevalent. About 60 per cent of the total area of the State was in Jagir areas, mostly in the districts of Jaisalmer, Barmer, Nagaure, Jalore, Jhunjhunu, Sikar and Bikaner. There were social chains of Jagirdars with a chain of intermediaries, such as tenants, sub-tenants, share-croppers, bonded labourers and agricultural labourers. The Jagirdars were collecting land revenue for the rulers and maintaining law and order in their regions of jagirs. They were collecting heavy land tax from the tenants and thus impoverishing them forever. The Jagirdari system enhanced the economic, social and political domination of the Rajput jagirdars over the tenants, agricultural labourers and villagers. In course of time, the nature and forms of domination of peasants have changed quite substantially.

After Independence, the Rajasthan government promulgated the Rajasthan Protection of Tenants Ordinance in June 1949 and Rajasthan Land Reforms and Resumption of Jagirs Act 1952, and again a number of times these Acts were amended by the Rajasthan Legislative Assembly. The main thrusts of land reforms were (i) the abolition of intermediaries (Jagirdars and Biswedars) tenancy reforms; (ii) ceiling on landholdings; and (iii) consolidation of holdings. The abolition of Jagirdars was completed in Rajasthan after the implementation of Rajasthan Tenancy Act 1955 and 1959. But the land reforms in terms of ceiling on landholdings and consolidation of holdings were not seriously implemented. Land ceiling limits were implemented in 1960 and thereafter were reduced from 336 acres of land. It was the highest in the country. During the Fifth Plan, measures of distribution of surplus land were regarded as a process that would lead to removal of poverty. It was recommended to redistribute the acquired land after the imposition of a ceiling among the small and marginal farmers. The provision of security of tenure of sharecroppers and temporary tenants also got attention and was executed to some extent. Till 1985-86 in the State 608.625 acres of land was declared under ceiling and 5,42,473 acres was taken possession and 3,91,822 acres were distributed among 72,295 landless tenants. Out of it 26,690 were Scheduled Caste people.

Apart from distribution of ceiling land, allotment of agricultural land, both in non-project areas and minor and medium command areas, was started in Rajasthan by The Rajasthan Land Revenue Act 1956. In it over 18 lakh acres of land was allotted to various social groups and out of it 4.565 lakh SC, 3.90 ST persons got 21.56 and 1,076 lakh hectares of land respectively. Most of the beneficiaries were landless tillers.

The tenancy reforms had given the tenants permanent rights and ownership of their land after giving marginal compensation to the landlords in the long run. Even after the Jagirdari abolition and tenancy reforms, landlords were controlling huge areas of land. To acquire land from their control, Rajasthan Tenancy (Amendment) Act 1960 for fixation of ceiling area and acquisition of surplus land came into force from 15th December, 1963 after receiving the approval of the President of India. A number of times, this act was amended to break the hold of the Benami transferred lands. But these Acts were not implemented properly due to manipulation and domination of the landlords. In 1982, legislation was passed to give land to share croppers who are the actual tillers, but it was also not implemented. Even now thousands of litigation cases are going on regarding ceiling and other land related laws. But these laws certainly changed the rural class structure and the tillers of the land became owners of the land to a great extent.

There had been a lot of obstacles in the implementation of ceiling legislation. It was a very difficult task for the authorities to acquire and distribute surplus land. The landlords challenged it in the courts and got stay orders from different courts. They used other tactics to thwart the legislation such as selling or transforming some parts of their land. Therefore, the distribution of land continues to be unequal and the distribution of productive surplus land amongst landless labourers or marginal farmers has not been sufficient. Land reforms failed to give land as an asset to all the rural poor and they continued to remain BLP formality depending on the government for grants in IRDP or JRY and other PAP programmes.

Excessive dependence on agriculture in certain districts leads to a lower rate of literacy and lesser urbanisation, and industrialisation. The density of population is very high in the districts of Dausa, Jaipur, Bharatpur and Alwar. Therefore, in this part of Rajasthan there is a larger concentration of poor people and there are more mouths to feed and more hands without work. This generates various social and economic problems such as hunger, disease, illiteracy, unemployment, and social tension. The district of Jaipur with 598 persons per sq. km had the highest density. Whereas Jaisalmer district with a persons per sq. km is the lowest. In 19 districts the density was more than the State average.

III. AGRARIAN REFORMS

In 66 years the different elected governments have given priority to agricultural development. About 50 per cent of the State budget was earmarked for rural and agricultural development. In the 2014-15 State budget, the Chief Minister, Vasundhara Raje has given importance to *bijili-sadak-paani* formula and sanctioned various plans for transport, water and electricity supply on 10th August, 2014 she presented her view on "Rajasthan 2020-way Ahead" during the first meeting on the Chief Minister's advisory council. She focussed on various issues pertaining to health, education, and others. CM announced the decisions to establish additional capacity of 6,500 MW electricity in next five years and construction of 20,000 kW of roads. These is training for a Master Plan for the towns and village having populations of more than 10,000 now the government of Rajasthan is directing its on infrastructure, investment, economic growth, health, nutrition, education and livelihood. But she also mentioned that 97 per cent of the state budget goes to salary, pension, loan and internist payment. Only three per cent of its budget is left for all the development activities. State government in looking towards more central assistance and planning to impose new taxes to generate internal resources. In it irrigation was the most important component. Therefore, land area under cultivation increased from 97.55 lakh hectares in 1951-52 to 2.3 in 1987-88. The area under irrigation increased more than three and a half times. It rose to 66.61 lakh hectares in 2010-11 from 11.71 lakh hectares in 1951-52. In Rajasthan, peasants were mostly cultivating only one crop in a year. But the irrigational facilities made available to them by canals and tube-wells slowly changed the crop-pattern. The total double cropped area in 1951-52 was only 4.42 lakh hectares which increased to 64.78 lakh hectares in 2011-12. It helped the State to become self-sufficient in foodgrain production which was a meagre 33.8 lakh tonnes. Production reached a record level of 220.50 lakh tonnes in 2011-12. Due to consistent drought in 2011-12 foodgrain production has declined in 2010-11. The oilseed production registered an impressive increase in Rajasthan. Production of oilseeds has increased manifolds since 1985-87. A real breakthrough in production of mustard oil has been achieved. During the last 64 years, it has been observed that the area under crop and production of crops has also undergone significant changes. Area under the rabi cultivation over the years increased substantially. Further, the production of different cash crops, cereals, pulses, foodgrains and oilseeds registered a substantial jump under the rabi. All this was possible only due to government institutional support and incentives built up in agriculture and allied fields.

In Rajasthan per capita food production has increased. In spite of that the growth of agricultural production is lower than that in many other States. The agrarian economy of other backward States is far better because of consumption of fertilisers per hectare of gross cropped area, use of other high-tech inputs such as tractors, electric pumps and oil engines.

Table 4.6: Size of Land Class-wise Holding and Area of SC/ST and Other during 1985-86

Holding	*Holdings (Lac nos.)*			*Total*	*Area (Lac Hec.)*			*Total*
	SC (%)	*ST (%)*	*Others*		*SC (%)*	*ST (%)*	*Others*	
Marginal Below 1 ha	2.196 (30.9)	2.791 (38.5)	8.62	13.611	1.136 (4.7)	1.304 (7.4)	3.97	6.41
Small (1-2 ha)	1.672 (23.6)	1.733 (23.9)	5.84	9.240	2.386 (9.8)	2.466 (14.1)	8.41	13.27
Semi-medium (2-4 ha)	1.462 (20.6)	1.527 (21.6)	6.84	9.826	4.126 (16.9)	4.268 (24.3)	19.53	27.92
Medium (4-10 ha)	1.247 (17.6)	0.977 (13.5)	7.64	9.868	6.672 (31.5)	5.832 (33.2)	47.71	61.21
Large (10 ha & above)	0.515 (7.30)	0.222 (3.0)	4.35	5.084	9.029 (37.1)	3.78 (21.0)	85.19	97.90
Total %age to the total holding	**7.092 (14.9)**	**7.25 (15.2)**	**33.29**	**47.629 100.00**	**24.34 (11.8)**	**17.55 (8.5)**	**164.81**	**206.714 100.00**

Source: *Agriculture Situation in India*, December 1988, Director of Economics & Statistics, Ministry of Agriculture, New Delhi and Agriculture Census: 1985-86, Rajasthan, Preliminary Report, Government of Rajasthan, Revenue Secretary and Agriculture Census Commissioner, Rajasthan.

The Table 4.6 shows that even after land reforms, acquisition and distribution of surplus land a large number of holdings and area of land are still with the social groups other than SC and ST. Out of the total 206.7 lakh hectares of land, 24.34 and 17.55 lakh hectares belongs to them. In the context of ownership of large holdings 10 and above hectares of land on 51 to 22 thousand of holdings are with the SC and ST. In contrast 435 thousand holdings are with the rest of the population. Only one-third of small holdings and area are with them. Due to the surplus land distribution they got these small holdings between shares in area operated which was 3.43 hectares for the SC and 2.42 hectares for ST respectively. It had been noticed that people of general categories were purchasing land from SC and ST. Therefore, suitable amendments have been made in the act to provide special protection to them. To prevent distress sales SC and ST tenants cannot transfer, sell, mortgage or otherwise transfer land to any other except SC and ST. It retained land within their social section.

Table 4.7: Agriculture Calculate Year 2010-11 in Social Community with Number of Area

Sl. No.	Land Holder	Holding (Lac nos.)					Area (lac Hec.)				
		SC (%)	ST (%)	Others	Institute	Total	SC (%)	ST (%)	Others	Institute	Total
1.	Marginal	372	593	1542	4	2511	191	279	766	2	1236
	Below 1 ha	14.81	23.62	61.41	0.16	100.00	15.43	22.54	61.87	0.16	100.00
2.	Small	230	265	1014	2	1511	327	373	1459	3	2162
	(1-2 ha)	15.22	17.54	67.11	0.13	100.0	15.13	17.25	66.48	0.14	100.0
3.	Semi-medium	178	170	984	3	1335	500	470	2796	8	3774
	(2-4 ha)	13.33	12.74	73.71	0.22	100.00	13.25	12.45	74.09	0.21	100.00
4.	Medium	135	79	911	2	1127	818	459	5627	14	6918
	(4-10 ha)	11.98	7.01	80.83	0.18	100.00	11.82	6.64	81.34	0.20	100.0
5.	Large	39	13	350	2	404	631	204	6127	82	7044
	(10 ha & above)	9.65	3.33	86.63	0.50	100.00	8.96	2.90	86.98	1.16	100
	Total	**954**	**1120**	**4801**	**13**	**6888**	**2467**	**1785**	**16775**	**109**	**21136**
	%age to the total holding in the State	**13.85**	**16.26**	**69.70**	**0.19**	**100.0**	**11.67**	**8.44**	**79.37**	**0.52**	**100.0**

In 2010-11 agriculture census, share of land holdings declined in context of SC and ST. It was 11.8 and 8.5 per cent in 1985-86 and it declined to 11.67 and 8.44 in 2010-11. It is due to purchase of land of SC and ST by newly constituted academic institutions, private universities and other enterprises other than agriculturalists. The Table 4.7 explains it.

IV. ASSET PROVISION

In rural Rajasthan land is still the basic source of livelihood. Therefore, the identification of BPL family is based on land ownership and production related to agricultural activities. At the bottom of society there are classes of landless workers and artisans. Most of them are from the SC, ST and OBC category. Their employment is usually seasonal and wages are not sufficient to permit savings. The number of those belonging to the upper castes among them are negligible. They are engaged in their skilled or unskilled occupations. Along with the class of landless labourers, there is the class of share-croppers. They possess some acres of small land and instruments of production such as fertilizers, ploughs, cattle, seeds, etc. Since their holdings are not economically viable, some of the members of their families are compelled to work as labourers and to go out for work. The incidence of ill-health, malnutrition and poverty is very high among them. They are low in socio-political and economic status and powerless even in PRI. They are doing well in cattle growing and trading of its products. The cattle population of the State as per the 1991 Census was 484 lakh and rose to 543 lakh in 1997, 1,087 lakh in 2003 and 1,211 lakh in 2007 which gives a ratio of almost 1:1 with human population in the State. During 2003 and 2007 cattle population increased by 11.44 per cent. The cattle population, however, has been increasing with every livestock census. In subsequent drought years a large number of cattle-owners migrated to neighbouring States for protecting their cattle during drought and famine.

In Rajasthan, animal husbandry is not merely subsidiary to agriculture, but is a major economic activity, specially in the arid and semi-arid areas, providing much needed insurance against frequently occurring scarcity conditions to the poor families. After crop production, animal husbandry is the most common activity in Rajasthan which is closely interwoven with agriculture and plays an important role in the rural economy by providing employment and stalling the household income, with wide variation in the region and households. A nationwide study, carried out by NCAER in 1990, found that revenue from milk sale alone accounted for 22 per cent of family incomes.

Livestock sector tops in rural employment with 4.5 per cent growth against 1.75 for all sectors and 1.1 for agriculture. This sector has also the highest potential for rural self-employment generation at the lowest possible investment per unit. Development of livestock sector, therefore, is the critical path-way to rural prosperity. Livestock management is labour intensive with a high concentration of women contributing to it. This sector, therefore, not only provides livelihood to rural poor, but is also an integral part of life of rural economy and is directly benefiting women and families of mostly below poverty line.

The level of production of important livestock products such as milk has increased from 31 lakh tonnes into 54.50 tonnes in 1996-97. Production of wool rose from 100 lakh kg in 1979-80 to 180 lakh kg in 1996. Similarly, production of meat witnessed more than 300 per cent increase. These livestock products were from rural areas and helped a lot in PAP. The three subsequent droughts have had a negative impact on dairy due to non-availability of fodder and water. The Government of Rajasthan is providing subsidies to cattle owners and co-operatives.

Rajasthan accounts for about 9.16 per cent of the total milk and 40 per cent of wool produced in the country. A concerted approach for the development of dairy in the State was initiated in 1971 under 'Operation Food'. The Rajasthan Co-operative Dairy Federation came into being in 1978 and has continued to undertake the task of dairy development through the 'Anand Pattern' three-tier co-operative structure.

V. INCOME AND CONSUMPTION SUPPORT

The composition of net State domestic product by broad sectors of economy from 1988-89 onwards at constant (1980-81) price reaffirms that the economy of the State continues to be agrarian in character. The contribution of the primary sector consisting of agriculture, animal husbandry, forestry, and mining to the NSDP has ranged from 44.45 per cent to 50.13 per cent, whereas the contribution of this sector to the Net National Product (NNP) was between 31.74 per cent and 34.9 per cent during the same period.

Causes of poverty in rural areas in Rajasthan are as follows:

1. Rapid population growth;
2. Lack of capital and infrastructure;

3. Lack of alternative employment opportunities other than agriculture;
4. Excessive population pressure on agriculture;
5. Illiteracy lack of skill training;
6. Regional disparity, desert, mountain and erratic rainfall;
7. Mismanagement in public distribution system; and
8. Corruption in policy formulation, implementation and evaluation of poverty elimination programme.

Government Initiative: To eliminate rural poverty, the following steps are being taken by the Government of Rajasthan:

Legal elimination of bonded labourers,

Abolition of Jamindari system and implementation of land reforms,

Antodaya programme,

Small Farmers Development Programme (SFDP),

Drought Area Development Programme (DADP),

Integrated Rural Development Programme (IRDP),

National Rural Employment Programme (NREP),

Jawahar Gram Samriddhi Yojana,

Mid-Day Meal Scheme,

TRYSEM Scheme,

Swarna Jayanti Gram Swarozgar Yojana,

Mahila Samriddhi Yojana,

Pradhan Mantri Gramodaya Yojana,

Sampurna Gramin Rozgar Yojana,

Indira Awaas Yojana,

Samagra Awaas Yojana,

Pradhan Mantri Rojgar Yojana, and

Bhamashah Yojana.

VI. TWENTY POINT PROGRAMME (TPP)

On 1st July, 1975 the Prime Minister, Indira Gandhi, gave the slogan of 'Garibi Hatao' (Removal of Poverty). It continues to be an elusive goal for politicians. The programme launched was further revised in the year 1982 in the Sixth FY Plan (1980-85) and also in 1986. Presently, the programme is being implemented for economic development and upliftment of the poorer sections of the society. It was discontinued in 1977-79 by the Janata Party Government and was started in 1980 when Congress (I) again came to power at the centre and in Rajasthan. The Congress (I) remained in power in Rajasthan and till 1990 it was an important PAP. Even the BJP-led government continued TPP as till 1995 the Congress (I) was the ruling party at the Centre and substantial Plan allocation was made for it. During 1998-99, Rajasthan government got the first prize in the implementation of TPP in all India level. In 1998 and 2008, Congress (I) again came into power and the BJP government captured power in December 2013. Now, their objective includes eradicating poverty, raising productivity, reducing income inequalities and removing social and economic disparities. Now it has 65 items and 20 items are being monitored including MGNREGS. In these programmes public interventions are made in the form of social employment programmes, social security measures (e.g., safety nets), infrastructural programmes and skill upgradation programmes. These programmes are in operation for nearly 40 years and have helped identify poor households in rural areas every year to cross the poverty line. In some cases non-poor have availed themselves of the benefits under this programme. Even the local leaders and institutions like Gram Sabha worked on partial way to help the non-poor.

The Government of Rajasthan followed the path of planned economic growth. It started various activities and incentives in the field of agriculture and rural development. The problems of poverty, malnutrition, inadequate employment and lack of infrastructural facilities in rural areas increased. The continuous efforts of the State government failed to check rising rural poverty and miseries of rural poor. Small Farmers Development Programme, Drought Prone Area Programme, Desert Development Programme, TSP, IRDP, TAD, IRY, etc. are being implemented by the District Rural Development Agencies (DRDA). The State government has made sufficient budget allocation for the employment generating programmes. But the benefits from these programmes have not substantially reached the poor population of the State. The rich peasants and other influential rural sections monopolised the major amount of incentives. They are getting subsidised electricity and are making huge profits from production of oil seeds, cotton and wheat but are not paying electricity bill and land revenue properly.

In addition to the above mentioned programmes the following steps were taken under the 20-Point Programme by the Government of India and Rajasthan for eradication of poverty.

1. Attack on rural poverty.
2. Strategy for agriculture dependent on rains.
3. Better utilization of irrigation water.
4. Bigger harvests.
5. Enforcement of land reforms.
6. Special programme for rural labour.
7. Clean drinking water.
8. Health for all.
9. Two child norm.
10. Expansion of education.
11. Justice for SC & ST.
12. Equality for women.
13. New opportunities for the people.
14. Residential houses for people.
15. Improvement of the urban slums.
16. New strategy for forestry.
17. Protection of environment.
18. Concern for consumer.
19. Energy for the villages.
20. A responsible administration.

In these plans small farmers were the target group. In 1977 a novel scheme of Antyodaya was implemented by the Janata Party Government to uplift the poorest of the poors in the villages by providing income generating assets through a mix of subsidy and loan. The food for work programme was also started to generate work and infrastructure like roads and canal. Only small money was spent by the government on rural development in the First Five Year Plan. In these Plans the amount spent on rural development was Rs. 04 crore, Rs. 12.52 crore, Rs. 14.48 crore, Rs. 3.00 crore and Rs. 19.24 crore respectively. Priority was given to capital formation in agriculture sector, improvement in the living standard of the poor, development of infrastructure and growth in social sector.

VII. FIVE YEAR PLAN PRIORITIES

It was in the Sixth Five Year Plan that the Government of India realised that a sizeable amount had to be provided for rural development if abject poverty in the rural areas was to be reduced. Consequently, an amount of Rs. 123.32 crore or 5.78 per cent of the total Plan expenditure was spent on rural development in the Sixth Plan (1981-85). In 1978-79 the Integrated Rural Development Programme (IRDP) was launched. It focused on reduction of unemployment in rural areas and provision of assets and inputs to the poor for enabling them to rise above the poverty line on a lasting basis. It was for the poorest among the poor consisting of small and marginal farmers, agricultural and non-agricultural labourers, rural artisans and craftsmen, SC, ST and persons living under BPL. Production assets and resources were provided to 150 lakh families during the Sixth Plan.

In the Seventh Plan, an amount of Rs. 207.69 crore or 6.68 per cent of the total Plan expenditure was spent on rural development. In the Eighth FY Plan (1992-97), an amount of Rs. 1021.76 crore or 8.88 per cent of the total outlay of the Plan was provided for various schemes of rural development in Rajasthan. Important schemes include the IRDP, Jawahar Rozgar Yojana (JRY), Drought Prone Area Programme (DPAP), Desert Development Programme (DD) and Employment Guarantee Programme (EGP). Top priority has been given to poverty removal, human resources development and to create durable assets for the benefit of all the villagers.

In the Eighth Five Year Plan (1992-97), allocation in agriculture and allied services was 1286.92 crore (11.91%) of the total Plan allocation. But in the Ninth Five Year Plan it is 1880.04 crore or 6.80 per cent of the total Plan.

To provide the following 7 Basic Minimum Services (BMS) on a uniform basis in the entire country in a time-bound manner with a view to alleviating poverty and improving the quality of life of people was the aim of this Plan; Safe drinking water in every habitation, according to national norm; provision of efficient primary health care for every group of 5,000 people; provision of public housing assistance to all the shelterless poor persons. Connectivity to all villages/habitations by providing an all-weather road; nutrition support to every child from the poor families during pre-school and elementary education stages; fair price shops to supply essential commodities through the public distribution system in every village/Panchayat; adequate arrangements for universal as well as compulsory primary education, especially of women and girl child in villages together with related measures for spread of literacy. This is a dream which need the thrust of the State as well as the Central government in 2014.

The Tenth Five Year Plan envisages establishment of specific monitorable targets covering economic, social and environmental dimension of development, including targets on reduction in poverty ratio, universal enrolment of children in schools, raising literacy rates, decline in infant mortality and maternal mortality rates, raising employment growth rate, improving coverage of villages in terms of access to safe drinking water, reducing illiteracy and gender gap, etc.

The Plan places critical responsibility on the Panchayat Raj institutions particularly with regard to improved delivery mechanism for poverty alleviation schemes and also improving accountability at the local level in the public provisioning of educational and health services.

The main thrust of different IX, X, XI, and XII Plans was to eradicate poverty through various agricultural and rural development programmes. Therefore, consistent Plan allocation in agriculture, rural development, irrigation and power increased in terms of investment and percentage of the total Plan allocation. In the Twelfth Plan emphasis is on inclusive development along urban facilities in rural area.

Periodic drought and scarcity conditions are a characteristic feature of Rajasthan. With its meagre water resources and perilous dependence on scanty and uncertain rainfall, it is most vulnerable to drought and famine conditions. The frequency of drought appears to have increased. During the 40 years from 1975 onwards the spectre of crop failure and drought has haunted the people of the State.

From the above mentioned different Five Year Plans programmes it may be mentioned that the Central government and Rajasthan Government had broadly taken six types of programmes towards alleviation of poverty.

These are:

1. Provision of employment through (a) wage employment and (b) self-employment in rural as well as urban areas.
2. Food security.
3. Development of disadvantaged people such as SCs, STs, OBCs, minorities, women, street children, destitute and persons suffering from disability.
4. Provision of basic minimum services.
5. Political empowerment of the poor.
6. National social assistance programme.

In the different sectors, Plan allocation percentage has come down. Investment is quite bigger than in VIII Plan. In real terms there has been a decline in the government's expenditure in PAP in the 90's.

The development of irrigation facilities is vital for agriculture and rural development. In spite of its vital importance, allocation in this sector has come down to 11.21 per cent from 16.69 per cent of Eight Plan. The ambitious Indira Gandhi Canal Project for irrigation and drinking water which was started in 1959 also suffers from insufficient allocation in this vital sector of rural economy. The economic reforms and programmes of structural adjustment which involve privatisation and globalisation failed to attract private investment, both domestic and foreign. In Rajasthan enough public revenues for funding rural development are not available and the State government is in difficulty to pay regularly to its employees. Hence, economic growth will suffer in the coming years. During Twelfth Plan 1997-02, emphasis was on poverty alleviation.

Periodic crop failures and droughts have affected the State's economy directly as well as indirectly. The Government is compelled to spend substantial funds on relief in years of drought. Periodic crop failures have kept the farmers and non-farm workers impoverished and debt-ridden. This phenomenon has depressed the State Domestic Product and per capita income to about 75 per cent of the national level. Dealing with drought requires both, short as well as long term strategies. While the State has performed well in managing droughts from one year to the next, the longer-term issues have yet to be tackled. Drought proofing the economy requires concerted effort on several fronts. These include more irrigation for larger areas; more importantly, it requires better water management in irrigated areas and change in the crop pattern.

VIII. AGRICULTURE SCENARIO

Agriculture has been a way of life and continues to be the single most important means of livelihood of the masses. Agriculture and the allied sectors play an important role in the State's economy. Agriculture in Rajasthan is primarily rain fed. The period of monsoon is short. Due to unstable weather conditions, farmers have to depend on both, rain fed and ground water agriculture.

Problem of Drinking Water

The ground water condition in the State has become quite alarming due to overexploitation in the last two decades. Water crisis across State deepened further as 172 out of total 243 Blocks in the State, only 25 Blocks are safe, 20 are semi critical in terms of ground water balance, 172 Blocks are over-exploited category, 24 are critical with two Blocks being completely saline. The average extraction of ground water in the State is 137 per cent of recharge with one Block having extraction of 600 per cent of the recharge.

The State also suffers from the problem of quality of available water. Out of the total water quality affected habitations of the country, 26 per cent belong to Rajasthan State only. There are 6,876 habitations affected from fluoride, 15,557 habitations from salinity, 11 habitations from iron and 1,397 habitations from nitrate. Thus, as many as 23,841 habitations suffer from water quality issue. In addition to this 27,850 habitations are only partially covered with drinking water supply. Poor quality of drinking water adds to serious health concerns also. In rural areas during summer, women are unable to take bath due to water crisis. Along with poor quality of water the availability of drinking water is a major problem in Rajasthan. In many districts women have to go 4 to 5 km to fetch water. People of many villages migrated to adjoining States. In a few villages youth are not getting married. Women are returning to their parent's home due to water crisis. Water problem is more serious in Alwar near National Capital region, with Bhilwara, Barmer and Bikaner districts on 24 July, 2014 State water resources Minister announced that there was no ban on digging tube well for drinking water purposes after obtaining prior permission even on dark zone. He said sufficient efforts would be made to provide drinking water to areas suffering from acute shortage of water.

Presently more than 90 per cent of water supply schemes are based on ground water. Due to overexploitation, the ground water sources are likely to be completely dry in the next 10 to 15 years. The Government of Rajasthan is taking deep interest for augmentation of the existing sources, improvement in the distribution system, replacement of filter plants and to address salinity and fluoride problems etc.

Irrigation

At the time of the formation of the State in 1949, a little less than 10 lakh hectares of area was irrigated, which was just 13 per cent of the total area under cultivation. This rose to 83.23 lakh hectares of area in the year 2011-12 bringing 32.01 per cent of the total area under irrigated cultivation. Though significant progress has been made, Rajasthan is still behind the national average. Further, 68.7 per cent of irrigated potential in the State is based on ground water, which has erratic assurance of water availability depending in turn on rainfall.

Famines, droughts and scarcity of food and fodder is a very common problem for the government of Rajasthan. In almost all famines and droughts more than a crore of people and cattle are affected by it. The Government has to manage heavy financial burden from its own resources or relief fund by the Government of India. During famine year State government suspended called off land revenue which reduces the revenue receipts of the government. In rural areas more people go to below poverty line and face uncertain economic situation. A large number of cultivators migrate to neighbouring States with their cattle. To mitigate droughts, Government of Rajasthan, along with 13 States deployed satellites in

Table 4.8: Year-wise position of Districts and Villages with Population (Human and Livestock) affected by Famine/Scarcity Conditions in the State

Year	*Number Affected*								
	Districts	*Percent to total*	*Villages*	*Percent to total*	*Population in lakhs*	*Percent to total*	*Livestock in lakhs*	*Percent to total*	*Land revenue suspended (lakh)*
1995-96	29	94	25478	62	273.82	62	282.29	58.22	210
1996-97	21	68	5905	15	55.29	13	72.60	14.97	30
1997-98	24	75	4633	11	14.91	3	29.37	5.37	3
1998-99	20	62	20069	49	215.07	48	295.78	54.12	170
1999-00	26	81	23406	57	260.79	58	345.60	63.23	130
2000-01	31	97	30583	73	330.41	74	399.69	73.13	310
2001-02	18	56	7964	19	69.70	15	69.73	12.73	46
2002-03	32	100	40990	97	447.80	98	451.63	91.91	430
2003-04	03	09	649	01	5.82	01	7.57	1.54	8.80
2004-05	31	97	19814	47	227.65	40	222.44	45.27	168
2005-06	24	75	15939	38	198.44	35	178.10	36.25	123
2006-07	28	88	11944	28	136.73	24	142.01	28.90	365
2007-08	12	36	4309	10	56.12	8	61.47	10.85	399
2008-09	12	36	7402	17	100.12	15	106.00	18.71	477
2009-10	27	82	33464	75	429.15	63	364.55	64.34	460
2010-11	2	6	1249	50	13.67	2	12.79	2.26	9.5
2011-12	7	21	3061	28	35.86	5	28.40	5.01	30.8
2012-13	12	36	8030	52	120.90	18	106.21	18.74	—

Source: *Economic Review* 2012-13 Government of Rajasthan, Jaipur.

2013. They will predict patchy monsoon on the basis of taluk and district level data. Now, Rajasthan can handle future droughts in case of scanty rain.

Vast Desert and Drought Prone Area

The State has been perennially prone to drought conditions. The deficient rainfall severely affects the State's economy and erodes the coping capacity of the people. Water, employment and protection of the livestock population often become the main concerns of the State Government adversely affecting other development efforts. The financial implications of these efforts are enormous. Despite increase in irrigated area in the State, agricultural production remains highly dependent on rainfall.

Water Supply

The State Government is implementing a number of schemes for providing potable water, both in rural and urban areas as the problem of clean and safe water in the State is very complex due to geographical diversities and limited availability of both, ground and surface water.

Rural Water Supply: Due to vigorous efforts of the State Government, the water problem is being solved gradually. The present status of villages/habitations covered with fully/partly drinking water facility is as under:

Table 4.9

Habitation	*Unit*	*Total*	*Covered upto December 2012*
Main Villages	Number	39,753	39,751
Dhanies	Number	81,380	67,232

Source: *Economic Review* 2012-13 Government of Rajasthan, Jaipur.

During the year 2014-15, nearly 3,173 villages/habitations are targeted to benefit from water supply against which 570 villages/ habitations of SC, 390 ST and 100 of minority community Rajasthan planning to provide safe drinking water Along with drinking water grid will be established to provide drinking water all over along with proposed 5 smart cities facilities made available to SC/ST busties.

IX. STATE FLAGSHIP PROGRAMMES

The State Government has announced a lot of policy measures and is implementing a number of very popular State Flagship Programmes (along with National Flagship Programmes) for the benefit of the people of the State. The State Government has been making efforts for improving the social and economic status of the people in the State. The State Government, for the upliftment of the common man and with a objective of ensuring that the benefits of schemes reach to the last man of the society, has identified its important public welfare schemes as Flagship programmes for greater emphasis and 15 State Flagship programmes are being implemented. The State Flagship programmes being run are as follows:

- Mukhyamantri Ann Suraksha Yojana;
- Mukhyamantri Nishulk Dava Yojana;
- Mukhyamantri BPL Jeevan Raksha Kosh Yojana;
- Rajasthan Janani Shishu Suraksha Yojana;
- Mukhyamantri Gramin BPL Awas Yojana;
- Affordable Housing Policy;
- Rajasthan Guaranteed Delivery of Public Services Act 2011;
- Rajasthan Right to Hearing Act 2012;
- Mukhyamantri Pashudhan Nishulk Dava Yojana;
- Mukhyamantri Shahari BPL Awas Yojana;
- Exemption from Interest to Farmers for timely Repayment of Loans Scheme;
- Mukhyamantri Uchcha Shiksha Chhatravritti Yojana, 2012;
- Rajiv Gandhi Digital Vidyarthi Yojana;
- Mukhyamantri Kaushal Vikas Yojana; and
- Rajasthan Gramin Sadak Vikas Yojana.

Today, there is an overall praise for these schemes of Rajasthan and several States have shown keen interest to implement them on similar pattern in their States. In 2014-15, Government of Rajasthan decided five important areas for the village development named as total development.

Education: The State Government is making concentrated efforts for improving the social and economic status of people through better development of education and educational infrastructure. The State is endeavouring to achieve the objective of total literacy through implementation of various programmes/schemes. In elementary education, there are 49,642 Primary Schools with more than 2.22 lakh teachers and 59,547 Upper Primary Schools with more than 2.51 lakh teachers wherein the total enrolment is 130.27 lakh. In view of achieving the goal of cent per cent enrolment and retention of children in schools in the age group of 6-14 years, Child Tracking System has been conducted and 12.10 lakh out of School and Never Enrolled Children have been identified through this survey. Intensive enrolment drive was conducted and out of school children were mainstreamed. At present, 15,497 Primary and 8,173 Secondary and 3,357 Senior

Secondary schools are in the government sector wherein 31.81 lakh students including 13.03 lakh girls are studying. There are many more lakh children who miss out on school, which is a huge impediment in their growth and capacity building in rural areas Children of 10+age are working as child labour in agriculture and animal husbandry. Thousands of them are migrating to urban areas and to more hazardous work.

Rajasthan Lowest Spender on Quality Education

Rajasthan is utilizing only 2 per cent grant allocated for elementary education on children's entitlements and quality of education which is among the minimum in the country, though it is spending 76 per cent of the grant on teachers. This was the conclusion of the annual Paisa report prepared by Accountability Initiative (a research group) and Centre for Policy and Research, New Delhi in collaboration with Assessment Survey Evaluation Research.

The report was realised in March 2013. The State received a total of Rs. 8312.59 crore grant for elementary education and Sarva Shiksha Abhiyan for 2012-13 from the Union Government. The report highlights that the State's spending on children and quality education is the lowest in Bimaru States.

The huge disparity in utilization of grants has affected the reading and learning levels of children in the State. Only 64 per cent students in Class I to III can read and write letters. The component on teachers is spent for their salaries, training and teaching inputs such as teaching and learning material.

Table 4.10: Funds Allocated, 2012-13

State	*Total amount (Rs.)*	*Per Student*
Rajasthan	8,312,59	116.17
Orissa	4,899.45	87.94
Bihar	11,311.21	55.16
MP	8,437.75	82.55
UP	22,283.10	113.77

The component-wise allocations show a prioritization towards teachers where the allocation increased from 67 per cent in 2010-11 to 76 per cent in 2012-13 with no change in budgeting on children and quality in the same period. These grants come under the School Facility Grant (SFG), the School Management Grant (SMG) and the Teaching Learning Material Grant (TLM).

The State's 58 per cent schools got all 3 grants as compared to the national average of 74 per cent schools. Altogether 70 per cent schools received School Facility Grant compared to School Management Grant which is 80 per cent; and Teaching Learning Material Grant is 91 per cent.

The allocation for elementary education has been increased by 11 per cent and SSA allocations by 30 per cent this year, making the average per student allocations at Rs. 11,509 annually. However, just 2 per cent of the amount was spent on children is seen as a major bottleneck in the education scenario in the State.

Table 4.11: Money Spent among Bimaru States on Children

Category	*Rajasthan*	*Orissa*	*Bihar*	*MP*	*UP*
Teachers	76%	26%	41%	50%	73%
School	16%	50%	41%	23%	11%
Children	2%	13%	14%	16%	9%
Management	4%	7%	2%	7%	3%
Quality & Misc.	2%	4%	2%	3%	4%

Source: *Times of India*, Jaipur, May 27, 2013.

It says that though the shortfall in separate toilets for girls has decreased from 21 per cent in 2010 to 13 per cent in 2011, it again went up to 15 per cent in 2012-13 (till November). It further says that 41 per cent schools reported shortfall of classrooms and 42 per cent recorded shortfall of playgrounds by October-November 2012.

X. STATUS OF EDUCATION IN RAJASTHAN

As per the 2011 Census, Rajasthan has recorded a literacy rate of 67.06 per cent compared to 60.41 per cent in 2001, registering a net increase of 6.65 percentage points during 2001-2011. The figures for male and female literacy rates are 80.51 and 52.66 per cent respectively in 2011. Maternal Mortality Ratio (MMR) in the State in 1998 was 508 per one lakh live births (as per Sample Registration System 1997-98). Whereas it slumped to about 318 as per SRS 2007-09.

Infant Mortality Rate (IMR) in the State remained stagnant for most of the nineties. However, in the new millennium, decline in IMR was sharper. The aggregate IMR declined from 85 in 1995 to 80 in 2001 to 67 in 2004 (*SRS Bulletin*, April 2006) and presently, it is 49 in (2013 C.H.T. July 2014).

The percentage of institutional births increased from a mere 12 per cent during NFHS-1 (1992-93) to 21.5 per cent during NFHS-2 (1998-99) and thereafter to 32.2 per cent during NFHS-3 (2005-06).

IHDR 2001 made it a point that devolution of power and decentralization of decision-making is a key to ensure human development as it would provide space to communities to access its determinates like Livelihood, Health and Education in a more efficient manner. This decentralization would accompany civil service reforms to promote accountability, efficiency and transparency. It would also help in ensuring inclusion of marginalized sections like women, SCs, STs, minorities and children.

There is a widespread disparity across the State and districts in terms of the parametres of Human Development Index (HDI) in the State. India ranked 135 among 187 countries of the world. The government have not done enough to improve education health and other facilities. The adverse geophysical conditions of Rajasthan coupled with low infrastructure have created these inter-regional imbalances and thus widened the intra-State/Regional disparity as shown in the Table 4.12.

Table 4.12: Intra-State Disparity in Human Development

Particular	*Education Index (NER_Lit15+)*	*Health Index*	*Income Index*	*HDI*
Highest Score	Kota (0.875)	Bikaner (08.63)	Ganganagar (0.825)	Ganganagar (0.787)
	Jhunjhunu (0.850)	Jhunjhunu (0.581)	Bhilwara (0.818)	Kota (0.787)
Median Score	Alwar (0.747)	Barmer (0.581)	Chittorgarh (0.585)	Jhalawar (0.614)
	Nagaur (0.747)	Ajmer (0.574)	Tonk (0582)	Nagaur (0.610)
Lowest Score	Jalore (0638)	Banswara (0.309)	Dholpur (0.230)	Banswara (0.425)
	Banswara (0630)	Dungarpur (0.282)	Churu (0.226)	Dungarpur (0.409)

Source: planningcommission.nic.in

Population explosion and increased standards of living have contributed to the increase in the number of BPL families and poor people. Eliminating poverty bringing poor to a minimum standard of life and decline in their percentage in the total population requires not only resources but also political will to execute family planning measures effectively.

CONCLUSION

To achieve equity in distribution of income and reorientation of the production process the government must guarantee gainful employment to one person in a family.

To conclude, it may be said that during the last fifty years, Rajasthan rural and agriculture development has created suitable infrastructure for its development in various plan and programmes. Although rural poverty in Rajasthan has been increasing over the time due to population explosion, it has also witnessed visible betterment in people's standard of living. There have been resources scarcity and natural calamities but the State is moving towards rural upliftment.

CASE STUDY: WOMEN MEMBERS OF THE PANCHAYAT

Case Study-I: Pyaree Bai Gamethi

Panchayati Raj institutions (PRI) became the grass root units of rural development by the 73rd Constitutional Amendment in 1994. These are the vehicles of socio-economic transformation in rural India. To make effective and meaningful functioning of PRI in 1994 one-third seats in PRI were reserved for women in the 73rd Constitutional Amendment. In a few States reservation for women in nearly fifty per cent. Most of the probationers have written their case study on women members of the Panchayat. They have given different glimpses of the women members and the finding overall were similar. They observed in the long run PRI will certainly empower women and they will play an active role in PRI, on their own without any male intervention. Such is the case of Pyaree Bai Gamethi, and others.

"Pyaree Bai was elected to the Panchayat for the first time unanimously. This year unanimous election was held for Dhar

Panchayat. The villages are having elections of the Panchayat conducted on the guidelines as per rules and regulation of State Election Commission through direct polling system; but as the Dhar gram is a well knit socially and culturally, the Panchayat board including the Sarpanch were elected unanimously without poll. This board consists of the following members:

The female members of the Dhar Panchayat were having poor socio-economic background. The elected female member is from a Scheduled Tribe and solely depends upon the on farm and off farm activities.

The female members co-operate with the males in agriculture activities when ploughing is on and also doing their household affairs including collection of fuel wood, bringing water, etc.

It is a general observation that the discussions and decisions are led by male members; but on some issues like development of their ward, literacy, and female health, they express their opinions strongly and positively and keep to that level and the result comes in common interest of the village or whole community.

All four female members were elected for the first time and represented their ward unanimously, but they did not know the powers, procedures and complete formation of the Gram Panchayat. They needed short training on the functioning and their powers.

As stated above all the four members were sensitive towards the developmental issues of the village. They were closely monitoring the village developmental work and expressing views in the common interest of the community; and they wanted to get more benefits for their ward also.

In conclusion, the members were active and had deep inclination towards development of their ward and village. They need training and feedback for the functioning of the Panchayat and their powers in PRI. In Rajasthan it is 33 per cent in all levels of PRI system at District Level Zila Parishad, Block level Panchayat Samitis and village level Gram Panchayat. In last twenty years women members of PRI are getting elected to their institutions on the basis of their own political-social activity, due to provision of the PRI Act, due support of the family and community, etc. Their role and involvement in PRI activities depends on now and by the help of whom they are elected.

The study of PRI representatives got attention of the researchers and policy planners. Therefore, it became a part of the training course of the young I.A.S. officers to make a detailed case study of the women representatives of PRI. In their study different aspects such as family background, social, economic, status, electioneering, participation in PRI activities, awareness about own powers and functions and contributions in the development of the village were examined. They found that. Those who got elected for the second or third terms are involved in activities and free from male domination as compared to the newly elected.

Case Study-II: Dr. Preetam Yashvant I.A.S. (P)—Lalibai Meena

In the study of tribal dominated village Preetam Yashvant has written about Lalibai Meena. She belongs to a rich peasant family and has her own tractor and thresher machine. Her husband got her elected by money and muscle power.

During the entire election, Lalibai made only one appearance outside her home when she had to file her nomination for election. Everyone in Uni knows it was Jagdeesh who was standing for election. It is not at all an anomaly in this area. It is simply understood that women have no role to play in politics and that the reservation for women is an uncomfortable irritant which has to be avoided by proxy.

"It is Jagdeesh who attends GP meetings and not Lalibai. Her signatures are procured from her home as and when required. And she dutifully writes her name in a barely legible script whereever her husband tells her. The concluding remark about her is as follows: she has no idea about the functioning of the Panchayat and does not care in the least. She is contented in letting her husband manage those matters. Her personal contribution to the development of the village is nil."

Case Study-III: Nathi Devi

One good example of women member of Panchayat is Nathi Devi. She is from a middle class family; her husband is in a government job and her family is educated. Nathi herself is eighth passed. She and her husband are social, and are always ready to help others. This was the reason of her victory in the elections.

"She attended all the meetings of the Panchayat and wards and actively participated in discussions, gave her views and suggestions; in fact she was more active than any other member. She also participated actively in Shiksha Sambal Mahabhiyan, Swasthya Chetna, Gram Sampark Abhiyan and other development activities. She was more interested in the sanitation programme, child centred initiatives run by ICDS, and programmes for mother care. Due to her continuous effort most delivery cases are institutionalized now."

Case Study-IV: Arti Dogra

Arti Dogra's case study of women member of the Panchayat Samiti is very inspirational. She is around 25 years old and this was her first tenure as an elected representative. Sohini was born crippled and unable to walk and needs to be carried from one place to another by some member of the family. Arti Dogra narrated the case as follows:

"In 2005, the local MLA who is from her community, promised her a ticket for the Panchayat elections. He says he was impressed by her desire to improve her life and her will to study despite her difficult circumstances. His involvement in her election helped her win by a huge margin. Sohini's life changed after this election. Suddenly she had a role to play and not just at the village level, but as a member of the Panchayat Samiti. A young girl who had never stepped out of Chitrawas was now expected to sit with administrative and political functionaries and frame plans for the development of the entire tehsil of Gogunda. It was truly an empowering moment for Sohini.

She takes keen interest in the working of the Panchayat. She engages the Panchayat Sachiv in conversations about NREGS. Her contention is that since the majority of the workers at EGS work sites are women, there should be lady mates recruited by the Panchayat as well. She believes that the Anganwadi in the village needs to be managed better. Her regret while speaking to the CDPO is that she herself did not manage to pass Class 10, else she would have applied to be the Anganwadi worker. In a subtle manner, she raises issues concerning women and children whereever she can. Since being elected, she has never missed a single Panchayat Samiti meeting except around the time her baby was born. She does say that initially she found it hard to understand what the BDO and the other officials spoke at the meeting, but slowly things started to make sense.

Hers is a story of an individual determined to make a change to her life despite extremely pressing circumstances. She has not allowed her physical inability or her gender comes on the way of what she believes she can do."

Case Study-V: Sohini Devi, According to the Description of Gaurav Goyal

Sohini Devi of Phalodi is an excellent example of devoted member of Panchayat who commands respect of the villagers. She got elected from a Ward reserved for OBC women, and is a housewife in a rural agricultural family whose main occupation is agriculture and animal husbandry. There has not been any political person from the family and she is the first person in politics. She does not have any child, and there are only two members in the family including her husband. The academic qualification of her husband is Secondary pass. Though she is literate, but she only knows how to read and write her name.

As the representative of the Ward, she attends all meetings of the Panchayat regularly. She takes active part in Panchayat meetings and also puts up issues related to her Panchayat firmly in Panchayat meetings and other forums. She is popularly known as '*Kaki*' (aunt) in the village. Almost every woman of the village associates with her and comes to her even for small problems and issues.

As she is just literate, she is completely oblivious of the powers and functions of a Panchayat member. But she knows that any problem, whether of an individual or of the community at large, can be taken to the meetings of the Panchayat and that she has the right to go to district headquarters and complain to the Collector about various departments like electricity, power, education and health.

Who is Tara Devi ?

Tara Devi elected from SC reserved, says that the woman reservation in Panchayats has helped in women empowerment. Though she is only eighth class pass, after becoming a member of the Panchayat she has gained immense self-confidence. She says that initially she was hesitant in coming out of the home and talking in general public. During her first term as member of the Panchayat she was accompanied by her husband to the Panchayat meetings. Slowly she started understanding office work and taking decisions on her own.

She admits that even at present her husband takes active part in the village developmental activities.

Case Study-VI: Widow Member

Anandhi narrated the story of a 62 years old widow member who was unanimously elected by the people of the Ward. She was asked to stand for elections by the entire Ward Sabha and she won unopposed. The reason was that this was a reserved Ward and all of them had great faith in her. He had the reputation of being a very helpful and selfless person and also very clean and honest.

Case Study-VII: Tina Soni

The woman member is a housewife in a rural agricultural family whose main occupation is agriculture and animal husbandry. She has five children and including her husband, there are 7 members in the family. Her husband is literate. Though she is literate but she knows only how to read and write her name.

Tina Soni observed that a woman representative attends all meetings of the Gram Panchayat regularly. She takes active part in Panchayat meetings and also puts up issues related to her Gram Panchayat firmly in Panchayat meetings and other forums. She is popularly known as 'Panch' in the village. Almost every woman of the village associates with her and comes to her even for small and petty problems and issues.

Though she takes active part in Gram Panchayat meetings and also puts up development issues related to her village forcibly in those meetings, yet she has not been able to get any major development work done in her village. She admits that the primary reason for her failure to get things sanctioned for her village is her ignorance about various schemes and programmes of the government and the processes for getting schemes sanctioned for the village.

Case Study-VIII: Dhaapu Devi Parmeshwaran

Described the importance of infuential caste leaders in selecting candidates for the post of Sarpanch in Dhava Gram Panchayat. Dhaapu Devi got elected by a huge margin and she just put her thumb impression on official papers.

Panchayat elections were held in Rajasthan recently in early 2010. Dhava is a huge Gram Panchayat with a population of 12,560 and so the post of Sarpanch is considered very prestigious. Being directly elected it is assumed that the individual who is really the choice of the people will win the post. When results were declared on 31 January Dhaapu Devi won by a margin of 1,800 votes.

Ideally such a comprehensive margin must mean that her reputation as a public worker is well established long before. But just as in most places in Rajasthan and perhaps all over the country, the reason for her success was that she belonged to the Patel community which is dominant comprising more than 35 per cent of Dhava's population. When the lots for allotment of seats were drawn by the district administration on 28 December, 2010. Dhava was reserved for OBC women category. Within two days influential members of the community assembled and decided that Kalluram's family should have the honour. Thus his wife elected with a healthy margin.

"What are her plans for the development of the Panchayat? her son, Kalluram intervenes and says roads, water, education and health in an almost rhetorical manner while she innocently looks at him." And further he has written: "Is gender empowerment anywhere in the list? As I prepare to take leave, Kalluram adds with great pride that a splendid dinner."

According to Parmeshwaran, "The most important thing that needs to be done is in the Family Planning front. With scarce resources and a poor standard of living, the vicious cycle of child labour or early wage employment, early marriage and more children needs to be broken. Things can improve only if people can be made to understand the benefits of small families. And that will happen only with educational opportunities to improve awareness, medical facilities to ensure safe delivery and child care, economic opportunities to sustain oneself and the family without needing the additional child labour income. NREGA, NRIIM and SSA with mid-day meals can offer partial answers to these complicated questions."

Case Study-IX: Bali Devi

The case study is of, "Bali Devi who got elected as a woman member of a Panchayat. Though she faced no difficulties getting elected, she is certainly just a face. Whatever work or participation that is expected of her, is either done by the male members of her family or the political leaders who used her as a mask. To the question of male domination is a confusing one in such a scenario. How can one consider this male domination when she herself did not care for elections and got elected only because of the vested interests of some powerful people of her Ward? And yet, with no effective female participation, the Gram Panchayat is indeed a completely male dominated one."

Case Study-X: Sharandeep Kaur Brar

Sharandeep Kaur Brar described the tale of Rasis Khatoon, the Sarpanch of Ardaka village which is not different. Belonging to a middle class Muslim family, this Matriculate lady has willingly surrendered all her decision making powers to her father-in-law. Brar describes, The State government has directed all local bodies in the State not to allow interference of family members of elected women representatives in the discharge of their official duties. Despite this the trend continues because the women Sarpanches themselves do not feel comfortable working with the government officials." She further said, "The seat was reserved for a woman, so I was chosen. She said that she never read the papers which were signed by her as the entire work was done by her father-in-law. People no longer call her by name. Sarpanch Sahib—this is her newly found identity." The Panchayat Secretary of the village criticizes this reservation as, according to him, it is hampering the speedy process of any government plan in the Panchayat. He told from his experience that in every meeting it is becoming difficult for these women leaders to take decisions on the spot, as they have to consult their husbands afterwards. So everything is being delayed. It is quite evident that less weightage is given to women due to the patriarchal and male dominated society and the old social taboos against women in the rural areas.

On the specific problems she faces being a woman head: she feels that people always expect her to behave like a woman. Being a lady it is difficult to meet the government officials and she cannot mix freely with other Panchayat members either. Lack of direct public contact is also a handicap for her and it is her belief that her husband can do things in a better way. During her 5-year term, she wants to resolve the water problem in her Panchayat, have roads constructed, bring electricity to every house in her village, create water supply in the time of drought. She is motivated to do things but feels that it is difficult for her to get projects implemented because she has not 90 per cent of the exponent in execution public works before.

She believes collective leadership works best for the people and hence it is important to ensure participation of all by the Sarpanch. Lack of sensitization among Block and Panchayat level officials hampers the functioning of women as officials. The male members here are reluctant to let go of power. Rasisa is an empowered woman, in the sense she is heading a village, taking decisions for its development and serving its people. But in the true sense this empowerment means nothing till she becomes independent politically, till her decisions are hers and not her family's, till she feels confident of being a woman and of herself. Rasisa is wise; she is intelligent, determined and enthusiastic too. All that is missing is the faith, the confidence that her family and her people need to have in her abilities.

Case Study-XI: Poorest of Poor

In their case studies officers have written stories of the poorest of the poor family in the village studied by them. A few of them narrated the story in the format provided to them that included historical sketch, socio-economic status, causes of poverty, day-to-day life, livelihood pattern, benefit given by government and lastly ability to overcome adverse circumstances by the family. In such a study case Joga Ram narrated the story of a poor family from Jhalawar district of Rajasthan. His description of the poor family is as follows:

"He is having a kutcha house thatched by straw and 2 rooms (rather compartments). No question of electricity in the vicinity! He lights his doomed house with a kerosene lantern, thanks to the fair price shop. And the elixir of life water is fetched by him from a nearby public hand pump by the exercise of certain ups and downs. For cooking he uses (as most of the villagers do) wood collected from fields and from the so called neighbouring forest (which was once there). And his smoked house like others also causes health problems especially for ladies of the house who cook."

According to Joga Ram Ashok Kumar is a landless labourer and he has ownership of no capital things. He is having no permanent source of income. He does not have any cattle (animal husbandry) to augment resources. Due to his landlessness he works casually in agriculture.

Case Study-XII: Rohit Gupta

The case study of Rohit Gupta is just the copy or photo-copy of the story of Jogaram. Preanted a year before him The name of district is same 'Jhalawar' but the name of the poor person, village and Block are different. Rohit Gupta has given eight reasons for being poor and his case studies are—

1. He was a child married at the age of 19. He had no maturity and understanding about the responsibility, etc., of post-marriage life (Child-Marriage).
2. He is eighth class educated but left school because of family pressure for earning so he started working at an early age to feed his family (Child Labour).
3. Just after marriage he was thrown out of the house because of differences with parents. Has parents said that his earning was less than what he spent.
4. His grandmother, Narbadi Bai is 70 years old and lives with him. She frequently gets sick and is being treated by him. He says that about Rs. 700 was spent last year on her health.
5. He has become father of a girl just 6 months back. Due to this certain amount of money was spent on delivery and post-delivery care (Parenthood timing).
6. He seems to be in a Cycle of Emotional Disappointment so his confidence and mental strength is not at the optimum mark.
7. After interaction with him it was found that even if Government organizes some training for him to become self-reliant and self-employed, he would not go unless it is in his village. He wants proximity to family and due to this reason he did not venture out of his village to search for a job.

The trainees failed to analyse the good human quality of the poor person. He is talking of his grandmother, he has taken his wife to hospital for safe delivery and is talking one of girl child. He is a satisfied person and looking for employment in the village.

Case Study-XIII: Muktanand Agarwal

He described his circumstances as follows. "The Head of this family was among one of the five children of a Bheel who had no source of income or employment. Jagdish inherited all these shortcomings and vices like unemployment, poverty and lack of skills from his father. The family migrated from a nearby village to this Panchayat around three years ago in search of livelihood. The family currently resides in a deserted kutcha house, which is no more than a hut, consisting of one room only. The house is located on the outskirts of the village in a lonely place. Thus, the family not only lacks the basic infrastructures for living but also has no social circle in the neighbourhood to support the family."

The poorest person is not adopting small family norms. He does not take his wife to hospital for safe delivery. Agarwal stated that, "The couple Jagdish and Sita have given birth to 6 children from 10 yr. old Gheesa to 5 yr. old Bhuri. All of them were delivered by untrained 'Dais'. Their mother is suffering from obvious bad health. Her children do not enjoy good health either. None of the children have ever seen the face of a school. Their conditions do not allow them to do so. Jagdish works as a domestic servant in the village nearby and earns about 12,000 per annum. His eight year old son Satyanarayan works as a contract labour, which is actually a kind of bonded labour, in the house of a nearby Thakur and gets around Rs. 500 monthly which is a big support for the family. Sita Devi, due to her bad status of health, suffers from lack of energy thus restraining her from any sort of employment. Some of the siblings go to graze the cattle of others and earn a meagre amount of money to support the family."

There are a number of development programmes for scheduled tribals in tribal sub-plan (TSP) in southern Rajasthan. He explained the poor family of Jagdish and Seeta Bheel is one of the examples that show how all the efforts made by the Government have failed to benefit the people who are living in tough conditions. They have to strive hard even for their day-to-day needs and have no strong support base that enables them to face the adversities of life.

Case Study-XIV: Sharandeep Kaur Brar

Most of the poor families in the village are without land and working as agricultural labourers in the village. Now, they are getting employment in MNREGA. Their family members includes mother and wife are also getting pension of Rs. 500 per month. It helps his family to survive at bare subsistence level. Changi Ram is a landless labourer and he has no ownership of capital things. He is having no permanent source of income. He does not have any cattle (animal husbandry) to augment resources. Due to his landlessness he works casually in agriculture and also works in the NREGA as a job card holder. His wife gets a monthly sum of Rs. 500 as disability pension and his mother gets the same amount monthly as a widow pension.

Case Study-XV: Self-Help Group

Four officers prepared their case study on the topic of Self-Help Group. They are Ravi Jain, Arti Dogra, Shilpa Ramesh Bigar, and Anandi. Their description and findings are positive regarding working and benefits of SHG. Ravi Jain's case study is based on KAMDHENU GROUP of Kotra village in Kota district. It was formed on 4th of February, 2003 with 10 female members, all STs. The facilitating agency for the formation of the group was an unknown NGO. This SHG was formed under SGSY.

The group members are all females, between 30 and 50 years ago of age, they are all scheduled tribes, and only a few are literate. Everyone knew how to do dairy work and get benefit out of it. There is marketing facility for the milk at the village itself. There is a milk cooperative society at Kotra. The members sell their daily milk produce to the dairy in the morning and evening and get paid on the spot. All the group members belong to BPL. SHG is earning good profit and have repaid bank loan at higher interest rate of 12 per cent.

The interest rates for SHG and other employment generating schemes for the poor people and peasants are on the higher side. In contrast the car and consumer item loans are on remarkably cheap rate at 7 to 9 per cent. Some measures have to be taken by the government for financing them at lowest rate.

The fodder is easily available for the animals in the village. The subsidy (50%) is provided under SGSY and rest 50 per cent is provided as bank loan to SHG members.

Arti Dogra says her case study based on new concept and related with the tribal area of Udaipur district. She describes these villages which are under the Policy of Joint Forest Management. It was formed on 7th July, 2002 for conserving and managing their depleting forest resource. They got permission for management of 217 hectares of forest land. Scattered hamlets and the vast extent of the resources made the management and undertaking of physical conservation activity very difficult. Therefore another SHG was given the management of the 27 hectares a sub-part of the total forest land.

SHG capacities were further built in terms of women leadership, decision-making processes, bank transactions and monitoring the physical interventions. The institutional building processes were mostly focussed through monthly meetings and by increasing women participation in those meetings. The SHG further took up the physical treatment of the 27 hectares of the forest plot after making a micro plan for the group. She finds out that in the same year people started the system of 2 households per day taking up the task of protection (chowkidari) of the plot. Under this system each household had an opportunity once every two months. As a result of the strict protection the fodder availability improved and the natural regeneration took place. In this way successful development of the forest started happening. In 2006 the 101 households received cash payment of Rs. 1,09,646 (One lakh nine thousand six hundred and forty six) in addition to the increased grass production from the Rs. 1,314 spent on grass seeding.

Case Study-XVI: Shilpa Ramesh Bigar

Shilpa described a SHG of SP. Ghoorghra village, Ajmer in which 32 years old Kanta Devi became a member. This is a very good success story of SHG, therefore, presented in original. "Kanta Devi became a member of the SHG group named 'Pooja Mahila Swayam Sahayak Samooh' which contained 12 other women who also happened to be from the low income earning households of the village. The training of the group as to how much they have to contribute, how to keep account of the money, etc., was told by the Saathin at the meeting. Initially she used to contribute Rs. 10 monthly in the group like all other members. This went on for six months and the group received a loan for the first time. Initially the loan amount was used for inter loaning and Kanta also availed loan of around Rs. 2,000 when she had to take her son to the hospital when he fell down and broke his leg. Inter loaning went on for

2 years and now that group was contributing Rs. 50 each. The group fund also increased.

Further in a Jajam meeting (monthly meeting conducted by Saathin at GP level) when four women including Kanta expressed that they wanted to start Kasheeda work Saathin noted the names and the group's name. Later the 4 women including Kanta accompanied by some 50 women from other villages and other Blocks were sent to Jaipur for three days training in Kasheeda work. After the training they were given sewing machines on loan.

Since there were already some women doing Kasheeda work, Kanta contacted the person who would supply them with material for work. Kasheeda work mainly consisted as I saw, of doing simple embroidery work on *odhanis* (*dupattas*) used by rural women as their daily wearing. The person would give every morning some three or four *odhanis* with designs already drawn on it and the threads. Kanta after completion of her work could complete at least 3 *odhanis*. The person would pay her Rs. 30 for each *odhani*. In this way she started earning around Rs. 90-120 daily.

Last year a dairy co-operative was formed in Ghooghra village and the people in the village started getting Rs. 20/ltr minimum for their milk. Further, an automatic self measuring machine has been provided at the milk collecting booths which helped people get proper price for their milk. SHG groups started taking loans for even buying cows and buffaloes, Kanta could avail loan for buying a buffalo and now she sells around 4-5 kg. of milk everyday and is earning around Rs. 2,500-3,000 every month. Now she speaks with confidence and she is doing both, her dairy work and embroidery work. She now has established direct contacts with the shops in Srinagar town from which she gets direct work order and material every week and has done away with the middleman."

The case study of Nandhi is almost similar to the one narrated by Shilpa. Therefore, these need not to describe it further. In Rajasthan SHG is working very well and providing employment earning and empowerment to the people.

Case Study-XVII: Dr. Sumeet Sharma

Four officers selected "Returns from agriculture performance in the last decade." The study of Sumeet Sharma is quite elaborate and based on real village situation. The study of Joga Ram, Rohit Gupta and Bishu Charan Mallik is almost the same. Sumeet Sharma narrated the actual situation of Roop Narain Patidar, who got education upto eighth class and is now doing mechanised farming on 90 acres of land. According to the report:

"He irrigated fields by a well which is equipped with an electric motor and has electricity connection. In case of non-availability of electricity, he uses a diesel pump set for irrigation. He has also got a set of drip irrigation system for irrigation. He uses fertilizers and pesticides as per the guidance of the local Agriculture Supervisor.

Although he has limited technological knowledge, but under the guidance, of the Agriculture Supervisor, he is applying progressive method. For a long time, he has been using hybrid seed and pesticides for good cultivation and increased yielding."

Sumeet Sharma made a few important suggestions for improving agriculture. These are as follows:

"1. Traditional agriculture is not profitable in prevailing conditions. We should use advanced agriculture appliances.
2. Time to time, guidance of Agriculture Supervisor regarding sowing, cultivation, pesticide and fertilizers are necessary.
3. Only certified seeds and best fertilizers and pesticides should be used.
4. Sowing time is a major factor for good production.
5. Time bound programme should be chalked out for sowing, irrigation, providing fertilizers and pesticides."

Case Study-XVIII: Sumeet Sharma, Social Security Scheme

Sumeet Sharma "Social Security Scheme Impact" on any poor house hold narrate different social Security scheme, process for getting this benefit according to him "In rural areas, several schemes sponsored by State and Central Government are being executed for social upliftment of the poor and needy person, i.e., Pension for Old Age, Widow and Handicapped persons. Apart from these, schemes based on rural employment and poverty alleviation are also being executed in rural areas which are executed through Gram Panchayats and other agencies, i.e., SGRY, Samvikas, SGSY, IAY, etc."

He pointed out that most of the rural women are not familiar about the scheme and not getting its benefit. This is also in case of Gheesee Bai. She was informed by the local revenue officer after one year. The Widow Pension application forms are available with Gramsevaks. Duly filled form has to be submitted to the Gramsevak. He verifies the information as per records available with Gram Panchayat that the person belongs to BPL family, and then the duly signed form is sent to the Patwari and ILR concerned for signature after verification of the social and financial status of the applicant which is based on house, income, agriculture land, etc. After verification by the Tehsildar concerned it is sent to the BDO for sanction.

After sanctioning Widow Pension, the financial and emotional status of Smt. Gheesee Bai has improved. She is feeling independent today. Her family is now getting food and basic needs properly. She looks satisfied and contented.

Sumeet Sharma suggests measures such as extensive joint survey should be initiated by Revenue, Development, Medical and Health Department regarding socio-economic status of each and every family village-wise. At last he has good feeling for elderly people and suggests action against those not taking care of their parents when they are of old age. He observed that "In rural areas, many widows and old age women are not being looked after by their own major sons. They are deprived by their own relatives. Such type of persons/ sons are evil for society and provision for criminal action against them is suggested. Such type of persons should be socially boycotted."

In 2009, Government of Rajasthan passed a social security act. According to this act older people must be bitterly looked after. If any government official is not taking care of their parents, they will be penalised for it. The Government will even deduct some part of their salary which will be given to their parents. The neglect of elderly people is not only a problem of rural areas, but even in urban areas it is a much more serious social evil. In urban areas many elderly people are lacking social interaction and feeling lonely. Even the rich family proper food and accommodation are not provided to them.

In Rajasthan 56 lakh poor and elder family are getting different types of monthly pension of Rs. 500 by the State Government. Most of these pensions started in Rajasthan in 2012-13.

Case Study-XIX: V. Sarvan Kumar and Case Study-Ravi Jain, Landless Labourer

Ravi Jain's case study-II is on landless labourer of Kota district. In this case the mother is working in the village and the son migrates to urban centre Kota for work and is getting Rs. 100 per day. Mother Hansabai is illiterate and also could not provide formal education to his son. Her son now realizes the importance of education. He wants his three sons to go to school and get a government job finally. All three attend school regularly and are in ninth, eighth and fifth classes. Hansabai is a BPL card holder and all six members of the family have been recorded in the card. The fact that she can get rice, wheat, sugar and kerosene from the PDS shop. It is a big relief to her.

Hansabai's dream is to expand her 2 room katcha house. She would also love to own some land and cultivate her own field. But her biggest ambition is, as mentioned earlier, that her three grandsons should get good education so that they do not end up being landless labourers like their father or grand-father. Hansabai and her son also wish that employment avenues, apart from agricultural labour, should be available within the village so that her son and grandsons would not have to leave the family in search of employment during lean season of agriculture.

Case Study-XX: Puran, Ceiling Land Beneficiary

Only two officers have written case studies on Ceiling and Beneficiary. They are Krishna Kunal and Puran. Both of them found that ceiling land beneficiary are cultivating their lands but have not got any other incentives from the government. Puran describes:

"The surplus land vested in the State government was allotted under section 16 of Rajasthan Tenancy Act 1955, to the said person. But the land came in dispute, which was resolved in the year 1980. Since then the land is in possession of Ram Nivas.

Before allotment he was a landless labourer, with no house, and life was very hard. He and his wife used to work as hired labour. Now he has a pucca house with two rooms and electricity connection in the house. His wife works on their own land as a family worker and he daily migrates to city to work as an industrial labourer.

CASE OF MATERNAL DEATH

Maternal mortality is a matter of grave concern. The magnitude of the problem can be judged simply by the fact that the 'Maternal Mortality Rate (MMR) of India is highest in the world. It is roughly approximately quarter of all the maternal deaths occurring worldwide. According to the Registrar General of India, the MMR or rate of deaths among women during or after pregnancy, declined by 16 per cent in 2011-12 from 2007-09. Although the MMR has dropped from 212 deaths in 2007-09 to 178 in 2010-12, India is still far behind the target of 103 deaths per 1,00,000 live births of 'United Nations Mandated Millennium Development Goals (MDG's)' to be achieved by 2015.

The reasons for maternal deaths are manifold and some of the major issues were tried to be understood by the officers at the grass roots level in their case studies.

In the case study presented by Ravi Kumar Surpur, he presented the example of Bhawan Rawat, a lady of mere 19 years, who after her second miscarriage, died later succumbing to postpartum haemorrhage. The report clearly states that the lady and the family in question had access to the medical care but still they did not pay heed to the medical advice and did not avail the medical care leading to the maternal death which was totally preventable. The report also questions the indifferent attitude of the husband and his family.

The case study of Saravana Kumar V. presents the scenario of a village in Ramganjmandi, Kota, where the case of Lady Bangibai, clearly demonstrated that despite availing the medical care and benefits of Primary Health Centre (PHC) and Community Health Centre (CHC), the maternal death occurred due to poverty, poor medical facilities in the nearby vicinity and lack of scientific treatment by private practitioners. This was mainly because of poverty where the need to get the daily bread is most important for survival. Death could have been prevented if proper financial support like 'Janani Suraksha Yojana' etc., were provided to the family.

Dr. Arushi Malik has presented a case of Raeesa from the family of Mr. Mukhram mate of village Jatiyama. She died after birth of her third child due to the fact that mainly proper medical attention was not provided to her. Despite being available she did not avail the medical care during her pregnancy and later also at the time of delivery. The study questions the medieval and indifferent attitude of the family and local Meo community, who do not believe in providing proper medical care to the mother and in medical advancements like contraceptives and family planning. The study raises the need to promote awareness of maternal care among the local people and religious leaders.

All the case studies clearly prove the fact that to control and reduce the MMR, a multi-dimensional approach is needed to vanquish the demon of maternal death. The cause of maternal death is multi-factorial, like inadequate medical care, poverty, indifferent attitude of the couple and family, religious sentiments, malnutrition, illiteracy etc.

It is high time now to take stringent actions to reduce the incidence of maternal deaths and also infant mortality. These actions should include raising awareness among people regarding maternal care, employing and taking support of more and more grass roots workers like ASHA, Anganwadi worker, *dais*, etc., to reach every nook and corner of the country. Also, the need is to increase the medical force and the network of health centres to provide adequate healthcare to the ever increasing population of India Government should also frame more policies to provide adequate financial stability to the families like the 'Janani Suraksha Yojana' which provides financial incentive to families if they have delivery at a hospital. Policies should also focus on providing maternal nutrition, immunisation and family planning.

Case Study: Ravi Kumar Surpur

The lady had gone to a primary health centre for ante-natal check up and she was told by the doctor that she was very weak and was having severe anaemia and should take adequate rest and have dietary supplements.

Last year the lady became pregnant and was advised not to go to work after her third month, by the lady doctor in the CHC. The PHC staff too got her registered with them and provided her with Iron tablets for two months and had asked her go once every month to the doctor. However, as bad luck would have it she and her husband had to stay at the work site for the period. At the end of the sixth month though she was not working, she developed pain. She was taken to a nearby private dispensary where they got her clear of her pain and suggested nothing serious. Not many tests which must be needed were performed.

Though not a case of typical maternal death which resulted due to poor medical facilities and lack of scientific treatments, this case reflects a clear case of how poverty can drive people to work even when they should be resting and how they value themselves and their lives.

Case Study: Dr. Arushi Malik

Respondent gave birth to a live female child. The reasons of her death were manifold-untrained birth attendant, malnutrition, and she had also not gone for check-ups during pregnancy. She had also not been immunised for Tetanus at the local health sub-centre and then she had the delivery done by her sister-in-law at home.

BIBLIOGRAPHY

A. Books

Anjani Kumar, *et al.*, (2007), "Performance of rural credit and factors affecting the choice of credit sources (Article)," *Indian Journal of Agricultural Economics*, Vol. 62, No. 3, July-September, pp. 297-313.

Bandyopadhyaya, Liberalisation and rural development (Article) (1995), *Mainstream*, Vol. Annual, 9 December, pp. 39-42.

Baruah, Joydeep, (2004), Competitive villages, rural enterprises and rural development: The Indian experiments and experiences (Article) *Political Economy Journal of India*, Vol. 13, No. 1-2, January-June, pp. 61-75.

Basu, Priya, (2005). "A Financial System for India's Poor" *Economic and Political Weekly* (hereafter *EPW*), Bombay, September 10, p. 4008.

Batellle, A., (1974), *Studies in Agrarian Social Structure*, Delhi, p. 126.

Bhalchandra Mungekar. (2004), India's Economic Reforms and the *Dalits. An Ambedkar Perspective*, Mumbai, p. 38.

Chamala, S. (2003), "Moneylender's positive image: Paradigms and rural development (Article)," *Economic and Political Weekly*, Vol. 38, No.17, 26 April-2 May, pp. 1713-20.

Chavan, Pallavi, (2008), Trends in rural banking in the era of financial liberalization (article), *Contemporary Perspectives: History and Sociology of South Asia*, Vol. 2, No. 2, July-Dec., pp. 314-48.

Das Gupta, R., (2001), "Rural banking and credit: Tale of many committees" (Article), *Economic and Political Weekly*, Vol. 36, No. 9, 3-9 March, pp. 733-37.

Das, Debabrata (2002), "State cooperative bank and rural Development: A case study" (Article), *Journal of Rural Development*, Vol. 21, No. 2, April-June, pp. 251-64.

Datt Ruddar, (2008), Dismalexperience of MNREGA: Lessons for the future (Article), *Mainstream*, Vol. 46, No. 17, 12 April, pp. 5-7.

Gena, H.C. (2006), "Rural gender integration through communityland management in Western India: IFFDC's experience in Rajasthan" (Article), *Political Economy Journal of India*, Vol. 15, No. 1-2, Jan.-June, pp. 80-90.

Jain, L.C. and Other (1985), *Grass without Roots: Rural Development under Government Auspices*, Sage Publications, New Delhi.

Jain, S.C. (1985), *Rural Development*, Rawat Publication, Jaipur.

Jayakumar, E.C. (1998), "Impact of development programme on scheduled castes and scheduled tribes: A critical appraisal" (Article), *IASSI Quarterly*, Vol. 17, No. 2, October-December, pp. 76-92.

Jha, Abhas Kumar (2000), "Lending to the poor: Designs for credit" (Article), *Economic and Political Weekly*, Vol. 35, No. 8-9, 26 Feb., pp. 606-09.

Karmakar, K.G. (2008), "Trends in rural finance" (Article), *Indian Journal of Agricultural Economics*, Vol. 63, No. 1, January-March, pp. 5-18.

Khemani, C.L. and Yerram Raju. B. (1987), How and Why of Rural Banking, Sagar Publication, New Delhi.

Kishwar, Madhu (2001), "Reassessing their lost wisdom and rights: Villages in Rajasthan overcome Sarkari dependence profile of Raendra Singh and his work" (Article), *Manushi*, No. 123, Mar-April, pp. 4-16.

Kripa Shankar, "No relief for rural sector" (Article) (2004), *Economic and Political Weekly*, Vol. 39, No. 32, 7-13, pp. 3575-80.

Krishna Murari, (2007), "Five decades of rural development: Emphasis on Panchayati Raj, poverty and unemployment," (Article), *Think India Quarterly*, Vol. 9, No. 1, Jan.-March, pp. 66-74.

Lalitha, B.S. Nagarajan, (1988), Self-Help Groups in Rural Development.

M.L. Chhipa (1992), *Monetary and Banking Development in India.*

Manimekalai, N. (2000), "Empowerment of women through self help groups (SHGs)" (Article), *Margin,* Vol. 32, No. 4, July-Sept., pp. 74-88.

Mehta, Shiv. R. (1984), *Rural Development Policies and Programmes: A Sociological Perspective*. Sage Publications, New Delhi.

Minocha, O.P. (2006), "Capacity building for development: An assessment of Pradhan Mantri Gram Sadak Yojana," *Indian Journal of Public Administration*, Vol. 52, No. 3, July-September, pp. 358-69.

Mishra, A.P., (1995), Rural Poverty in India: Problems in Planning and Strategy for Poverty Alleviation. Deep and Deep Publishers, New Delhi.

Mishra, Baidhanath (1991), *Poverty, Unemployment and Rural Development.*

Nambiar, ACK, (2002), Village economy: The question of self reliant and sustainable development (Article), *Indian Journal of Regional Science*, Vol. 34, No. 1, June, pp. 30-36.

Narayanamoorthy, A. (2006), "Rural infrastructure and agricultural output linkages: A study of 256 Indian districts." *Indian Journal of Agricultural Economics*, Vol. 1, No. 3, July-September, pp. 444-59.

Narayanasamy, N. and others (2001), "Efficacy of participatory methods: A micro-probe in a rural cluster" (Article), *Journal of Rural Development*, Vol. 20, No. 2, April-June, pp. 273-97.

Padhy, Kishore Chandra (1986), *Rural Development in Modern India*, B.R. Publishers, New Delhi.

Pai, Padmakar, Y.A. and Arun Suel (1986), *Rural Industrialization and IBIL*, New Delhi.

Phand, Shahji, (2007), Adarsh Gaon Yojana: Way towards Gandhi's dream village: Self-sufficient, prosperous and peaceful, (Article), *Journal of Rural Development*, Vol. 26, No. 2, Apr-June, pp. 207-25.

Ram, P. *et. al.* (2009), "Understanding the distribution of BPL cards: All India and Selected States." (article), *Economic and Political Weekly,* Vol. 44, No. 7, 14-20 December, pp. 66-71.

Ramaswamy, S. (1984), *Management for Rural Development*, Publication Division, GOI, New Delhi.

Ramchandran, V.K. (2003), "Financial liberalization and rural banking in India" (Article), *Marxist*, Vol. 19, No. 1, Jan-March, pp. 20-45.

Ramulu, Ch. Bala, (1996), "Human resource development and liberalisation policy: A study of rural employment programmes in India" (Article), *Indian Journal of Public Administration*, Vol. 42, No. 3, July-September, pp. 462-74.

Rao, R.V. (1987), *Rural Industrialization in India*. Concept Publishing Co., New Delhi.

Rawal, Vikas, (2004), "Rural Banking: Agenda for change" (Article), *Social Scientist*, Vol. 32, No. 7-8, July-August, pp. 58-63.

Rayappa, P. Hanumantha and Mutharayappa, R., *Backwardness and Welfare of Scheduled Castes and Scheduled Tribes*, New Delhi.

Reddy, Y. Gangi (2000), Swarnjayanti Gram Swarojgar Yojana (SGSY) in Rajasthan: A few observations (Article), *IASSI Quarterly*, Vol. 19, No. 1, July-September, pp. 38-57.

Roy, Indrajit, (2001), "Prospect of linking agricultural markets to rural development" (Article), *Mainstream*, Vol. 39, No. 21, 12 May, pp. 26-28.

Saha, Rahul, (2007), Micro-financing rural India: A review of self help group banking in India, (Article), *Man and Development*, Vol. 29, No. 2, June, pp. 65-80.

Sanjeev Kumar, (2005), Development programmes, Panchayati Raj and well-being of the rural poor: Lessons from Bhilwara, Rajasthan (Article), *Journal of Health and Development*, Vol. 1, No. 1, Jan-March, pp. 36-46.

Satish, P. (2007), "Rural infrastructure and growth: An overview", (Article), *Indian Journal of Agricultural Economics*, Vol. 62, No.1, January-March, pp. 32-51.

Shivamaggi, H.B., "Banking infrastructure for rural sector" (Article), *Economic and Political Weekly*, Vol. 32, No. 43, Oct. 97, 25-31, pp. 2782-84.

Shiveniah and (1985), *Improving Delivery System for Others Rural Development*, NIRD, Hyderabad.

Singh, C.M. (1988), *Dynamics of Rural Development Administration,* Spick & Span, New Delhi.

Singh, D.R. (1987), *Rural Youth*, Chug Publications, Allahabad.

Singh, A. (1985), *Rural Development and Banking in India,* Deep & Deep Publications.

Singh, Harvinder (2007), "Improving retail penetration of banking services in rural India" (Article), *Man and Development*, Vol. 29, No. 2, June, pp. 65-80.

Singh, Surjeet (ed) (1991), *Rural Credit issues for Ninties*, Oxford IBH Publishing Pvt. Ltd.

Srivastava, A.K. (1986), *Integrated Rural Development Programme in India*, Deep & Deep Publications.

Sundaram, I.S. (1986), *Voluntary Agencies and Rural Development*, B.R. Publishing, New Delhi.

Von Pischke, J.D. (1985), *The Political Economy of Specialized Farm Credit Institutions in Low Income Countries*. World Bank Staff Working Papers No. 446.

B. Reports

Government of Rajasthan, Memorandum to the Fourteenth Finance Commission, February, 2014.

Government of Rajasthan, Jaipur, Budget 2013-14.

Annual Economic Report Government of Rajasthan, Jaipur, 2013.

Rural Banking and Microfinance (Article), *Economic and Political Weekly*, Vol. 40, No. 12, 19-25 March, 2005, pp. 1224-35.

Report of the committee to review institutional credit for agriculture and (CRAFICARD), Bombay, 1991

Report of the Desai Expert Working Group on Agricultural Financing by Commercial Banks.

Report of the Dantwala Committee on Review of the Working of Regional Rural Banks.

Report of the Functional Committee on Coordination of Short Term, Medium Term and Long Term Credit 1964.

Report of the National Commission on Agriculture, Ministry of Agriculture, New Delhi, 1976.

Rural Development in India: Some Facets NIRD, Hyderabad, 1979.

Report of the Shivaraman Committee to Review Arrangements for Institutional Credit for Agriculture and Rural Development (CRAFICARD).

Report on Development of Drought Prone Areas—National Committee on the Development of Backward Areas, Planning Commission, Government of India, New Delhi — September 81.

Integrated Agricultural Development in Draught Prone Areas Report by the Task Force on Integrated Rural Development Planning Commission, Government of India, 1973.

Report of the Study Team on Agricultural Credit Institution in Rajasthan. RBI 1973.

Improvement in Draught Prone Regions—A View from Within Joint Field SPC NABAR, By AMLK. Gupta (IIM) IIM

Rural development schemes in India: Salient features and the physical and financial achievements (Article), *Spatio-Economic Development Record*, Vol. 13, No. 4, July-Aug., 2006, pp. 33-43.

Critical neglect of social banking (Article), *Economic and Political Weekly*, Vol. 39, No. 21, 22 to 28 May, 2004, pp. 2072-78.

Annual Report 2003-2004. Ministry of Social Justice and Empowerment, Government of India, New Delhi, p. 6.

C. Periodicals and Journals

Agricultural Development Income Distribution and Social Shange, *Orissa Economic Journal*, Vol. XIV (1), 1981.

5

Socio-Economic Profile of Rural Himachal Pradesh

B.A. DABLA

SECTION I
HIMACHAL PRADESH: AN INTRODUCTION

1. Origin and History

Himachal Pradesh is a State in north-west of the Union of India. While literal meaning is region of snowy mountains, it is considered as *Deva Bhoomi* (Land of the Gods). It is spread over 56,019 sq. km and is bordered by the States of Jammu & Kashmir on north, Punjab on west and south-west, Haryana and Uttar Pradesh on south, Uttrakhand on south-east and Tibet in the east. The Aryan influence in this area dates back to the *Rig Veda* period. After the Anglo-Gorkha war, the British colonial administration came into power. It was initially in Punjab under the rule of Maharaja Ranjit Singh till 1857. In 1950, Himachal was declared as a Union Territory but after 1971, it emerged as the State of Indian Union.

The history of H.P. areas dates back to the time when the Indus Valley Civilization flourished between 2250 and 1750 BCE. The tribes of Dagis, Halis, Dhaugris, Dasa Kinnars, Kirats and Koilis were original inhabitants in the area from pre-historic era. During the Vedic period, small republics known as '*Janapada*' existed till these were dominated by Gupta Empire. After a brief period of supremacy by King Harshvardhana, the area was divided into several local rulers/ chieftains, including some Rajput principalities. These kingdoms enjoyed certain degree of independence, but it was devastated by the Muslim rulers. At the beginning of tenth century, they marched through the lower hills and captured a number of forts. In addition, several hill states acknowledged the Mughal suzerainty and paid regular tributes to them. A martial tribe, Gorkha, came to power in Nepal in 1768. It consolidated its military power and expanded its territories by annexing Sirmour and Shimla. With the rise of the leadership of Amar Singh Thapa, the Gorkhas laid attack in Kangra and defeated its ruler in 1806 with the help of some provincial chiefs. But, they could not capture Kangra fort which led to their debacle. At that time, Raja Ram Singh recaptured the fort of Siba from Ranjit Singh is Samvat 1846.

This led to the Anglo-Sikh War and local rulers came in direct conflict with the British along the *tarai* belt after which the latter expelled the former from the provinces of Sutlej. In this situation, the British emerged as the paramount powers. Bit, at the time of 1857, people in the hill states were not politically alive and active like the people in other parts of the country. Some among them were compelled British against the mass revolt such as rulers of Chamba, Bilaspur, Bhagal, and Dhami. The British territories in the hills came under British Crown after Queen Victoria's proclamation of 1858. During this British period, these states experienced some progress. At the time of World War I, all hill rulers sided with the British and remained loyal to its rule.

After Independence in 1947, the Chief Commissioner's province of Himachal Pradesh came into being on 15 April, 1948. It comprised hill districts around Shimla and southern hill areas of former Punjab. Himachal Pradesh. Became part C State on 26 January, 1950 with the implementation of Constitution of India. It became Union Territory on 1 November, 1956 and on 18 December, 1970 the State of Himachal Pradesh Act was passed by Parliament and the new State came into existence on 25 January, 1971 and thus it emerged as the eighteenth State of Indian Union.

2. Geography and Climate

Himachal Pradesh is a hilly State situated in the western Himalayas. It is completely mountainous with elevation from about 1,148 ft. to 19,685 ft. above the sea level. The drainage system is composed of rivers and glaciers. Himaliyan rivers criss-cross the entire mountain chain. In fact, the rivers here are older than the mountain system. The State provides water of the Indus and the Ganges basins. The drainage system of the region are the Chandra Bhaga or the Chenab, Beas, Sutlej and Yamuna. These rivers are perennial and are fed by snow and rainfall. They are protected by the extensive cover of natural vegetation.

There is variation in climatic, conditions of Himachal Pradesh due to extreme variation in elevation. The climate varies from hot and sub-humid tropical in the southern ranges with more elevation. The State has areas like Dharamsala that receives very heavy rainfall as well as areas like Lahaul and Spiti that are cold and rainless. In general, Himachal Pradesh experiences three seasons: hot weather, cold weather and rainy season. Summer lasts from mid April till the end of June and most parts become very hot with average temperature ranging from 28°C to 32°C. Winter lasts from late November to mid March. Snowfall is common in alpine tracts, i.e., in the higher and Trans-Himalayan areas.

3. Total Population

The total population of Himachal Pradesh in 2001 was as given in Table 5.1:

Table 5.1: Total Population of Himachal Pradesh (Rural/Urban, Male/Female), 2001

	Males No.	*Females No.*	*Total No.*	*%age*
Rural	2,756,073	2,726,246	5,482,319	100.00
Urban	331,867	263,714	595,581	100.00
Total	**3,087,040**	**2,989,960**	**6,077,900**	**100.00**

Source: Economic Survey of Himachal Pradesh, Economics and Statistics Department, Himachal Pradesh.

In the same census year, the religious composition of population in Himachal Pradesh was as mentioned in Table 5.2:

Table 5.2: Religious Composition of Population Himachal Pradesh, 2001

Religion	*Males No.*	*Females No.*	*Total No.*	*%age*
Hindus	2,939,150	2,861,072	5,800,222	95.43
Muslims	66,173	53,339	119,512	01.97
Christians	4,220	3,467	7,687	00.13
Sikhs	38,118	34,237	73,355	01.19
Jains	750	658	1,408	00.02
Others	212	213	425	00.01

Source: Economic Survey of Himachal Pradesh, Economics and Statistics Department, Himachal Pradesh.

(iii) According to the census reports of 2011, the total population with various compositions was as follows:

4. Scheduled Caste/Scheduled Tribe Population

(i) The population of SCs and STs in Himachal Pradesh in the year 2001 was as shown in the Tables 5.3 and 5.4 below:

Table 5.3: SC Population in Himachal Pradesh, 2001

Rural/Urban	*Male No.*	*Female No.*	*Total No.*
Total	763,333	738,837	1,502,170
Rural	710,166	692,884	1,403,050
Urban	53,167	45,953	99,120

Source: Economic Survey of Himachal Pradesh, Economics and Statistics Department, Himachal Pradesh.

Table 5.4: ST Population in Himachal Pradesh, 2001

Rural/Urban	*Male No.*	*Female No.*	*Total No.*
Total	122,549	1,22,038	244,387
Rural	118,388	118,672	237,060
Urban	7,527	4,161	3,366

Source: Economic Survey of Himachal Pradesh, Economics and Statistics Department, Himachal Pradesh.

5. Administrative Set-Up

Himachal Pradesh has distributed the entire State into 12 administrative units which are called districts. In fact, the district unit has emerged as the most crucial administrative unit. The names of these districts are as follows:

- Bilaspur
- Chamba
- Hamirpur
- Kangra
- Kinnaur
- Kullu
- Lahaul & Spiti
- Mandi
- Shimla
- Sirmaur
- Solan
- Una

Below the district administrative set-up, there are other important and functional administrative units such as sub-district, town, Block, tehsil and village.

6. Education

Hamirpur district, stands among the top districts in the country for literacy. Literacy among women also stands impressive. The standard and quality of education in the State has reached to a considerably high level in comparison to many other educationally advanced States. It has several reputed educational institutions for higher education. The Himachal Pradesh University (HPU), Shimla, the NIT, Hamirpur and Jaypee University of Information Technology, Waknaghat are some of the pioneer institutes located in the State. Himachal Pradesh Agricultural University (HPAU), is one of the most renowned hill agriculture institutes in the world. It has made a unique contribution for teaching, research and extension education in horticulture, forestry and allied disciplines in the country. The State has got Indira Gandhi Medical College and Hospital. Besides that there is Himachal Pradesh Dental College which is the first recognized dental institute in the State. Moreover, there are globally reputed schools which contribute to the educational development at the national level.

The role of the State in Himachal Pradesh has proved very productive and purposeful in the educational development in the States. The State government has recently decided to start three nursing colleges to further create awareness about health care needs and health care system in the State. There are over 10,000 primary schools, 1,000 plus secondary schools and more than 1,300 high schools functioning in Himachal Pradesh. In order to meet the constitutional obligation to make primary education compulsory, Himachal Pradesh has now emerged as the first State in India to make elementary education accessible to every child in the State.

7. Review of the Economy

The economy of Himachal Pradesh has transformed radically from the most backward State to one of the advanced State of India, which has given it the role as a leader in Hill area Development. It stands an ideal destination for investment in power and tourism sectors. Responsive administration and favouable macro-economic conditions have induced a competitive environment for the growing and expanding economy in the State. In general, the economy of Himachal Pradesh maintains the growth rate of 6.2 per cent in the current financial year which stands better in comparison to the national growth rate.

The States Gross Domestic Product (GSDP) at factor cost at constant (2004-05) prices in 2012-13 is estimated at 44,480 crore as against 41,908 crore in 2011-12 registering a growth of 6.1 per cent during the year as against the growth rate of 7.3 per cent during the previous year. At current prices, the GSDP is estimated at 73,710 crore as against 64,957 crore in 2011-12 showing an increase of 13.5 per cent during the year.

The per capita income (PCI) at current prices witnessed an increase of 11.6 per cent from 75,185 in 2011-12. The increase in total State domestic product is attributed to be 9.5 per cent increase in primary sector, 10.00 per cent in community and personal services sectors, 6.2 per cent in transport and trade, 4.8 per cent in finance and real estate, whereas the secondary sector increased by only 3.4 per cent. Foodgrains production, which was 15.44 lakh MT during 2011-12 has increased to 15.68 lakh MT during 2012-13.

The economic growth in Himachal Pradesh is predominantly governed by agriculture and its allied activities showed not much fluctuations during 1990s as the growth rate remained stable. The decade showed an average annual growth rate of 5.7 per cent which is at par with its national level. The economy has shown a shift from agriculture to industries and services as the contribution of agriculture and allied sectors in total State domestic product has declined from 57.90 per cent in 1950-51 to 55.50 per cent in 1967-68, 26.50 per cent in 1990-91 and to 14.42 per cent in 2012-13. The share of industries and services sectors has increased proportionately. The declining share of agriculture sector did not, however, affect the importance of this sector in the State economy. It is the major contributor to the total domestic product and has overall impact on other sectors and government attaches high priority to this sector.

The State has made significant progress in the development of horticulture. The topographical variations and altitudinal differences coupled with fertile, deep and well drained soils favour the cultivation of temperate to sub-tropical fruits. The region is also very suitable for cultivation ancillary horticultural produce like flowers, mushroom, honey and hops.

During the year 2013-14, 8.28 lakh tonnes of fruits were produced in Himachal Pradesh and it is envisaged to bring 3,000 hectares of additional area under fruit plants against which 3,917 hectares of area has already been brought under plantation and 9.48 lakh fruit plants of different species were distributed up to December 2013. Growing of off-season vegetables has also picked up in the State. During the year in 2012-13, 13.98 lakh tonnes of vegetables were produced.

The hydropower is emerging as a powerful mechanism for speedier economic growth and overall development in the State. The power policy of the State attempts to address all aspects like capacity addition energy security, access and availability, efficiency, environment and assured employment to people in H.P.

High priority has also been accorded to tourism, which has emerged as the major sector in the economic development of Himachal Pradesh. The government and private sector equally have developed appropriate infrastructure for its development which includes public utility services, roads, communications, airports, hotels, transport facilities, water supply, civic amenities and other necessary services. The very significant rise has been noticed in the tourist arrival in Himachal Pradesh during last few years as revealed in Table 5.5.

Table 5.5: Arrival of Tourists in Himachal Pradesh (in lakhs)

Year	Indian Tourists	Foreign Tourists	Total No. of Tourists
2005	69.28	2.08	71.36
2006	76.72	2.81	79.53
2007	84.82	3.39	88.21
2008	93.73	3.77	97.50
2009	110.37	4.01	114.38
2010	128.12	4.54	132.66
2011	146.05	4.84	150.89
2012	156.46	5.00	161.46

Source: Economic Survey of Himachal Pradesh, Economics and Statistics Department, Himachal Pradesh.

8. Socio-economic Measures

The Government of Himachal Pradesh has made some specific and systematic socio-economic efforts in the last few years to achieve overall development in the State. Some of these socio-economic measures are as mentioned below:

- An amount of Rs. 1,000 is being provided to eligible literate unemployed youths under skill development scheme.
- Social security pension was increased from Rs. 450 to Rs. 500 per month.
- Senior citizens of the age 80 and above are provided an old age pension of Rs. 1,000 per month.
- Free travelling facility in HRTC buses to all students of government schools.
- Free travelling facility to new born and their mothers from hospital to home.
- 12 per cent of the total State budget is spent on the agrarian economy per sectors of the State. 5,84,568 Kisan Credit Cards have been issued by the banks and an amount of Rs. 2660.31 crore was distributed till 2013.
- Under Kisan Call Centre Scheme, the farmers can get any information on agriculture by dialling toll free telephone any time in the day.
- Under weather based crop insurance scheme, 41,333 farmers were covered in the State.

- Under Horticulture Technology Mission, the Central government has approved an action plan for Rs. 43.08 crore.
- Under Rajiv Gandhi Ann Yojana, 36,82,000 consumers were provided 3 kg wheat and 2 kg rice every month.
- Essential commodities are supplied on subsidized rates to all ration card holders in the State.
- The Per Capita Income in the State has touched the level of Rs. 83,899 in 2012-13.
- 8,432 MW hydro power has been harnessed out of 23,000 MW identified potential. During the year 2012-13, 1,815 million units of electricity were generated.
- 424 generic medicines free of cost were provided at the State hospitals.
- Out of 40 chronic diseases, free of cost treatment to all the children under 18 years of age are being provided in the State.
- Under NREGA Yojana 160 lakh man days were generated and 4,09,999 households were benefited.
- 7,064 houses are sanctioned under Indira Awas Yojana provide shelter to the homeless rural poor in Himachal Pradesh.
- 24×7 customer self service on Web Portal is operational for the help of dealers.
- Under Rajiv Awas Yojana construction subsidy has been increased from Rs. 48,000 to Rs. 75,000.
- Mahila Mandal Protsahan Yojana is implemented in the State to motivate and encourage the Mahila Mandals in sanitation activities and the reward of 131.04 lakh has been kept for this purpose during 2013-14.
- Under Mahila Shakti Bima Yojana, all women living below poverty line are covered in case of their death or disability.
- To improve the educational status of deprived sections of society, various kinds of scholarships/stipend are provided by the State government at various stages and different fields.
- Government has started running of girl's hostels in educationally backward Blocks in the State to bridge the gap in the male and female literacy rates.

- The students of 10th and 12th classes in government schools were provided 5,000 notebooks under Rajiv Gandhi Digital Vidyarthi Yojana.
- Scholarship of Rs. 75,000 each is provided to the students selected in IIT, IIM, AIIMS under Mukhya Mantri Protsahan Yojana.
- A total of 28,923 students have been benefited in the State under post-Matric scholarships.
- Under the Information and Communication Technology (ICT) project, different subjects from ninth to twelfth classes will be taught with the help of LCD-TV and LCD-project.
- The BETI HAI ANMOL Yojana has been started to change the negative attitude towards the girl child. A provision of birth grant of Rs. 10,000 is deposited in the local post office in favour of the girl born in BPL family (2 girls) till she attains the age of 18 years.
- The marriage grant has been increased to Rs. 25,000 from Rs. 21,000 under Mukhya Mantri Kanyadaan Yojana.
- Inter-caste marriage and widow remarriage grant has also been increased to Rs. 50,000 from Rs. 25,000.
- Under Indira Gandhi Matritva Sahyog Yojana, there is provision of providing cash incentive of Rs. 4,000 and has now been enhanced to Rs. 6,000 after implementation of Food Security Act to pregnant and lactating women of 19 years of age.
- Implementation of National Rural Health Mission (NRHM) with the involvement of local government institutions for ensuring better health care facilities at the door step of people has been started in the State.
- Under Matri Sevab Yojana free institutional deliveries of expectant mothers are done in all government hospitals.
- Himachal Pradesh has the distinction of being the first State in the country to commission the Statewide Area Network (HIM-SWAN) and e-Samadhan.
- It is the only State in India which has provided horizontal connectivity to 1,350 government office in the country.
- Finally, Himachal Pradesh has been adjudged the best State in the fields of Health and investment.

SECTION II
SOCIO-ECONOMIC PROFILE OF HIMACHAL PRADESH (DISTRICT-WISE)

In this section, an explanation of the socio-economic profile of Himachal Pradesh will be carried out as follows:

1. District Bilaspur

(i) ***Geography and History***: (a) This district lies between 31°12′35″ and 31°35′45″ north latitude and between 76°23′45″ and 76°55′40″ east longitude in the outer hills of the Himalayas next to the Punjab plains and forms a part of the basin of river Sutlej which flow meandering across it for about 90 km. It covers an area of 1,167 sq. km. Its boundaries touch Una, Hamirpur, Mandi and Solan districts. Sutlej is the main river which passes through the middle of this district and divides it into equal parts.

(b) The erstwhile ruling family of Bilaspur claims its descent from Chandarwanshi Rajputs who reigned at Chanderi in Bundelkhand region of Madhya Pradesh. The place now forms part of the Guna district. It is said that the seventh ruler of Chanderi kingdom handed over it to his son and sought his fortune in a shrine. The capital of ruling dynasty continued to be located at Kothahlur till 1600 AD when their hair Bir Chand fled at Sunhani across the river Sutlej along with mother where he settled. He returned to Kotakhlur after conversion to Islam. He got himself installed as the King. He kept his capital at Sunhani on the side of Sutlej. In 1650 AD, when Deep Chand succeeded as Raja of Kahlur, he decided to shift his capital. It is generally believed that he accompanied with 2 Hindus and 2 Mohammadans and sought new site for the capital and finally chose left bank of Sutlej known as Beas Gufa. He built a palace there and founded a town on the river side which was later on called Bilaspur. Since then it continues as the major town, though it was submerged in the Govind Sagar in 1954. Subsequently a new township at an elevation of 673 metres above sea level emerged.

(ii) ***Population and Demography:*** (a)The total population and its male-female and rural-urban composition of District Bilaspur in the year 2001 was as follows:

Table 5.6: Total Population (Male-female and rural-urban) 2001

Total/ Rural/Urban	*Total*	*Males*	*Females*	*%age*
Persons	340,885	171,263	169,622	100.00
Rural	318,934	159,488	159,446	100.00
Urban	21,951	11,775	10,176	100.00

Source: Economic Survey of Himachal Pradesh, Economics and Statistics Department, Himachal Pradesh.

While the total area is 1,167 sq. km, the density of population in the State is 282. The sex ratio in the population in 2001 was 990 (females per 1000 males).

(b) The district consists of two tehsils, Ghumarwin and Bilaspur Sadar. In 1980, the State government created a separate sub-tehsil called Naina Devi at Swarghat. Again in 1984, a new sub-tehsil namely Jhandutta was created. Administratively, the district is divided on the pattern of following units:

Sub-divisions	—	02
Tehsils	—	03
Sub-Tehsil	—	01
C.D. Blocks	—	136
Municipal Committees	—	02
Notified Area Committee	—	02
No. of villages		

(c) Bilaspur has been a town from 1891 and 1901 census. In 1931, it was classified as town. Naina Devi is a place of religious importance and was declared as a town in 1951 after Independence. In the year 1961, it got the municipal committee. After 1981 Census, Shah Talai has been classified as notified area committee.

(iii) (a) ***Literacy and Education***: Bilaspur had the following literacy rate in the year 2001:

Persons/Total	77.75%
Males	86.04%
Females	69.55%

(b) The educational level attained in the district in 2001 was as follows:

Table 5.7: Educational Level attained in the District, 2001

Sl. No.	*Level of education*	*Persons*	*Male*	*Female*
1.	Without any level	3,082	1,600	1,482
2.	Below Primary	38,795	20,811	17,984
3.	Primary	67,592	31,464	36,128
4.	Middle	42,373	23,255	19,188
5.	Matric/Higher Secondary	68,148	42,670	25,478
6.	Graduate and above	11,726	7,928	3,798
	Total	**2,311,733**	**127,738**	**103,995**

Source: Economic Survey of Himachal Pradesh, Economics and Statistics Department, Himachal Pradesh.

(iv) ***Types and Number of Workers***: According to the Census reports of 2001, this district had the types and number of workers as is noted in the Table 5.8:

Table 5.8: Types and Number of Workers in District Bilaspur, 2001

Sl. No.	*Types of workers*	*Total/people*	*Male*	*Female*
1.	Total No.	166,708	89,425	77,283
	(a) Cultivators	114,244	44,068	70,176
	(b) Agricultural labourers	2,923	1,792	1,131
	(c) Household workers	2,727	2,172	555
	(d) Other workers	46,814	41,393	5,421
2.	Main workers	110,652	69,356	41,296
3.	Marginal workers	56,056	20,069	35,987
4.	Non-workers	174,177	81,838	92,339

Source: Same as above.

(v) ***Largest SCs***: In this district, there were three largest SC communities and their population was as follows:

Table 5.9: Population of Three Major SC Communities in the District, 2001

Sl. No.	*Name of SC community*	*Total*	*Male*	*Female*
1.	Chamar, etc.	45,068	22,921	22,147
2.	Julaha, etc.	19,935	10,086	9,849
3.	Lohar	8,966	4,600	4,366

Source: Same as above.

(vi) ***Largest STs***: In this district, there are three major STs and their population is explained below:

Table 5.10: Population of Three Major ST Communities in the District, 2001

Sl. No.	*Name of ST community*	*Total*	*Male*	*Female*
1.	Gujjar	9,108	4,683	4,415
2.	Jadd, etc.	24	17	7
3.	Gadd	18	12	6

Source: Economic Survey of Himachal Pradesh, Economics and Statistics Department, Himachal Pradesh.

(vii) ***Amenities and Infrastructural Facilities***: This district has 965 villages and amenities/facilities to the people living there as mentioned below:

Primary schools	544 villages
Secondary/Senior Secondary schools	102 villages
Primary health centres	19 villages
Drinking water facilities	965 villages
Electricity (power supply)	962 villages
Electricity (agriculture)	16 villages
Paved approach roads	513 villages
Middle schools	168 villages
Medical facilities	230 villages
Primary health sub-centres	135 villages
Safe drinking water	963 villages
Electricity (domestic)	370 villages
Bus service	574 villages
Posts and Telegraph	572 villages

(viii) ***Trade and Commerce***: Three towns of Bilaspur, Ghumarwin and Naina Devi are important for trade and commerce in the fields of foodgrains, steel furniture, wooden furnitures, shutters, grills and metal splints.

(ix) ***Tourist Places***: The places of tourist attraction in the district are Bhakra Dam, Gobind Sagar Lake, Reghunathji Temple, Gopalji Temple, and Kandnor Bridge.

(x) ***NGOs***: The following NGOs are active in the district:

- — Mahila Mandal Jabli (1990)
- — Manav Sewa Sansthan (1989)
- — Samaj Sudhar Kala Sangam Sanskriti Sangathan (1991)
- — Social Action through Research Centre (1990)

(xi) ***Fairs and Festivals***: The main/major fairs/festivals in the district are as under:

(a) *Bachhretu Naun Fair*: It is one of the famous fairs in the district. It begins on the night of last day of Chaitra (April) and lasts up to 1st Vaisakha in the evening.

(b) *Barnot Fair*: It is held for a day in Asvina (October) at Jhanduta.

(c) *Basant Panchmi Fair*: This fair is said to be about 350 years old and begins a day before Basant Panchmi and ends on this day in the month of Magha (January).

(d) *Bhadra Amavasya*: It falls on the last day of dark half in the month of Bhadra (August) every year. It is also called Kusha Patni Amavasya.

(e) *Bhel Fair*: It is held at Bhel near a Dev Temple on 3rd and 4th Asvina (September) every year for two days.

(f) *Gauri Tij*: It falls on the third day of bright half in the month of Magha (January). It is locally called Gauntri. The women fast on this day for the welfare of their husbands and children.

(g) *Gugga Bhater Fair*: This fair is held in every big ground in front of the Gugga temple and lasts for two days from Gugga Navami to Ekadashi during the dark half in the month of Bhadra (August).

(h) *Naina Devi Fair*: In a small town, this fair is celebrated in one corner of Bilaspur.

2. District Chamba

(i) ***Geography and History***: (a) The district Chamba is bounded on north-west by J&K, on the north-east and east by Ladakh and Lahaul and Bara Bengal area of Himachal Pradesh, on the south-east and south by district Kangra and Gurdaspur District of Punjab. It is situated between north latitude 30°11′ 30″ and 33°13′ 6″ and east longitude 75°49′ and 77°3′ 30″ with an estimated area of 6,528 sq. km. and is surrounded on all sides by lofty hill regions. The territory is completely mountainous with altitude ranging from 2,000 to 21,000 feet.

(b) It is believed that this area was at time inhabited by certain Kolian tribes, which were later, subjugated by the Khasas which too came under the sway of Audyumbaras. From the Gupta period, the region was under the control of Thakurs and Ranas. In 500 AD, a legendary hero, Maru, migrated to this area. His successors continued to rule the area and gave it the name of their daughters, Chamba. The district is the only State in northern India to preserve a well-documented history from 500 AD. Its high mountain ranges have given it a sheltered position and helped in preserving its centuries old relics and inscriptions. The rulers of Chamba had occasional fights with their neighbours like the Mughals but their damage was seldom serious. By late eighteenth century, the Sikhs forced the hill states to pay tribute to them. Maharaja Ranjit Singh systematically deposed the hill princes but spared Chamba in lieu of the services Wazir Nathu had rendered him. In 1817, he had saved Singh's life by offering his horse at a critical moment. When the Sikhs were defeated by the British, Chamba was taken under the control of British and subjected to the annual tribute. Later, the British developed cordial relations with the local rulers and introduced various reforms. Raja Sahila Verman unified the territory and, therefore, divided Chamba in five zones known as Mandals and now called Wazarats which are Bharmour, Chamba, Bhattiyat, Churah and Pangi.

(ii) ***Population and Demography***: The total population of this district is as follows:

Table 5.11: Total (Rural-Urban and Male-Female) Population, 2001

Sl. No.	*Rural/Urban*	*Persons*	*Males*	*Females*	*%age*
1.	Rural	426,345	216,704	209,641	100.00
2.	Urban	34,542	18,514	16,028	100.00
	Total	**460,887**	**235,218**	**225,669**	**100.00**

Source: Economic Survey of Himachal Pradesh, Economics and Statistics Department, Himachal Pradesh.

(iii) ***The Population of SCs and STs***: The population of SCs and STs in this district was as shown in the two following Tables 5.12 and 5.13:

Table 5.12: SC Population in the District, 2001

Sl. No.	*Rural/Urban*	*Persons*	*Males*	*Females*
	Total	92,359	46,940	45,419
1.	Rural	86,150	43,761	42,389
2.	Urban	6,209	3,179	3,030

Source: Economic Survey of Himachal Pradesh, Economics and Statistics Department, Himachal Pradesh.

Table 5.13: ST Population in the District, 2001

Sl. No.	*Rural/Urban*	*Persons*	*Males*	*Females*
1.	Rural	115,701	57,812	57,889
2.	Urban	1,868	1,038	830
	Total	**117,569**	**58,850**	**58,719**

Source: Economic Survey of Himachal Pradesh, Economics and Statistics Department, Himachal Pradesh.

(iv) ***Types and Number of Workers***: The district Chamba has the following types and number of workers as mentioned in Table 5.14:

Table 5.14: Types and Number of Workers in District

Sl. No.	*Types of workers*	*Persons*	*Male*	*Female*
1.	Total workers	230,452	126,718	103,734
	(a) Cultivators	167,590	74,839	92,751
	(b) Agricultural labourers	1,655	984	671
	(c) HHI workers	2,780	1,574	1,206
	(d) Other workers	58,427	49,721	33,731
2.	Main workers	128,452	94,721	33,731
3.	Marginal workers	102,000	31,997	70,003
4.	Non-workers	230,435	108,500	121,935

Source: Economic Survey of Himachal Pradesh, Economics and Statistics Department, Himachal Pradesh.

(v) ***Largest SCs in the District*:** The three largest SCs and their population (male-female) is given in the Table 5.15:

Table 5.15: Three Major SC in District Chamba

Sl. No.	*Name of the caste*	*Persons*	*Male*	*Female*
1.	Hali	31,698	16,658	16,040
2.	Sipi	16,907	8,425	8,482
3.	Chamar, etc.	10,416	5,311	5,105

Source: Economic Survey of Himachal Pradesh, Economics and Statistics Department, Himachal Pradesh.

Table 5.16: Three Largest STs in District Chamba

Sl. No.	*Name of the ST*	*Persons*	*Male*	*Female*
1.	Gaddi	91,789	45,721	46,068
2.	Pangwala	15,875	7,962	7,913
3.	Gujjar	8,302	4,315	3,987

Source: Same as above.

(vi) ***Literacy and Education*:** The literacy rate in Chamba district in 2001 was follows:

(a) Total Persons — 62.91%

(b) Males — 76.41%

(c) Females — 48.85%

The level of education attained in the district reveals in the Table 5.17.

Table 5.17: Three Largest STs in District Chamba

Sl. No.	*Level of education*	*Persons*	*Male*	*Female*
1.	Without any level	4,356	2,536	1,818
2.	Below Primary	72,121	40,141	31,980
3.	Primary	75,341	46,242	29,099
4.	Middle	34,228	22,580	11,648
5.	Matric/Higher Secondary	51,105	35,031	16,071
6.	Graduate and above	8,997	5,985	3,012
	Total	**246,169**	**152,533**	**93,636**

Source: Same as above.

(vii) ***Amenities and Infrastructural Facilities*:** The district had total number of 1118 inhabited villages and amenities-facilities available were as mentioned below:

Primary schools	— 852
Middle School	— 290
Secondary Schools	— 172
Medical Facility	— 300
Primary Health Centres	— 28
Primary Health Sub-centres	— 190
Drinking water facility	—1,118
Safe drinking facility	—1,108
Electricity (power supply)	—1,111
Electricity (domestic)	— 962
Electricity (agriculture)	— —
Bus service	— 402
Paved approach roads	— 333
Posts, Telegraph and Telephone	— 571

(viii) ***Places of Tourist Attraction*:** The following places are of the tourist attraction in the district:

Chamba: Shiva temples, Chandra Gupt temple, T.B.S. Museum and Natural Tourism site at Dalhousie.

(ix) ***Fairs and Festivals*:** The following are the major and famous fairs and festivals celebrated in the district:

Bharari Devi fair	— held at Kakirra Village on 2-3 Asadha (June)
Dehri Ghat Jatar	— annually on 1-4th Asvina (September)
Ghatasni Mata fair	— 4th night of Jyaistha (May) every year
Kiunr Jatar	— In the Month of Bhadra (August)
Lakkh Data's Chhinj	— In the month of Asadha (June)
Mindal Jatar	— In the month of Bhadra (August)

Minjar fair	— In the month of Sravana
Nag fair	— On 4th Sravana every year
Phool Jatar	— In the month of Asvina (October)
Radha Rathaniv fair	— On Full Moon day of Bhadra month
Saho Jatar	— 15-16 Vaisakha (April)
Shiv Shakti fair	— 10th day of bright Moon in Bhadra (August)
Minghal fair	— In the month of September
Tisagarh Jatar	— In the month of Bhadra (August)

3. District Hamirpur

(i) ***Geography and History***: (a) This district is situated between 76°18′ to 76°44′ east longitude and 31°25′ to 31°52′ north latitude. The tract is hilly covered by Shivalik range. The elevation varies from 400 to 1,100 metres having the configuration ranging from almost flat lands that border river Beas to the heights of cliffs and precipitious slopes of hill ranges. There are 3 principal ranges which run in south-easterly direction. It is situated at lower elevation and comparatively warmer but has some hilly ranges covered with pine forests. It is well connected by roads from all sides.

(b) The history of Hamirpur is closely associated with the Katoch dynasty which ruled the area between Ravi ad Sutlej rivers in the olden days. During *Mahabharata* period, it was a part of old Jallandhar-Trigarta empire. It is believed that in ancient period the rulers of Gupta dynasty had established their sovereignty over this area. But, with the passage of time, all rulers went away and the area came under the control of Ranas of Mewar and the Katoch dynasty became predominant in eighteeth century. These rulers built a fort in Hamirpur. In the nineteenth century, the British made Kangra and Hamirpur as a district.

(c) This district remained a part of Punjab till 1966 when these areas were merged in Himachal Pradesh. As a result of rearrangement of districts in the merged areas in 1972, Hamirpur was created as a separate district with two tehsils of Barsar and Hamirpur. In the year 1980, three more tehsils, Tira Sujanpur, Nadaun and Bhorang were created with the further reorganization.

(ii) ***Population and Demography***: The total population of Hamirpur district in 2001 is shown in Table 5.18.

Table 5.18: Total Population of Hamirpur District, 2001

Sl. No.	*Rural/urban*	*Persons*	*Males*	*Females*	*%age*
1.	Rural	382,494	180,366	202,128	100.00
2.	Urban	30,206	16,277	13,979	100.00
	Total	**412,700**	**196,593**	**216,107**	**100.00**

Source: Census, 2001.

The sex ratio (females per 1,000 males) of population in the district was 1,099, while the density was 369. The district had an area of 1,118 sq. km. At, present, the district has five tehsils as mentioned below:

- Hamirpur
- Bhoranj
- Sujanpur
- Barsar
- Nadaun

The district has also been divided into six development Blocks mentioned below:

- Hamirpur
- Bhoranj
- Sujanpur
- Bijhari
- Nadaun
- Bansan at Touni Devi

(iii) ***SC and ST Population***: The population (male-female and rural-urban composition) of SCs and STs in the district is given in the Tables 5.19(a) and 5.19(b):

Table 5.19(a): Total Population of SCs in the District, 2001

Sl. No.	Total/rural/urban	Population	Males	Females
1.	Rural	93,350	46,002	47,348
2.	Urban	5,189	2,740	2,449
	Total	**98,539**	**48,742**	**49,797**

Source: Census, 2001.

Table 5.19(b): Total Population of STs in the District, 2001

Sl. No.	Total/Rural/Urban	Population	Males	Females
1.	Rural	18	13	05
2.	Urban	137	79	58
	Total	**155**	**92**	**63**

Source: Census, 2001.

(iv) ***Types and Number of Workers*:** The various types of workers in the district Hamirpur were as shown in Table 5.20 below:

Table 5.20: Different Types of Workers in the District, 2001

Sl. No.	Types of workers	Persons	Male	Female
1.	Total workers	205,405	100,067	105,338
	(a) Cultivators	143,535	46,900	96,635
	(b) Agricultural labourers	3,291	1,773	1,518
	(c) HHI workers	2,916	2,247	669
	(d) Other workers	55,663	49,147	6,516
2.	Main workers	119,870	69,496	50,374
3.	Marginal workers	85,535	30,571	54,964
4.	Non-workers	207,295	96,526	110,769

Source: Census, 2001.

(v) ***Major SC and ST Communities*:** The three major communities of SCs and STs inhabiting in this district and their population (with male-female proportion) in noted in the Table 5.21 (a) and 5.21(b):

Table 5.21 (a): Three Largest SC Communities in the District, 2001

Sl. No.	*SC community*	*Persons*	*Male*	*Female*
1.	Charmar, etc.	48,047	24,053	23,994
2.	Julaha, etc.	21,927	10,551	11,376
3.	Lohar.	10,402	5,077	5,325

Source: Census, 2001.

Table 5.21 (b): Three Largest ST Communities in District, 2001

Sl. No.	*Name of the ST*	*Persons*	*Male*	*Female*
1.	Generic tribes, etc.	109	65	44
2.	Jad, etc.	16	05	11
3.	Kanaura, etc.	12	10	02

Source: Census, 2001.

(vi) ***Amenities and Infrastructural Facilities***: The total number of inhabited villages in the district in 2001 was 1,635 and amenities-facilities available in these villages are as mentioned below:

Primary schools	— 555
Middle School	— 224
Secondary schools/Sr. Secondary Schools	— 163
Medical facility	— 289
Primary Health Centres	— 16
Primary Health Sub-centres	— 153
Drinking water facility	—1,635
Safe drinking facility	—1,634
Electricity (power supply)	—1,619
Electricity (domestic)	— 370
Electricity (agriculture)	— 7
Bus service	— 891
Paved approach roads	— 733
Posts, Telegraph and Telephone	— 930

(vii) ***Places of Tourist Attraction***: The places of tourist attraction in the district are as follows:

- Mahadev Temple
- Devi Temple
- Rest House
- Bilikesher Temple at Naudaun

(viii) ***Fairs and Festivals***: The people celebrate the following fairs and festivals on the following days:

- Kahika fair — celebrated for three days
- Holi — celebrated throughout the district for several days.

4. District Kangra

(i) ***Geography and Histroy***: Lying 526 km, north-west of New Delhi, Dharamshala is the headquarters of Kangra District in Himachal Pradesh. The Kangra valley stands one of the most pleasant, relaxing and spiritual places in the Himalayas. The upper Dharamshala is well wooded with oak, cedar, pine and other timber yielding tree and offers finer views. Lord Elgin the British Viceroy of India liked Dharamshala so much that he had sent a proposal to the British monarch to make it the summer capital of India, but it was ignored. Till India attained independence in 1947, Macleod Ganj and Forsyth Gunj continued to serve as health resorts and resting places for British rulers. This situation changed when government of India granted political asylum to the 14th Dalai Lama in 1959. In the following year, he was allowed to make McLeod Ganj his headquarters.

(ii) The present Kangra district came into existence in September 1972 consequent upon the reorganizations of districts in Himachal Pradesh. It was the largest district in composite Punjab in terms of area till it was transferred to Himachal Pradesh in November 1966. At that time, this area was shifted along with Shimla, Kullu and Lahaul-Spiti.

(iii) ***Population and Demography***: The total population in the district Kangra has been showed in Table 5.22:

Table 5.22: Total Population of the District (Male-Female and Rural-Urban), 2001

Sl. No.	*Total Rural/Urban*	*Persons*	*Males*	*Females*	*%age*
1.	Rural	1,266,745	623,259	643,486	100.00
2.	Urban	72,285	37,995	34,290	100.00
	Total	**1,339,030**	**661,254**	**677,776**	**100.00**

Source: Census, 2001.

The total area of this district of Himachal Pradesh is 5,739 sq. km. While the sex ratio (females per 1000 males) stands at 1,025 in 2011, the density of population in this district is 233. The district has six tehsils as under:

- Nurpur
- Palampur
- Hamirpur
- Kangra
- Dehragopipur
- Kullu

(iv) ***SC and ST Population***: The total population (with male-female and rural-urban proportion) in the district in 2001 was as follows:

Table 5.23(a): Total Population of SCs in the District, 2001

Sl. No.	*Total Rural/Urban*	*Population*	*Males*	*Females*
1.	Rural	268,721	134,232	134,489
2.	Urban	10,819	5,626	5,193
	Total	**279,540**	**139,858**	**139,682**

Source: Census, 2001.

Table 5.23(b): Total Population of STs in the District, 2001

Sl. No.	*Total Rural/Urban*	*Population*	*Males*	*Females*
1.	Rural	1,372	748	624
2.	Urban	225	121	104
	Total	1,597	869	728

Source: Census, 2001.

(v) ***Types and Number of Workers*:** This district has the following types and number of workers as noted in the Table 5.24:

Table 5.24: Types and Number of Workers in the District, 2001

Sl. No.	*Types of workers*	*Persons*	*Male*	*Female*
1.	Total workers	588,994	336,447	253,547
	(a) Cultivators	335,357	134,574	200,783
	(b) Agricultural labourers	39,534	23,801	15,733
	(c) HHI workers	19,345	11,538	78,07
	(d) Other workers	194,758	165,534	29,224
2.	Main workers	336,649	242,236	94,413
3.	Marginal workers	252,345	93,211	159,134
4.	Non-workers	750,036	325,807	424,229

Source: Census, 2001.

(vi) ***Literacy and Education*:** In the district in 2001, the general literacy situation is explained below:

Total Persons — 80.08%

Male — 87.54%

Females — 73.01%

The general educational level attained in the district is given in Tables 5.25:

Table 5.25: Levels of Education in the District, 2001

Sl. No.	*Level of education*	*Persons*	*Males*	*Females*
1.	Without Level	11,092	5,785	5,307
2.	Below Primary	163,622	89,138	74,484
3.	Primary	259,382	118,127	141,255
4.	Middle	174,315	92,156	82,159
5.	Matric/Higher Secondary	287,036	166,871	120,166
6.	Graduation and above	44,916	28,229	16,687
	Total	**940,505**	**500,383**	**440,122**

Source: Census, 2001.

(vii) ***SC and ST Communities*:** The three largest/major SC-ST communities inhabiting in this district are identified with their population is given in Tables 5.26 (a) and 5.26(b).

Table 5.26 (a): Three Largest SCs in the District, 2001

Sl. No.	*SC Community*	*Total*	*Males*	*Females*
1.	Chamar, etc	101,358	50,752	50,606
2.	Julaha, etc.	34,875	17,113	17,762
3.	Lohar	26,608	13,388	13,220

Source: Census, 2001.

Table 5.26 (b): Three Largest STs in the District, 2001

Sl. No.	*ST Community*	*Total*	*Males*	*Females*
1.	Bhot, etc.	1,358	722	636
2.	Generic tribes, etc.	71	44	27
3.	Pangwala	55	31	24

Source: Census, 2001.

(viii) ***Amenities and infrastructural Facilities*:** There are 3,610 total number of inhabited villages in the district. These villages have the amenities and facilities as given below:

Table 5.26 (c): Amenities and Infrastructural Facilities in the Village

Sl. No.	*Amenities/Facilities available*	*No. of Villages*
1.	Primary Schools	1869
2.	Middle Schools	725
3.	Secondary/Higher Secondary Schools	466
4.	Medical facility	786
5.	Primary Health Centre	48
6.	Primary Health Sub-centre	430
7.	Drinking water supply	3619
8.	Safe drinking water	3617
9.	Electricity (power supply)	3602
10.	Electricity (domestic)	1455
11.	Electricity (agriculture)	75
12.	Bus service	2127
13.	Paved approach road	1767
14.	Posts and telegraph	2220

Source: Economic Survey of Himachal Pradesh, Economics and Statistics Department, Himachal Pradesh.

(ix) ***Places of Tourist attraction***: The following places can be considered as places of tourist attraction:

- Kareri Lake
- Lam Dal Lake
- Lord Elgin Tomb
- Jawalamukhi old fort at Nurpur

(x) ***Fairs and Festivals***: The people in the district celebrate the fairs and festivals as mentioned below:

- Kali Devi fair on 1st Tuesday of Jyaistha (May) every year
- Shiama Kali fair on 20th Jyaistha (June) every year
- Vrajeshwari fair twice a year
- Seri fairs
- Cattle fairs

5. District Kinnaur

(i) ***Geography and History***: (a) A mountainous area, ranging from 23,206,816 metres, Kinnaur district is one of the smallest districts in India by population. It is famous for the Kinnaur Kailash, a mountain sacred to Hindus, close to the Tibetan border. The district was earlier known as Chinit tehsil of the former Mahasu district, came into being as an independent district in May 1960. Before independence in 1947, Kinnaur valley was a part of erstwhile Bushahr state with headquarters at Rampur.

(b) By the beginning of fourteenth century, the area of kinnaur was divided in 7 parts, locally called *sar khund*. In the medieval period, though some of the hill states were attacked and made tributary to the Mughal emperor, in Delhi, Bushahr state could not be reached. Later on, Shimla hill states for, 1803 to 1815, the states of Bushahr faced the menace of Gurkha invasions. The tract between Sutlej and Jamuna rivers came under British protection by the treaty of 1809 between Ranjit Singh and British. It seems clear that, during the princely days, Kinnaur valley acted as a bulwark to the Bushahr state. However, with the lapse of paramountcy, Kinnaur then known as Chini tehsil was merged to form a part of Mahasu district. In fact, the Chini tehsil covered entire Kinnaur valley beyond Wangtu which was created in 1891 by the then ruler and this continued till 1960. Afterwards, the importance of reorganizing border area and realized and in view of ethnic and cultural considerations, the areas in Rampur tehsil were reorganized into a separate district of present Kinnaur.

(ii) ***Population and Demography***: The district had the total population (with male female and rural urban proportion) in 2001 is given below:

Table 5.27: Total Rural/Urban Population and Demography in the District

Sl. No.	*Total Rural/Urban*	*Persons*	*Males*	*Females*	*Percentage*
1.	Rural	78334.00	42173	36161	100
2.	Urban	00000.00	00	00	00
	Total	**78334.00.**	**42173**	**36161**	**100**

Source: Census, 2001.

The total area of this district is 6,401 sq. km. While the sex ratio in population (females per 1000 males) is 857, the density of population is 12.

(iii) ***SC and ST population***: The SC and ST population in Kinnaur district in 2001 reflects Tables 5.27(a) 5.27(b):

Table 5.27 (a): SC Population in the District, 2001

Sl. No.	*Total Rural/Urban*	*Persons*	*Males*	*Females*
1.	Rural	7625	3972	3653
2.	Urban	0	0	0
	Total	**7625**	**3972**	**3653**

Source: Census, 2001.

Table 5.27 (b): ST Population in the District, 2001

Sl. No.	*Total Rural/Urban*	*Persons*	*Males*	*Females*
1.	Rural	56268	27583	28685
2.	Urban	0	0	0
	Total	**56268**	**27583**	**28685**

Source: Census, 2001.

(iv) ***Types and Number of Workers***: The major types of workers and their number working the Kinnaur district in 2001 was as shown in the Table 5.28:

Table 5.28: Types of Workers and their Number in the District, 2001

Sl. No.	Type of workers	Total	Males	Females
1	Total workers	47811	28041	19770
	(a) Cultivators	30977	14018	16959
	(b) Agri. Labourers	1101	767	334
	(c) HHI workers	871	576	295
	(d) Other workers	14862	12680	2182
2	Main workers	40313	25033	15280
3	Marginal workers	7498	3008	4490
4	Non-workers	30523	14132	16391

Source: Census, 2001.

(v) ***Literacy and Education***: The Literacy rate (male-female) in the district in the year 2001 was as follows:

Total literacy rate — 75.20%
Males literacy — 84.30%
Females literacy — 64.40%

The situation of education can be explained in terms of levels of education attained by people in the district. In this regard, the details are given in the Table 5.29.

Table 5.29: Different Levels of Education Attained in the District

Sl. No.	Type of workers	Persons	Males	Females
1.	Without level	775	394	381
2.	Below primary	13,424	7,031	6,393
3.	Primary	14,945	8,736	6,209
4.	Middle	9,158	5,630	3,528
5.	Matric/Secondary	11,537	8,114	3,423
6.	Graduate and above	2,069	1,679	390
	Total	**51,913**	**31,589**	**20,324**

Source: Census, 2001.

(vi) ***Major SC and ST Communities***: The three largest SC and ST communities in the district were as noted in Table 5.30(a) and 5.30(b).

Table 5.30 (a): Three Largest SC Communities in the District

Sl. No.	*Type of workers*	*Persons*	*Males*	*Females*
1.	Kri, etc.	3335	1722	1613
2.	Julha, etc.	1138	585	553
3.	Chamar, etc.	1130	608	522

Table 5.30 (b): Three Largest ST Communities in the District

Sl. No.	*Type of workers*	*Persons*	*Males*	*Females*
1.	Kri, etc.	55973	27391	28582
2.	Julha, etc.	130	75	55
3.	Chamar, etc.	74	38	36

(vii) ***Amenities and Infrastructural Facilities***: The district had a total number of 234 villages and the amenities and facilities available in 2001 were as mentioned below:

Table 5.30 (b): Amenities and Infrastructural Facilities Available in No. of Villages

Sl. No.	*Amenities available*	*No. of villages*
1.	Primary Schools	158
2.	Middle Schools	76
3. •	Secondary/Sr. Secondary schools	60
4.	Medical facility	77
5.	Primary Health Centres	17
6.	Primary Health Sub-centres	32
7.	Drinking water facility	196
8.	Safe drinking water	188
9.	Electricity (power supply)	232
10.	Electricity (domestic)	160
11.	Electricity (agriculture)	6
12.	Bus service	90
13.	Paved approach road	78
14.	Post and telegraph	138

Source: Economic Survey of Himachal Pradesh, Economics and Statistics Department, Himachal Pradesh.

(viii) ***Places of Tourist Attraction***: In the district, the following places/sites are attracting tourists in large numbers:

- Buddhist Monastery
- Wall paintings at Kinnaur
- Natural tourism

(ix) ***Fairs and Festivals***: In district Kinnaur, the following fairs and festivals are celebrated by the people:

- Agtarang fair
- Bang Kayangon the full moon of Paush
- Bishu festival on 1st-2nd Vaisakha (April) for two days
- Dakhraini festival on 1st Sravana (July) for 3 days
- Jagang fair on 3rd of Magh for a day
- Mang fair on 18th of Magh for a week
- Rokfo festival on 1-3 Phalguna (February) every year
- Fulaich in the monsoon month of Bhadrapada.

6. District Kullu

(i) ***Geography and History:*** (a) Kullu was probably the most ancient state next to Kashmir and Kangra. The Chinese pilgrim, Hiuen Tsang described it as kiu-lu-to situated at 117 miles to the north-east of Jalandhar. According to historical sources, it was founded in the first century AD by Behangamani Pal who came from outside. The people of higher valley of Kullu were suffering under repressive regimes of Thankurs of Spiti and their rule continued till 1450.

Reference may be made to Raja Jagat Singh (1637-1672) belonged to Jihna Rana, above Manali and opposite to Naggar. It was during his regime that the famous idol of Rghunathji was brought from Ayodhya and installed at the temple of Sultanpur (Kullu). The Rajas adopted Vaishnava dharma and gave away the whole kingdom to Raghunathji by placing the image on the *gaddi* and himself became vice-regent. Since the, Rajas of Kullu ruled the state in the name of Raghunathji.

(b) Like other hill states, Kullu had its ups and downs till it was ceded to the British Empire in 1846 according to Lahore agreement along with other trans-Sutlej states.

(c) Kullu was made a sub-division of Kangra district. Lahaul-Spiti was attached to Kullu for administration. In 1960, it was made a separate district. Kullu too was declared a district in 1963 and was a part of Punjab up to October 1966. On reorganization of State in November 1966, Kullu was declared as a district of Himachal Pradesh.

(ii) ***Population and Demography***: The total population of Kullu district in the year of 2001 is given in Table 5.31:

Table 5.31: Total Population (Male-Female and Rural-Urban) in the District, 2001

Sl. No.	*Total Rural/Urban*	*Persons*	*Males*	*Females*	*Percentage*
1.	Rural	351478	181131	170347	100
2.	Urban	30093	16885	13208	100
	Total	**381571**	**198016**	**183555**	**100**

Source: Census, 2001.

The total area of this district was 5503 sq. km. While the sex ratio (females per 1,000 males) was 927 in 2001, the density of population in the same year was 69.

(iii) ***SC and ST Population***: The total population of the SCs and STs in this district is given in the Table 5.32(a) and 5.32(b).

Table 5.32 (a): SC Population in the District, 2001

Sl. No.	*Total Rural/Urban*	*Persons*	*Males*	*Females*
1.	Rural	103418	52961	50457
2.	Urban	4479	2385	2094
	Total	**107897**	**55346**	**52551**

Source: Census, 2001.

Table 5.32 (b): ST Population in the District, 2002

Sl. No.	*Total Rural/Urban*	*Persons*	*Males*	*Females*
1.	Rural	9344	4644	4700
2.	Urban	2007	1020	987
	Total	**11351**	**5664**	**5687**

Source: Census, 2001.

(iv) ***Types and Number of Workers***: The min types and their number of workers in Kullu district in the year 2001 has been entered in Table 5.33:

Table 5.33: Types and their Number of Workers in the District

Sl. No.	Type of workers	Total	Males	Females
1.	Total workers	216513	119395	97118
	(a) Cultivators	164646	78736	85910
	(b) Agri. Labourers	5590	22952	2638
	(c) HHI workers	2733	1613	1120
	(d) Other workers	43544	36094	7450
2.	Main workers	166715	100140	66575
3.	Marginal workers	49798	19255	30544
4.	Non-workers	165058	78621	86437

Source: Census, 2001.

(v) ***Literacy and Education***: The district Kullu had literacy rate in 2001 as follows:

Total literacy rate	— 72.90%
Males literacy	— 83.98
Females literacy	— 60.88

The level of education attained in the district in 2001 was as given in Table 5.34:

Table 5.34: Levels of Education in the District, 2001

Sl. No.	Type of workers	Persons	Males	Females
1.	Without level	3747	1855	1892
2.	Below Primary	65666	35285	30382
3.	Primary	68910	39897	29013
4.	Middle	35947	22313	13634
5.	Matric/Sr. Secondary	53725	35938	17787
6.	Graduate and above	11636	8356	3280
	Total	**239649**	**143655**	**95994**

Source: Census, 2001.

(vi) ***SC and ST Communities***: The district had the three largest SC and ST communities as given in Tables 5.35 (a) and 5.35(b):

Table 5.35 (a): Three Largest SC Communities in the District, 2001

Sl. No.	*Name of SC Community*	*Total*	*Males*	*Females*
1.	Kri, etc.	75911	38871	37040
2.	Julha, etc.	15497	7905	7592
3.	Chamar, etc.	6111	3179	2932

Source: Economic Survey of Himachal Pradesh, Economics and Statistics Department, Himachal Pradesh.

Table 5.35 (b): Three Largest ST Communities in the District 2001

Sl. No.	*Name of SC Community*	*Total*	*Males*	*Females*
1.	Kri, etc.	5407	2728	2679
2.	Julha, etc.	2106	1035	1071
3.	Chamar, etc.	1461	699	762

Source: Economic Survey of Himachal Pradesh, Economics and Statistics Department, Himachal Pradesh.

(vii) ***Amenities and Infrastructural Facilities*:** The Kullu district had a total number of 172 inhabited villages and following facilities/ amenities were available:

Table 5.35 (c): Amenities and Infrastructural Facilities Available in No. of Villages

Sl. No.	*Amenities and Infrastructural facilities available*	*No. of villages*
1.	Primary Schools	171
2.	Middle Schools	122
3.	Secondary/Sr. Secondary schools	96
4.	Medical facilities	140
5.	Primary health centres	13
6.	Primary health sub-centres	98
7.	Drinking water facility	172
8.	Safe drinking water	172
9.	Electricity (Power supply)	172
10.	Electricity (domestic)	123
11.	Electricity (agriculture)	2
12.	Bus service	111
13.	Paved approach road	82
14.	Posts and telegraph	112

Source: Economic Survey of Himachal Pradesh, Economics and Statistics Department, Himachal Pradesh.

(viii) ***Places of Tourist Attraction***: The following are the places of tourists attraction in district Kullu:

- Kullu Valley
- Kullu Dussehra
- Hot water spring at Manikaran
- Gurdwara at Manikaran
- Rest House
- Vashishtha Hot water spring
- Natural Scenery at Manali

7. District Lahaul and Spiti

(i) ***Geography and History***: (a) This district of Himachal Pradesh was at one time separate Himalayan waziries or cantons of the Kullu sub-division which formed a part of Kangra district. Now, the district comprises two different mountain tracks, known as Lahul and Spiti, though they have different origins.

(b) Lahaul had been changing hands between the rulers of Ladakh and Kullu. In later seventeenth century, Lahaul passed into the hands of the Kullu chief. In 1840, Maharaja Ranjit Singh took over Lahaul along with Kullu and ruled it till 1846 when the area came under the British. Till 1940 Lahaul was administered through local jagirdars/Thakurs. In the late 1030s, the power and influence of Wizier of Lahaul started declining. In 1941, a separate sub-tehsil of Lahaul and Spiti was formed which existed till 1960 when it got the status of a district.

(c) In 1941, Spiti was constituted into a separate sub-tehsil of Kullu sub-division. Later on, in 1960, Spiti was taken into a sub-division with its headquarters at Kaza.

(ii) ***Population and Demography***: The total population of this district in 2001 has been noted the Table 5.36:

Table 5.36: Total Population in the District, 2001

Sl. No.	*Total Rural/Urban*	*Persons*	*Males*	*Females*	*Percentage*
1.	33224	18441	14783	14783	100
2.	33224	18441	14783	14783	100
3.	00	00	00	00	00

Source: Census, 2001.

The total area of this district in 2001 was 5,503 sq. km. While the sex ratio (females per 1,000 males) in 2001 was 927 and density of population in the same year was 69.

(iii) ***SC and ST Population*:** This district had the SC and ST population in 2001 as shown in Table in 5.37 (a) and 5.37 (b):

Table 5.37 (a): SC Population in the District, 2001

Sl. No.	*Total Rural/Urban*	*Persons*	*Males*	*Females*
1.	Rural	2605	1386	1219
2.	Urban	00	00	00
	Total	**2605**	**1386**	**1219**

Source: Census, 2001.

Table 5.37 (b): ST Population in the District, 2001

Sl. No.	*Total Rural/Urban*	*Persons*	*Males*	*Females*
1.	Rural	24238	11952	12286
2.	Urban	00	00	00
	Total	**24238**	**11952**	**12286**

Source: Census, 2001.

(iv) ***Types and Number of Workers*:** The district had the types and their number of workers in 2001 as shown in Table 5.38:

Table 5.38: Types and their Number of Workers in the District, 2001

Sl. No.	Type of workers	Persons	Males	Females
1.	Total	21088	12604	8484
	(a) Cultivators	11160	4751	6409
	(b) Agri. I Labourers	339	171	168
	(c) HHI workers	138	49	87
	(d) Other workers	9453	7633	1820
2.	Main workers	19209	11795	7414
3.	Marginal workers	1879	809	1070
4.	Non-workers	12136	5837	6299

Source: Census, 2001.

(v) ***Literacy and Education***: In this district the literacy rate in 2001 were as mentioned below:

- Total literacy rate — 73.10%
- Males literacy — 82.82%
- Females literacy — 60.70%

The level of education attained in the district were attained as given in Table 5.39:

Table 5.39: Different Levels of Education in the District, 2001

Sl. No.	Level of education attained	Total	Males	Females
1.	Without level	1333	605	728
2.	Below Primary	5282	2825	2457
3.	Primary	5439	3420	2019
4.	Middle	3288	2238	1050
5.	Higher/Sr. Secondary	5098	3660	1438
6.	Graduate and above	1164	975	189
	Total	**21609**	**13726**	**7883**

Source: Census, 2001.

(vi) ***SC and ST Communities***: The district had the following largest SC and ST communities in 2001 in Tables 5.40(a) and 5.40(b):

Table 5.40 (a): Three Largest SC Communities in the District, 2001

Sl. No.	*Name of SCs*	*Total*	*Males*	*Females*
1.	Chanal	1286	623	663
2.	Lohar	872	461	411
3.	Hesi	170	84	86

Source: Census, 2001.

Table 5.40 (b): Three Largest ST Communities in the District, 2001

Sl. No.	*Name of SCs*	*Total*	*Males*	*Females*
1.	Bhot, etc.	17215	8436	8779
2.	Swangla	6778	3358	3420
3.	Lahula	88	39	49

Source: Census, 2001.

(vii) ***Amenities and Infrastructural Facilities***: The district Lahaul and Spiti had 287 inhabited villages in the year 2001 and below-mentioned amenities/facilities were available:

Table 5.41: Amenities and Infrastructural Facilities available in No. of Villages

Sl. No.	*Amenities and Infrastructural Facilities available*	*No. of Villages*
1.	Primary Schools	189
2.	Middle Schools	57
3.	Secondary/Sr. Secondary Schools	42
4.	Medical facility	65
5.	Primary Health Centres	9
6.	Primary Health Sub-Centres	34
7.	Drinking water facility	287
8.	Safe drinking water	266
9.	Electricity (Power supply)	250
10.	Electricity (domestic)	—
11.	Electricity (agriculture)	167
12.	Bus service	67
13.	Paved approach road	156
14.	Posts and telegraph	

Source: Economic Survey of Himachal Pradesh, Economics and Statistics Department, Himachal Pradesh.

(viii) ***Places of Tourist Attraction***: The following are the places of tourist attraction in district:

- Rewalsar Lake with temple and *gurdwara*,
- Prashar lake,
- Kamrunag lake with temple and gurdwara, and
- Ancient temple of lord Shiva at Karsong.

(ix) ***Fairs and Festivals***: The people in this district celebrate the fairs and festivals as follows;

- Ahar fair on 25th Vaisakha (April) every year.
- Bulak Rupi fair on every Saturday in Asadha (June) and Agrahayana (November) every year.
- Birshu-ki-Atar on 3rd Vaisakha (April) every year.
- Chauran fair on 20th Vaisakha Bikrami (May) every year.
- Chauntra fair in the monthy of Jyaistha (June).
- Chindi fair on 18-21 Sravana (August) every year.
- Chirhnu on the Sankrant of Sravana.
- Gada Gusain fair on 14th-15th Sravana (July) every year.
- Guma fair on 6th, 7th and 9th Vaisakha every year.
- Jogindernagar fair on 24th Chaitra (March) every year.
- Kau fair on 2nd of Asadha (June) every year.
- Lahaul fair on 5th of Vaisakha every year.
- Machhayal fair on 1st Vaisakha every year.
- Mahun Nag fair on 2nd-3rd Jaiystha (May) every year.
- Navle on 9th Jyaistha (May) every year.
- Shitla Devi fair on 9th Jaiystha every year.
- Shivaratri fair in the month off Phalguna every year.
- Tramat fair on Asadha Sankrant (June) every year.

8. District Shimla

(i) ***Geography and History***: (a) Shimla district, the present day capital of Himachal Pradesh., lies between the longitude 77°0″ and 78°19″

east and latitude 30°45″ north. It is bounded by Mandi and Kullu in the north, Kinnaaur in the east, the State of Uttranchal in the south, Sirmaur in the west. The elevation of the district ranges from 300 to 6,000 metres. The topology of Shimla is rugged and tough. It derives its name from Shimla town which was once a small village. The present day Shimla came into existence from September 1972 on the reorganization of districts in the State.

(b) The history of Shimla goes back to nineteenth century, the period of Anglo-Gurkha War. In 1804, the Gurkhas, after suffering severe defeat by Sikhs, commenced to ravage the states and hills surrounding Shimla. By 1808, the invaders had conquered all fortified posts and extended their ruthless rule until people appealed to the British for help. The British forces under Sir David Orchterlony took over the hill states and majority of hill chiefs joined the British army. The battle of Malaon in May 1815 ended the rule of Gurkhas and these areas came under the British protection. The Maharaja of Patiala was rewarded with land in the neighbourhood of the areas now comprising Shimla.

(c) Present day Shimla comprises of 19 erstwhile hill states mainly Balson, Bushahr, Bhaji and Koti, Darkoti, Tharocha and Dhadi, Kumharsain, Khaneti and Delath, Dhami, Jubbal, Keothal, Rawinggarh, Ratesh and Sangri, Shimla district in its present form came into existence from September 1972 on the reorganization of districts of the states.

(ii) ***Population and Demography***: The total population of Shimla district in 2001 was as shown in the Table 5.41:

Table 5.41: Total Population Male-Female and Rural-Urban in the District, 2001

Sl. No.	*Total/rural/urban*	*Total*	*Males*	*Females*	*%age*
1.	Rural	555269	285305	269964	100.00
2.	Urban	167233	95691	71542	100.00
	Total	**722502**	**380996**	**341506**	**100.00**

Source: Census, 2001.

The total area of the State is 5131 sq. km. While the sex ratio (females per 1,000 males) in 2001 was 896, the density of population in the same year 141.

(iii) ***SC and ST population***: The population of SCs and STs in this district was as mentioned below:

Table 5.42 (a): SC Population in the District, 2001

Sl. No.	*Total/rural/urban*	*Persons*	*Males*	*Females*
1.	Rural	162494	85523	79971
2.	Urban	26293	14655	11618
	Total	**188787**	**97178**	**91609**

Source: Census, 2001.

Table 5.42 (b): ST Population in the District, 2001

Sl. No.	*Total/rural/urban*	*Persons*	*Males*	*Females*
1.	Rural	2057	1141	916
2.	Urban	2055	1171	884
	Total	**4112**	**2312**	**1800**

Source: Census, 2001.

(iv) ***Types and Number of Workers***: The types and number of workers in this district in the year 2001 was as shown in Table 5.43:

Table 5.43: Types and Number of Workers in the District, 2001

Sl. No.	*Types of workers*	*Persons*	*Males*	*Females*
1.	Total worker	370223	219133	151090
	(a) Cultivator	237490	110658	126832
	(b) Agri. labourers	9814	5898	3916
	(c) HHI Workers	4392	3071	1321
	(d) Other workers	118527	99506	19021
2.	Main workers	305709	196700	109008
3.	Marginal workers	64514	22433	42081
4.	Non-workers	352279	161863	190416

Source: Census, 2001.

(v) ***Literacy and Education*:** The literacy situation in this district prevailed as shown below:

Total literacy	— 79.72%
Male literacy	— 87.19%
Female literacy	— 70.07%

Different levels of education attained in the district in the year 2001 were as noted in the Table 5.44:

Table 5.44: Levels of Education attained in the District, 2001

Sl. No.	*Type of workers*	*Persons*	*Males*	*Females*
1.	Without level	11640	5781	5859
2.	Below Primary	97060	50412	46648
3.	Primary	114805	61974	52831
4.	Middle	78995	46040	32955
5.	Matric/Sr. Secondary	153284	97133	56151
6.	Graduate and above	48464	32346	16118
	Total	**504330**	**293745**	**210585**

Source: Census, 2001.

(vi) ***SC and ST Communities*:** The largest SC and ST communities in this district, with their population, were as identified in Table 5.45 (a) 5.45(b):

Table 5.45 (a): Largest SC Communities in the District, 2001

Sl. No.	*Name of Community*	*Persons*	*Males*	*Females*
1.	Kri, etc.	139006	70787	68219
2.	Chamar, etc.	10566	5787	4779
3.	Lohar	8774	4618	4156

Source: Census, 2001.

Table 5.45 (b): Three Largest ST Communities in the District, 2001

Sl. No.	*Name of SC Community*	*Total*	*Males*	*Females*
1.	Kanaura, etc.	3024	1671	1353
2.	Bhot, etc.	520	332	188
3.	Generic tribes, etc.	282	153	129

Source: Census, 2001.

(vii) ***Amenities and Infrastructural Facilities***: The district has, 2,520 villages and the amenities/facilities available in these villages are given below:

Table 5.45 (c): Amenities and Infrastructural Facilities in No. of Villages

Sl. No.	*Amenities and Infrastructural Facilities available*	*No. of villages*
1.	Primary Schools	1363
2.	Middle Schools	453
3.	Secondary/Sr. Secondary schools	288
4.	Medical facility	396
5.	Primary Health Centers	53
6.	Primary Health Sub-Centers	256
7.	Drinking water facility	2519
8.	Safe drinking water	2493
9.	Electricity (power supply)	2508
10.	Electricity (domestic)	1921
11.	Electricity (agriculture)	69
12.	Bus service	938
13.	Paved approach road	477
14.	Posts and telegraph	1218

Source: Economic Survey of Himachal Pradesh, Economics and Statistics Department, Himachal Pradesh.

(viii) ***Places of Tourist Attraction***: In this district, the tourist attraction places are as mentioned below:

- Winter sports at Kufri.
- Golf course at Naldehra.
- Ancient Tibetan temple.
- Laxmi Narain temple at Rampur.
- Anging at Rohru.
- Durga Temple at Hatkoti.
- Summer festival at Shimla.

(ix) ***Fairs and Festivals***: In this district, the following fairs and festivals are celebrated by the people:

- Athakoda festivals on Magha (January) each year.

- Barara fair on first on Jyaistha (May).
- Bhoj fair in the month of Agrahayana (November).
- Bhunda Rohru on 4th of Asvina.
- Chakrana fair on 4th of Asvina at Chakrana.
- Charayoli fair on first night of Bhadra (August).
- Deoth Dhar fair on 26th Sravana (August).
- Dudh Bahli fair on 12-13th Asadha (June).
- Fag fair in the month of Chaitra (March).
- Jagra on Panchmi day of Bhadra (August).
- Laul fair on 14 Kritika (April).
- Lavi fair on 14 Kartika (November).
- Mahasu Jatar on 3rd Tuesday of Vaisakha (May).
- Patti Jubbar fair 6-7 of Asadha (June).
- Rampari-ki-Jatar on first day of Asadha (June).
- Seoni Dussehra on next day of Navratra.
- Shwani fair on the day of Snana Purnima.
- Shilgiri-ka-Bishu on 4th and 5h of Jyaistha (May).
- Suskar festival in Phalguna (February).
- Tohar 15th of Pausa (December).

9. District Sirmaur

(i) ***Geography and History***: (a) This district is the south-eastern district in the State which is largely mountainous and rural. It includes the towns of NahanLeu-nana, Sarahan, Paonta Sahib and Shivalik Forest Park at Suketi. It has a common border with Haryana and Uttarakhand. The district is known for its fertile land and farmers here grow grains as first option.

(b) According to some experts, the subjects of Sirmaur state approached the Raja of Jaisalmer to give one of his sons as the rules of their state which was conceded and one of his sons was crowned as ruler of Sirmaur. Ever since, the name of Prakash in its princely family is continued till today. After rise and fall of different rulers, good and bad for a long time, the British Commander moved towards this state in 1826 and imposed the local ruler choice. The most important aspect of one of last rulers of Sirmaur, Maharaja Rajendra Parkash, was freedom fighter in the state. He played a dominant role in mobilizing the public opinion against the British rule which led to the British government action related to state's succession to the Union of India and final merger in Himachal Pradesh.

(ii) ***Population and Demography***: The Total population (male-female and rural-urban) of this district in 2001 is given in the following Table 5.46:

Table 5.46: Total Population of the District, 2001

Sl. No.	*Total/rural/urban*	*Total*	*Males*	*Females*	*%age*
1.	Rural	409362	214150	195212	100.00
2.	Urban	91195	56141	35054	100.00
	Total	**500557**	**270291**	**230266**	**100.00**

Source: Census, 2001.

The total area of the district is 1936 sq. km. Which constitutes 3.49 per cent of the total area of the of the State and ranks ninth amongst the districts. While the sex ratio (number of females per 1,000 males) in 2001 was 852, the density of population in the same year was 258. The district was carved out of Solan and Arkti tehsils of the Mahasu districts and tehsils of Kandaghat and Nalagarh of the then Shimla district.

(iii) ***SC and ST Population***: The total population of SCs and STs in this district in 2001 was as noted in the Table 5.47:

Table 5.47 (a): Total Population SCs in the District, 2001

Sl. No.	*Total/rural/urban*	*Total*	*Males*	*Females*
1.	Rural	127395	65609	61786
2.	Urban	13247	7407	5840
	Total	**140642**	**73016**	**67626**

Source: Census, 2001.

Table 5.47 (b): Total Population STs in the District, 2001

Sl. No.	*Total/rural/urban*	*Total*	*Males*	*Females*
1.	Rural	3179	1721	1458
2.	Urban	363	231	132
	Total	**3542**	**1952**	**1590**

Source: Census, 2001.

(iv) ***Types and Number of Workers***: The types and number of workers in Solan district in the year 2001 was as given in the Table 5.48:

Table 5.48: Types and Number of Workers in the District, 2001

Sl. No.	*Types of workers*	*Persons*	*Males*	*Females*
1.	Total workers	263445	165277	98168
	(a) Cultivators	143630	63062	80568
	(b) Agri. Labourers	6309	3735	2574
	(c) HHI Workers	3291	2138	1153
	(d) Other workers	1100215	96342	13873
2.	Main workers	172274	137209	35065
3.	Marginal workers	91171	28068	63103
4.	Non-workers	237112	105014	132098

Source: Census, 2001.

(v) ***Literacy and Education***: The Solan district had the literacy situation in 2001, the details of which are given in the Table 5.49:

Total literacy	— 76.57%
Male literacy	— 84.75%
Female literacy	— 66.89%

The educational levels prevailing in the district Solan in the year 2001 were as follows:

Table 5.49: Levels of Education attained in the District, 2001

Sl. No.	*Type of workers*	*Persons*	*Males*	*Females*
1.	Without level	4363	2421	1942
2.	Below Primary	62747	34577	28170
3.	Primary	88573	47859	40714
4.	Middle	58832	35886	22946
5.	Matric/Sr. Secondary	94957	64099	30858
6.	Graduate and above	22900	14580	8320
	Total	**332410**	**199444**	**132966**

Source: Census, 2001.

(vi) ***SC and ST Communities***: The largest SC and ST communities inhabiting in the district were identified as given in Tables 5.50(a) 5.50(b):

Table 5.50(a): The Largest SC Communities in the District, 2001

Sl. No.	Name of Community	Persons	Males	Females
1.	Chamar, etc.	52147	27242	24905
2.	Kori, etc.	35801	18348	17453
3.	Julaha, etc.	19496	9920	9576

Source: Census, 2001.

Table 5.50 (b): Three Largest ST Communities in the District, 2001

Sl. No.	Name of Community	Total	Males	Females
1.	Gujjar	2891	1523	1368
2.	Kanaura, etc.	469	295	174
3.	Genric tribes, etc.	67	48	19

Source: Census, 2001.

(vii) ***Places of Tourist Attraction***: The below mentioned places are the places of tourist attraction in Solan district:

- Cricket stadium at Chail.
- Indira Holiday home at Kandaghat.
- Central Research Institute at Kausali.

(viii) ***Fairs and Festivals:*** The people in Solan district celebrate the following fairs and festivals:

- Harat fair in the month of Kartika (October).
- Khardar fair in the month of Asadha (June) every year.
- Koti fair on 7th of bright half in the month of Jyaistha (May).
- Mal Purnima in the month of Asvina (October).
- Sair fair in Arki during Asvina (October).
- Shalogra fair in Asvina (October).
- Solan fair 2nd Sunday of Asadha (June) every year.

11. District Una

(i) ***Geography and History***: (a) The district share its borders with Hoshiarpur district of Punjab. Its terrain is plain with small hills. It has been identified as a main industrial hub. In the recent past, it has turned as a transit town for travels going to Dharamsala or other locations in the Himalayas.

(ii) It is believed that the present Una district was formally a part of erstwhile Kangra state. It was mostly ruled by the Katoch family of Kangra. During the Mughal period, it remained loyal to the Mughals, especially, Akbar and helped them always. In the year 1877, the British government in India restored to Raja Ran Singh the *jagir* in Jaswan, including the family garden at Amb. The area was ruled by the successive family kings.

The present district of Una until November 1966 was one of the tehsils of Hoshiarpur district. Consequent upon reorganization of Punjab all hill areas including Una was transferred to Himachal Pradesh. Till September 1972, it remained as tehsil of the then Kangra district. In the same year, the Himachal Pradesh government reorganized the Kangra district into three districts, Una, Hamirpur and Kangra. At present, the Una district consists of two sub-divisions, three tehsils, two sub-tehsils and five development blocks.

(iii) ***Population and Demography***: The total population of this district in 2001 was as given in the following Table 5.51:

Table 5.51: Total Population in the District, 2001

Sl. No.	*Total/rural/urban*	*Persons*	*Males*	*Females*	*%age*
1.	Rural	408,849	203,724	205,125	100.00
2.	Urban	399,424	20,800	18,624	100.00
	Total	**448,273**	**224,524**	**223,749**	**100.00**

Source: Census, 2001.

The total area of this district is 1,540 sq. km. While sex ratio in population (number of females per 1,000 males) was 997, the density of population in the district was 291.

(iv) ***SC and ST Population***: The total population of the SCs and STs in the district in the year 2001 was as given in the Tables 5.52 (a) and 5.52(b):

Table 5.52 (a): SC Population in the District, 2001

Sl. No.	Total/rural/urban	Persons	Males	Females
1.	Rural	93,128	47,532	45,535
2.	Urban	7,460	3,925	3,535
	Total	**100,588**	**51,457**	**49,131**

Source: Census, 2001.

Table 5.52(b): ST Population in the district, 2001

Sl. No.	Total/rural/urban	Persons	Males	Females
1.	Rural	22	13	9
2.	Urban	29	29	2
	Total	**51**	**40**	**11**

Source: Census, 2001.

(v) ***Types and Number of Workers*:** The major types of workers and their numbers in the district in 2001 were as recorded in the Table 2.53:

Table 2.53: Types and Number of Workers in the District, 2001

Sl. No.	Major types of workers	Persons	Males	Females
1.	Total workers	201,658	118,768	82,890
	(a) Cultivators	115,171	49,048	66,123
	(b) Agri. Labourers	11,330	7,032	7298
	(c) HHI workers	3,986	2,474	1,512
	(d) Other workers	71,171	60,214	10,957
2.	Main workers	119,050	92,212	26,838
3.	Marginal workers	82,608	26,556	56,052
	Non-workers	246,615	105,756	140,859

Source: Census, 2001.

(vi) ***Literacy and Education:*** The literacy situation in the district prevailed in 2001 whose details are given below:

- Total literacy — 80.37%
- Males literacy — 87.73%
- Females literacy — 73.18%

The levels of education attained in this district in 2001 were as shown in the Table 5.54:

Table 5.54: Different Levels of Education in the District, 2001

Sl. No.	*Level of education*	*Persons*	*Males*	*Females*
1.	Without level	3,377	1,635	1,742
2.	Below Primary	55,738	30,232	25,506
3.	Primary	88,129	40,125	48,003
4.	Middle	57,583	31,704	25,879
5.	Matric/Higher Secondary	93,782	56,542	37,240
6.	Graduation and above	13,646	8,198	5,448
	Total	**312,278**	**168,450**	**143,828**

Source: Census, 2001.

(vii) ***SC and ST Communities***: In this district, three largest SC and ST communities were identified as follows:

Table 5.55 (a): Three Largest SC Communities in the District, 2001

Sl. No.	*SC community*	*Persons*	*Males*	*Females*
1.	Chamar, etc.	60,180	30,915	29,265
2.	Julaha, etc.	13,624	6,919	6,705
3.	Lohar	10,723	5,356	5,367

Source: Census, 2001.

Table 5.55(b): Three Largest ST Communities in the District, 2001

Sl. No.	*ST community*	*Persons*	*Males*	*Females*
1.	Kanaura, etc.	25	24	1
2.	Generic Tribes, etc.	22	13	9
3.	Lahaul	3	3	0

Source: Census, 2001.

(viii) ***Amenities and Facilities***: The district has 758 total inhabited villages and the amenities facilities available there in 2001 were as follows:

1. Primary schools 415
2. Middle schools 193

3.	Secondary/Sr. Secondary schools	145
4.	Medical facilities	284
5.	Primary Health Centres	12
6.	Primary Health Sub-Centres	131
7.	Drinking water facility	756
8.	Safe drinking water	756
9.	Electricity (power supply)	756
10.	Electricity (domestic)	389
11.	Electricity (agriculture)	26
12.	Bus service	489
13.	Paved approach road	450
14.	Posts and telegraph	555

(ix) ***Places of Tourist Attraction:*** The following places were considered as the places of tourist attraction in this district:

- Una Fort.
- Baba Kadhari fair.
- Gurudwaras.
- Samadhi of Baba Rudra Nand.

(x) ***Fairs and Festivals*:** The people of this district celebrate the following fairs and festivals:

- Chintpurni fair (Mata da mela) thrice a year in Chaitra (March), Shrawana (July) and Asvina (September).

SECTION III
SECTOR-WISE RURAL SOCIO-ECONOMIC PROFILE OF HIMACHAL PRADESH

1. Economic Sectors

(i) ***Agriculture and Horticulture:*** (a) Agriculture is the main occupation of the people of Himachal Pradesh which is the only State in the country whose 89.96 per cent of population in 2011 lives in rural areas. So, dependence on agriculture is prominent as 70 per cent of the total workers are engaged in this sector. About 15 per cent of total GSDP comes from this sector. The average holding size comes to 1.04 hectares and 87.03 per cent of the total holdings in 2005-06 was with small and marginal farmers. The agro-climatic conditions in the State are congenial for the production of cash crops like seed potato, off-season vegetables and ginger. There are four distinct seasons with respect to rainfall which is received during monsoon season.

(b) In 2012-13, 15 per cent of State Domestic product was generated by agriculture and allied sectors. In the same year, the foodgrains production was achieved at a record level 15.68 Lakh mts, while as production of potato and vegetables was 1.83 lakh metric tonnes and 13.80 lakh metric tonnes.

(c) The emphasis in Himachal Pradesh is on increasing productivity levels besides diversification towards high value crops. Due to increasing shift to commercial crops, the area under foodgrains is gradually declining which reduced to 798.31 through hectares in 2012-13.

(d) So, the emphasis has been laid on distribution of seeds of high yielding varieties to the farmers. In this connection, adoption of plant protection measures is of paramount.

(e) In order to maintain the fertility of the soil during each season, soil samples are collected from the farmers and analysed in the soil testing laboratories. During 2012-13, 1.23 lakh numer of soil samples were collected and 1.22 lakh number of soil health cards were issued.

(f) The organic farming is becoming popular being suitable, environmental friendly and health concern to all concerned. For organic farming, incentive at Rs.10,000 per hectare (50%) and for certification Rs. 10,000 per hectare is being provided for three years. Fertilizer is a single input which helps in increasing the production to a great extent. The level of consumption of fertilizers has increased in the State to 48,129 tonnes in 2012-13.

(g) In view of the propensity of farmers to borrow money, credit flow for purchase of inputs is being made available by the banks. In 2013, 5,84,568 Kisan credit cards were issued by the banks. Moreover from 2013-14 the existing NAIS has been withdrawn by the government of India and in place a new C.S.S. of NICP will be implemented. Himachal Pradesh State seed certification agency registered growers in different areas for heavy seed production.

(h) The regulated markets established in the State provide useful services to farmers. A modernized market complex at Solan is functional at present.

(i) Total area under tea is 2,300 hectares with a production level of 8-10 lakh kgs.

(j) Under agriculture mechanization, new farm implements or machines and testing of these machines are popularized among the farmers.

(k) Seed village programme has been initiated in the State in order to meet local seed requirements besides facilitating supply of seeds at lower cost and in shorter time.

(l) The Department of Agriculture is implementing two soil and water conservation schemes which are: (i) Soil Conservation works, and (ii) Water Conservation and Development.

(m) The Department has a project on production of cash crops by Adoption of Precision in Farming Practices through Poly House Cultivation. The NABARD has sanctioned a project of 154.92 crore for 4 years from 2008-09. Up to March 2014, 13,500 poly houses have been constructed.

(n) Under RKVY, an expenditure of 77.40 crore has been anticipated for 2013-14 by Agriculture and allied departments. The total allocation of 55 crore has been made under general Plan.

(ii) ***Horticulture:*** (a) the particular suitability of Himachal Pradesh has resulted in shifting of land-use pattern from agriculture to fruit crops in the recent past. The area under fruits which was 792 hectares in 1950-51 with total production of 1,200 tonnes increased to 2,18,303 hectares during 2012-13.

(b) Area under apple has increased from 400 hectares in 1950-51 to 3,025 hectares in 1950-61 and to 1,06,440 hectares in 2012-13.

(c) During 2012-13, the procurement price of apple, mango and citrus fruits increased by 50 paisa per kg under Market intervention scheme over the previous year and 34,000 M.T.C. grade apple fruit valued to 22.00 crore has been procured under this scheme.

(d) Litchi is also gaining ground in certain regions of the State. Mango and litchi are fetching better market prices. New fruits like kiwi, olive, pomegranate, pecan and strawberry are fast promoted areas.

(e) To bring diversification in horticulture a total area of 342 hectares has been brought under flower cultivation up to December 2013.

(f) During 2013-14, farmer have been covered under Weather Based Crops Insurance Scheme for apple who have insured their 38,69,715 trees for which the government has borne 25 per cent premium share of 6.16 crore.

(g) About 4,300 farmers have been benefited till December 2013 under various schemes such as HTM, RKVY and NMMI.

(h) The H.P.M.C. has sold about 974.45 lakh processed products in the domestic market during 2013-14. It has also procured about 831.35 MT apple juice and about 18,889.55 MT of apples in the same period. Till November 2013, fruits and vegetables worth 323.50 lakh has been supplied to different institutions by HPMC.

(iii) ***Animal Husbandry***: (a) Livestock is an important integral part of the economy of Himachal Pradesh. The major contribution of livestock products in 2012-13 was 11.39 lakh tonnes of milk, 1,650 tonnes of wool, 107,000 million eggs, and 4,000 tonnes meat. The milk production and its per capita availability is shown in Table 5.56 below:

Table 5.56: Milk Production and Per Capita Availability

Sl. No.	*Year*	*Milk production (lakh tonnes)*	*Per capita availability (gram./day*
1.	2012-13	11.39	455
2.	2013-14 (estimated)	11.63	465

Source: Economic Survey of Himachal Pradesh, Economics and Statistics Department, Himachal Pradesh.

(b) The State has the following infrastructure for the treatment of livestock in December 2013.

Animal Health Disease Control	— 1
State level Veterinary Hospital	— 1
Policlinics	— 7
Sub-divisional veter. Hospital	— 49
Veterinary Hospitals	—282
Central Veter. Dispensaries	— 30
Veterinary Dispensaries	—1762

(c) For improving the quality of sheep and wool, the flock strength of farms are 2,047 in the year 2012-13 and 175 Rems were distributed to the breeders.

(d) Dairy production is an integral part of Animal Husbandry and earning of small and marginal farmers. During 2012-13, 7.45 lakh semen straws for cows and 2.63 lakh semen straws for buffaloes. In the same year, 0.80 lakh litre of LN2 gas was produced. Artificial insemination facility is being provided through 2,092 institutions and 7.00 lakh cows and 2.00 buffaloes are likely to inseminated in 2013-14.

(e) During 2012-13, the thirteenth Livestock Census was conducted by the Central government.

(f) The following schemes and measures have been launched in Himachal Pradesh for the development of livestock sector:

- Doodh Ganga Yojana for providing bank loan of 5 lakh for purchase of 10 cows, 18 lakh for those who could chain milk transportation system, 24 lakhs for milk products making units, and 25 per cent subsidy to SC/SR farmers;
- Livestock Insurance scheme to save owners from loss in the event of death of high yielding cattle and buffalo;
- National project on cattle and buffalo development;
- Backyard poultry farming to develop the poultry sector;
- Assistance to State for control of animal diseases;
- Bhed Palak Samriddhi Yojana;
- Shepherd insurance scheme;
- Benefits to sheep breeders;
- Chaff Cutter on 75 per cent subsidy;
- Establishment of mild-based industries; and other development efforts.

(iv) ***Fisheries***: (a) The commercially important fist species in Gobind Sagar and Pong Dam reservoirs have become a tool for upliftment of local population. About 4,900 fishermen depend directly on reservoir fisheries for their livelihood. During 2013-14, cumulative fish production was of level of 5,900 MT valued at 4094 lakh. The production of two major reservoirs was 1385.00 MT valued at 917.00 lakh to December 2013.

(v) ***Tourism***: (a) This industry in Himachal Pradesh has been given very high priority and government has developed appropriate infrastructure for its total development. For the year 2013-14, an allotment of 2838.71 lakh has been made for this purpose. At present, about 2,769 hotels. Having bed capacity of about 61,497 are registered with the department of Tourism. In addition, about 500 home stay units were registered in the State having about 1,350 rooms.

(b) Moreover, the government of India has decided to initiate the following projects/measures for the development of tourism in Himachal Pradesh.

- Integrated development of Buddhist Circuit in the State.
- Integrated development of Una-Nandaun as a tourist destination in Himachal Pradesh.
- Integrated development of Shimal suburbs as a tourist circuit.
- Integrated development of Tourist Transit Zone in the State.

(c) The department of Tourism has prepared the plan for the planned and sustainable development of tourism sector, tourism policy and sustainable for Dharamshala. This department and HPTCC along with private hoteliers participated in more than 30 fairs and festivals during 2013.

2. Social Sectors

(i) ***Education***: (a) The literacy rate in the State, according to 2011 Census reports, was 82.80 per cent (males 89.53% and females 75.93%).

(b) *Elementary Education*: At present, there are 10,886 notified primary schools in Himachal Pradesh and 2,349 are not notified. Attempts are being made to provide schools at this level for disabled. To encourage enrolment, reduce dropout rate, and enhance retention rate, the following measures have been initiated:

- Poverty stipend scholarships,
- Girls attendance scholarships,
- Scholarships for army personnel,
- Scholarships for students belonging to IRDP families,

- Pre-Matric scholarships for SC students, and,
- Pattern scholarship.

The SSA was also launched in the State to ensure universal access, enrolment, removal of gender basis, retention and completion of elementary schooling by all 6-14 age groups in the State.

(c) *Out of School Children:* The NER at the elementary stage is more than 99 per cent which shows there are negligible number of children who are out of school. For identified 2,414 out of school children, age and class appropriate education is ensured through NRBCCs. A total of 18,211 CWSN were identified suffering from disability and have been integrated in formal schools. Nearly 1,332 in-service teachers have been trained in the field of disability till date. Various physiotherapy occupational therapy and speech therapy were provided on priority basis.

- IEP was prepared for every child and goals were fixed for every three months.
- Some special children having good level of understanding are being trained for small vocations such as candle making.
- Parents counselling session with the help of trained RTs and counselors under home based programme have been started in Himachal Pradesh.
- Trained teachers are providing support in the community involvement for children.
- Orientation of teachers and other supportive staff is an important aspect of SSA.
- 3-day care centres in primary schools have been established in Shimla, Mandi and Kangra.
- Medical assessment camps for CWSN are organized every year and aids and appliances were provided to the concerned children.
- No to and fro local bus fare to the CWAN along with one attendant.
- Braille books and enlarged print books are provided to the concerned.
- Barrier free access made available in 2,875 schools.
- For monitoring of IE activities, SSA has designed the monitoring proforma.

- It was observed that nearly 99 per cent of children at elementary level were declared successful.
- NPEGEL is being implemented at elementary level in 8 district where the rural female literacy rates are below the national average.
- In KGBVs girls are being imparted skill education along with normal studies.
- Now, the emphasis is on diagnostic teaching instead of promoting rote method and single line paper pencil test.
- HPSMA constantly monitoring the SSA programme implementation, State teams from DIETS have been constituted and 700 schools and all KGBVs have been monitoring 67 educational Blocks.
- All the BRCs are being regularly trained in a phased manner with different activities.

(d) *Quality of Education*: The following measures under SSA have been started to enhance quality of education in Himachal Pradesh:

- Curriculum and text book renewal.
- Teacher training programmes.
- Organizing TLM exhibitions/Bal Melas.
- Establishing functional libraries.
- Quality improvement programme like Aadhar.
- Computer aided learning.

(e) *Technical Education*: Department of Technical Education in Himachal Pradesh was established in 1983. Today, it has the following functional technical institute:

- IIT — 1
- NIT, Hamirpur — 1
- NIFT, Kangra — 1
- J.N. Govt. Engineering College — 1
- ABV Institute of Engg. Colleges — 1
- Privately managed Engg. Colleges — 17
- Govt. polytechnics — 15
- Private polytechnics — 18
- ITIs — 82

- The present intake in the existing technical institutions is as under:

Degree level	—	7,980
B. Pharmacy	—	1,000
Diploma level	—	10,858
ITIs/ITCs	—	33,506
Total		53,344

(f) Modular Employable Skills under the Skill Development Initiative Scheme, vocational training is being provided to those workers seeking certification of their skills, school drop outs, unemployed youth and ITI graduates to improve their employability. The total number of 23,688 candidates has been trained under the scheme and 327.87 lakh has been spent so far.

(ii) Health

(a) *Health and Family Welfare*: The Health and Family Welfare Department in Himachal Pradesh is providing services which include curative, preventive, promotive and rehabilitative services through the following health network:

Civil hospitals	—	55
Community health centres	—	47
Primary health centres	—	476
ESI dispensaries	—	11
Sub-centres	—	2065

Moreover, the government is strengthening the existing infrastructure by providing modern equipments, specialized services, increasing the medical and paramedical staff in the medical institutions. During the year 2013-14, the following health and family related activities were carried out:

- 4,27,667 blood slides were examined, out of which 136 were found positive.
- Under national leprosy eradication programme, the prevalence rate has been reduced to 00.21 per 10,000. During

the previous year, 103 new cases of leprosy are under treatment.

- Under the national T.B. Control Programme, 1 T.B. sanctorum, 12 district T.B. centres, 50 TB units and 180 microscopic centres having a provision of 310 beds were functioning in the State. 10,935 cases of this disease and sputum tests of 60,685 were carried out.
- Under programme for control of blindness, 17,781 cataract operations were performed against the target of 23,100 operations.
- Under the national family welfare programme, 5,077 sterilizations, 13,425 IUD insertions, 21,518 OP Users and 85.574 CC Users were done.
- Under the universal immunization programme, the following were carried out during 2012-13:

Table 5.57: Name of Immunization in Himachal Pradesh 2012-13

Sl. No.	*Name of Immunization*	*Target*	*Achievement*
1.	D.P.T.	114000	71614
2.	Polio	114000	71678
3.	BCG	114000	79087
4.	Hepatitis-B	114000	71559
5.	Vit. A Doze	114000	69222
6.	DPT (5-6 years)	116000	76852
7.	T.T. (10 years)	116000	93152
8.	D.P.T. Booster	117000	68900
9.	Polio Booster	114000	68930
10.	T.T. (16 years)	129000	11163
11.	T.T. (PW)	131000	72773
12.	I.P.A.	131000	62434

Source: Economic Survey of Himachal Pradesh, Economics and Statistics Department, Himachal Pradesh.

- Under National Aids Control Programme, 1,06,899 persons screened out of which 397 HIV positive cases were detected. A total of 49 ICTC centres are providing counselling and testing services in the State. 17 clinics are providing STI/RTI services functioning in the State.

- Under anti-retroviral treatment programme, 3 ART centres at IGMC are functioning in Shimla.
- Under targeted interventions, 13,962 persons have been provided STI services and 27,522 were referred to ICTC.
- Under NRHM, 24 hour emergency were provided to 573b Rogi Kalyan Samitis in hospitals. A sum of Rs. 1,032 crore has been distributed.

(b) *Medical Education*: At present, Himachal Pradesh has two medical colleges in Shimla and Tanda. Besides four dental colleges are in private sector at Sundernagar, Solan, Nalagarh and Paonta Sahib. The seats in nursing institutions have been increased from 580 to 660. 11 ITIs have been upgraded as centre of excellence and 252.00 lakh have been received as central assistance for modern machinery, equipments, honorarium/remuneration and training of teachers.

(iii) Social Welfare Programmes

(a) *Social Security Pension Schemes*: The following schemes/ programmes/measures were adopted in Himachal Pradesh:

Table 5.58: Social Security Pension Schemes Functions

Sl. No.	*Name of the Scheme/ Programme*	*Functions performed*
1.	Old age pension	70% of disabled provided assistance
2.	Disability Relief Allowance	Rs. 500 p.m. provided to above 45 years widows and deserted women
3.	Widow/Deserted/Ekal Nari pension	Provided Rs. 500 per month to 1,482 lepers.
4.	Rehabilitation allowance to Lepers	Provided to above 60 years old age.
5.	I.G. National old age pension	Provided pension to widows of 40-79 age group
6.	I.G. National Widow Pension	Functions performed

1. Award for inter-caste marriage	Rs. 50,000 per couple as incentive money
2. Housing subsidy	Rs. 75,000 per family for house construction
3. Training in Computer application	Rs. 1200 p.m. provided to all SSC/ST/BPL
4. Follow up programme	Rs. 1500 per beneficiary of SC/ST/BC
5. Compensation to victims of ST/SC family	Relief provided to the concerned families

Source: Economic Survey of Himachal Pradesh, Economics and Statistics Department, Himachal Pradesh.

(b) *Welfare of Disabled*: The following schemes/measures were adopted for helping the disabled persons in the State:

Table 5.59: Welfare of Disabled Schemes Functions

Sl. No.	*Scheme/measure*	*Functions performed*
1.	Disabled scholarship	Assistance provided to disabled persons
2.	Marriage grant for disabled	Grant of Rs. 8,000-15,000 to one who marries the disabled
3.	Awareness generation	Helping NGOs for working with disabled
4.	Self-employment	provided assistance for self initiative of disabled
5.	Skill enrichment	Rs. 1,000 p.m. for vocational rehabilitation Training
6.	Scheme of awards	Incentives to best disabled individuals
7.	Institutions of children with special needs	—
8.	Disability rehabilitation centres	Provide assistance to disabled
9.	SC Sub-plan	Various schemes implemented

Source: Economic Survey of Himachal Pradesh, Economics and Statistics Department, Himachal Pradesh.

(c) *Child Welfare*: The following schemes/programmes were started in the State:

- Mukhyamantri Bal Sudhar Yojana to look orphan/destitute children;
- Bal/Balika Suraksha Yojana for financial assistance to children;

- Integrated child protection scheme to contribute for welfare of overall welfare;
- Integrated Child Development services which included Beti Hai Anmol Yojana—Post-birth grant, scholarship for education;
- Kishori Shakti Yojana for improvement of nutrition, health and development status of adolescent girls;
- RG Scheme for empowerment of adolescent girls; and
- Supplementary Nutrition Programme.

(d) Women Welfare

- State Home Mashobra to provide shelter, clothing education, etc. to young girls, widows, deserted and destitute women;
- Mukhya Mantri Kanyadaan Yojana to provide marriage grant of Rs. 25,000 to destitute girls;
- Self-employment scheme for women;
- Widow remarriage scheme to help in rehabilitation after remarriage of widows;
- Mother Teressa Asahai Matri Sambal Yojana to provide assistance to 3000 per child per annum to BPL destitute women;
- I.G. Matritva Sahyog Yojana to improve the health status of pregnant and lactating women and infants; and
- Financial assistance for Victims of Rape Scheme.

(iv) Rural Development

The main objective of this programme are the implementation of poverty alleviation, employment generation and area development schemes in rural areas in the State. The following State and centrally sponsored developmental schemes are functional in Himachal Pradesh.

(a) National Rural Livelihood Mission (NRLM) for generation of self-employment activities;

(b) Watershed Development Programme to develop wastelands/ degraded lands, drought prone and desert areas;

(c) Indira Awas Yojana to benefit BPL families for the construction of new houses;

(d) Matri Shakti Bima Yojana which covers all BPL women of 10-75 years;

(e) Rajiv Awas Yojana to provide financial assistance of 75,000 to poor families;

(f) Total Sanitation Campaign to bring about an improvement in quality of life in rural areas and accelerate sanitation coverage. The following physical facilities were provided under this scheme:

Table 5.60: Sanitation Campaign Scheme Facilities

Year	*IHHL*	*School toilet*	*Anganwari toilet*	*Sanitation Camp.*
2012-13	5183	1215	1066	163
2013-14	7218	206	16	52

Source: Economic Survey of Himachal Pradesh, Economics and Statistics Department, Himachal Pradesh.

(g) Mahila Mandal Protsahan Yojana to encourage Mahila Mandals in Sanitation Campaign;

(h) Nirmal Gram Puruskar to give a fillip to the total sanitation campaign;

(i) M.V. Sampooran Swachhta Puruskar (MVSSP) to boost the sanitation campaign; and

(j) School Sanitation Reward Scheme under which cleanest government primary and middle schools were rewarded.

SECTION IV
RURAL SOCIO-ECONOMIC PROFILE OF HIMACHAL PRADESH: 10 VILLAGE CASE STUDIES

After presenting the Rural Socio-economic profile of Himachal Pradesh in district-wise and sector-wise framework, this profile is explained in terms of village case studies carried out by IAS officers during their training period. The details of these 10 village case studies are given below:

Table 5.61: Details of Village Case Researcher's Name

Sl. No	Year	Name of village	Tehsil/Block	District	Name of Researcher
1.	2004-2006	Jandour	Pragpur	Kangra	C. Paulrasu
2.	2004-2006	Nagchala	Dalh	Mandi	Priyanka Basu Ingty
3.	2004-2006	Ambwala-Sainwala	Nahhan	Sirmaur	Mamta
4.	2005-2007	Bharara	Tissa	Chaamba	Riteshb Chauhan
5.	2005-2007	Sadwan	Pragpur	Kangra	Meera Mohanty
6.	2006-2008	Dalah	Padhar	Mandi	Priyatu Mandal
7.	2007-2009	Charri	Rait	Kangra	Shainanol A.
8.	2008-2010	Katipari	Drang	Mandi	Ashish Singhmar
9.	2008-2010	Kirri	Mehla	Chamba	Kadam S. Vasant
10.	2009-2011	Basehar	Padhar	Mandi	Rohan Chand Thakur

Source: Economic Survey of Himachal Pradesh, Economics and Statistics Department, Himachal Pradesh.

Village: Jandour, Block: Kangra, District: Kangra

(a) ***Village:*** This village is at a distance of 1055 km., from Dharamshala and is situated near Pong Dam lake. It is well connected by a metal road to the headquarters and has most of

(b) ***Population and Demography:*** The total population in the village was as follows:

Table 5.62: Population and Demography in Decadal Growth

		1919	*2001*	*Decadal growth*
01	Population	919	1441	56.80
02	Males	456	719	57.60
03	Females	463	722	57.80

Source: Village Study Reports CRS, LBSNAA, Mussoorie.

The caste-wise population in the village was as follows:

Table 5.63: Caste-wise Population in the Village

1.	SC	155	10.70
2.	ST	00	00.00
3.	OBC	45	3.10
4.	Others	1241	86.20

Source: Village Study Reports CRS, LBSNAA, Mussoorie.

(c) ***Basic Amenities/Faciltities Available***: The following amenities/facilities were available in the village at the time of research:

Electrification	—Yes	Approach road	—Yes
Primary school	—		
Primary health sub-centre	—Yes	High school	—Yes
PDS shop	—Yes	Drinking water source	—Yes
Public telephone	—Yes	ICDS Centre	—Yes
Panchayat bhawan	—Yes	Street lights	—Yes

(d) ***Education***: The literacy rate in the village in 2001 was 65 per cent for males and 55 per cent for females. There were 1 AWC, 2 Primary schools, 2 Primary schools, 2 High schools and a private college. The enrolment and attendance in schools was as follows:

Table 5.64: Literacy Rate in the Village in 2001

Classes	*Students Male*	*Present Female*	*Total Male*	*Strength Female*
I	3	6	3	6
II	4	6	4	6
III	6	7	6	7
IV	10	11	10	11
V	10	12	10	12
VI	12	21	12	21
VII	13	13	13	13
VIII	14	18	14	18

Source: Village Study Reports CRS, LBSNAA, Mussoorie.

The primary school have facilities such as drinking water, toilet, play ground, black board, separate teaching rooms and school buildings.

(e) ***Health***: There are three government health centres and private services available in the village. The IMR was as follows:

- No. of births last year — 21 males and 19 females
- No. of deaths in last year — 13 males and 12 females
- No. of infant deaths in last year — 1 male and 00 females

The PHC and sub-PHC in the village provide immunization, ante-natal care, pediatrics care and contraceptives and IUD insertion, etc. ANM visits very often and government and private practitioners are present, number of institutional deliveries are more than the domestic deliveries. Most prominent diseases in the village include anemia and low blood pressure. The major cause of ill health is malnutrition, poverty and lack of private health care.

(f) ***Land Detail***: The land details (in acres) in the village are mentioned below:

Total land in acres	—658.5	Land for cultivation	—119
Land under forest cover	—242.5	Waste land	—150
Pasture and grazing land	—147	Land for homestead	—2.5
Net sown area	—119	Community land	—00

The pattern of land ownership was 1 acre with 169, 1-3 acres with 39, 5-10 acres 1 villager.

Land by ownership had the following pattern:

Less than 01 acre	—169 (67.87%)	1-3 acres	—40 (16.6)
3-5 acres	—39 (15.66%)	5-10 acres	—1 (00.40%)

The land assigned under land reforms was land taken in possession, land distributed and land actual possession was 15.00 acres equally. The SCs got 12.00 acres of land.

(g) ***Agriculture***: The crops grown in the village are wheat (December-January), rice (May-June) and maize (June-July). The inputs of wheat and rice are as follows:

Wheat	Fertilizer	40 kg urea and cow dung at the value Rs. 600
	Labour	Ploughing and harvesting at the cost of Rs. 750 and Rs. 2000
	Seeds	24 kg. per ha at the cost of Rs. 1800
	Pesticides	At the cost of Rs. 600
	Yield	800 kg. per acre at Rs. 6.6 per kg.

Rice	Labour	Transplanting, plugging and harvesting at the cost of Rs. 2500, Rs. 2000 and Rs. 3500.
	Seeds	24 kg per Ha at the cost of Rs. 250 and Rs. 750
	Pesticides	At the cost of Rs. 1500
	Yield	1250 kg. per acre

There is a fair price shop in the village and nearest grain market is 15 km away. There is no DPAP/CAD programme in operation.

(h) ***Employment conditions***: The employment conditions in the village reveals in the following details:

Tea shop	—2	Cosmetic shop	—1
Sweet shop	—3	General store	—4
Tailoring shop	—1	Rice mill small	—2
Steel furniture making	—2	Wooden furniture making	—4

(i) ***Migration***: Out migration to Mukherian and Garipur has been experienced in 5 per cent of population in the village for seeking market job.

(j) ***Panchayat***: There is one Panchayat in the village and Mukhya is a female, aged 53 years and belongs to Rajput and owns 4 acres land. Other members belong to SC, OBC and general castes and own 0.5 to 1.25 acres land.

(k) ***Status of Women***: Generally, women play equal role to their counterparts. Their activities are confined to household work, agriculture fields, rearing cattle, collecting fuel wood, and fodder from far off places. Women are not suppressed in the society and their voices are heard. Dowry is not demanded but people give household articles to their daughters at the time of marriage. The extreme form of *pardah* is not in practice. Married women cover their faces. The women are usually busy with domestic and agricultural activities.

(l) ***Poverty Alleviation Programmes***: The following schemes were implemented in the village:

(a) ***Swarnjayanti Gram Swarozgar Yojana (SGSY)***: There are 47 families, including 12 SC families, have been slected by the Gram Sabha for loans of 10,000 each for buying cows.

(b) ***Sampooran Gramin Rozgar Yojana (SGRY)***: In the year 2004-05, five link roads and footpaths have been constructed under this scheme and 406 mandays were generated benefiting 10 persons of the village at the cost of Rs. 62,929.

Village Nagchala, Block Balh, District Mandi

(a) The village Nagchala is situated on Chandigarh-Manali national highway No. 21 between Mandi and Sundernagar. It is 11 km away from Mandi district headquarters. It is in the heart of Balh valley, the most fertile in Himachal Pradesh. The Dalikar forest is at the distance of 15 km from the village.

(b) ***Population and Demography***: The total area of the village is about 231 hectares out of which 126 hectrares are under cultivation. The total population of the village in 2001 was 1,438 (males 722 and females 716) as per Census records. There are 174 families out of which 100 families belong to SCs whose population is 780. All families in the village profess Hindu religion. This village is well connected by road to the Bank in Mandi, zonal hospital in Mandi and vegetable market in Mandi. This connectivity has helped in the prospect of the people in the village.

(c) ***Education***: There is 1 government Primary, Upper Primary and Middle school in the village. Nearest High School is about 2 kms. There are 3 private schools. The government school has its own building, drinking water facility, playground, black boards and class rooms. The student strength of this primary school is as follows:

Table 5.65: Student Strength of Primary Schools in Villages

Classes	*Male Students*	*Female Students*	*Total*
1st	3	2	5
2nd	3	3	6
3rd	4	3	7
4th	4	2	6
5th	8	6	14
6th	2	4	6
7th	1	4	5
Total	**25**	**24**	**49**

Source: Village Study Reports CRS, LBSNAA Mussoorie.

There are 285 students enrolled in all schools, out of which 182 belong to the SC community and 102 to other castes. In last 10 years, girls have gone ahead of boys in these schools. For higher education, the villagers go to Himachal Pradesh University or its affiliated colleges. 32 boys have gone to college in last 10 years. The literacy rate in the village is 87.50 per cent (males 90.00% and females 85.00%).

(d) ***Health Status*:** There is no hospital, dispensary, primary or secondary health centres and midwifery centre for child welfare centre in the village. There are no private practitioners. The nearest hospital is the community health centre in Ratti at the Block Headquarters. There are no signs of any chronic diseases in the village. The infant mortality rate seems 10 per 1,000. Most the villagers use safe drinking water from pipelines. There seems no difference between the sanitary conditions of SCs and non-SCs. There are no proper draining facilities. Latrines are not being used. Since no medical facility is available, all deliveries take place at home in traditional way.

(e) ***Land and Agriculture*:** The total area of the village is 584 hectares. There is one irrigation and one water tank in the village which is used for irrigation purposes. For the rest of 50 per cent cultivated land, there is no source of irrigation. The type of land in the village are mentioned below:

Cultivated land	—	126 hectares
Forest land	—	29 hectares
Pasture and grazing land	—	4 hectares
Land for homestead	—	19 hectares
Community land	—	1 hectare
Miscellaneous land	—	52 hectares
Net sown area	—	126 hectares

While the market value of irrigated land is Rs. 30000 per bigha and unirrigated land 15000 per bigha. About 320 acres is under food cultivation and 59 acres under non-food cultivation. There are 287 cultivating land owners and cultivate 232 acres. There are no landless agricultural labourers in the village. The breakup of families in terms of their land holdings is given below:

1-5 acres	—162 families	5-10 acres	—12 families

The land revenue for different kinds of land is as follows:

Table 5.66: Land Revenue for Different Kinds of Land

Dhani Abbal	61 acres	1.02 bigha
Sailabi Abbal	2 acres	0.6 bigha
Barani Abbal	232 acres	0.76 bigha
Bagicha Abbal	12 acres	0.80 bigha
Bagicha Barani faldar	86 acres	0.12 bigha
Banjar	6 acres	0.15 bigha
Total	**399 acres**	

Source: Village Study Reports CRS, LBSNAA, Mussoorie.

Crops sown and harvested in the rabi season include wheat, barley, and pulses. In the *Kharif* season, crops like maize, paddy, mah, moong and rajma are sown and harvested. Ploughs made of iron are normally used in the village having 20 tractors. Manure and chemical manures are used in the village. 1000 kg. Of wheat seed, 600 kg. Of maize, 1800 kg. Of paddy seed were procured from the government for the villagers during 2005.06. The village is not self sufficient in food. The deficiency is met by purchasing foodgrains from the cooperative societies and by doing labour. The agricultural wages is between 80-100 or 10-12 kgs of wheat.

(f) ***Livestock:*** There are about 400 oxen, 250 buffaloes and 80 cows. There is no public grazing ground. There are 18 horses, 10 mules, 60 sheep and 25 goats and 100 poultry birds in the village. Villagers breed their own cattle through traditional and modern means.

Village: Ambwala-Sainwala, Block, Nahan, District: Sirmaur

(i) ***The Village***: This village, which has total area of 422.85 acres, is located at a distance of 9 km from district headquarters near the Kala Amb industrial area. It is connected by a metal road to the district. The village has got the distance to block headquarters 9 km, nearest but stop 5 km, nearest railway station 58 km, nearest twon 9 km, nearest market 9 km, nearest bank 9 km, nearest railway station 58 km, nearest PHC 0 km and nearest grain storage facility 18 km. The following amenities are available in the village:

Electrification	— Yes	Approach road	—Yes

Primary school	—Yes	Middle school	—Yes
Veterinary dispensary	—Yes	PDS shop	—Yes
Drinking water facility	—Yes	Public telephone	—Yes
ICDS Centre	—Yes	Panchayat bhawan	—Yes

(ii) ***Population and Demography***: In 2001, the village population was 1408 (718 males and 690 females), with 798 CSs, 42 OBC and 27 STs. Others comprised 541 people. The main language used in the village is Hindi. The IMR in the village is 2 per 1000.

(iii) ***Educational Status***: The literacy rate in the village in 2001, was 86.90 per cent (males 70.80% and females 78.90%). The following educational institutions were functional in the village.

	Government	Private
AWC	Yes	No
Primary school	Yes	No
Middle school	Yes	No

The enrolment and attendance in the school was mentioned below:

Table 5.67: Enrolment and Attendance

Class	*Students present*		*Out of total strength of students*	
	Males	*Females*	*Males*	*Females*
I	3	6	4	6
II	15	7	19	8
III	9	13	11	18
IV	–5	3	6	6
V	9	10	10	13
VI	13	19	22	25
VII	11	14	19	16
VIII	11	6	14	13

Source: Village Study Reports CRS, LBSNAA, Mussoorie.

The Primary school has got the following amenities:

Drinking water facility	— Toilet availability
Play ground	— Black board
Own building	— Class rooms

(iv) ***Health Status***: The government has provided the following health facilities in the village:

- Anm Sub-Centre
- Sub-PHC
- PHC and CHC

(v) ***Land Details:*** According to revenue records, the village had following kinds of land in acres:

Land for cultivation	—187.15	Fallow land	—48.66
Land under forest cover	—140.52	Waste land	—54.69
net sown area	—187.85	Community land	—1.57

(vi) ***Agricultural Land Allied Activities***: The village has the crops of wheat, gram, masoor dal, sarson, rice, maize and sugarcane. The area under one crop cultivation is 9.47 acre, while the area under multi-crop is 180.90 acre. The nearest grain markets are Paonta and Nariagarh.

(vii) ***Employment Conditions***: The occupational types and number of persons involved are as shown below:

Agricultural labourers	— 26 households 10%
Cultivators	— 170 households 50%
Household industry	— 00
Others (government employees)	— 150 household 40%

The non-farm activities undertaken by villagers are as follows:

Tea shop	— 3	Sweet shop	— 3
General store	— 4	Tailoring shop	— 3

(viii) ***Panchayat***: There is one Panchayat in the village for which elections were held in December 2005. The Mukhya is a female land owner, 35 years of age and belongs to SC.

Village: Bharara, Block: Tissa, District: Chamba

(i) ***The Village***: This hilly village is at the distance of 25 km from Block headquarters and 80 km from district headquarters.

(ii) ***Education***: The literacy rate in the village was 60 per cent for all persons (males 75% and females 45%). The situation is not positive mainly because most of the teachers posted in this village do not join. It is considered for far flung areas. The educational infrastructure in the school provided by SSa consists of 4 class rooms, one kitchen, one play ground and 2 more additional rooms. There are 3 teachers managing 8 classes. The students sit on the ground mat. There is heavy drop out rate because children are engaged in agricultural activities. Girls education after eighth class is not encouraged. There are no private educational institutions in and around the village.

(iii) ***Health and Sanitation***: The average expenditure on health is about Rs. 5,000 per year. The villagers suffer mainly by diseases like tuberculosis, rashes and anemia. The main health problem comes from bad sanitation. Most of the villagers defecate in the open and only 2 per cent in the village has toilets in houses. The sense of personal hygiene was also found missing. The village had only one ANM sub-centre which was inadequate for villagers. Most of the ladies while giving birth to their children engage a *dai* which often results in their bad health. IMAR and MMR were not available.

(iv) ***Land and Agriculture***: The different types of land in the village is mentioned below:

Total land	— 1056 acres	Land for cultivation	— 309
Fallow land	— 19	Pasture and grazing land	—684
Waste land	— 205		

The following was the pattern of distribution of land ownership;

Less than 1 hectare	— 215	1-3 hectares	— 4

People in the village mostly follow 2 crop regime, one *kharif* and second rabi season. There is no irrigation facilties in the village and agriculture is entirely dependent on rainfall. The agricultural productivity of the land is also not much. While some farmers use HYV seeds, many do not use the same. They use chemical fertilizers for cost consideration. Most of the produce is used for self-consumption and surplus produced is very less. The proportion of agricultural labourers in the village is very less. Most of the villagers engage family labour for cultivation purpose. The wages paid is around Rs. 70 per day.

(v) ***Occupational Pattern***: The occupational pattern of the village is self-cultivation. The next major occupation is manual labour. The village also have some people in government service. With the introduction of NREGA/HPREGS, most the people are found assured employment for the whole year. There is not much migration in the village because they prefer to stay at home than to go out of village. However, about 20 villagers have gone out in search of work. In general, unemployment and under employment are acute in the village. Though poverty exists in the village, it is getting access to safe drinking water, electricity and elementary education.

(vi) ***Poverty Alleviation Programmes***: In the village of Bharara, the following poverty alevation schemes were introduced and implemented.

(a) *SGRY*: It has been a major success. But, it faced certain problems. First, apart from roads, the focus on other durable assets is almost nil. Second, the wage rate to be paid under this programme is very less than the other prevalent rates in the local market.

(b) Other successful welfare programmes include specifically Vidhayak Kshetriya Nidhi Yojana and Vikas Mein Jan Sahyog Yojana.

Village: Sadwan, Block: Pragpur, District: Kangra

(i) ***The Village***: This hilly village is located at 5 km away from Block headquarters and 68 km from district headquarters.

(ii) ***Population and Demography***: In the year 2001, the village had total population of 667 (349 males and 328 females. In 1991, it was 502 (262 males and 240 females). Most of the families have got nuclear households. The socio-economic impact of population growth manifests in depletion and competition for scarce resources.

(iii) ***Infrastructure***: The village lacks higher secondary school and ITI, motorable road and no modes of irrigation. The yield from land is not much and most of the produce remains for self consumption. The villagers have no access to health centre, the railhead is 38 km away from the village. The private practitioner is in the town 3 km away.

(iv) ***Education***: The educational status of the village is above national average. Education of children and young adults is near 100 per cent Most of the girls are not allowed to continue education after middle stage. It was observed that students performed well at the primary level than at the higher level. The educational infrastructure reflects in 3 classrooms, one kitchen, one playground, one toilet and 2 additional rooms in the school in the village. There are 3 teachers managing 5 classes. There were 3 drop outs from the school. The school serves mid-day meals regularly. It has higher number of illiterate people, though figures are not available.

(v) ***Health and Sanitation***: In the village, the average expenditure on health in a year is Rs. 5,000. The villagers suffer from fever common cold and seasonal ailments such as dysentery, and common cold. Most of the villagers defecate in the open and 5 per cent of the village families have some kind of toilet. The sub-PHC though in working condition is understaffed with no modern facilities and equipment. ANM visits very often and health practitioners are present in the village. Among the family planning methods, the use of contraceptives is very common. The institutional delivery is rare in the village. Same is the case with child care. But, IMR and MMR is very low.

(vi) ***Land and Agriculture***: The villages mostly grow two crops and the entire production is used for self consumption.

The distribution of land ownership in the village had following pattern:

Less than 01 hectare	— 766	1 to 3 hectares	— 18
3-5 hectares	— 7	5-10 hectares	— 4

The agricultural productivity of the land is not much sometimes fetching 50 kg per canal. Some houses use HYV seeds while many use fertilizers massively. The surplus produced is very less. The proportion of agricultural labourer in the village is also less.

(vii) ***Occupational Pattern***: Most of the villagers are self cultivator. The next occupation is manual labour. Some villagers are also government employees. The non-farm economic activities revolve around the following:

Tea shop	—2	Cosmetic shop	—1	Sweet shop	—1
General store	—1	PDS shop	—1	Tailoring shop	—2

The seasonal unemployment is very high, especially during the rainy season. But, there is no migration from the village. Only about 20 villagers have gone out for seeking the jobs.

Unemployment and under employment is very acute, but poverty is not very high.

(viii) ***Poverty Alleviation Schemes***: The following schemes were introduced and implemented in the village.

(a) *SGSY*: The group which has taken up this scheme has made in some concerned fields. Some land was put to productive use under this scheme.

(b) *SGRY*: This scheme has been able to generate a lot of employment opportunities in terms of mandays work. However, it faces some problems.

(c) Other social welfare programmes in the village have been successful in cases of Vidhayak Kshetriya Vikas Nidhi Yojana and Vikas Mein Jan Sahyog Yojana.

Village: Delah, Block: Drang, District: Mandi

(i) ***The Village***: Delah is an average village which is situated about 30 km from Mandi town. It is situated on both sides of the national highway and approach to village is easy, though all areas are not well connected.

(ii) ***Population and Demography***: The total population of Delah in 2001 was 705 (males 355 and 35 females). It included 103 SCs, 70 STs and 532 other castes. The pressure of population in the village has resulted in small landholdings, even less than one hectare.

(iii) ***Infrastructure***: Delah has got electricity and telephone service, there are Block, tehsil offices, schools, colleges and SDM office. The Anganwadi centre is located at a distance of 5 km. Primary and Senior Secondary schools, CHC and other amenities are available in this village.

(iv) ***Education***: The educational status of the village is not satisfactory. While the overall literacy rate in the village was 65 per cent, male and female rates were 80 per cent and 50 per cent respectively. This literacy rate cuts across caste and sex. There is good primary school with 4 classrooms, one kitchen, one playground, and two additional rooms. 3 teachers manage 8 classes. The main reason for drop outs seems to be the engagement: The manual labour in agriculture is done in during growing and harvesting season. There is not a single private school in the village. The activity of mid-day meals is going on normally in the school.

(v) ***Health and Sanitation***: Lifestyle diseases like obesity and diabetes are absent from the village. However, on common diseases, the villagers spend Rs. 5,000 on an average per annum. There is not even minimum standard of sanitation in the village. Mostly people defecate in the open and 2 per cent in the village have latrines. While there is no PHC, the CHC is in the nearby village. Most of the ladies do not have institutional delivery and a *dai* is engaged for this work at home. Child immunization and child health get the same treatment.

(vi) ***Land and Agriculture***: There are following types off land in the village:

Total Land	— 615 acres	Land for cultivation	—179
Land under forest cover	— 100	Pasture & grazing land	—105
Waste land	— 2	Net sown area	—179
Miscellaneous	— 50		

The pattern of distribution of land ownership was as follows:

1 hectares	— 47	1-03 hectares	— 22
3-05 hectares	— 18	5-10 hectares	— 17

The people in the village follow two crop regime, one kharif and second rabi. Some farmers use HYV seeds, many of them use chemical fertilizers. Most of the produce grown in the village is used fro self consumption. The proportion of agricultural labourers is very less. The standard of wages is high as it is 75 and 100 rupees per day, as is paid under NREGA.

(vii) ***Occupational Pattern and Employment***: Most of the villagers are self-cultivators. The occupation in the village is government service, especially in Class IV. The rest are totally dependent on the farm produce for their livelihood. NREGA has provided some relief to them. The non-farm activities are done by manual labour as road laying, bricks laying, and stone laying. Seasonal unemployment is very high in the village but the villagers do not opt for out-migration. Only about 20 people have gone for migration. Though unemployment and underemployment is acute in the village, poverty is not very high.

(viii) ***Poverty Alleviation Programmes***: People of the village have been much benefited by PAPs such as SGRY, SGSY, IAY, VVMJS, VKVNY and by HPREGS and NREGA.

Village: Chari, Block: Rait, District: Kangra

(i) ***The Village***: Chari village is 6 km away from block and 10 km from district headquarters.

(ii) ***Population and Demography***: The village had the following population in 2001:

Total Population	— 2592	Males	— 1377
Females	— 1215	SCs	— 542
OBCs	— 2050		

The housing pattern in the village is oriented towards the nuclear family. The socio-economic impact of population growth manifests in the competition for limited resources such as drinking water.

(iii) ***Infrastructure***: The village is electrified and has all-weather approach road. It has a primary health sub-centre, PDS shop, primary and middle schools. The village has no modes of irrigation for its farms.

(iv) ***Literacy and Education***: While the male liateracy rate in the village was 85 per cent and that of females it was 80 per cent, both of which are above the national average. There are 2 primary schools, one middle school and 3 aganwadi centres. The school has 4 class rooms, one kitchen, one playground, 2 additional rooms, toilets and blackboards. The mid-day meal is going on normally in the school.

(v) ***Health and Sanitation***: Though villagers consider themselves as healthy, they usually spend Rs. 5,000 on an average per annum on health expenditure. The common diseases in the village are tuberculosis, anemia and rashes. Most of the people defecate in the open and only some families have constructed toilets. There is a PHC and sub-PHC in the village, but not well maintained and well stocked. The ANM is not a regular visitor. Maternity and child care is not satisfactory. Most of the ladies gave births at their homes with the help of *dai*.

(vi) ***Land and Agriculture*:** The details about distribution of land in the village follow:

Land	Hectares	Land	Hectares
Total land	—228,4221	Land for cultivation	—86.22
Land under forest—	63.12	Community land	—19.46

The pattern of land ownership in the village is as under:

Below 1 hectare	— 32	1-20 hectares	— 00
Landless	— 00		

The village follow a 2 crop regime, one *kharif* and second *rabi* season. Some farmers use HYV seeds, while many do not use the same. Traditional ploughing is still popular. Most of the production is used for self consumption. The proportion of agricultural labourers in the village is very less. The average wage rate in the village is 70 per day.

(vii) ***Occupational Pattern*:** Most of the activities performed in the village are related to agriculture. The second occupational group is that of government employees, especially in the Class IV cadre. In additional to cultivation and cattle rearing, basket making and handloom weaving is done in the village. The non-farm activities are unskilled manual labour. Seasonal unemployment is very high especially during rainy months but there is not much out-migration. Only 20 persons have out of village for searching jobs. However, there is some degree of in-migration. In the village, though unemployment and underemployment is acute, poverty is very high.

(viii) ***Poverty Alleviation Schemes*:** Various Programmes, especially SGRY, have been popular and effective. Other such programmes like SGSY, IAY, VMJS, VKVNY and NREGA have helped the villagers significantly in many ways to the tune of Rs. 7,500 annually.

(ii) ***Population and Demography***: The population of the village in the year 2001 was as under:

Table 5.68: Population and Demography of the Village in 2001

Category	Persons
Males	310
Females	304
SCs	135
STs	31
Others	448
Total Population	**614**

Source: Census 2001.

Most of the families are of nuclear type in the village. The Socio-economic impact of population growth has been felt in the competition for limited resources.

(iii) ***Infrastructure***: The village is electrified, has all-weather approach road, one primary health sub-centre, one PDS shop and primary and middle school but with no street lights. There is no mode of irrigation of the farms and entire agriculture depends on rains. In fact, the village has subsistent mode of production.

(iv) ***Literacy and Education***: While the male literacy rate was 80 per cent, that of females was 70 per cent which are above the national average. There are 3 anganwadi centres. The literacy rate cuts across caste and sex. The village has a school having 4 classrooms, one kitchen, one playground, two additional rooms, own building, toilets and blackboards. The mid-day meals are going on nicely.

(v) ***Health and Sanitation***: The common diseases prevalent in the village are fever, diarhoea, rashes and anemia. Most of the health problems are because of open defecation and no proper sanitation. Maternity care and child care is least available. They call for *dai* at the time of delivery.

(vi) ***Land and Agriculture***: The pattern of types of land in the village was as follows:

Total Land	—153.22	Land for cultivation	—84.60
Land under forest cover	—21.60	Fallow land	—18.00
Pasture and grazing land	—7.40	Community land	—00.63

The pattern of landownership in the village was as follows (household wise):

Landless	— 00	Less than 1 acre	— 27
1-3 acres	— 10	3-5 acres	— 03
5 acres	— 00		

The village follows a 2 crop scheme, *kharif* and *rabi*. The agricultural productivity is not much. Some farmers use HYV seeds, while others use chemical fertilizers. The traditional ploughing is in vogue in the village. The whole production is self consumed.

(vii) ***Occupation Pattern***: Most of the villagers are cultivators. The next major occupation is the manual labour. The third occupation is government employment in lower cadre jobs. Some villagers are engaged in the work provided by NREGA. The non-farm activities are related to unskilled manual labour.

Though seasonal unemployment is acute, there is not much out migration in search for jobs. However, there is some degree of in-migration. Unemployment and underemployment is very high but there is not very high poverty in the village.

(viii) ***Poverty Alleviation Programmes***: NREGA stands the popular PAP in the village. It has benefited people massively as it involved unskilled labour in the village. Other PAPs include IAY, VMJS, VKVNY, etc.

Village: Kirri, Block: Mehla, District: Chamba

(i) ***Population and Demography***: The village Kirri had the population in the year 2001 as follows:

Table 5.69: Population and Demography in Village Kirri in 2001

Category	Persons
Males	— 525
Females	— 491
SCs	— 501
STs	— 30
OBCs	— 00
Others	— 485
Total population	**1016**

Source: Census 2001.

Other details of population show that as a result of this natural resources have been affected and level of landholding has been decreased. It has also resulted in low cost sanitation, falling nutrition level, access to medical facilities and insufficiency of food, firewood, fodder, etc.

(ii) ***Infrastructure***: The village has an approach road and higher secondary school. There are no modes of irrigation for farms. For this, the village depends on rain only. It has a sub-health centre.

(iii) ***Literacy and Education***: The average literacy rate is 60 per cent, the male-female literacy rate was 75 per cent and 45 per cent. The village school has 4 classrooms, one kitchen, one playground, 2 additional rooms, toilets, own building and blackboards. The mid-day meals are served regularly.

(iv) ***Health Sanitation***: The diseases most common in the village are tuberculosis, rashes and anemia. Though villagers feel themselves healthy, an expenditure of Rs. 5,000 per annum per family is incurred by them. There is no PHC or sub-PHC. Even ANM's visits are irregular. The maternity and child care is least available.

(v) ***Land and Agriculture***: The village has the following pattern of distribution of land:

Total Land	— 1,056 acres	Land for cultivation	— 309
Fallow land	— 19	Pasture & grazing land	— 684
Waste land	— 205		

The following is the pattern of landownership in the village:

Landless	— 00	Less than 1 hectare	— 215
1-3 hectares	— 04	3-10 hectare	— 00
Above 20	– 00		

The village follow 2 crop regime, *kharif and rabi*. The agricultural product is not much, but all that is self consumed in the village.

(vi) ***Occupational Pattern***: Majority of the villagers are cultivators. The next major occupation in the village is manual labour. Some people are engaged in lower cadre government service. The rest of dependent on the farm produce. The non-farm activities are undertaken by unskilled manual labour and other jobs in non-agricultural sector. In the village, the seasonal unemployment is very high, but out-migration takes place. In fact, some in-migration has been observed. Though unemployment and underemployment is acute in the village, but poverty graph is not very high.

(vii) ***Poverty Alleviation Programmes***: NREGA is the most popular PAP in the village as it has been more effective. Other PAPs include IAY, VMJS, VKVNY and programmes run by PS/ZP. NREGA has benefited Rs. 7,500 per annum to per beneficiary.

Village: Basehar, Block: Padhar, District: Mandi

(i) ***The Village***: Basehar comprises five hamlets. Chamah is at a distance off 4 km from the national highway. All the residents of the village are Hindus and about half of them are SCs. The status of women reflects in their voice in household affairs. The days of joint family in this village seem numbered as most brothers live in separate houses. Most of the houses in the village are traditional with wooden exterior. Though there is an approach road to the village, there is no bus service.

(ii) ***Population and Demography***: According to 2001 Census, the total population in the village is 718 with 353 (about 50%) belong to SCs. The sex ratio is 983, with females 347 (roughly 49%). The average annual growth rate of 3.44 per cent existed during 1981-1991. Rapid population growth has led to increased pressure on limited land.

(iii) ***Education***: The village has a government Primary school in Chamah. For secondary school, the children have to go to Padhar. The literacy rate among males is marginally higher than among females. In the village school, there are 35 students and 3 teachers (equal to the national ratio of 40 : 01). There is a government college in Padhar which has reduced the drop out rate in the village. Most of drop outs become lorry/truck drivers or mechanics.

(iv) ***Health***: People in the village have to go to Padhar for CHC or to district hospital for medical needs. Most of the deliveries in the village happen at the CHC Padhar. For immunization of children the villagers approach the same CHC. The IMR and MMR are at lower level. However, preference for a male child is common.

(v) ***Land and Agriculture***: The total area of the village is 368 acres, out of which 162 acres and 101 acres are under cultivation and under forest respectively. While pasture and grazing land is 64 acres, the waste land is 40 acres. There is one solitary case of tenancy in the village. Almost no family in Basehar is landless. Majority of the operational landholdings are 1-3 acres. The total sown area is 152 acres. Most of the land used for cultivation was Barani land. In order to improve the application of water to land, water had been diverted from small streams through cement drains. NREGA has been helpful in this case.

(vi) ***Occupational Structure***: Most of the villagers are cultivators. There are two government employees also. Farming is the most single crop and in well irrigated areas, experience of vegetable growing has been started. There are couple of families who have opened shops in Padhar. However the fact stands that agriculture remains the dominant occupation.

(vii) ***Poverty Alleviation Programmes***: MNREGA stands popular and most effective PAP in the village and has benefited all sections and groups in the village. The SGSY programme is used by the residents to set-up SHGs. Of these, 4 are based on Diary farming and one was of sericulture. It has benefited close to 40 households.

6

Summing Up

C. ASHOKVARDHAN

The objective of fast, inclusive and sustainable growth depends on the development of human and institutional capabilities.

HUMAN CAPABILITIES

Human capabilities tend to raise the productive capacity of our economy. Proper development of human capabilities will also ensure that our growth is more inclusive in the sense that the marginalized and disadvantaged sections of our society will be more able to access the opportunities thrown up by the growth process.

Life expectancy level in India remains lower than in any emerging market economy and it is appropriate to plan for significant improvement in this regard. The decline in the child sex ratio rings an alarm.

India has a young population. To reap this demographic dividend we must ensure that our younger citizens come into the labour force with higher levels of education and skill. The MDM scheme has ensured retention in schools. However, the learning outcomes for a majority of children continue to be disappointing. The quality of teachers and even more important, their motivation and accountability are to be ensured. Addressing the quality issue in our schools is critical for the effective development of human capabilities as also for achieving the objective of equality of opportunities.

At present, less than 30 per cent of outpatient and less than half of inpatient health care capacity of the country is in the public sector, and the majority of the population relies on private health care provision which is highly expensive. Coverage of both rural and urban areas, through the National Health Mission, will require additional resources in the public sector.

Attainment of good health outcomes is not just by curative care. We have to give attention to public health. We have to focus on clean drinking water and sanitation.

INSTITUTIONAL CAPABILITIES

Institutional capabilities of institutions like PRIs and ULBs need special attention. Training and Manpower development is in a disarray at the level of local bodies as also at the State and Central Government levels. There is lack of motivation at various levels. Government systems are largely process-driven. They are not outcome-oriented.

Delivery of public services in many States is hampered by weak institutional capacity. We may have to devise mechanisms for measuring the extent of public satisfaction with public services and publicizing the results. Greater involvement of citizens organizations can help Governments identify problem areas.

There is a plethora of regulatory bodies staffed by former bureaucrats but bereft of specialists with domain knowledge.

Infrastructure provides the basic support system for various sectors of the economy. Small enterprises are dispersed widely and have to rely on the general infrastructure available. Their ability to compete successfully, which is critical for growth to be employment generating and inclusive, depends on the quality of this infrastructure.

AGRICULTURAL GROWTH

There is evidence that wherever land productivity has improved and greater water security has been delivered, small and marginal farmers working on MGNREGA sites have reverted back to farming and allied livelihoods. There is also evidence that MGNREGA is enabling crop diversification, particularly into horticulture, wherever it has adequately converged with schemes of agricultural departments. An important lesson from this experience is that it is the quality of assets created, which will determine whether MGNREGA can go beyond the safety net to become a springboard for entrepreneurship, even at the lowest income levels.

For achieving the agricultural growth of 4 per cent during the Twelfth Plan, action is needed on many fronts including provision of basic support services such as technology and irrigation infrastructure, access to credit, good and reliable seeds and improved post-harvest technology. The bulk of the growth will come from diversification towards horticulture, animal husbandry and fisheries.

The greatest potential for improving productivity is in the rainfed areas, which account for 55 per cent of net sown area and where most of the poor live. Land productivity is low in these areas, but a combination of effective water management combined with better seeds, promotion of soil health and a focus on investments combined with efforts to improve infrastructure can make a big difference. Rainfed farming requires a natural resource management perspective with a farming systems approach focusing on producing diverse products that mutually reinforce each other and stabilise the system. These areas require knowledge and institutional investments on many fronts. There have also to be diverse livelihood options such as livestock and fisheries.

Some of the Government's key inclusiveness promoting programmes, such as MGNREGA can make a major contribution in improving land productivity, if the projects under it are structured to increase on-farm productivity. Properly designed and converged, MGNREGA can contribute to creating positive synergy with agricultural growth.

CORE INDICATORS

The following core indicators reflect the vision of rapid, sustainable and more inclusive growth in education and health:

EDUCATION

- Mean years of schooling to increase to seven years by the end of the Twelfth Five Year Plan.
- Enhance access to higher education by creating two million additional seats for each age cohort aligned to the skill needs of the economy.

- Eliminate gender and social gap in school enrolment (that is, between girls and boys, and between SCs, STs, Minorities and the rest of the population) by the end of the Twelfth Five Year Plan.

HEALTH

- Reduce IMR to 25 and MMR to 1 per 1,000 live births and improve Child Sex Ratio (0-6 years) to 950 by the end of the Twelfth Five Year Plan.
- Reduce Total Fertility Rate to 2.1 by the end of the Twelfth Five Year Plan.
- Reduce under-nutrition among children aged 0-3 years to half of the NFHS-3 levels by the end of the Twelfth Five Year Plan.

GENDER CONCERNS

With progressive devolution of powers to PRIs and an increasing number of States mandating 50 per cent reservation for women in PRIs, new opportunities are emerging for making development planning processes gender sensitive and child friendly at the grass roots level. Ending gender-based violence against women, including improvement in the adverse and deeply declining child sex ratio, is the crying need of the hour.

According to the 2011 Census, women account for 586.47 million in absolute numbers and represent 48.46 per cent of the total population of the country. On the health front, implementation of the National Rural Health Mission has resulted in an improvement on many indicators pertaining to gender. There has been an increase in literacy amongst women from 53.67 per cent (Census 2001) to 65.46 per cent (Census 2011). The challenge, however, remains in bridging the gender gap which stands at 16.68 per cent. The gender differential in education is declining, particularly at the Primary level. There is a need to address the issues of retention of girls is schools, quality of education and the provision of separate toilets, sibling care facilities, and so on.

From 1993-94 to 2009-10, women's participation in the labour force has decreased substantially from 36.8 per cent to 26.1 per cent in rural areas and from 17 per cent to 13.8 per cent in urban areas as indicated by NSSO data.

Special efforts have to be made to promote skill development of women from traditional skills which help women break the gender stereotypes and move into employment requiring higher skill sets. Skill development will have to be seen as a vehicle to improve lives and not just livelihoods of women. The curriculum should, therefore, include inputs that help women to assert themselves individually and collectively.

The promotion of enterprises of home-based workers, self-employed workers and small producers has to be an essential component of women development plan. The plan strategy must identify such women workers and support their enterprises through setting up of common facility centres to ensure all important services including technology and skill training, entrepreneurship training, market information, access to institutionalized credit, power and other infrastructure and related facilities.

There is a need to review the SHG interventions and ground realities to determine how SHGs may better serve the interests of poor women, and suggest changes required in overall SHG policy frameworks.

Existing formal institutions must recognize women's roles and needs in various fields of agricultural activity and must ensure the participation of women farmers in designing programmes for technical training and research. Technology transfer to women would be prioritized in all aspects of farming and farm management, including dry land farming technologies, animal husbandry, forestry, sustainable natural resource management, enterprise development, financial management and leadership development.

Endowing women with land is an important instrument for empowering them economically and strengthening their ability to challenge social and political gender iniquities. There are three main sources of land for women: direct government transfers, purchase or lease from the market and inheritance.

Existing traditional industries like leather, handlooms, handicrafts and sericulture, existing publicly funded institutions will have to be activated to identify the industry's market potential and skills. State policies will have to be encouraged to publicise the opportunities in these industries among potential women entrepreneurs and give assistance to them is their ventures.

The Ministry of Women and Child Development and the Ministry of Panchayati Raj in collaboration with other Ministries must promote several activities including especially (i) Capacity building and training modules on women's programmes for government functionaries and officers, (ii) Pre-election preparation of women candidates and voters, intensive training of elected Panchayat women representatives; and (iii) gender budgeting and gender audit in rural and urban local bodies.

The SC women should be provided with good quality house-sites in the joint names of both the wife and husband. In view of particular vulnerability faced by SC women and children and migrant labour, special programmes and interventions should be drawn up for them, particularly in the fields of education and health. Similarly, there has to be greater focus on awareness building among tribal women about policies, programmes, schemes and legislations meant for them by using various print and electronic media. There has to be a focus on the implementation of the Scheduled Tribes and other Traditional Forest Dwellers' (Recognition of Forest Rights) Act 2006. Within the Scheduled Tribes, a special category called the PVTGs (Particular Vulnerable Tribal Groups) has been identified. A special scheme needs to be developed targeting women of these communities.

FOCUS ON SOCIAL INCLUSION

An inclusive growth process provides opportunities for all to participate in the growth process combined with schemes that would either deliver benefits directly or more importantly help these groups to benefit from the opportunities thrown up by the general development process. Across social groups, the incidence of poverty has been most pronounced among the SCs and STs. Even though the incidence of poverty among these groups has declined over the years, the head count ratio (HCR) for SCs and STs remains higher than the national average. Over the years, several steps have been taken to bridge the gap between these mariginalised groups and the rest of the population. But gaps still persist and further efforts are needed.

The Eleventh Five Year Plan (2007-12) adopted a three pronged strategy for the socio-economic development of the disadvantaged groups including the SCs and STs:

1. **Social Empowerment**—Removing existing and persisting inequalities besides providing easy access to basic minimum services with a top priority assigned to education as the key factor in social development.
2. **Economic Empowerment**—Promising employment-cum-income generation activities with an ultimate objective of making them economically independent and self-reliant.
3. **Social Justice**—Striving to eliminate all types of discrimination with the strength of legislative support, affirmative action, awareness generation and change in the mind-set of the people.

The principal goals for the twelfth Five Year Plan (2012-17) towards the empowerment of the Scheduled Castes, will be:

1. To ensure the security and dignity of all persons belonging to the Scheduled Castes, especially women and put a complete end to all forms of 'untouchability' and discrimination against them.
2. To bring members of the SCs—both men and women—at par, to the maximum possible extent, with their non-SC/ST counterparts, in terms of all development indices, viz., education, health, nutrition, housing, income generation and employability.
3. To empower SCs to participate in nation-building, on an equal basis with others.
4. To effectively implement SCSP as the essential instrument for accomplishing inclusive growth.

Unlike the SCs who are dispersed throughout the country, STs have traditionally been concentrated in about 15 per cent of the country's geographical areas, mainly forests, hills, undulating and inaccessible areas. Because of the remoteness of location of most of the ST population, the extent to which they can benefit from general development programmes is more limited and the need for special programmes is greater than for SCs. The Human Development Report

2011 of the Planning Commission candidly admits that though the consumption expenditure of Scheduled Tribes has been rising over time, the rate of increase was lower than the all-India average. Between 1993-94 and 2004-05 the share of the tribals amongst the poor in the country increased from 15.83 to 20.49 per cent. Lagging of scheduled tribes reflects the fact that geographical seclusion has limited their access to new self-employment opportunities. Similar gaps continue between literacy levels and health indicators of STs and the general population and have widened over the years.

Economic development among the tribals largely depends upon agriculture and its allied activities. Besides, forest resources and minor forest produce contribute substantially to the tribal economy. This calls for capacity building in diversifying their livelihood sources.

The success of PESA hinges critically on the effective functioning of the Gram Sabha. There is much to be desired in the effective functioning of the Gram Sabha and there is a large measure of exclusion of women. There is also the exclusion of those who are poorer or whose voice is weaker. This calls for a dedicated cadre of social mobilisers at each GP level, specifically assigned with the task of mobilizing the Gram Sabha and ensuring the effective participation of the marginalized, as also spreading greater awareness of laws such as PESA and Scheduled Tribes and Other Traditional Forest Dwellers (Recognition of Forest Rights) Act and key flagship programmes of the Government.

A clear and categorical provision should be made in the Panchayati Raj Acts or the Revenue Laws through a notification under Para 5(1) of the Fifth Schedule to empower the Gram Sabha to restore the unlawfully alienated land to its lawful owner.

COMMON PROPERTY RESOURCES

Any discussion on rural development will remain incomplete without a mention of the Common Property Resources and their contributions to people's livelihood, such as in household income, livestock sustenance, etc. CPRs assume importance from an ecological perspective as well. Proper development and management of these common lands is critical in the success of a watershed as they are often located along the watershed ridges. In recent years there has been a steady decrease in all kinds of common lands and pastures, village forests, ponds or even burial grounds. This is due to diversion of CPRs for urbanization, industrial, mining, homestead and development purposes.

A long term perspective on CPRs should be evolved through developing landuse plans of each village. CPR should be defined according to its importance to support rural livelihoods and ecology. The following categories of land should be considered as common property land resource:

- Cultivable wastes and fallows other than current fallows.
- Common pastures and grazing lands.
- Protected and unclassified forests.
- Private land to which common access may exist.

There should be a minimum percentage of CPLR (Common Property Land Resource) of the total land in a village. The capping should be decided by the PRIs. Based on the criticality of CPRs, a complete ban on diversion should be approved unless their conversion is in the larger interest of all the users and ecology. To identify and estimate the magnitude of CPRs in the country, the National Sample Survey Organization should enumerate this in every round.

The development model for CPR should be similar to the JFM model. The rights over the management and use of CPRs should be assigned to users. For proper management of CPR, the role of the community-based institutions, the Central and State Governments, and civil society, especially those working on it, are critical.

There should be heavy penalty on resource rich farmers who encroach upon such lands. It is high time to safeguard existing *de jure* CPRs. Funds should be made available and investment should be made for their development. Also, the diversion of existing *de jure* CPRs should be banned. Disputes over CPRs should be resolved on priority and for this purpose, the Government should initiate fast track and time-bound processes.

Finally, building greater public awareness is the need of the hour. People's perspective on CPRs should be thoroughly understood and taken into consideration while designing public interventions.

In a similar context, it is necessary to point out that collective leasing for the women cooperatives should be permitted in respect of the cultivable wastelands and other Government lands whose use has undergone a change so as to permit leasing out. The wasteland should be under the management of the Gram Sabha as is the practice in several States. It should be unequivocally recognised that it is the landless poor who have the first charge on the Government lands whose changed land-use permit leasing out.

Index